Reason
and
Horror

REASON AND HORROR

CRITICAL THEORY, DEMOCRACY, AND AESTHETIC INDIVIDUALITY

Morton Schoolman

Routledge
Taylor & Francis Group
New York London

First Published in 2001 by
Routledge
29 West 35th Street
New York, New York 10001

Published in Great Britain by
Routledge
11 New Fetter Lane
London EC4P 4EE

This edition published 2011 by Routledge:

Routledge
Taylor & Francis Group
711 Third Avenue
New York, NY 10017

Routledge
Taylor & Francis Group
2 Park Square, Milton Park
Abingdon, Oxon OX14 4RN

Copyright © 2001 by Routledge

Routledge is an imprint of the Taylor and Francis Group.

All rights reserved. No part of this book may be reprinted or reproduced or utilized in any form or by any electronic, mechanical, or other means, now known or hereafter invented, including photocopying and recording, or in any information storage or retrieval system, without permission in writing from the publishers.

Library of Congress Cataloging-in-Publication Data

Schoolman, Morton.
   Reason and horror: critical theory, democracy, and aesthetic individuality / by Morton Schoolman.
     p. cm.
   Includes bibliographical references and index.
   ISBN 0-415-93027-8—ISBN 0-415-93028-6 (pbk.)
           1. Individualism.   2. Democracy.   3. Aesthetics.   4. Enlightenment.   5. Reason.
6. Holocaust, Jewish (1939–1945)—Causes.   I. Title
JC571.S3782 2001
126—dc21
                                                                                                         00-065334

For my mother,

Helene C. Schoolman

Who Dreamt of Being Reconciled

with the World

To catch the truth of madness, "one would have to bend an attentive ear to the whispers of the world and try to perceive the many images that have never been set down in poetry and the many fantasies that have never reached the colors proper to the waking state."

                        Michel Foucault,
                        Madness and Civilization

CONTENTS

Acknowledgments xi

ONE   INTRODUCTION: REASON AND HORROR   1

INDIVIDUALITY BEFORE THE HOLOCAUST 2

Formal and Aesthetic Reason / 2   Aesthetic Reason, Aesthetic Individuality, Aesthetic Sensibility / 5   Reading *Dialectic of Enlightenment* / 7   Aesthetic Individuality and the Aesthetics of Tragedy / 11   From a Genealogy of Reason to Aesthetic Theory / 13

SURFACES 14

Individuality as an Aesthetic Problem / 15   Adorno: A Sensibility to Violence, Creativity without Form—Nietzsche: Creativity with Form, without a Sensibility to Violence / 16   Whitman: The Aesthetic Problem from the Point of View of the Artist (the Creator) / 19   Aesthetic Individuality in Democratic America / 23

INDIVIDUALITY AFTER THE HOLOCAUST 26

PART I
INDIVIDUALITY BEFORE THE HOLOCAUST   27

TWO   REASON AS A "MURDEROUS PRINCIPLE"   29

DIFFERENCE AND THE BIRTH OF THINKING 30

DIFFERENCE AND MAGICAL THINKING 33

DIFFERENCE AND MYTHICAL THINKING 36

DIFFERENCE AND THE ENLIGHTENMENT OF MODERN TIMES 40

THREE   *DIALECTIC OF ENLIGHTENMENT* AS A GENEALOGY OF REASON   52

RHETORICAL OVERLAY VERSUS LINEAR HISTORICAL NARRATIVE 52

INDIVIDUALS IN POSSESSION OF OURSELVES   55

   A Conflict of the Faculties, Its Hierarchical Resolution, and Identity as Self-Contradiction / 55   Self-Identity and the Triumph of Formal Reason / 58   An Ideal Form of Aesthetic Individuality / 60   Methodological Reflections on the Possibility of Aesthetic Individuality / 62   Modern Subjectivity and Artless Thinking / 65   Aesthetic Individuality as Art / 67

"THE TERRIBLE BASIC TEXT *HOMO NATURA* . . . THE ETERNAL BASIC TEXT *HOMO NATURA*"   69

   The Task of Translation / 69   Equivalence / 70   Sublation / 71   Forgetting and the Rise of Enlightenment as a System of Domination / 72   The Autonomy of Formal Reason and Social Order / 75   Genealogy, the Universalization of Formal Reason, and Private Property / 76   Capitalism and Violence to Difference / 79

FOUR   **AESTHETIC INDIVIDUALITY BY ANALOGY: *DIALECTIC OF ENLIGHTENMENT* AND THE BIRTH AND DEATH OF TRAGEDY**   85

"SPREAD OVER POSTERITY LIKE A SHADOW THAT KEEPS GROWING IN THE EVENING SUN"   85

   The Birth of Tragedy and the Concept of Aesthetic Individuality / 86   Analogy from the Apollinian and the Dionysian: Art Deities and Forms of Thought / 87   Analogy from the Greek Dionysian Festival: Aesthetic Form and Forms of Thought / 92   Analogy from Attic Tragedy: The Ideal of Aesthetic Individuality / 97   Analogy from "Aesthetic Socratism:" Socratic Reason and Enlightenment as "Murderous Principles" / 104

RECONCILIATION AND THE ALLIANCE BETWEEN KANT AND HEGEL, OR HEGEL WITHOUT THE ABSOLUTE, KANT WITHOUT THE SUPERSENSIBLE   106

AESTHETIC INDIVIDUALITY AND THE DESTRUCTION OF THE JEWS   114

FIVE   **RECOVERING AESTHETIC INDIVIDUALITY FROM ART: AESTHETIC REASON IN ADORNO'S *AESTHETIC THEORY*   117**

THE AESTHETICS OF DARKNESS   120

   Beauty and the Unknown / 122   Trace and the Unknown / 124   Rationality, Mimesis, and the Unknown / 125   Spirit and the Unknown / 127   Expression and the Unknown / 128

REASON AND DARKNESS   130

NO TRESPASSING   133

THE GREAT DIVIDE   135

"A MUSIC WHOSE SOUL KNOWS HOW TO ROAM AND BE AT HOME AMONG GREAT BEAUTIFUL SOLITARY BEASTS OF PREY" 138

NIETZSCHE'S DREAM, ADORNO'S NIGHTMARE 144

THE MARRIAGE OF LIGHT AND DARK 145

PART II
SURFACES   147

SIX   AN ETHIC OF APPEARANCES   149

UP FROM THE DEPTHS, ONTO THE SURFACES OF THE WORLD 149

NIETZSCHE'S PURE SURFACES 150

THE CREATIVE WILL AND ITS DESTRUCTION OF DEPTH 157

INTO THE UNKNOWN 165

    Nonidentity and the Unknown / 166   Perspectivism and the Unknown / 169   God and the Unknown / 171

AN ETHIC OF APPEARANCES / 173

    Mystery, Wonder, and Delight in Appearances / 174   Appearance and Difference / 178   The Sufficiency, Equality, and Uniqueness of Appearances / 180   An Intimacy with Appearances / 183

SEVEN   INDIVIDUALITY AS A POETIC FORM OF LIFE   185

A POETIC FORM OF LIFE 186

EVERY EXISTENCE HAS ITS IDIOM 188

    The Distant Brought Near / 191

REPRESENTING A WORLD 194

    Representing Surfaces Descriptively / 195   Representing Surfaces Metaphorically / 202

PRESENTING A WORLD 206

    Forcing Surfaces and Depths / 209   Attachment and Self-Creativity / 214   Discontinuity / 217   A Constitutive Interest in Difference / 222   The Aesthetic Value of Surfaces and Nietzsche's Marriage of Light and Dark / 224

EIGHT   DEMOCRACY AS AN AESTHETIC FORM OF LIFE   230

TECHNOLOGY, MODERNITY, AND DIFFERENCE 231

DEMOCRACY, MODERNITY, AND DIFFERENCE 232

CONTENTS

DEMOCRACY, DIFFERENCE, AND POETRY 235

DEMOCRACY AND AESTHETIC EDUCATION 237

DEMOCRATIC TIME, DEMOCRATIC SPACE 240

NINE AESTHETIC INDIVIDUALITY AS A DEMOCRATIC ACHIEVEMENT 248

TOCQUEVILLE'S AESTHETIC SENSIBILITY 250

TOCQUEVILLE'S BLINDNESS TO DEMOCRATIC DIFFERENCE 253

The Large Differences of Aristocratic Societies / 257 The Small Differences of Democratic Society / 263

THE AESTHETICS OF SMALL DIFFERENCES 270

Democracy's Mimetic Dimension—Self-Creativity and Aesthetic Presentation as Imitation, or Individuality From the Point of View of the Artist (the Creator) / 271 Representing Difference: A Sensibility to Violence in the Aesthetics of Individuality / 282 Individuality's Orientation to the Surfaces of Small Differences / 285 Individuality's All-Inclusive Orientation to Small Differences / 286 Individuality's Orientation to the Equality, Sufficiency, and Uniqueness of Small Differences / 286 Individuality's Receptivity to Small Differences / 288 Attachment and Intimacy / 290 Individuality's Indifference to Difference in Its Depths, the Unknown, and the Indeterminacy of Surfaces / 292 The Logic of Identity "as" Difference / 296

AESTHETIC INDIVIDUALITY AS A DEMOCRATIC ACHIEVEMENT 298

TEN CONCLUSION: INDIVIDUALITY AFTER THE HOLOCAUST 300

A MORALLY DISTINCTIVE DEMOCRATIC INDIVIDUALITY 301

THE MORAL AND THE AESTHETIC 307

NOTES 311

INDEX 329

ACKNOWLEDGMENTS

Reason and Horror originally grew out of my dissatisfaction with the failure of political and social theorists to bring the critical theory of Max Horkheimer and Theodor Adorno to bear on the problem of individuality in modern democratic society. In the wake of Horkheimer and Adorno's powerful and dire appraisal of the fate of the modern "subject" in a Western world shaped by the process of enlightenment, there seems to have been a general disregard for the need to reexamine, in light of their work, the character of the individual who is the very center of democracy. A tacit consensus seems to have formed around the view that rather than offering a renewable source of critical analysis, Horkheimer and Adorno's contribution to this issue concluded with the interpretation of their work taking shape in the three decades following the defeat of Fascism. To the exclusion of other possibilities, this tradition of interpretation emphasizes dimensions of their work tracing the disappearance of the individual in late capitalism, who is swept up into a future perpetuating the rationality responsible for the horrors of the past. The approach I take here runs contrary to this tradition. By drawing upon the critical theory of Horkheimer and Adorno and entering it into dialogue with the thought of Nietzsche, Whitman, and Tocqueville, I attempt to theorize a new form of individuality.

"Aesthetic individuality," I believe, has been developing gradually in modern democratic society from its very birth, nurtured by democracy's most fundamental institutions, practices, and principles. By creating the modern self and its world in ways that depend on and promote the flourishing of the great diversity of differences that surround it, aesthetic individuality serves as a barrier to the evil of punishing those who are different by virtue of their race, religion, gender, ethnicity, or sexual identity, among other forms of difference for which individuals and groups are treated punitively. Aesthetic individuality's distinctive quality is that it serves as a barrier to the evil of holocaust and genocidal extermination.

To the extent to which it has been realized, my project has been contributed to generously over the past several years by friends, colleagues, and students. I am especially indebted to Bill Connolly, whose work on identity and difference posed important challenges to my idea of an aesthetic form of individuality, and to George Kateb, whose contributions to a theory of democratic individuality, and contagious love for the art of Walt Whitman, formed the inspired background for my work. I am grateful to George Kateb and Shadia Drury for extensive comments on the entirety of *Reason and Horror*, which improved its arguments considerably, and to Bill Connolly, Jane Bennett, Dick Flathman, Tom Dumm, Tracy Strong, Stephen White, and Nancy Love for reading and commenting on chapters of the manuscript when they were first completed. Correspondence with David Lenson regarding the meaning of Nietzsche's arguments in sections of *The Birth of Tragedy* was invaluable. I owe a special debt to Gary Gossen, Judith Johnson, Marilyn Masson, and John Pipkin for considering my work in a study group that has provided the Emersonian friendship out of which agonistic debate becomes most fruitful, and to Angelo Frascarelli, for the time spent discussing the finer points of music theory. My thanks to Jack Gunnell, Peter Breiner, Bruce Miroff, David Kettler, and George Marcus for comments on my presentation of chapter 6 at our local chapter meeting of the Conference for the Study of Political Thought, and to faculty and students at the University of Massachusetts, University of Calgary, and Amherst College for comments on chapters 5, 7, and 8, respectively, at colloquiums to which I was kindly invited to give presentations. During the past several years graduate students in my seminar on contemporary political theory, especially Jim Freeman, Kevin Cameron, Philip Brendese, Chris Price, Mine Doyran, Jeff Hilmer, Leah Murray, David Parisi, Mike Rogers, Brian Schmidt, Jason Scruton, and Frank Vander Valk, have offered comments and criticisms that have been as insightful and useful as any I have received from other quarters. I am grateful to Helen Desfosses, Frank Thompson, and Bill Hedberg for their friendship and support, and to my family, Maureen, Ethan, and Rachel, whose love and encouragement helped me to see this project to completion. Finally, I am grateful to Eric Nelson, my editor at Routledge, whose professionalism and thoughtfulness make it possible for an author to produce his best work.

This book is dedicated to the memory of my mother, Helene Schoolman, for whom a democratic society bringing enlightenment to power by breaking the bounds of enlightenment would have provided a home.

ONE

Introduction: Reason and Horror

Keeping company with the many explanations marshaled over the decades for the rise of German Fascism and its extermination of the Jews, one constant suspicion may be held in common at this late period of modernity by all who have thought about those events. Those who participated in the crime of the Holocaust did so in the wake of some terrible sea change that had been effected in the human spirit. If such a fear does haunt us, perhaps through all our efforts to lay blame for the Holocaust elsewhere so that we can feel less vulnerable precisely where we may have become the weakest, then the thesis of this work will resonate. The destruction of the Jews was the consequence of the destruction of the aesthetic features of what the Western philosophical tradition since John Stuart Mill more narrowly understood as "individuality." "Aesthetic individuality," as I will call it, disappeared with the triumph of a form of rationality whose progress led inevitably to the Holocaust. Set forth in *Dialectic of Enlightenment*, I will argue in part I of *Reason and Horror*, this is Max Horkheimer and Theodor W. Adorno's discovery.[1] It is the sea change in the human spirit from which the horror of the Holocaust followed.[2]

Yet, although the eclipse of aesthetic individuality and the event of the Holocaust are related so necessarily in Horkheimer and Adorno's text, the intellectual autonomy they required to entertain even the possibility of an exception to this thesis was foreclosed by the horror of the extermination. In *Twilight of the Idols* Friedrich Nietzsche captures the relationship between reason and horror that must have prevailed at that moment in 1944 when Horkheimer and Adorno first wrote of the "indefatigable self-destructiveness of enlightenment," of the path not to a truly human condition but rather to "a new kind of barbarism" on which the process of enlightenment seemed to have launched humankind.

> The fanaticism with which the whole of Greek thought throws itself at rationality betrays a sense of emergency: one was in peril, one had only *one* chance: either to perish or—*be absurdly rational*.[3]

It is not that their extreme reaction to the state of emergency defined by the horror of the Holocaust gave birth to the concept of an aesthetic form of individuality, or more generally to an "aesthetic reason" that would secure rationality in the midst of madness. To the contrary, Horkheimer and Adorno's "pathologically conditioned" response to horror, as Nietzsche goes on to describe the Greeks' reaction to the peril of internal warfare from which they labored to free themselves with their uncompromising rationalism, assumed the opposite form. Horkheimer and Adorno's pathology lay in their belief that "formal reason," as they referred to it, which from the very birth of human thought propelled enlightenment on an irreversible and unwavering trajectory toward the Holocaust, could so utterly eliminate the aesthetic form of reason with which it had been locked throughout history in primordial struggle.

My argument in part II emerges from a recognition that the self-destructive process of enlightenment rooted in an "absurdly" powerful formal rationality was Horkheimer and Adorno's desperately conceived explanation for an event whose horror absolutely determined that they could offer no alternative reply. While they mark the Holocaust as the culmination of the history of enlightenment, the aesthetic form of individuality they believe a horror-bound formal rationality destroyed to bring about the Holocaust nevertheless survived elsewhere, I will contend. To borrow Alexis de Tocqueville's expression, as the "consequence" of democratic institutions and practices, aesthetic individuality becomes a democratic achievement, the singular product of a democratic society. Aesthetic individuality becomes a new and increasingly prevalent form of democratic individuality. *Dialectic of Enlightenment* enables us to speak of an "individuality before the Holocaust," of an aesthetic individuality whose eradication issued in horror, and of an "individuality after the Holocaust," of this same aesthetic individuality that did not vanish everywhere, as Horkheimer and Adorno claimed, but was seeded in the bedrock of modern democratic society. If it can be shown that aesthetic individuality survived the process of enlightenment to flourish within a democratic form of life, then the destruction of the Jews and of all other forms of "difference" the Jew symbolically represents may be an event to which democracy proves resistant. Through the aesthetic form of individuality to which it gives birth, democracy erects barriers to evil.

INDIVIDUALITY BEFORE THE HOLOCAUST

To read *Dialectic of Enlightenment* as their response to the Holocaust, horror becomes the emergency that compelled Horkheimer and Adorno to produce a concept of reason beyond the bounds of reason, which is what I understand Nietzsche to mean by a pathologically conditioned absurdly rational idea of reason.[4] What is required first, then, is an understanding of their concept of reason, the task to which chapter 2 is devoted, though some introductory remarks will be useful in getting our bearings for that discussion and for the chapters that follow.

Formal and Aesthetic Reason

At the outset of what will become the long history of the development of reason, essentially the historical process of enlightenment, Horkheimer and Adorno argue, out of fear of the threat to its self-preservation posed by the appearance of an unknown world surrounding it, thinking's strongest impulse is to render known what is unknown. From the very birth of thinking, fear of the unknown provokes reason to make transparent a world that is dark and fathomless, bringing an end to the danger the unknown threatens. As what is unknown ultimately is unknowable, however, the world to some extent must elude thought, no matter how exhaustive its concepts. What reason believes it knows to be true of the world is, in part, therefore, an illusion, although this insight is itself unavailable to a form of reason driven single-mindedly by its fear of an enchanted world. And perhaps it is an illusion in greatest part, because as the world is finally unknowable, it is not possible for reason to estimate how much of the world it has grasped. Enlightenment, first as a world-historical process that extends from the birth of thinking onward, and then as the culmination of this process in the cultural self-understanding of the West designated as "the Enlightenment," is reason relentlessly pursuing knowledge of the world that in part is illusory, yet without a reflective understanding of the known's illusory nature.

Reason's illusion is not merely a malformation of thought. It is also, and most importantly, a malformation of the *object* of thought, a malformation of the unknowable world that is forever different from reason's every thought of it. For if the world is unknowable, and reason in its determination to abolish its fear of the unknown creates an illusory image of a world always exceeding the range of thought, then reason's illusions have re-formed a world that objectively is otherwise. Reason has imposed form on an unfathomable world essentially different from the way it is represented in thought. What is different about the world has been abolished in reason's drive to rid the world of the unknown and thinking of its fear of the unknown. Herein lies the meaning of enlightenment as Horkheimer and Adorno conceptualize it. Enlightenment is precisely this elimination of difference or, more emphatically, of all the difference in the world, because enlightenment is the process through which reason seeks to make the world known in its entirety. Whereas in its early history reason represents the world as other than it is, in-itself, later in its development reason through science and technology acquires the power to effect a wholesale transformation of the world on the basis of its illusory representations. Enlightenment in a twofold sense is consequently the expression of a violence to difference that inheres deeply in the nature of thought—in reason's impositions on the world of the forms in which it represents the world as the object of thought, and in the transformation of the world in accordance with these forms.

Unless we think of the progress of reason as the equivalent of the historical process of enlightenment, as the force of Horkheimer and Adorno's argument encourages us to do, reason is not simply and only hostile to difference. Only "formal" reason, which becomes increasingly hegemonic as enlightenment on its way to and through the modern world wends its way successively through each developmental stage of thought, unleashes its violence on the world. Formal rationality is expressed in cognitive strategies that render the unknown world known by representing it in ways that identify only those elements each thing belonging to it shares with everything else, while omitting those qualities which differentiate them. Each thing, unknowable in-itself and essentially different from thought's every representation of it, and thus different from everything else represented in thought, is represented in terms of its commonalities with other things, through which it appears to be the same. Differences become known as formal rational thinking represents them in a form through which they are made to resemble that from which objectively they are distinct. Yet, where formal reason through representation of the commonalities of the objects of thought effaces what is different among them, knowing the world's diversity of differences by making them appear the same, other properties of reason recognize that the world's differences are not entirely available to thought. "Aesthetic" reason, as I shall refer to the form of rationality Horkheimer and Adorno contrast with formal reason, is distinguished by its quality of receptivity. Aesthetic reason is receptive to the diversity of differences of which the world is composed when it acknowledges the fathomlessness of the world and affirms that its meaning and value are mysterious and that all it contains exceeds the boundaries of thought and is essentially different from reason's representations. If life is this diversity of differences, then in its acknowledgment of the unknown and its affirmation of mystery, both of which constitute thinking's receptivity to differences in all their infinite diversity, aesthetic reason's receptivity affirms life.[5] And formal reason, which eliminates differences through their assimilation to images representing only commonalities and exterminates differences that cannot be so represented in thought, is hostile to life.

Formal reason and the aesthetic form of rationality with which Horkheimer and Adorno contrast it—reason that finds what is unknown and different from thought to be an obstacle to its emancipation from fear, and reason unafraid of the unfathomable in which it finds the source of its receptivity to the diversity of different forms of life—are the two forms of reason whose conflict defines the historical process of enlightenment. As I will show in the following chapter, in *Dialectic of Enlightenment* they trace the conflict of these forms of reason through several stages. Each stage in turn marks the further ascendancy of formal reason and the steady devolution of its aesthetic counterpart until the struggle is resolved with the dominion of formal rational thought. Beginning with preanimistic thinking through magic and myth to the Enlightenment of modern times, at each of these stages the power of formal reason to purge the world of what lies outside the boundaries of thinking and is different from reason's thought of it is enhanced. The Holocaust represents the capacity of formal reason to exterminate not just the Jew but difference as such. For as Judaism embodies difference in its most abstract form, the destruction of the Jews likewise represents the destruction of the last line of ideological resistance to formal reason's power to impose form on the world, ridding it of what is unknown and appears threatening to its self-preservation. Adopting a straightforward exegetical approach to *Dialectic of Enlightenment* in chapter 2, I review the stages through which reason's violence to difference escalates until it reaches its apotheosis with the Holocaust.[6]

Aesthetic Reason, Aesthetic Individuality, Aesthetic Sensibility

Long before this catastrophic event, however, as early as the birth of thinking and also in magic, Horkheimer and Adorno find evidence for the aesthetic form of rationality that opposes the violence in thought, which as their study of Homer's *Odyssey* proves, then surfaces dramatically at the stage of thought dominated by a mythical view of the world. Although Horkheimer and Adorno never explicitly refer to the form of rationality acknowledging the unknown and receptive to difference as "aesthetic" reason, there can be no doubt that this is its proper reference. As I will argue in chapter 3, they discover the embodiment of aesthetic rationality in the individuality they attribute to Odysseus, who models the struggle to free thinking from formal reason's dominion so that it may incorporate an acknowledgment of the world's fathomlessness and a receptivity to difference. In Odysseus's encounter with the lure of the Sirens they explore an episode in the *Odyssey*, symbolic for the history of thought, when his aesthetic capacity to experience enchantment *directly*, the capacity in which his aesthetic individuality is anchored, turns into aesthetic contemplation, the *indirect* experience of enchantment through art. After partially relinquishing the formal rational mastery that has enabled him to avoid the dangers to his self-preservation threatened by an enchanted world, Horkheimer and Adorno argue, Odysseus at first is immediately engaged by their music. While the directness of his experience suggests that the two opposing forms of reason were moving toward some sort of harmonious relationship, Odysseus as his ship passes beyond the Sirens continues to gaze after them as though they were merely works of art. It is at this moment in the evolution of thought, I will propose, when Odysseus's original receptivity to difference assumes the form of art, that in retrospect we realize the form of rationality that throughout his journey had defined his individuality as receptivity is an *aesthetic* orientation to the world. Aesthetic individuality is revealed clearly at that moment when enlightenment spoils myth's anticipation of a resolved division within reason between its will to make the world known and its will to affirm the unknown, between its fear of what lies outside of and is different from thought and its receptivity to such difference. Beyond myth formal reason continues to be developed by the process of enlightenment, while at the stage of myth enlightenment has arrested the aesthetic individuality with which Odysseus had embraced the world's darkness, as he had in his encounter with the Sirens through his receptivity to a direct experience of enchantment. Individuality, in the aesthetic form in which it appeared "before the Holocaust," shedding its fear of the unknown to become receptive to difference, has been displaced to art, which confirms its aesthetic nature.

Reason's aesthetic receptivity, the third chapter demonstrates, is at the heart of individuality as Horkheimer and Adorno conceptualize it. Likewise, the chapter's explanation of art as the repository of individuality's displaced aesthetic features justifies my introduction, in chapter 2, of the term *aesthetic* to describe the receptivity to a world of difference that opposes formal reason's relationship of violence. Both of these discussions are integral to a larger project that occupies chapter 3, the reconstruction of *Dialectic of Enlightenment*. If our interpretation of this work were to progress no further than an account of the stages of enlightenment through which reason advances to the Holocaust, the final impression would be that of a linear historical development of reason that unfolds with the inertia of an unvarying and unremitting force. Indeed, so much so does the course of enlightenment seem to follow a predetermined course that with the hegemony of formal reason and its eclipse of aesthetic individuality in modernity there are several inevitable consequences for thinking. At the conclusion of Horkheimer and Adorno's linear historical narrative, reason's aesthetic capacity to think the world could ever be different from its every thought of it has been ruined so thoroughly by the process of enlightenment that we no longer can imagine reason could be anything other than formal rationality. In effect, formal reason constitutes a sphere of rationality that defines the parameters within which all thinking proceeds. Our thinking is so determined by formal reason that we cannot account even for a reader who has the ability to grasp enlightenment's catastrophic implications for "difference." Yet, as readers we do grasp these implications, and surely Horkheimer and Adorno expect that they will not elude us, at least not entirely.

Dialectic of Enlightenment, I contend, is thus paradoxical. At one level it presupposes the existence of a reader who at another level, that of the text's linear historical narrative, is shown to have vanished without a trace in the wake of enlightenment. Of course, it is not that there is either a reader or there is not, but that the reader that escapes the historical fate to which Horkheimer and Adorno's narrative claims it has succumbed has instead been made rather precarious by the historical forces threatening it with extinction. So precarious has the reader been made by the process of enlightenment, perhaps all that remains of a historically earlier and robust aesthetic reason and aesthetic individuality is an aesthetic *sensibility* awakened at the conclusion of their work to establish the reader's connection to their argument. No matter how precarious the reader, though, once our recognition of the paradoxical character of their argument has led us to the aesthetic sensibility that prevails against enlightenment to allow *Dialectic of Enlightenment* to become accessible to a reader, a strategic interpretive move becomes possible. We then are drawn back into the narrative structure of the text to discover how a form of aesthetic reason could have survived the history of disenchantment to which it was argued to have been lost. Put differently, since the preservation of an aesthetic sensibility belies the argument of the linear historical narrative, we are encouraged to entertain the possibility that Horkheimer and Adorno's work contains a second and deeper argument that does not agree with the narrative structure at the manifest level of their text.

With this possibility in mind, I pursue a reconstruction of *Dialectic of Enlightenment* as a "genealogy of reason." By the reconstruction of *Dialectic of*

Enlightenment genealogically, textual evidence may be found indicating that at some point in its past reason may not have been so perfectly shaped by enlightenment as its linear historical narrative proves. Aesthetic reason may have had some chance to resist enlightenment. The relationship between formal and aesthetic reason may have been otherwise than the domination of the former over the latter. Consequently, at some stage of thought the evolving identity of the modern world and of all those in it may have been received as a *contingent* formation, or one offering *possibilities* for aesthetic individuality *other* than its displacement to art. If so, these earlier possibilities for aesthetic individuality may have been inherited by the late modern world in the diminished form of an aesthetic sensibility, or perhaps in some other form that even outstrips the aesthetic sensibility that appears to be all that has survived the onslaught of enlightenment. A line of inquiry enabling us not only to account for the survival of a sensibility qualifying us to be readers of *Dialectic of Enlightenment* but also to recover the possibility for a more developed form of aesthetic individuality in the present becomes available when *Dialectic of Enlightenment* is reconstructed as a genealogy of reason. Genealogy potentially places us on the threshold of an enlightenment for which Horkheimer and Adorno had held out hope, an enlightenment that through the aesthetic transformation of reason breaks through the historical limitations of an enlightenment of violence.

Reading *Dialectic of Enlightenment*

Adopting a two-tiered interpretive strategy, I approach *Dialectic of Enlightenment* as though it were a text divided against itself. Though it is unequivocally a linear historical narrative of enlightenment that empties the world of contingent possibilities for aesthetic individuality, on the one hand, it becomes equally a genealogy of reason that recovers contingency in history to loosen formal reason's hold over us. Guided by this genealogical interest, I retreat to Horkheimer and Adorno's examination of myth, for it is at the mythical stage of thought, they argue, when enlightenment initially appears as the progress of formal over aesthetic reason. It is unlikely that an aesthetic orientation to the world could have persisted beyond myth if at this stage there had not been some contingent opportunity to counter the assault of formal rationality that inaugurated enlightenment as the architect of reason's future history. No matter how insignificant, if there is some contingency to be discovered in the history of enlightenment, in other words, it will be found at the stage of myth. To be sure, as seen through Horkheimer and Adorno's discussion of Homer's *Odyssey*, Odysseus's aesthetic receptivity to the enchanted world through which he must make his way home to Ithaca at first appears to be the victim of a fateful process of enlightenment. His trials and their outcomes appear to be determined in advance by a contest in which one world-historical principle steadily cedes to the ascendancy of the other. Odysseus appears, in every instance, to be an object of formal reason.

Against the inevitability guaranteed by this linear historical narrative, however, Odysseus, considered genealogically, refuses to be ruled by a principle of reason that operates over his head and behind his back. Rather than a world-historical conflict of which Odysseus's struggles are symbolic, the conflict between a formal and an aesthetic orientation to the world becomes a conflict within his own thinking, essentially within his self, and as such one over which he has some power. Especially in the poignant episode in which he encounters the Sirens, which with the genealogical turn of interpretation in chapter 3 will move to the forefront of my discussion, we witness Odysseus exercising some control over his fate. By having himself lashed to the mast of his ship so that he could experience their mysteries directly, though without risking his self-preservation, Odysseus forges a compromise between a formal rational orientation and an aesthetic receptivity to the world. Through this *compromised* form of aesthetic individuality, as I describe it, Odysseus permits himself an aesthetic experience of enchantment. At the same time, however, because his self-preservation and identity are never endangered and his crew is able to hold fast to its homeward course, the principle of formal reason underlying his approach to negotiating dangers that appear to be posed by an enchanted world is not reconstituted in the least. In the *Odyssey*, I argue, Horkheimer and Adorno consequently discover evidence that at the mythical stage of thought formal reason's first decisive challenge to an aesthetic receptivity to the world is not entirely victorious. Aesthetic reason is subordinated to formal rationality, but not subdued, and Odysseus's individuality has not yet been sacrificed to an identity whose relation to the world eventually would be governed exclusively by formal reason. Contingency, the possibility that beyond this historical point Odysseus's future could have been otherwise than the way we know it to have unfolded, as could the futures of those who would have inherited the partially unconquered form of his aesthetic individuality, is installed at the moment of his compromise.

On the basis of the compromised form of aesthetic individuality through which Odysseus avoids sacrificing the aesthetic dimension of his experience, it becomes possible to clarify the features of aesthetic reason and to project an *ideal* of aesthetic individuality that would entail the transformation of enlightenment. With this ideal I conceptualize a fully developed form of aesthetic individuality whose receptivity is the articulation of an undistorted human nature that, in turn, neither reproduces formal reason's distortion or destruction of outward nature's diversity of differences nor threatens the self-preservation of identity. Beyond these conceptual insights, however, Odysseus's *encounter with* the Sirens finally does not suggest that mythical thought yielded the degree of contingency that might have altered the direction of the process of enlightenment away from the horrors to which it inevitably led. From the standpoint symbolized by Odysseus at the stage of thought reached by myth, the subsequent history of enlightenment might have been other than it became only if the contingencies that were then available to the Western cultural constellation he represents became a legacy for future generations.

As we shall see, though, the compromise Odysseus strikes with formal rationality to create space for an aesthetic receptivity to difference—that is being squeezed out of history by the fate to which he has been subjected by the process of enlightenment—is but a fleeting independence that momentarily problematizes the linearity of Horkheimer and Adorno's narrative. What appeared as a contingent opportunity to oppose formal reason by insinuating into the tightly woven fabric of history an aesthetic form of individuality that could shape, as well as be shaped by, the history of enlightenment is quickly suppressed. Odysseus fails to exploit the contingencies his compromise opens to him, and the aesthetic receptivity to an enchanted world of difference expressed in his encounter with the Sirens is displaced to art. Continuing on his journey home to Ithaca, Horkheimer and Adorno argue, Odysseus passes through the stages of enlightenment as they are traced out by the *Odyssey*, and he becomes symbolic of the fate the process of enlightenment visits upon modernity. Odysseus's affirmation of aesthetic individuality gives way to the hegemony of formal reason and to the creation of the modern subject with the Enlightenment of modern times. Individuality's aesthetic existence is effectively ended, which unbridles the violence inherent in thought and exposes all the difference in the world to reason as a murderous principle. What contingency we inherit from myth is the pale reflection of that briefly created by Odysseus. Odysseus's compromised form of aesthetic individuality is bequeathed to us in the form of art, rather than as the contingent opportunity he possessed before his direct aesthetic experience of an enchanted world turned to aesthetic contemplation. At most, all we possess is the aesthetic sensibility embodied in artworks to which aesthetic individuality has been displaced by formal rational thought. Enlightenment continues unabated, while the aesthetic sensibility that found refuge in art allows us entry to a text that, as narrative, teaches us only of our fate, though, as genealogy, accounts for a sensibility that has escaped that fate to enable a reader who at least can conceptualize aesthetic individuality and reconstruct its history.

Although it may be suspected that I have adopted a genealogical approach to *Dialectic of Enlightenment* out of deference to current methodological trends, my real motive lies elsewhere. In part it is informed by my belief that Nietzsche must be credited with having the greatest influence on Horkheimer and Adorno's thought. While the matter of his real bearing on their work must be left for another time, *Dialectic of Enlightenment*'s structural resemblance to Nietzsche's later genealogies appeared to me so striking that circuitously, at least, my reconfiguration of this work as a genealogy of reason establishes his presence emphatically. What becomes most important in the course of my argument, however, are the new interpretive possibilities that open up when *Dialectic of Enlightenment* is approached as a genealogy. At the same time, I do not concentrate on its genealogical dimensions to the exclusion of other methodologies prominently at work in

Horkheimer and Adorno's argument. In particular, in the concluding sections of chapter 3 I will propose that the genealogical design of *Dialectic of Enlightenment* does not explain the progress of enlightenment beyond the Enlightenment of modern times. Whereas genealogical categories enable Horkheimer and Adorno to plot the ascendancy of formal reason from the birth of thinking to the Enlightenment, to complete their analysis of the evolution of enlightenment they turn to Marxism. With the aid of Marxist categories they are able to show how property relations and formal reason develop in and through each other until the latter becomes universal, and how as a consequence of securing the universalization of formal reason capital becomes responsible for the murderous history of enlightenment since the Enlightenment. Even where they rely on economic categories to explain the development of formal reason from the Enlightenment through the several stages of liberalism, though, there is also a degree of continuity in their use of genealogical concepts. To take Horkheimer and Adorno's argument as a whole, then, the Enlightenment marks the dividing line in a history of enlightenment between a past development of formal reason that cannot be understood without being reconstructed genealogically and a future development of formal reason that to be understood must be seen to correspond increasingly to a linear narrative as capitalist relations unfold.

As I already have indicated in a preliminary way, though, as I draw out the structural similarities of Nietzsche's genealogical method to *Dialectic of Enlightenment* in chapter 3, and the genealogical framework of Horkheimer and Adorno's work is thrown into relief, it will become evident that they offer us more than a metanarrative of reason's destruction of difference. Approaching *Dialectic of Enlightenment* genealogically, we have begun to see, allows us to account for a reader who they believe has been interdicted by the history of enlightenment to the point of becoming an "imaginary witness," the term they use in the "Notes and Drafts" to their text. Short of this genealogical account, *Dialectic of Enlightenment* cannot be critically redeemed, for if we were unable to discover a historical basis for a reader, far more than the new interpretive possibilities that a genealogical approach opens to us would be lost. Lost, as well, would be the possibility of discovering in our own historical period some evidence for the aesthetic form of individuality a genealogy of reason recovers. As I will show, approaching their work as a genealogy reveals that Horkheimer and Adorno carry out what Nietzsche in his own work had called a "translation" of "man back into nature," a translation—or what we more recently understand to be a "deconstruction"—of modern subjectivity back into individuality. With this genealogical translation they are able to recall individuality's original aesthetic properties before it evolved into a different form as a consequence of a struggle within thought between two qualitatively different types of thinking. Recovering their genealogical reconstruction of the concept of aesthetic individuality allows us to imagine our own relationship to difference as becoming free of violence and to inquire into the conditions under which this relationship might be developed, as I will do in part II of my argument, even if within the framework of Horkheimer and Adorno's own work such a possibility is no more than utopian.

Finally, by developing the resemblance between Horkheimer and Adorno's and Nietzsche's genealogical practices, my intention is to generate a certain openness to the argument I follow with in chapter 4: that the concept of aesthetic individuality we find in *Dialectic of Enlightenment* has an even more fundamental Nietzschean connection. Nietzsche's *The Birth of Tragedy*, I will argue, furnishes a historical model of the origin and decline of aesthetic reason that resembles Horkheimer and Adorno's nearly to the last detail. Nietzsche's work not only entails a concept of an aesthetic receptivity to the world mirrored in *Dialectic of Enlightenment* but likewise explains its destruction by a principle of rationality identical to the principle of formal reason that animates the process of enlightenment as Horkheimer and Adorno present it. By developing the parallels between *The Birth of Tragedy* and *Dialectic of Enlightenment* through a series of analogies drawn between the two texts, I clarify the concept of aesthetic individuality that first became available to us by approaching Horkheimer and Adorno's work as a genealogy. And as the parallels prove to be nothing less than stunning, they shore up my claim that by virtue of its counterpart aesthetic characteristics in Nietzsche's work, the concept of individuality Horkheimer and Adorno offer is undoubtedly aesthetic.

Aesthetic Individuality and the Aesthetics of Tragedy

As Nietzsche reconstructs it genealogically in *The Birth of Tragedy*, the history of Hellenic culture develops as a struggle between two principles, the Dionysian and the Apollinian. Because there is not one but several outcomes to this conflict, the art and thought of ancient Greece will vary during its epic stages depending on which of these principles dominates at a given time. With the structure of *Dialectic of Enlightenment* already well established as the background to my discussion of his work, it will be evident that the conflict that Nietzsche describes finds its virtual facsimile in Horkheimer and Adorno's study, and not just with regard to the process of enlightenment considered synoptically.

Among the key moments in Nietzsche's arguments, I will contend, we find predecessors to the interpretive scenarios through which Horkheimer and Adorno offer different forms of aesthetic individuality. Nietzsche's recollection of the Greek Dionysian festival, for example, relates the Apollinian and Dionysian principles in a way that is duplicated in Horkheimer and Adorno's construing of the way in which, in his encounter with the Sirens, Odysseus forges and then resolves a compromise in his individuality between its formal and aesthetic qualities. Similarly, Attic tragedy, whose birth Nietzsche describes as arising from the balanced coupling of the Apollinian and Dionysian, is imitated by the ideal of aesthetic individuality implicit in *Dialectic of Enlightenment*. Replicating the structure of the relationship between the Apollinian and Dionysian principles in

Attic tragedy, Horkheimer and Adorno's ideal of aesthetic individuality equally incorporates the principles of formal and aesthetic reason. Normatively speaking, it then drives their critique of enlightenment and its destruction of aesthetic individuality. And it does so in much the same way that Nietzsche's model of Attic tragedy drives his critique of the death of Attic tragedy brought about through the changes in Greek drama and culture that commenced with the art and science of Euripides and Socrates. As I will try to show, there can be no doubt that the dramatic parallels between *The Birth of Tragedy* and *Dialectic of Enlightenment* are underpinned by Horkheimer and Adorno's belief that formal reason shares the *modus operandi* characterizing the principle of Socratic reason as Nietzsche described it. In relation to the individual's aesthetic receptivity to all the difference in the world, formal no less than Socratic reason is a "murderous principle," as Nietzsche so unforgivingly judged the principle of enlightenment responsible for the death of Attic tragedy and with it the destruction of the Hellenic aesthetic receptivity to being.

When the analogies between the two texts all have been drawn, it will be clear that in every important respect *The Birth of Tragedy* conceptually prefigures the entire course of enlightenment as it is deciphered in *Dialectic of Enlightenment*. So clear, in fact, that as we listen to each work echoing the other's analysis of the destruction of the aesthetic receptivity to the world that distinguishes the highest stage of Greek culture, it will be tempting to dwell on the future raw consequences of enlightenment as they are commonly laid out in both texts. There is a shared conviction more telling, however, than Horkheimer and Adorno and Nietzsche's agreement that we are denied our deepest, aesthetic experience of a world by an enlightenment that necessarily subjects it to the mastery of formal reason. It is Nietzsche's aesthetic ideal modeled by Attic tragedy and reproduced in Horkheimer and Adorno's aspiration for an aesthetic enlightenment that will come to power to transcend the historical limits of an enlightenment of violence. By valuing our aesthetic experience of the world above all, such an enlightenment would protect the ways in which the world is different from our every thought of it, the world as it appears in its diversity of differences, thus ending the domination of formal reason.

Nietzsche's ideal, though, does celebrate an aesthetic experience that at its extreme appears to know the world in the precise way that the Socratic logic to which he objects purports to know the world, that is, in its essence. Acknowledging this ambiguity in his aesthetics, I defend Nietzsche against the charge that his theory of Attic tragedy reflects a philosophical allegiance to the possibility of reconciliation. Here, again, I find him aligned with Horkheimer and Adorno, who attack both the process of enlightenment and the cultural period of the Enlightenment for nurturing forms of thought that entail a belief in reconciliation. Reconciliation is e/Enlightenment's illusion that the world can be known as it is, in-itself, the expression of reason's deepest cognitive need to free itself of its fear of the unknown by making the world transparent, the need that underlies every thought of the world shaped by formal rationality. Nietzsche's aesthetics affirms reason's unbridgeable separation from the world for which Horkheimer and Adorno, I argue, through an alliance between Kant and Hegel, find grounds in the "concept," the work performed by thought when it recognizes that it can know the unknowable world always and only in part, and that the greatest part may remain unknown. By affirming the ontological divide at the root of conceptual thinking, in other words, Nietzsche's aesthetics affirms the form of thought at the heart of individuality as Horkheimer and Adorno allow us to develop it aesthetically. Formal reason's drive to cross the unbridgeable divide between thought of the world and the world as it is, in-itself, which is the physical and mental space within which difference is located, is consequently hostile to the aesthetic nature of individuality and to aesthetic individuality's conception of the world as unknown and essentially different from its every thought of it.

With the argument of chapter 4 the comparative analysis of *The Birth of Tragedy* and *Dialectic of Enlightenment* has served to clarify the concept of aesthetic individuality embedded in Horkheimer and Adorno's text and to support my claim that they do, in fact, contribute a concept of aesthetic individuality. Yet the comparison of these two great works does not rewrite the history of enlightenment that buried individuality's aesthetic experience of the world in art. At the chapter's conclusion I briefly revisit the event to which the process of enlightenment is hurled. As Judaism is the incarnation of difference, the destruction of the Jews is the most extreme escalation of enlightenment's determination to purge thinking of the uncertainty ineradicably inscribed in conceptual thought. As does the concept, the Jew represents the unknown, though in its most elusive form. Exterminating the Jew is thus enlightenment's most "advanced" achievement, as it proves that no form of life other than art can withstand the progress of formal reason to preserve thinking that constitutes aesthetic individuality's receptivity to the world in its infinite diversity of differences. Confined to art, to which in the history of enlightenment it was displaced, aesthetic individuality becomes a matter for aesthetic theory, the focus of chapter 5.

From a Genealogy of Reason to Aesthetic Theory

As chapter 5 opens, formal reason has crushed individuality's capacity to be receptive to the world aesthetically except through the medium of art, so that the aesthetic properties of individuality now must be recovered conceptually from the work of art in which they took refuge. Adorno's *Aesthetic Theory*, I argue, is precisely this recovery. Both the compromised and the ideal forms of aesthetic individuality differentiated out of *Dialectic of Enlightenment* by approaching it as a genealogy of reason, which were lost to the artwork as a consequence of enlightenment, now can be reconstructed by aesthetic theory only more generally as aesthetic reason. By fully recovering the concept of aesthetic reason from art, aesthetic theory defines what it means to be receptive to the world aesthetically, and thus restores the philosophical basis for the theory of aesthetic individuality that I will develop in part II of my argument. As the study of aesthetic reason through the study of art, aesthetic theory proves that to be receptive to the world aesthetically—to be receptive to the world as aesthetic reason orients art receptively—is to take the world to be unknown and unknowable and the darkness of the world to be an absolute barrier to the discovery of truth, so that the world always is recognized as different from thought's every representation of it. Art consequently sets limits to enlightenment, chastens reason by purging it of the violence in thought, and by providing the unknown as the first principle of its creativity teaches how an aesthetic form of individuality receptive to difference can be creative against a background of mystery where the world is held to be unknowable. Unfettered by the aesthetic idealism that the work of art lays bare the essence of every existence it takes as its aesthetic object, emancipated from the chimerical notion that art is able to reveal truths to which all artistic work should be directed, aesthetic creativity explodes, becoming nearly indeterminate, as does the creativity of an aesthetic individuality that takes aesthetic reason from art as its first principle.

SURFACES

With part I, "Individuality before the Holocaust," concluded, a project in conceptual retrieval has been completed. What was lost is again found: a concept of an aesthetic individuality that stands in opposition to the nightmare of the historical process of enlightenment is recovered from Horkheimer and Adorno's *Dialectic of Enlightenment*. Although its importance is not to be underestimated, an aesthetic sensibility that allows us to unlock the secrets of its history is the only sign that aesthetic individuality has survived in any other than a conceptual form. As the historical artifact of aesthetic individuality, by itself an aesthetic sensibility offers no real hope for changing the future trajectory of enlightenment unless it inspires a renewed search in the late modern world for the aesthetic individuality for which it provides evidence. Guided by the concept of aesthetic individuality retrieved from enlightenment's historical ruins, should we not next consider whether aesthetic individuality might not have been made entirely extinct by enlightenment? To put it boldly, should we not now undertake the task of completing Horkheimer and Adorno's critique of enlightenment by searching for evidence of aesthetic individuality in addition to the sensibility that appears to be its only legacy? Failing to take this next step, would we not then succumb to the same horror that pathologically conditioned their metanarrative of reason gone uncontrollably and irreversibly mad?

In the four chapters that make up "Surfaces," part II of *Reason and Horror*, I first develop the concept of aesthetic individuality from the point it was left after being recovered from art through Adorno's aesthetic theory. This project revolves briefly around Adorno and Nietzsche in chapter 6, and then is fleshed out through the poetry and prose of Walt Whitman in the remainder of that chapter and in the two that follow. While Whitman's contribution to this effort is decisive, each of these thinkers contributes uniquely and indispensably to the conceptual properties of aesthetic individuality. Once its conceptual dimensions are developed fully, in chapter 9 I look for evidence of aesthetic individuality in a democratic society by way of an examination of Alexis de Tocqueville's *Democracy in America*, an approach for which I offer justification early in that discussion. Relying on his understanding of democratic America, I *redescribe*, in the aesthetic terminology I developed through Adorno, Nietzsche, and Whitman, Tocqueville's analysis of the forms of thought and action that the "equality of condition," as he refers to democratic equality, encourages each individual in a democratic society to adopt. Evidence for aesthetic individuality as a democratic achievement rests on the possibility of redescribing, in aesthetic terms, Tocqueville's argument about the forms of thought and action fostered by equality. What behavior Tocqueville carefully observed though conceived in other terms, I will show to be aesthetic through and through.

Individuality as an Aesthetic Problem

As a consequence of his earlier collaboration with Horkheimer, and then subsequently through his *Aesthetic Theory*, we have seen, Adorno has enabled us to conceptualize individuality as an aesthetic problem. Adorno's own contribution to this problem, as I summarize it at the outset of chapter 6, constitutes its foundation. An aesthetic form of individuality eroded through the historical process of enlightenment is sublimated in art and reappears conceptually as aesthetic reason. Through the philosophical reflections of aesthetic theory, aesthetic reason, the rationality internal to the artwork, illuminates a contradiction belonging to aesthetic representation that speaks to the nature of thinking as well as to the nature of art. Aesthetic theory shows that, like the object of art, the object of thought evades representation, that there is a persistent "difference" between the identity of an object and our every thought of it. According to aesthetic theory, the rationality of the artwork demonstrates that the identity of the world we believe we can know by dint of reason escapes it. Through art we learn that by striving to abolish the difference between the world and our every thought of it, as enlightenment requires, so that we eliminate the fear bred by the uncertainty in the persistence of difference, thinking mistakenly equates its representations with the world it represents. By virtue of this equation, art teaches, thought compels the world to bear the illusory form of identity imposed upon it and to suffer the violence of appearing to be something other than it is. Aesthetic rationality thus installs the unknown as the limit to enlightenment and is sensitive to the violence accompanying every act of thought that attempts to cross the unbridgeable divide between the known and the unknown.

If we now take aesthetic reason to be the defining quality of individuality, aesthetic individuality's receptivity to the world will proceed from its recognition of an essential difference between the identity of the world, and of anyone and anything in it, and the world as individuality represents it. Each object, each living and nonliving thing, will be represented as composed of depths that are unknowable and a surface, a realm of appearance, on which reason cannot but remain. Unknowable, every object now appears as a world in-itself, so that we can speak of a "world of worlds." Out of respect for the fathomlessness of the identity of difference, aesthetic individuality will confine itself to the surfaces of the world and of everyone and everything in it, which will be to adopt a receptivity to appearances that leaves their identities, their differences in their fathomless depths, alone and unknown. Aesthetic individuality's experience of the world will be divided, confined to the surfaces of the world that in their impenetrable depths are mysterious, its creativity inspired by the mystery and wonder of the unknown while unencumbered by the desideratum to subject creativity to a truth reason seeks to discover in the depths. Aesthetic individuality's every representation will be free of the violence that accompanies representations that reason fails to acknowledge are, at least in part, impositions of form on an unknowable world.

Adorno: A Sensibility to Violence, Creativity without Form—Nietzsche: Creativity with Form, without a Sensibility to Violence

Adorno's contribution to conceptualizing individuality as an aesthetic problem is not unproblematic, however. Insofar as aesthetic individuality confines its experience of the world to its surfaces and abstains from trying to penetrate its depths, its receptivity effectively denies any knowledge of the identity of the world that would inform and guide its relationship to it, which had been the prerogative of reason in its pursuit of truth. Aesthetic individuality cannot know what form its *creativity* ought to assume when confined receptively to the surface of a world. To put it simply, aesthetic individuality's creativity is in want of *aesthetic form*. Nevertheless, the image of the world as a surface with fathomless depths that we draw from Adorno's aesthetics is indispensable to an individuality whose ethic cultivates, out of respect and care for difference, an aesthetic sensibility to the violence inflicted on difference by thought guided by enlightenment ideals.

Whereas Adorno forces us to bracket aesthetic individuality at the moment its creativity becomes problematic, I will argue in chapter 6, Nietzsche orients individuality creatively to the surfaces of the world by "envisaging the aesthetic problem from the point of view of the artist (the creator)," as he writes in *On the Genealogy of Morals*.[7] From the artist's point of view, Nietzsche is proposing, creativity is expressed and developed through aesthetic form, which he wants us to think of as the medium through which individuality can create, or represent, itself and the world, as does the artist.[8] Surfaces, or the ways in which each of us and the world and all it contains appear, are the artist's objects of aesthetic representation, but acquire depth—and this is decisive—*only* through the meaning and value belonging to the image of the surface when it is first created by the artist through the medium of aesthetic form.

As I will show, to emphasize the co-originality of value, meaning, and creativity through aesthetic form, Nietzsche cleverly conceives of surfaces metaphorically as "mirrors" in which their depths appear only as the "reflections" of the image of how a surface can be creatively formed or represented.[9] As the mere reflection of an image created on the surface of the world, depth, figuratively speaking, has no weight, and thus is no source of gravity weighing creativity down. To put it differently, thought of as mere reflections, depths release individuality from captivity to values and meanings that, when privileged as truths, are imposed upon its creativity as authoritative norms and standards it must subserve, as though they were depths belonging to a surface all along, an objective foundation that should govern creativity on the surface above. And with the idea of depth as the reflection of a creation on a surface, Nietzsche is stressing that the depth of any particular meaning or value created is open to interpretation. Indefinite in meaning and value, depth confers a corresponding indeterminacy upon the identity of its creator. Through the interpretive openness of the meaning and value of individuality's creation, individuality's own identity becomes something different than it appears to be, a surface with a fathomless depth, deeper in meaning and value than the image in which it has represented itself. Hence Nietzsche's approach to the aesthetic problem, the problem of creativity, from the point of view of the artist, enables us to imagine individuality originating meaning and value without proscription, and creating an identity that differs from its appearance, that is as different from its appearance as may be the depths of an image's reflection as it appears in the surface of a mirror.

Such creativity earns the individual "nobility," the quality with which Nietzsche distinguishes individuality. Those incapable of originality are fated to resent those who are noble. Out of their resentment, they collectively "say no" to the values and meanings originated by nobility by constructing and universalizing moral systems that demonize nobility as "otherness" while valorizing the collective identity of the herd. To Nietzsche, moral truths are depths—values and meanings—that the power of the collective universalizes, and in their universalization cease to be reflections of their origins and take on an illusory objectivity. As depths normatively grounding thought and action, universal moral truths become weights subduing creativity by holding it hostage to values and meanings not of its own making, which undermines individuality's creativity on the surface. Surfaces and depths are consequently inverted. No longer a reflection of creativity on the surface, as truth depth is transformed into "reality" and the surface and its creations into mere manifestations of the underlying reality. Since in the moral universe reality connotes the value accorded truth, losing the totality of surface possibilities to the reality of the depth further diminishes the value of creativity on a surface already devalued through its enslavement to moral imperatives.

It is through the concepts of surface and depth, then, that Nietzsche establishes the conditions for aesthetic individuality's relationship to the world. Receptive to the surface of the world, individuality's creativity on a surface is "light" in two metaphorical senses. Its creativity is light when unencumbered by the pull of gravity exerted by the deadening depth of truth below, to become the light reflecting the meaning and value of images created on a surface as its depths.[10] Yet, I shall also ask what would be the relationship of Nietzsche's aesthetic individuality to Adorno's depths, the fathomless depths of a world whose identity is forever unknown? After all, Adorno's depths do not weigh individuality down as do the heavy, inert depths of moral truth. Unknown, unfathomable depths free individuality from the belief that the ideas and images of the world it forms illuminate its depths, free thought from the hubris that it can know the world in its depths and from the limitations on creativity that such truth prescribes. Freeing individuality from the illusion of reconciliation, Adorno rescues from the violence of representation all that the world contains, whose identities necessarily elude and thus remain different from thought, by confining individuality's aesthetic receptivity to the surface.

In the course of my discussion it will become clear that both Nietzsche and Adorno orient individuality receptively to the surfaces of the world, though with a decisive difference. Once Adorno's idea of a world possessing an identity with fathomless depths confines creativity, or representation, to the world's surfaces, individuality is left to imagine the form of its aesthetic relationship to the world. Creativity is in want of form beyond individuality's reflective understanding that unless its experience of the world remains divided, the world falls victim to a process of enlightenment that extinguishes difference by seeking to know the world in its depths. Nietzsche, to the contrary, confines individuality creatively to the surfaces of the world, though without being mindful of Adorno's depths below. Nietzsche's formulation of an aesthetic relation *excludes* the possibility that a fathomless depth, unavailable to thought, might lie divided from us beneath the surfaces on which individuality creates its images of the world in all their values and meanings. In that event, Adorno's depths become a mere extension of Nietzsche's surfaces, mere layers of the surface and as depths indistinct, collapsed to the surface and integral to the foreground on which individuality's creativity explodes when emancipated from the limitations imposed by the foundations, the "fathomable" depths, underlying moral truth. Adorno's depths would be re-formed by the creative transformations of the surface, their identity subjected to the violence of the forms of representation to which the surface is subjected, their plight veiled by depths construed to be the mere reflections of individuality's images of the surface.

It is evident, I will argue, that there is an irreconcilable contradiction between the ways in which Nietzsche and Adorno relate individuality aesthetically to the surfaces and depths of the world. On a general level, surfaces and depths are the poles around which Nietzsche's ideas of individuality and creativity revolve, and they circulate powerfully though tacitly throughout Adorno's thinking. By means of these concepts as they work when Nietzsche and Adorno are taken together, the two central dimensions of aesthetic individuality—creativity and a sensibility to violence in the ways individuality creatively forms itself and the world—are fleshed out. While both Nietzsche and Adorno constitute an aesthetic relation to the world as receptivity to its surfaces, however, the identity of difference in its depths that Adorno's aesthetics protects from the impositions of representation are violated by Nietzsche's idea of creativity, becoming assimilated to the surface on which individuality's images of the world are formed. If we are to preserve for aesthetic individuality the aesthetic sensibility to difference that Adorno's aesthetic theory recovers, we must discover a way to enfold this sensibility within Nietzsche's model of creativity. Aesthetic individuality must be conceptualized in a way that weds Nietzsche's idea of aesthetic creativity on the surfaces of the world to Adorno's idea of an aesthetic sensibility to its depths. With this conceptual challenge, which I show will be met by Whitman's work, we have the fully developed formulation of individuality as an aesthetic problem, to which the remainder of chapter 6 and the two chapters that follow are devoted.

Whitman: The Aesthetic Problem from the Point of View of the Artist (the Creator)

Whitman's prose, though especially his poetry, I will demonstrate, not only affirms but draws inspiration from an experience of the world divided between the world as it can be known and the world as it remains unknown. If it were not for a certain innocence in his enthusiastic embrace of technological progress, the philosophic motifs that in all their poetic variations spring from Whitman's recognition of the unknown would qualify him as no less an opponent of the Enlightenment than Nietzsche and Adorno. Whitman's conviction that the world is unfathomable is evident from arguments he frames poetically. As its animating principle, the unknown enables the poet to form images distinguishing between the depths, the fathomless qualities, of the world's diversity of differences, and the surfaces of differences through which poetic creativity is to unfold. Every thing and every one existing is different from everything and everyone else, on its surface different from the surface of every other, and different in its depths from the way it appears on the surface.

The poet is drawn irresistibly to the world when engaged by the world's sheer diversity of differences, an engagement that becomes possible for the poet once the identity of everyone and everything of which the world is composed, and hence the identity of the world itself, is acknowledged to be unknowable in its depths, a surface with a fathomless depth. Acknowledged to be unknown, different in their depths from how they appear, surfaces cease to be reducible to deeper, shared properties that would blind the poet to the differences among them by urging him to attend to their commonalities. As for Adorno, for Whitman differences appear among surfaces when surfaces are acknowledged to be unknown in their depths. Poetic creativity is inspired by surfaces that by virtue of their differences each become highly visible and absorbing, and to which the poet becomes receptive when out of a recognition of the unknown he cultivates an indifference to fathomless differences in their depths, an indifference to the identity of difference. For Whitman, individuality realizes its creativity when it relates to the world just as the poet relates to the world through poetry, aesthetically—receptive to the world's surfaces through an acknowledgment of the unknown and an indifference to the world's depths. Only on the surface of the world will individuality discover the sheer diversity of different forms of life, and in this diversity the images through which to form itself and the world as the poet forms his poetry and through his poetry forms the world.

Following Nietzsche's suggestion, then, I envisage the aesthetic problem, the problem of individuality, from the point of view of Whitman, the artist (the creator). I consider Whitman's point of view, in other words, as that of an artist addressing the problem of individuality's creativity in aesthetic terms, which is what I believe to be his interest to begin with. Accordingly, the aesthetic forms of Whitman's poetry, which constitute the point of view through which he takes the world as an object of his creativity, become a model for individuality's own aesthetic creativity and receptivity to the world. Taking Whitman's poetic forms as the model for aesthetic individuality, I initially focus on his poetic forms as modes of aesthetic representation, the ways in which they allow him to represent the world in poetic images. In light of a reconstruction of what I describe as the representational logic of his poetic forms, Whitman's images appear to be created through a mode of aesthetic representation that agrees with Adorno's criteria for what determines aesthetic receptivity to the world. Obedient to this logic of representation, the poetic forms through which Whitman's images are created acknowledge the world to be unknown in its depths, distinguish the world's surfaces from its unfathomable depths on the basis of the unknown, and conceive of every surface as different and an image through which poetry is formed and forms the world. Because the assumption underlying Whitman's poetry is that the world is different from its poetic representations, the identity of all the difference in the world remains concealed beyond the representational reach of poetic images created through an aesthetic receptivity only to the surfaces of the world's diversity of differences.

Now, if individuality were to form the world as Whitman's poetry forms the world, as I argue he intends, or in Nietzsche's terms, if it were modeled on the aesthetic point of view provided by Whitman's poetic forms, individuality would relate to the world as Whitman's poetry is related to the world. Individuality's own logic of representation, the form of its creativity, in other words, would be purged of the violence that Adorno attributes to the representations of the world rooted in the illusory belief that the identity of a fathomless world, its meaning and its value, can be known. Receptive to the world aesthetically, individuality's creativity would leave the world's differences alone in their depths. The aesthetic receptivity to the world in which Whitman's poetic forms place individuality would subdue the violence of mastery as it subdues the violence of representation accompanying the illusion of reconciliation, the illusion of knowing the identity of a world that in its depths is essentially unknowable. By bringing his poetry to bear on individuality as an aesthetic problem, I will show that from Whitman's point of view, the point of view of the artist (the creator), poetry proves that individuality can be guided by an ethical sensibility to the violence in the ways its representational practices creatively form the world.

It is not only in its representational dimensions that Whitman's poetry meets the aesthetic desiderata according to which Nietzsche and Adorno encourage us to conceptualize aesthetic individuality. While Whitman's poetry offers individuality a model of aesthetic representation that incorporates Nietzsche's vantage point on aesthetic creativity and Adorno's sensibility to violence in the way creativity forms the world, it also provides a model of aesthetic "presentation" whose ethic is no differently principled. Whereas chapter 6 maps the aesthetics of individuality modeled on Whitman's poetic forms of representation, chapter 7 considers his poetry as a model for how individuality creates, or *presents*, the *self* through the images in which others and the world can be aesthetically represented. From Whitman's aesthetic point of view, I argue, presenting or creating the self first requires representing the world. Aesthetic presentation presupposes aesthetic representation.

The key to the relationship between aesthetic representation and presentation appears in Whitman's great poem "Song of the Open Road." There he speaks of the world of "objects" that we all share—things and people and their cultures and all they contain—a world of worlds, Whitman wants us to understand, whose meanings "call from diffusion [our] meanings and give them shape!"[11] By this I take Whitman to mean that individuality forms itself by imitating the forms in which others appear, so that individuals form themselves through the surface forms or shapes belonging to others and other things to which their self-creativity orients them aesthetically. Aesthetically speaking, there is a constitutional moment when the identity individuality can create at first belongs to someone or something else, which individuality appropriates as a vehicle through which its own identity can creatively unfold on its own surface and in its own depths. Individuality is what enables us to become diverse beings by creating ourselves aesthetically through the world's different surfaces, and through our diversity to become different from ourselves, from who we were or who we are, and different from others as we individuate ourselves by newly developing the depths of the surfaces we adopt. The world's diverse surfaces become available to individuality's creativity, however, only when in the manner of the representational logic of Whitman's poetic forms individuality affirms the unknown as the ethical principle that orients it receptively to the surface of the world. Only through individuality's affirmation of the unknown can it become receptive to surfaces, whose multiplicity then would serve as the vehicles through which individuality creates itself differently on its surface and in its depths.

Individuality's affirmation of the unknown, however, is but the philosophical precondition for the aesthetics of its self-creativity. Although affirming the unknown orients individuality receptively to the surface where it finds the plurality of forms through which it can create and re-create itself, individuals can become only as diverse as the diversity of the objects they can be receptive to and represent aesthetically. Individuality's aesthetic receptivity and representation are intimately bound up with the form of life in which individuality is situated. Unless that form of life is inclusive of the world's diversity of differences, unless it is *democratic*, as I argue in chapter 8, individuality is denied the opportunity to be receptive to and to represent the multiplicity of surfaces through which it can present itself differently. Without democracy, in other words, individuality is unable to become aesthetic. Such a tight connection between aesthetic individuality and democracy already is anticipated by Whitman's poetic forms. As we shall see, the representational logic of Whitman's poetry is radically inclusive of the diversity of differences through which its creativity unfolds, so much so that it seems entirely appropriate to describe his poetic forms as democratic through and through. By orienting individuality receptively to all the difference in the world through a logic of poetic representation that is democratic, Whitman's poetry proves that it is its democratic form of representation that makes aesthetic creativity possible. And while the representational logic of aesthetic receptivity to the diversity of different surfaces establishes its connection to democracy, the connection appears to run in the opposite direction as well. Democracy is aesthetic when it, too, I will try to demonstrate, strains to include all differences. For Whitman, the aesthetics of individuality and the aesthetics of democracy consequently run hand in hand. Moreover, when aesthetic individuality is realized through an aesthetic, democratic form of life, the possibilities for self-creativity increase exponentially to the point where the individual's relationship to time and space is dramatically altered. As an aesthetic form of life, I will show, democracy provides an aesthetically receptive individuality with the representational means to overcome the finiteness of its existence. In a word, democracy offers an aesthetic individuality a form of immortality.

As the connection between aesthetic individuality and a democratic form of life is developed, I make it clear that Whitman also intends a connection between aesthetic individuality and democracy in America, and between America and modernity. Whitman's idea is that America can create modernity out of itself by fostering a democratic form of life inclusive of all the world's cultural differences, past and present, in one New World. Once we grasp the relationship between democracy, America, and modernity as Whitman understands it, it becomes evident that the modern, American, democratic world, and the aesthetic form of individuality for which it provides the foundation, are aesthetic achievements because they all create their identities through the same representational logic characteristic of Whitman's poetic forms. Whitman's poetry is a model not only for an aesthetic form of individuality but for the aesthetic form of life embodied by America, whose essentially democratic constitution defines the aesthetic nature of its collective identity and the identity of modernity.

With chapter 8 concluded, the concept of aesthetic individuality has been fleshed out completely and democracy has been foregrounded as the political form of life within which aesthetic individuality in its representational and presentational dimensions can flourish. Part II of my argument therefore comes unavoidably upon the question on which its final chapter will focus. If aesthetic individuality requires a democratic form of life, can we not then find evidence for aesthetic individuality in modern democratic society? To answer to this question, though only provisionally, of course, I examine Alexis de Tocqueville's *Democracy in America* and proceed on the understanding that this great work offers the uncontested point of departure for contemporary analyses, not only of America but of democratic society generally.

Aesthetic Individuality in Democratic America

My approach to Tocqueville is to *redescribe* his work in the aesthetic terms I have developed in the previous three chapters of part II, to determine if there is a correspondence between the aesthetic form of individuality conceptualized through Whitman's poetry and the form of individuality produced by democracy as Tocqueville describes it. Turning to Tocqueville for evidence of aesthetic individuality in democracy, I discover that each of the elements belonging to Whitman's poetic forms appears in the relationships individuals form as a consequence of the "equality of condition," as democratic equality was called in *Democracy in America*. To put it concisely, individuals in a democracy form relationships to one another in precisely the ways that Whitman relates individuality receptively and creatively to the world and to everyone and everything in it through the representational and presentational dimensions of the aesthetic forms of his poetry. My approach has several steps.

Although he did not speak of aesthetic individuality, or even of individuality to any significant extent, Tocqueville is deeply interested in difference, a term he uses synonymously with inequality, and with the ways individuals relate to difference, which is what my concept of aesthetic individuality problematizes. By thematizing his interest in the relations to difference in which individuals become implicated due to the encouragements provided by democracy's equality of condition, I am prepared to look for evidence of individuals' forming an aesthetic relationship to one another in all relations to difference in democratic America as they are described by Tocqueville. Before doing so, however, I must next engage Tocqueville's claim that differences in democracy disappear, for if he is correct about the disappearance of difference, there would be no differences to which individuals could form an aesthetic relationship. In response to Tocqueville's claim, I show that he narrowly conceptualizes difference as the "large class" differences of aristocratic society. While these differences disappear in Tocqueville's reading of democratic equality, his allegiance to an aristocratic concept of large class differences *blinds* his conceptual framework to other sorts of differences that continue to prevail within democracy. Once Tocqueville's argument about the disappearance of difference is clarified in relationship to large, aristocratic class differences, we then are left with differences other than large differences that have not disappeared but of which a conceptual framework equating difference with large differences could not have taken account. *Small differences*, as I term them, are those differences beyond the conceptual boundaries of Tocqueville's large, aristocratic class differences, and include the entire range of nonclass social differences, such as multicultural differences. Nonclass small differences are not small in any quantitative sense but are so called only to distinguish them from the large, aristocratic class differences that conceal them from view.

Having introduced a concept of difference into Tocqueville's theoretical framework that is far more inclusive of differences than large class differences, I direct my attention to the *relation* to difference that the democratic equality of condition encourages individuals to form. Here, as does Tocqueville, I focus on the "passion for equality," as he calls it, that the equality of condition ignites. Pursued passionately by all who benefit from the equality of condition, equality for Tocqueville initially translates into individuals' *acute sensitivity* to the differences they perceive between themselves and others, and then, most importantly, into an unflagging determination on the part of each individual to *overcome* these differences. With my revision of Tocqueville's conceptual framework, however, now the passion for equality also means overcoming all small differences. This third step shows how the equality of condition produces in individuals a relationship to the widest sort of differences that continually proliferate within democracy and allows us to raise the issue that places us on the threshold of redescribing Tocqueville's argument in the aesthetic terms I culled from my examination of Whitman. How does the passion for equality fueled by the equality of condition express itself? Or more pointedly, what occurs in a democratic society when individuals overcome the small differences they discover between themselves and others?

In one of his most brilliant interpretations of American democratic life, Tocqueville proposes that driven by a passion for equality that constrains them to be acutely sensitive to the least perceived difference, individuals "borrow" and "copy," "emulate" and "imitate" one another. Democracy, I will contend as I redescribe Tocqueville's argument in aesthetic terms, possesses what I call a mimetic dimension, through which individuals imitate each other and in doing so come to resemble those differences they mark for imitation. In the perpetual throe of a passion for equality, individuals overcome differences between themselves and others by becoming different, specifically by adopting the form of difference taken by another, *exactly as Whitman in his poetry imagines individuality doing*. It thus is inaccurate, I will insist, to read Tocqueville simply to be arguing that democratic society molds all of its members in the same identical image so that eventually there will be no differences among them, as this is an incomplete and misleading picture of the way he depicts individuals forming themselves in a democracy. Individuals create themselves aesthetically through a mimetic relation to others, indeed, through a mimetic relation to all others. Tocqueville conveys the image of each individual in a democracy becoming different in all the ways all others in democratic society are different. It is an image of an individual who, becoming different through imitation, is at the same time itself and someone else. Becoming different in the way others are different and different in those ways from itself, an individual develops identities that are many "identities"—many and often contradictory ideas, notions, and desires—in one. Individual identity becomes multiplicitous.

After finding the individual's mimetic relation to others to be the form in which individuality creates itself in a democracy, to be its Nietzschean, presentational dimension, so to speak, I examine the representational logic of this relationship to determine if it incorporates Adorno's ethical sensibility to violence. Here the question is whether the individual who has been shown to create itself aesthetically does so through a relationship whose structure reproduces all the elements of Whitman's poetic forms. As does the form of individuality's relationship to the world that we explicated in Whitman's poetry, I will show, the aesthetic form adopted by each individual within a democratic context orients individuality receptively to the surfaces of differences, and confines it to the surface as well. Confined receptively to the surface and indifferent to the identity of difference in its depths, the democratically encouraged form of aesthetic individuality allows what lies below the surface to remain unknown. Through its aesthetic receptivity individuality remains innocent of the violence to difference that throughout the history of enlightenment accompanied every effort to say what the identity of difference is. Consistent with the ethical requirements of Adorno's aesthetics, self-creativity occurs through its receptivity to the surfaces of others and other things, through which every individual may create itself differently on its own surface and in its depths.

As we learn in chapter 9, then, democracy not only produces an aesthetic form of individuality but an aesthetic individuality that, like Whitman's poetry, meets the conceptual criteria that emerge from enfolding Adorno's ethical sensibility to violence into Nietzsche's approach to creativity from the point of view of the artist. Among the implications for democracy of discovering that aesthetic individuality is a democratic achievement, I am interested predominately in one. For individuals whose relationship to the world is aesthetic, I propose, identities are constituted in relationship to those who are different according to a logic that *undermines* the development of the resentment from which a slave morality grows. By virtue of their receptivity to differences, in particular, to the surfaces of differences through which their own self-creativity unfolds, individuals would not convert difference into forms of "otherness" as they do where resentment and its moral imperatives prevail. Difference would no longer be victimized. Democracy, to the extent it produces aesthetic individuality, would not visit the horrors of holocaust and genocidal extermination upon those who are different.[12]

INDIVIDUALITY AFTER THE HOLOCAUST

To the extent to which democratic society produces aesthetic individuality, we can speak figuratively of "individuality after the Holocaust." What we are speaking of literally, though, is a form of individuality that in the wake of the Holocaust seems to embody the features of the aesthetic receptivity whose destruction, Horkheimer and Adorno argued, led to the destruction of the Jews, but whose democratic cultivation safeguards difference and allows it to be regarded as the source of aesthetic individuality's self-creativity. On the basis of my examination of Tocqueville's analysis of the dynamics of democracy in America, we should infer that since the aesthetic dimensions of individuality appear to be rooted in equality, which is democracy's most fundamental institutional principle, aesthetic individuality would be a strong if not the dominant tendency in democratic life. Before we suppose this to be the case, however, the question of the presence of aesthetic individuality in democratic society should be joined in a second way, which is the topic of my concluding chapter.

By considering George Kateb's *The Inner Ocean: Individualism and Democratic Culture*, I intend to explore in a preliminary way the matter of whether there may be sources of morality in late modern democratic society that would not thwart the development of aesthetic individuality but complement and perhaps nurture it.[13] In one of the most original and provocative studies of democratic individuality in contemporary political theory, Kateb offers evidence showing that a form of individuality produced by democracy is, for its greatest part, "morally distinctive" in nature, and he provides an explanation for how it is produced that is essentially Tocquevillian, though he concentrates on democratic institutions and practices other than those I have highlighted. My approach to Kateb will be first to explicate his concept of a morally distinctive individuality and its genesis and then to consider briefly whether it contributes to the development of individuality's aesthetic qualities. Hence Kateb's work will enable us to determine whether democratic society creates moral beliefs and dispositions that contest Nietzsche's critique of the moral life of democracy. And it will provide a more certain grasp of whether we can speak of individuality after the Holocaust, of an aesthetic form of individuality through which democracy will avert the reason and horror of the past.

PART I

Individuality
BEFORE
THE HOLOCAUST

"For fear—that is man's original and fundamental feeling. . . . Such prolonged ancient fear, at last become subtle, spiritual and intellectual—at present, me thinketh, it is called *Science*."

> Friedrich Nietzsche,
> *Thus Spake Zarathustra*

TWO

Reason as a "Murderous Principle"

I believe it only appropriate to begin a discussion of Horkheimer and Adorno's *Dialectic of Enlightenment* at that point to which their own discussion leads us once it concludes. For above all other responses to this deeply disturbing and despairing work, it is a sensibility belonging to each of us to which the argument at its end finally appeals. It is precisely this sensibility that enables the implications of this great work and the force of its rhetorical structure to be grasped, in retrospect and for the first time, as it were, ameliorating its harshest claims, which if evaluated in a stricter analytical context would be dismissed as implausible, if not outrageous. In advance of our considering the work as a whole, the first challenge is to capture the sensibility that can offer such an access to *Dialectic of Enlightenment*. Goethe's *The Sorrows of Young Werther* provides as perfect an illustration of this sensibility as we are likely to discover. In his letter of August 18 Werther writes to his dearest friend,

> That generous and warm feeling for living Nature which flooded my heart with such bliss, so that I saw the world around me as a Paradise, has now become an unbearable torment, a sort of demon that persecutes me wherever I go.... It is as if a curtain has been drawn away from my soul, and the scene of unending life is transformed before my eyes into the pit of the forever-open grave.... There is not one moment which does not consume you and yours, and not one moment when you yourself are not inevitably destructive; the most harmless walk costs the lives of poor, minute creatures; *one* step of your foot annihilates their painstaking constructions, and stamps a small world into its ignominious grave. My heart is worn out by the consuming power latent in the whole of Nature which has formed nothing that will not destroy its neighbor and itself. So I stagger with anxiety, Heaven and Earth and their weaving powers around me. I see nothing but an eternally devouring and ruminating monster.[1]

While Lotte's unrequited love for Werther may have precipitated his suicide, as a prelude to this catastrophic romantic episode it would seem that Werther's painfully acute sensibility virtually had paralyzed his affirmation of life. Werther's insight is horrifying, insisting as it does on the principle that, in some sense perhaps, each act of life is at the same time an unavoidable occasion for death and destruction. Through Werther's fate Goethe means to prove that once we come to understand that the most innocent expressions of living cast worlds into oblivion, believing in life or in the possibility of life without domination is an illusion. Goethe urges us to discard as pretense the belief that life simply can live, and then, once we do, perhaps with Werther we, too, are to relinquish our claim to life. Werther's sorrows articulate the relentless logic that animates Horkheimer and Adorno's *Dialectic of Enlightenment*, in which they hold Fascism to be the most fully developed expression of reason and ultimately significant less as a historic abomination than as the absolute denial of life embodied in all forms of life. Fascism, like the principle of annihilation Werther discerns to be endemic to life, inheres in reason. Werther's sensibility, or the sensibility the delicacy of his relation to the world now awakens in each of us, suspends the outrage with which without reflection we must hastily deny the plausibility of Horkheimer and Adorno's claims about the relationship between reason and barbarism.

As does Goethe's rueful narrative, the sensibility that Horkheimer and Adorno's work awakens compels us to adopt an extreme position. Indeed, there can be no more extreme position. Werther's suicide asks us to respond not to the end of one life but to the sacrifice of all living in life's fateful and unbroken reversal of life that it represents. Similarly, Fascism is not the collapse of the Enlightenment, but represents the process of enlightenment since the origin of thought as a continuous inversion rather than an advancement of thinking. At the moment Horkheimer and Adorno demonstrate that enlightenment culminates in Fascism, they intend for us to recollect the entire evolution of enlightened thought up to that stage not as a history wherein what is unknown progressively becomes known and thought's enrichment is halted by the onslaught of barbarism. Rather, Fascism is construed to be the final and undisguised expression of the innermost tendency of thought to *exterminate* the unknown, to exterminate what is different about the world from our thought of it. As the world-historical telos of reason, the onset of Fascism is meant to arouse an *aesthetic* sensibility alerting us to the violence to difference intrinsic to thinking.

DIFFERENCE AND THE BIRTH OF THINKING

Alerted to reason as a "murderous principle," to recall Nietzsche's judgment of Socratic reason in *The Birth of Tragedy*, we turn to the earliest, or "preanimistic," stage of thought taken up by Horkheimer and Adorno, corresponding to the birth of enlightenment. "Thought originated," Horkheimer and Adorno propose, "in the course of liberation from a terrifying nature."[2] Interpretations of this proposition generally conclude that Horkheimer and Adorno are saying simply that thought originates to rescue us from what in nature threatens our self-preservation. To read them in this way, however, would mistakenly attribute a certain brute facticity to the threat nature and the world surrounding us pose, which they deny. To the contrary, it is not nature specifically that threatens self-preservation but its terrifying *appearance*, an appearance rooted not in nature's indomitable power but in its opacity. From its beginning thinking is bound up inextricably with an image of nature as the unknown and pursues the elimination of the world's unfathomable qualities through a process of enlightenment that rids it of the unknown and the terror it threatens. "Man imagines himself free from fear," they submit, "when there is nothing more unknown (*wenn es nichts Unbekanntes mehr gibt*)."[3] Thinking, by its own nature, is driven to form impressions that fail to distinguish between what in nature is actually threatening and what is simply unfamiliar and unknown and may not be threatening at all. Or what is but the same thing, thinking fails to distinguish between what it knows to be threatening and what is different from what it knows. It is whatever in nature is different from what thinking knows that is unknown and threatening. It is *difference* that is terrifying. To eliminate the unknown and the terror it provokes is to eliminate difference.

At its birth, Horkheimer and Adorno thus insist, thinking is imprinted by nature with a dread of the unknown. Acting in accordance with this tendency in its nature, thought proceeds to defend itself from what is unrecognizable by converting all the difference it encounters in the world into an unthreatening world of familiar forms. It is this idea that lies at the core of *Dialectic of Enlightenment*. The "specific origin of thinking" possesses a "universal perspective (*universale Perspektive*)" from which it always has been inseparable.[4] Reason's universalistic orientation, through which thinking abolishes difference by conceiving abstractly of differences in terms of commonalities among them, enables reason to find things everywhere the same. Throughout the long process of enlightenment, we shall see, in order to render the unfamiliar familiar and the unknown known a cognitive imperative installed at the ground of thinking compels thought to construct identities among differences, confining representation to the commonalities among them. Universality arises first and foremost as a property of thought, and not of the objects of thought, which first and foremost are particulars, each different from the other. The violence in thinking resides in this universalistic orientation intrinsic to knowing, whereby reason obliterates what differences there are in nature and the world by identifying them only according to what form they possess in common.

At thought's preanimistic stage, thinking's orientation to nature necessarily unfolds within the framework of a dualistic opposition that appears to entail, in part, a sort of primitive Cartesianism. As Horkheimer and Adorno describe it, thinking's relationship to nature historically emerges in the form of a contradiction between subject and object as the (species) subject's instinctive self-understanding of its own needs is paired with its image of nature as *mana*, meaning, most importantly, that nature is thought to be a force or power in virtue of being unknown, and terrifying in its utter fathomlessness. It is as though subjectivity's certainty of maintaining its own existence can be achieved only by first forswearing the possibility of any intuition of nature whatsoever, thus converting nature into a terrifying abstraction that permits it to be dominated for the satisfaction of needs. Yet, nature or *mana* as unknown does not unequivocally support subjectivity's instrumental relationship to the world about it. Though a fathomless nature is threateningly alien to subjectivity and as the terrifying unknown everything within it is "primary and undifferentiated," which attaches a uniform, common identity to all that nature contains, as the unknown, nature also is experienced as difference.[5] By virtue of being unknown, nature is experienced as being *indefinitely more* than whatever needs it serves and as something to be feared. Transcending its instrumental relationship to nature, subjectivity also experiences as enchanted the same world it perceives to be objectively fathomless and terrifying. As Horkheimer and Adorno put it, when the

> tree is no longer approached merely as tree, but as evidence for an Other, as the location of *mana*, language expresses the contradiction that something is itself and at one and the same time something other than itself, identical and not identical.[6]

At this earliest stage of thought, then, thinking is oriented to the world ambiguously, as it were, at odds with itself within. With the concept of *mana*, at one level of understanding thinking identifies nature as useful though terrifying, an object to be subdued while feared. Yet in the awe of enchantment with which nature is received, thinking also is tacitly aware of the mysteriousness of nature and hence of the limits to the identity thinking imposes upon nature. Importantly, the image of nature as objectively terrifying is not only an imposition or projection of thought on nature (what Adorno in his subsequent work will refer to as "identitarian thinking"[7]) but "the *echo* of the real supremacy of nature in the weak souls of primitive men."[8] Thinking, we can say of it at this stage of thought, at some deeper level of understanding is able to acknowledge the "in-itself" of the being of the world, a difference between its every thought of the world and the world as it is or may be essentially, a difference that perpetually lies indefinitely and inscrutably beyond the difference that thinking "identifies" as being one way and never any other. While there is violence in thinking that identifies difference as objectively terrifying, there is likewise a transcendence of the violence in thought through its aesthetic receptivity to difference beyond the identity of difference, difference as constantly fathomless, a "superior power" imprinted obscurely as an "echo" in our attempts to identify it. It is thinking's recognition of the unknown and aesthetic receptivity to difference that the process of enlightenment at first will force into remission and then eventually extinguish altogether. What then will remain of thought, in other words, is only its capacity for converting all the world's differences into a world of commonalities where everything resembles everything else. What will remain of thought is thinking's capacity for inflicting violence on difference. Enlightenment reduces thought to "formal reason."

With regard to the "formal" tendency in thought that becomes dominant through the process of enlightenment, along with the Cartesian dimensions of Horkheimer and Adorno's argument, variations of a Kantian theme appear to surface early in *Dialectic of Enlightenment*. Whatever difference thinking encounters remains forever opaque, being-in-itself, while what thinking believes it knows of its fathomless object, nature's terror, for instance, is only the identity brought to nature by thought from the outside. In the face of the terror of the unknown, Kantian-like thing-in-itself, however, thought deceives itself into thinking that the identity it attributes to nature belongs to it universally, such that nature's terror and the instrumental relationship to which it gives rise are sustained by an illusion of certainty. Consequently, the "untruth" of enlightenment consists in the fact that what is known of the world, its identity, is already presupposed from the start in that it is simply a form imposed by a subject whose thought is unavoidably constrained by its fear of the unknown. Enlightenment proves to be a perversion of the Kantian notion that all knowledge is, in some sense, self-knowledge. Unable to extricate itself from a drive for self-preservation whose tenacity is rooted in a confusion between what is horrifying and what is unknown, reverting to its own nature in every thought that at a deeper level seeks to raise itself above nature, reason reduces nature and the world of differences in all their diversity to mere resistance to abstract thought. Knowing is overcoming resistance, substituting thought of the universal features of an object for the object itself, placing the unique difference belonging to an object of thought into servitude to terms alien to what is essentially different about it, servitude as domination. Thinking is "ruthless" and enlightenment "totalitarian." While Horkheimer and Adorno share Kant's distrust of knowledge and, at least implicitly, embrace his idea of things-in-themselves or some such idea not far removed, as I will make clear in the following chapter, they clearly radicalize his view of the ontological relationship between thinking and being.[9]

If this conception of reason appears implausible, it may already have been forgotten that its recognition must be the fruit of an aesthetic sensibility to the violence to difference inherent in thought awakened by the onslaught of barbarism. This is one of the dilemmas of modernity thrust on us by enlightenment, a dilemma of which Horkheimer and Adorno were painfully aware. When cultures that are wholly the products of enlightenment believe their practices to be immune to such evil, the long historical process of enlightenment has purged their capacity to reflect upon the violence to difference hidden within the distant origins of their own cultural forms of thought. When we discover this to be precisely Horkheimer and Adorno's claim as we trace the stages of their reconstruction of enlightenment, the virtue of enlisting Goethe to capture the interpretive sensibility they leave us with at the conclusion of *Dialectic of Enlightenment* is not without justification. Together with a damaged capacity for reflection, a blind confidence in reason born of enlightenment thwarts any interest modernity might develop in closely inspecting the natural origins of its own thinking. Why this is necessarily so becomes evident as we examine Horkheimer and Adorno's concept of reason in light of each of the remaining stages through which enlightenment passes on its way to Fascism.

DIFFERENCE AND MAGICAL THINKING

At its magical stage, thought undergoes its first demonstrable shift toward an eclipse of its capacity to be aesthetically receptive to difference. Certain features essential to aesthetic thinking persist, though. In particular, magical thought continues to represent the world nonidentically by constructing understandings that resemble the preanimistic idea of *mana*. In magic nature's nonidentity, the idea that the being of nature is indefinitely more than can be known through its representations appears as a belief in an animated spirit thought to inhabit the natural world in different forms. An enchanted worldview, magical thought's peculiar rationality grounds nature's nonidentity in two ways.

On the one hand, as Horkheimer and Adorno explain, "in magic there is *specific representation*. What happens to the enemy's spear, hair or name," which are believed to possess his spirit, "also happens to the individual." Thought of the "nature of things" as "always the same" is *not* a "proposition of magical invocation," which occurs only as enlightenment progressively brings about a metamorphosis in thinking through which it arrives at an "identity [that] constitutes the unity of nature."[10] By this they mean that magic, contrary to the formal rational thinking fostered by enlightenment, establishes an intimate connection between what thinking represents (in this case, the individual) and the way in which it is represented in thought (by spears or hair). The specificity of the individual, the individual in-itself, is not effaced in such a representation by an identity that abstractly equates the individual with others of his or her kind, as though by virtue of being represented by a possession or a body part one individual becomes the equivalent of any other who may be represented in the same way. Indeed, insofar as specific representation recognizes the uniqueness of an object, its quality of being "here and now," as Horkheimer and Adorno call it, its difference from others of its kind is marked off. As a mimetic function of thought first appearing prominently in magic, specific representation articulates the qualitative distinctions among the world's diversity of differences. Objects so identified are rendered "unfit for exchange," such that their value is not reducible to commonalities allowing them to be thought of as objects that are the same as or equivalent to others. On the other hand, the relation between the representation and the represented, between identity and the identified, is not so specific that the representation stands in for what is being represented. Whenever identities substitute for whatever in the world is identified, the assumption is that the identified is known, which suppresses the difference between the object and its representation, the cognitive act of thought wherein its violence lies. Where it does not mistake the invocation of the object for the object invoked and substitute the former for the latter, magical thinking affirms the difference between an object and its identification, affirms its nonidentity, which is the difference belonging to an object that can never be known. In both of these ways magic is aesthetically receptive to the unfathomable difference in every object represented and affirms thinking's capacity to experience difference.

Nevertheless, although by encompassing difference magic enriches thinking's relationship to the world, in Horkheimer and Adorno's reading magic's intention is not primarily to relate us to the world aesthetically, receptively to difference in all of its diversity, but to increase our control over nature. While through invocation magic represents the specificity, uniqueness, the *hic et nunc* of the world, it does so for the purpose of bringing about desired ends. What happens to the individual's spear is supposed to happen to the individual the spear represents. So from the standpoint of the terror the enemy threatens, the relation of magical thought to "equivalency" ultimately is ambiguous. As Horkheimer and Adorno argue, when the "shaman wards off danger by means of its image . . . [e]quivalence is his instrument."[11] Their purpose in stressing the importance of the "equivalency" between the object and its representation is to demonstrate that mastery is achieved through a substitution (what is done to the image of danger affects the danger itself) that distorts the object in thought even before the actual behavior of the object would be magically altered. But they press this argument still further. Generally, in the symbolism of shaman priests, "sign and image were one. Just as hieroglyphs bear witness, so the word too originally had a pictorial function."[12] Where the image thinking takes to be the equivalent form of an object becomes a "sign," then thinking has moved from the practice of substituting images for particular objects toward defining *thought itself as substitution*. Magic articulates the tendency of enlightened thought to increasingly *formalize* reason in this way. Enlightenment purges reason of mimetic properties that would enable it to represent substantive qualities that distinguish each object as an object different from every other.

To take Horkheimer and Adorno's argument about magical thought as a whole, at one extreme, they are saying, in the form of magic, enlightenment offends the world by representing its diversity through equivalencies that obscure and suppress differences that other properties of magic are, however, receptive to aesthetically. Far more seriously, at the other extreme, to the degree that thought is overwhelmed by terror of the unknown and the logic of equivalency in magical thinking prevails, magic foreshadows the annulment of ways to represent the world's diversity other than through equivalence. Through magic the process of enlightenment then anticipates the destruction of difference and of thinking's ability to be receptive to difference aesthetically that will occur when the process of enlightenment culminates in its cultural self-understanding as "the Enlightenment." With the Enlightenment, they conclude, what "was different is equalized" and the qualities distinguishing differences "are dissolved in thought."[13] And when the "identity of everything with everything else is paid for in that nothing may at the same time be identical with itself," that "is the verdict which critically determines the limits of possible experience."[14] Today enlightenment leaves no other way to represent and experience difference receptively than through art and the aesthetic sensibility it preserves, which in their estimation is the only aesthetic form of thought the fully enlightened world continues to have in common with thinking at its birth, with magic, and with myth.

DIFFERENCE AND MYTHICAL THINKING

As does magic, mythical thought, too, Horkheimer and Adorno argue, honors *mana*, which "lives on in the radiant world of Greek religion."[15] With its plurality of divinities—gods and goddesses, demigods, heroes and heroines—Greek mythology deifies the broadest range of cultural characteristics, beliefs, and practices. Myth offers a "mode of apprehension," they suggest, that celebrates differences within the human and natural worlds, collectively represented by mythological figures as worlds replete with powers and mysteries beyond the powers of human understanding. Myth implicitly conceptualizes the world without loss of its *hic et nunc* or of an experience of its here and now by recognizing that its great diversity of differences possesses qualities beyond the reach of thought. Among other examples of mythical reason they site the *Odyssey*'s Polyphemus, whose "mind itself, his thinking, is lawless, unsystematic, and rhapsodical," who consequently cannot solve the "mental problem of the way in which his invited guests [Odysseus and his crew] can escape from the cave."[16] His "thoughtlessness" is essentially unlike an enlightenment rationality that converts the world's differences into a uniform material amenable to calculations serving human ends and experienced universally as the same. The mythical world of Polyphemus is filled with wonders, a world of worlds experienced receptively as diverse and always different so long as its opacity, its quality of being wondrous and unfathomable, is sustained by thought.

Despite the aesthetic receptivity to difference nurtured by myth, however, it is the tendency toward enlightenment and the subversion of myth's receptivity to all the difference in the world that dominates mythological thought. Through its epic narratives mythology engages in a program of disenchantment that uproots its own animistic foundations. By overcoming superstition myth enables the mind to think of its essential task as securing the sovereignty won with the mastery of nature that frees thinking from fear of the unknown. "Mythology itself," Horkheimer and Adorno declare, "set off the unending process of enlightenment."[17]

As Horkheimer and Adorno approach the Homeric epic, in fact, it is as though the origin of myth had little to do with Greek culture's search for answers to basic questions about the creation of the world and its species, natural processes, and events. Rather, myth arose for the very purpose of rationalizing an enchanted world whose terrors threaten extinction. Put simply, the intention of myth is enlightenment. When the *Odyssey* is taken up in *Dialectic of Enlightenment*, Odysseus is treated not merely as an interpretive symbol for the historical process of enlightenment. Odysseus becomes enlightenment's proper metaphor and illuminates not only decisive stages in the history of enlightenment but the actual forces that are expressed at each of these stages, the struggles through which these forces play themselves out, and the principles consolidated in the resolution of these struggles.

This is evident, for instance, in the analysis of the episode of the Sirens, which is the key to Horkheimer and Adorno's critique of enlightenment and will move to the forefront of my discussion in the following chapter.[18] Odysseus discovers a way to become aesthetically receptive to the lures of the Sirens while protecting himself from their dangers and insulating his men from their temptations so that he can give himself up to the promise of happiness the demigodesses represent. Having himself lashed to the mast of his ship by his crew and requiring that they stop up their ears with wax, Odysseus sees that he and his men stay the course that leads them away from the wonders of nature threatening their self-preservation. Here, Horkheimer and Adorno argue, myth is combined with the imperative of rational labor to prevail *over* myth, demonstrating that the Enlightenment of the fully developed modern world already is present in the ancient world. The heroic Odysseus proves himself to be little more than the "prototype of the bourgeois individual," through whose calculations essentials of the process through which the history of enlightenment will develop become transparent.[19] Thinking, in Odysseus's struggle with an animistic world, can be observed translating its superstitious perception of the unknown as a threat to its survival into a form of reason that masters terror. Labor, with wax-plugged ears adopting an attitude of strategic detachment from the differences belonging to an enchanted world, represents the transformation of the diversity of being into a material form uniformly irrelevant to any considerations other than its manipulation and control. Enlightenment appears to be a world-historical process whereby a war between two kinds of thinking is resolved as the domination of "formal" reason (which Horkheimer and Adorno alternatively refer to as "regulative" reason) over an aesthetic rationality possessing a receptivity to the "heart of the world," as Nietzsche in *The Birth of Tragedy* referred to the "in-itself" of nature ruled by Dionysian powers.

With each adventure Odysseus extends the conquest of enlightenment over myth until the entire meaning of the Homeric world is the triumph of formal reason. Formal reason is shown to be the thread that runs through and unifies the sagas of the *Odyssey*, destroying mythical forces and thus myth itself on behalf of a principle of reason contained in myth. "There is no work which offers more eloquent testimony to the mutual implication of enlightenment and myth than that of Homer," Horkheimer and Adorno write. In this "basic text of European civilization" epic and myth "do not so much emerge from and contrast with, as expound and elucidate, one another."[20] As they reconstruct the episode of the Sirens and others to explain how myth and enlightenment mutually expound and explicate each other, certain dimensions of formal reason already thematized are foregrounded, which in the course of their analysis of the *Odyssey* they will show to be definitive of the process of enlightenment.

One of these dimensions, self-preservation, serves prominently as the basis for conceptualizing others. Although the "unequivocal purposiveness" of Odysseus's self-preservation is the driving need behind his destruction of myth and the disenchantment of the world, the conquests of formal reason he represents and that ensure self-preservation are ironic, for each act of self-preservation entails self-sacrifice. An "immense though superfluous sacrifice is required," Horkheimer and Adorno propose, "against sacrifice itself."²¹ In all of the *Odyssey*'s tales examined in *Dialectic of Enlightenment* in some detail—his escape from the Sirens, from Polyphemus, and from Circe—Odysseus is able to preserve his life only at great cost to himself, a cost signified in these episodes by the perpetual "flight (*Fluchtbahn*) of the individual [Odysseus] from mythic powers."²² By "flight of the individual" they mean not only the sacrifice of the real happiness that would have accompanied Odysseus's willingness to relinquish mastery over the mythical powers of nature. It must mean, too, as I have intimated, the more important sacrifice of the self's capacity to be aesthetically receptive to a world composed of differences and to have experiences that are different from what formal rational thinking allows us to know and expect of the world. For if formal reason sacrifices whatever does not contribute to the "ultimate context of self-preservation," then it must sacrifice, as well, whatever in the *self* contradicts the drive for self-preservation.²³ Enlightenment must sacrifice an aesthetic receptivity to the world as it is, in-itself, as it goes about its business of interpreting the world's differences as unknowns apparently threatening the self's preservation.

This second and I think more consequential form of sacrifice is apparent in each of the three spectacular episodes of the *Odyssey* studied by Horkheimer and Adorno. In each tale its god or demigod fills the world with wonder and sets it apart as a world of qualitatively different experiences from the experiences of Odysseus's own world. So, for instance, when Odysseus saves his life and the lives of his men from Polyphemus and cleverly outwits the monster Cyclops by referring to himself as "Nobody," in Greek, *Udeis*, thereby exploiting the play in the similarly sounding "Odysseus," Horkheimer and Adorno conclude that in "words,"

> Odysseus discovers what is called "formalism" in fully-developed bourgeois society: [words'] perennial obligation is paid for by the fact that they distance themselves from every fulfilling content, and at a distance refer to every possible content —to Nobody as to Odysseus.²⁴

In other words, since the abstract form of the "word" (words as such, all words) is a universal that includes within it all possible cases ("every possible content") of that person, thing, or event that it represents, every word introduces a "distance" between it and any particular case ("every fulfilling content") to which it specifically refers. Because the word "Nobody" refers to no *one* (to no particular case) at all, Odysseus's ingenious response to Polyphemus privileges the formal relationship, the distance, between universal and particular. Just as the particularity (the "here and now") of Odysseus, Odysseus himself, remains, in the name of "Nobody," entirely beyond the reach of the Cyclops, so too is his particularity entirely beyond the reach of the universal form of every word. Odysseus's response to Polyphemus represents the loss of the way in which the universal is also intended to refer to a particular (Odysseus) that is *different* from the universal (from Nobody, the word). That Odysseus is not (the same as) Nobody is lost because, not meant to refer to Odysseus (or any one at all) in particular, Nobody only has a universal form, which suppresses the difference between Odysseus and all the others to whom a universal abstractly and commonly refers. Odysseus must elude Polyphemus by resorting to the universal form of the word, because the revelation of his name, of his particularity or difference, would cost him his life. Though guaranteeing his self-preservation, formal reason's universalistic orientation at the same time prevents Odysseus from relating aesthetically to the world in terms of his and the world's differences. Formal reason, enlightenment, making the world "known" through the word, forecloses on an aesthetic relationship between Odysseus and the world, and his receptivity to all the difference in the world is lost to him.

The sacrifice of the individual's aesthetic ability to relate to the world receptively is similarly threaded through Horkheimer and Adorno's examination of text weaving the tales of the *Odyssey* together. No matter what enchanted, unknown seas and territories Odysseus explores and that lead him from one adventure to another, he never fails to find his way. Odysseus "anticipates the work of the compass . . . no part of the sea remains unknown to him."[25] Once measured by the meaning of animistic forces inhabiting it, space is emptied of all its qualitative value by the objective measurements of human reason. Dark, forbidding, spiritualized space quickly becomes disenchanted, secularized space. Space, we might say of their argument, becomes "Kantian," a form imposed on whatever lies outside of human reason by human reason itself. Neutralized by reason, the space of the sea is experienced not as filled with wonders different from what is familiar, but as though it were a space independent of every different thing it contains, of "every fulfilling content," to recall their words, that occupies it.

If we look more closely at these instances where an aesthetic receptivity to the world is sacrificed, another characteristic of formal reason further crystallizes through the loss to Odysseus of all the difference in his world. Common to the tale of the Cyclops and the trope of navigable seas is the element of equivalence, which again operates according to the logic we first encountered at the magical stage of thought. Where every different sea with all of its multidimensional qualities is reduced to the one dimension of quantitative spatial measurement, there is only a single vast measurable *identical* sea. Where all seas are equivalent, all equivalent seas are the same and experienced as the same. Likewise, Odysseus's cunning by disclosing his identity but not keeping to his agreement to reveal his name deceives the Cyclops and breaks his promise. By substituting the similarly sounding *Udeis* for his own name, Odysseus adopts the formal rational logic of equivalence to transform what is different, as Odysseus is different from Nobody, into what is the same, as Odysseus sounds the same as *Udeis*. In effect, the terms of the agreement were honored, yet the spirit of the agreement and its good faith commitment were not. Odysseus's cunning resembles the fetishized contract of capital, where the substantive inequality between classes is concealed in the formal equivalence of so much labor power for so many wages. As Horkheimer and Adorno put it, in his negotiations with Polyphemus Odysseus practiced "[d]eception as a mode of exchange in which everything proceeds as it should, where the contract is fulfilled and yet the other party is deceived."[26] Just as the qualitative difference in the power between the classes is destroyed through the contract by the equivalency it establishes in the quantitative relation between labor and wages, so, too, in his deception is Odysseus's lie equivalent to truth. "Cunning (*die List*)," they argue, summarizing the logic of equivalence according to which the self is sacrificed through its pursuit of self-preservation, "is the means by which the adventuring self loses itself in order to preserve itself. The seafarer Odysseus cheats the natural deities, as does the civilized traveler offering them colored glass beads in exchange for ivory."[27] If cunning is a form of equivalence, they are saying, then equivalence is the form by which the world is mastered, its spirit dominated, and all the difference in the world suppressed.

Inevitably, at this point, the mistaken impression will be formed that Horkheimer and Adorno's critique of the process of enlightenment is a critique of thought only, and that what plagues thinking is not actually visited upon the world. After all, thus far formal reason appears to destroy our aesthetic capacity for receptivity, and not the world of difference to which we can be aesthetically receptive. As they make clear, Odysseus flees from myth, leaving the enchanted world behind. Should it not then seem that it is only Odysseus's aesthetic experience of the world that is disenchanted, and not the enchanted world itself? Perhaps it should be recalled that magic and myth mark the origin of the evolution of enlightened thinking, and that Horkheimer and Adorno search there for the emergence of properties of thought that increasingly predominate and that change the world as their relationship to the world changes. Formal reason does affect far more than our aesthetic capacity to be receptive to the world. It determines the fate of the modern world and of the world as a whole insofar as the modern world determines the world's fate. But for Horkheimer and Adorno what goes wrong with reason is not peculiar to modern thought only, but is there in embryo from the beginning of thinking. Yet this lesson is likely to be overlooked unless there continues to be an aesthetic sensibility to what is, ineradicably, a violence in reason as such. Without this sensibility, Horkheimer and Adorno's argument will just seem to be a caricature of the predicament of reason in modernity.

DIFFERENCE AND THE ENLIGHTENMENT OF MODERN TIMES

Greek philosophy constitutes the transition between myth and science, between the time formal reason begins its ascendancy over the aesthetic faculty in thinking with which it struggles and the moment when enlightened thought, which assumes that the shape of reality universally parallels its rationalized form in thought, could begin to affect the world. Pre-Socratic thought anticipates this transition, Horkheimer and Adorno maintain, where the principles of its cosmologies, the "moist, the indivisible, air, and fire, which [are held] to be the primal matter of nature, are already rationalizations of the mythic mode of apprehension.... [T]he equivocal multitude of mythical demons were intellectualized in the pure form of ontological essences."[28] But the decisive rationalization of myth constructing the terms of philosophical discourse until the Enlightenment occurs in Platonic thought. Plato's theory of forms initially rationalizes myth by absorbing the patriarchal gods of Olympus into the philosophical *logos*. Because the idea of universal forms nevertheless sublimates the connection in myth, perpetuated by the Greek deities, between thought and nature in all of its diverse qualities, however, Plato's forms are reconfigured in his last writings when "numbers" are equated with "Ideas." With this further rationalization of myth, Horkheimer and Adorno conclude, thinking has now largely achieved the level of abstraction that "expresses the longing of all demythologization: number became the canon of the Enlightenment."[29] Greek thought represents the stage of enlightenment when thinking develops forms of rationalization that neither tolerate any thought of spirit inhabiting nature, as had magic, nor settle for an escape from animistic forces, as had mythical thought. Rather, enlightenment proceeds in Greek philosophy as a process of rationalization that subjects the animistic forces of nature to a transformation in thought so that nature can be transformed in practice.

During the Enlightenment of "modern times (*neureren Zeit*)," as Horkheimer and Adorno distinguish the Enlightenment as only one stage in the world-historical process of enlightenment, the more highly developed form of rationalized thought whose earlier version is found in Plato's later writings completely displaces its less rationalized counterpart. The classical notion that universal forms correspond to particular qualities in nature and the world was taken by philosophy to be a Trojan horse secreting in mythical powers under the guise of reason. Bacon reintroduces the Platonic attack on universals through concepts of science and nature that disarm philosophy by severing its connection to difference, in the judgment of Horkheimer and Adorno, who recall Voltaire's description of him as the "father of experimental philosophy." Bacon's postulate of a universal science stressed the unity of nature. In scientific discourse nature is to be conceived abstractly only as uniform matter throughout, calculable and manipulable, rather than as differentiated into a multiplicity of different qualities represented by universals. After Bacon scientific abstraction will manage without the philosophical image of nature filled with meaning that is sustained by universal concepts. These were "abandoned" as metaphysics and assessed as being "memorials" of mythic powers despite philosophy's attempts to preserve its categories by redefining them in a way relevant to modernity, which further crippled philosophical thought already disabled by the assault on universals.

With the advent of the scientific abstraction of nature during the Enlightenment, the formalization of thought initiated by the process of enlightenment at its magical stage virtually is completed. Most importantly, with the formalization of reason in science, Horkheimer and Adorno observe, "to the extent that its preferred function is that of a symbol for neutral procedures . . . thought appears meaningful only when *meaning has been discarded.*"[30] Science condemns the belief in the existence and possibility of a meaning that belongs objectively to nature *before any other thought* of the world. As Horkheimer and Adorno describe this development,

> [t]here is said to be no difference between the totemic animal, the dreams of the ghost-seer, and the absolute Idea. On the road to modern science, men renounce any claim to meaning. They substitute formula for concept, rule and probability for cause and motive.[31]

Whatever meanings or semblances of meanings have been said to inhere in nature—all animistic spirit, all mythical figures, all qualities, all value—scientific practice alleges, become simply anthropomorphic inventions. Science aggressively disqualifies any form of representation that would fail to pose a barrier to an objective meaning imputed to nature. It exchanges the "word," which as a universal, we recall, is a vehicle for meaning through its reference to "every fulfilling content," for the sign, the mere symbol, which allows all of nature to be translated into formulaic equivalencies. At the summit of enlightenment, science thus reproduces the hostility to meaning implicit in Odysseus's deceit of the monster Cyclops appearing at the dawn of the ascendancy of formal rationality. And as they are lost to Odysseus, the particularities of nature in all their differences from thought are lost to modernity in the drive for self-preservation, which as Horkheimer and Adorno explain precisely and powerfully, is the very "constitutive principle of science."[32] Formal reason is "the intellectual expression" of a system of mechanized production whose singular purpose is the preservation of ways of life anchored in the domination of nature.

Due to the progress of formal reason, then, there has been an important development. Through the level of abstract representation realized through formulaic equivalence, science achieves real mastery over nature. Thinking will no longer flee from mythological forces. By reducing the world to a single, meaningless form, by equating truth with formal reason, science excludes the possibility that thought could think of the world as indefinitely different from thought and as composed of a diversity of differences that prefigure an aesthetic receptivity to the world based on the dual suppositions that the world is both ultimately unknowable and meaningful in-itself. Science eliminates difference, which, as the unknown, enlightenment must eradicate so that the world acquires the transparency upon which mastery depends. Though "progress" over myth, enlightenment is no different from myth in its denunciation of what falls outside of its epistemological assumptions. For science and myth the idea of the unknown is taboo. "Enlightenment," Horkheimer and Adorno say famously, "is mythic fear [of the unknown] turned radical," thus summarily capturing the sense in which the "dialectic of enlightenment" refers to the sublation in ever new forms of thought of the violence in reason with which the world has been threatened from the beginning.[33] In view of their reconstruction of the process of enlightenment from the birth of thinking through to the Enlightenment of modern times, should we not again recall Nietzsche's description of Socratic reason in *The Birth of Tragedy* to say that with the Enlightenment formal reason is poised to become in practice what from the beginning it had been in thought, a "murderous principle"?

Perhaps this is an exaggeration. Is it a histrionic interpretation of *Dialectic of Enlightenment*, even exceeding the aesthetic sensibility to the violence in thought that Horkheimer and Adorno's argument first requires of us so that we can understand the work as a whole? Are there not also dimensions of thought, particularly in the philosophical thought of the Enlightenment, that oppose the process of enlightenment, check its drive to dominate nature, and uncover explanations for thinking's single-mindedness? To the contrary, Horkheimer and Adorno maintain, for on the way from myth to the formal rational logic of modern science "thought has lost the element of self-reflection," the capacity for self-understanding that lies at the root of resistance to enlightenment.[34] What they mean by self-reflection and how it may be lost will be further considered where I take up Kant and Hegel's contribution to their idea of a form of thought that is opposed but at the same time vulnerable to enlightenment.[35] As Horkheimer and Adorno conceptualize thinking, I will propose, the properties of thought that create the possibility for self-reflection are the same that enable thinking to be aesthetically receptive to difference and to the world as a world of fathomless differences. As enlightenment formalizes reason and erodes our capacity to be receptive to the world aesthetically, in other words, our capacity to engage in self-reflection and to oppose enlightenment decays. To this point, though, it is at least apparent that when reason is formalized to the furthest possible extent—when in the course of enlightenment the adoption of signs that exclude all meaning other than what mastery means to mechanized production is equated with the discovery of truth—then the basis on which thinking would be able to inquire into its own meaning is purged from thought. Held hostage to the logic of formal reason, thinking necessarily assumes a neutrality in relation to the ends that formal reason serves and is blinded to any meaning outside of itself that could act, if only hypothetically, as a standpoint from which its own commitments could be examined self-consciously and questioned. As Horkheimer and Adorno put it, the "notion of the self-understanding of science contradicts the notion of science itself."[36] And by eliminating any trace of self-consciousness enlightenment does away with the "classic requirement of thinking about thought."³⁷ Once enlightened thought is without a reflective capacity, whatever actions of which it is capable, whatever different forms of life may be destroyed in its path, are not given the second thought of reflection. Horkheimer and Adorno express this development in the strongest possible terms. "Abstraction, the tool of enlightenment," they explain, "treats its objects as did fate, the notion of which it rejects: it liquidates them."³⁸

It may be objected that Horkheimer and Adorno's critique neglects important teachings of the Enlightenment that erected barriers to the process of enlightenment as they understand it, especially Kant's critiques on which the Enlightenment's contribution to moral discourse is largely based: and further objected that the scientific will to domination was not unopposed by philosophy, as their argument about the eclipse of reflective thinking proposes. While they do not deny there is ambiguity in the Enlightenment's relationship to formal rationality, they believe that overall its moral concepts bear witness to a futile attempt to find replacements for religious precepts that had constrained the progress of enlightenment by perpetuating social institutions and political ideologies resilient to the attack of formal reason. They stress the Enlightenment's success in forcing moral principles to part company with religion so that morality could be adjusted to the imperatives of capitalism. After crippling religion by tying its beliefs to myth and superstition, the Enlightenment rationalized religious-moral truths by redefining them in philosophical terms that accord with the goals of a society realizing its interests through the maxims of scientific rationality. Indeed, Horkheimer and Adorno's most damning indictment of this tendency in the philosophical thought produced by the Enlightenment is their critique of Kant, which appears as a subtext running through the main arguments of *Dialectic of Enlightenment*.

Portraying Kant as an accomplice of the process of enlightenment, their critique should come as something of a surprise. For we might reasonably expect that by focusing their critical attentions on his work they at least would find in it a source of moral-ethical opposition to enlightenment, even if it were somewhat equivocal. In particular, we would expect them to turn the Enlightenment against the process of enlightenment by cultivating Kant's ontological distinction between a phenomenal world known to the senses and a supersensible world unknown in-itself. By means of this distinction the fathomlessness of Kant's unknown being-in-itself would prove to be the absolute limit to enlightenment and a wellspring from which they could draw support for the idea that a world essentially different from however thought identifies it acquires a certain intrinsic meaning and moral authority over its fate, even if this were not the intended purpose of Kant's two-world thesis. To be sure, as I have suggested earlier and will argue further on, there appears to be a quite powerful Kantian moment of precisely this sort implicit in *Dialectic of Enlightenment*, which is carried over even more prominently into Adorno's *Aesthetic Theory*. Given the Kantian dimensions of their idea of the unknown, it would seem all the more reasonable to expect Horkheimer and Adorno to enlist Kant as their ally by exploiting the critical potential of his supersensible realm.

In the context of Horkheimer and Adorno's concern with the Enlightenment's failure to post opposition to enlightenment, however, Kant's ontology appears to be a no-less-impotent response to the advance of formal reason than the religious-moral tenets his two-world thesis protects. Although they do not confine their critique of his thought to his ontology, which is only one of the several features of Kant's thought that are each by turn considered quite briefly, in Horkheimer and Adorno's view Kant's ontological claims are the most egregious example and proof of philosophy's complicity with the process of enlightenment.

Despite its analytical tone, one of the most startling lines in *Dialectic of Enlightenment* is composed with Kant's divorce between appearance and reality obviously in mind. In the same thought in which they decry enlightenment's ruthless domination of the being of the world, Horkheimer and Adorno implicitly attack the in-itself as an ontological concept with which Kant's philosophy creates the illusion that being escapes the process of enlightenment unscathed, even though the development of its logic paves the way in theory for the extermination science then can carry out in practice. "There is no form of being in the world that science could not penetrate," they declare, "but what can be penetrated by science is not being."[39] These few chilling words place in stark relief the consequences of enlightenment's will to power as they are meted out to forms of life whose meaning is utterly alien to the logic of formal rationality. Worlds of being are simply integral to a scientific system of enlightenment, an unreflective form of knowledge that "copes most proficiently with the facts and supports the individual most effectively in the mastery of nature."[40] In Kantian terms, though, the worlds of being that science "penetrates," that is, in practice as well as in theory, remain unknown in themselves and hence, ontologically speaking, are seen to be neither penetrated nor mastered in the least. Through Kant's ontology the Enlightenment becomes an accomplice of enlightenment. In the final analysis, what for Kant was the great achievement of the Enlightenment, "understanding guided by reason," is only the historical process of enlightenment through which *formal reason* unself-consciously and unreflectively comes to fruition, as Horkheimer and Adorno translate Kant's ideal of man's emergence from intellectual immaturity. It is Werther's nightmare all over again, where the devastation of life follows from the life that lives unaware of life. This also becomes poignantly clear in their study of the work symbolizing the relationship between enlightenment and the morality of modernity.

If Odysseus is a metaphor for the evolution of enlightenment, and an especially appropriate metaphorical representation up to the stage where the Enlightenment turns formal reason against the world to physically transform into a common identity or form all the difference from which thought earlier in its history had fled, then the Marquis de Sade's Juliette (*Histoire de Juliette*) is

Dialectic of Enlightenment's metaphor for the fate of the world since the Enlightenment. "Juliette believes in science," Horkheimer and Adorno explain, she "makes the scientistic the destructive principle."[41] Their reference, of course, is to Juliette's infamous sexual practices, which convert the body and spirit into an instrument of pleasure with the assistance of highly developed expressions of formal reason—technique, method, discipline, control, manipulation, and so forth. Sexuality reveals the true potential of enlightenment and implications of mastery. Juliette's perverse and sacrilegious practices are not attempts to extend the definition of sexual normality, but are rather actions celebrating values that civilization has tabooed. By endorsing the "opposite" of its morality, Horkheimer and Adorno argue, Juliette seeks compensation from civilization for the value judgment it levels against desires it has outlawed. Juliette appears to engage the established terms of moral discourse in a reversal where "[g]oodness and benevolence become sin [and] domination and oppression become virtue."[42] Yet, they argue, Juliette is implicated in a framework ultimately having nothing to do with morality. Indeed, it is "when all ideologies have been abrogated" by enlightenment, when formal reason has emptied life of all belief in the objective possibility of meaning, in other words, that Juliette's compensation in their estimation is far less a reversal than a complete "transvaluation of values," by which they mean to suggest as well that Nietzsche is implicated in the logic of enlightenment. Juliette is the highest expression of enlightenment, not the Enlightenment's "other." Enlightenment frees Juliette to think and act without regard to values, for formal reason allows only that the world is meaningless and that there is no evidence for values in any event.

Unconstrained by moral frameworks, Juliette's thoughts and actions are as without conscience as the logic of formal reason is without reflection. And Juliette's actions do not stop with the systematic domination of the body and spirit for the sake of pleasure. Pleasure is exacted with a brutality whose techniques are perfected through a precision that is virtually scientific. Moreover, what is true for the bedroom should be true for society at large. Juliette's strength lies in having the courage to do what is forbidden, and in doing *in* those who do not. Juliette's resolve, Horkheimer and Adorno point out, is expressed through the words of her friend Princess Borghese. " 'Are pretexts necessary in order to commit a crime? ...The weak and unsuccessful must perish; this is the first proposition of *our* philanthropy.' "[43] But the weak and unsuccessful are only those who continue to affirm the possibility of some independent meaning and value. In effect, those whose differences locate them normatively outside the framework of formal reason that neutralizes values are those who become the victims of disciplines combining pleasure and brutality in which they are unable to participate. As Horkheimer and Adorno conclude, stressing the extent to which enlightenment has been released from aesthetic elements of reason that orient it to the world as though it were meaningful in itself, for the "*chronique scandaleuse* of Justine and Juliette ... is the Homeric epic with its last mythological covering removed: the history of thought as an organ of domination."⁴⁴

Of the values that Juliette's theory and practice refute, love is the one of greatest consequence, which is destroyed through its dissociation from pleasure. Pleasure is incompatible with "bourgeois love," which is itself a form of resistance to pleasures that undermine a unique regard for the individual who valorizes faithfulness. "In love," as Horkheimer and Adorno put it, "enjoyment was coupled with a deification of man, who vouchsafed it; it was the human emotion proper."⁴⁵ Without love and the loyalty and care for the body and spirit that it entails, the pursuit of pleasure can be developed to its furthest extreme. The formal logical means of acquiring pleasure through mastery and domination becomes fetishized, and pleasure is reduced to a means rather than consummated as an end, as in love. "Enjoyment becomes the object of manipulation," they explain, "until, ultimately, it is entirely extinguished in fixed entertainments." Just as Juliette's association of pleasure and brutality presages the violent extermination of all difference toward which enlightenment hurls us, the absorption of pleasure into the logic of formal reason anticipates a different kind of annihilation of difference, though one perhaps not less violent if by now our aesthetic sensibility to the violence in thought has been awakened. Juliette's pleasures as fixed entertainments already anticipate the culture industry.

With the opening lines of *Dialectic of Enlightenment*'s essay on mass culture, any thought that Horkheimer and Adorno's critical approach is informed primarily by a sociological interest in the ways in which modern capitalism reproduces itself or how other social tendencies are expressed in cultural phenomena must be set aside. While their critique of mass culture in their work as a whole certainly serves these ends, as Adorno's own reflections confirm, "The Culture Industry: Enlightenment as Mass Deception" puts a much finer point to it.⁴⁶ When they declare "*Kultur heute schlägt alles mit Ähnlichkeit*"—today culture strikes everything with sameness—they mean by "strike" that violence is endemic to culturally formative processes and by "sameness," or resemblance or commonality, that violence leaves its mark in cultural formations compelled to share one and the same identity.⁴⁷ Modern culture, in short, destroys difference. Individuality and the differences individuality continues to express are illusions. Proof of this lies additionally in the fact that the sameness with which culture is stricken is hardly confined to capitalism but prevails over cultural terrains wherever formal reason prevails. "Even the aesthetic activities of political opposites," they argue, "are one in their enthusiastic obedience to the rhythm of the iron system. The decorative industrial management buildings and exhibition centers in authoritarian countries are as much the same as anywhere else."⁴⁸ The allusion, of course, is to the German Reich, and further associates a peculiar kind of violence, Fascism, with formally rationalized cultural systems.

"Equivalency," the principle of formal reason whose logic could be discerned in embryo at the stage of magical thought, achieves hegemony through mass culture. Horkheimer and Adorno are relatively unconcerned with the specific goods produced by the culture industry, but rather focus on practices by which consumers are classified, organized, and labeled so that all become implicated in a process of cultural formation whose values are uniform throughout the "thinly veiled identity of all industrial culture products."[49] Equivalency among products creates a virtual equivalency among individuals, what they refer to as the "rule of complete quantification." Consumers have no needs that cannot be fulfilled and for which there is no denominator common to any and all other needs. Cultural production in every sphere of culture is obedient to a formula according to which every product in its particulars is shaped. "Because of his ubiquity," Horkheimer and Adorno point out by way of illustrating the logic of the culture industry, "the film star with whom one is meant to fall in love is from the outset a copy of himself. Every tenor voice comes to sound like a Caruso record, and the 'natural' faces of Texas girls are like the successful models by whom Hollywood has typecast them."[50] Conventions within the culture industry to which new productions are subjected are maintained with such strictness that "only the copy appears."[51] And conventions must be intensified all the more to guarantee the outcome of the culture industry's relentless pressure to produce new cultural goods, meaning that there can be none of the creative tension between established and budding cultural forms that expresses itself in an individuality of style. So pervasive is the logic of equivalency that the "totality" of the culture industry consists only of "repetition."[52] The whole and the part, universal and particular, identity and difference are alike.

The consumer no less than the producer of mass culture receives one message, that self-preservation means "fitting in or being left behind." Horkheimer and Adorno invoke the Kantian notion of the subject as a measure of how little subjectivity the culture industry actually tolerates with this desideratum. On this occasion damning Kant with faint praise, they point out that even though the Kantian subject already reflected a diminished bourgeois subjectivity unable to constitute the formal categories that shaped its experience of the world, it at least created the world through forms that—although given with an ontological finality—belonged to the subject. As Horkheimer and Adorno put it, "Kant's formalism still expected a contribution from the individual, who was thought to relate the varied experiences of the senses to fundamental concepts; but industry robs the individual of his function."[53] As the institutional embodiment of the formal rational elements of reason that were developed through the historical development of the subject, as the "subject" prevailing over the subject, mass culture does not even require formal rational thinking from its consumers or producers, who with all of their reactions scripted in advance are simply types reproduced in every product. From the standpoint of mass culture, subjects have lost their identity as subjects and bear only the common identity presupposed by the "thinly veiled identity" among cultural goods. "Ironically," Horkheimer and Adorno note, conveying an insight that captures the degree to which subjectivity has become irrelevant to mass culture, "man as a member of a species has been made a reality by the culture industry."[54] If there is a sense in which individuals persist as subjects, it is as examples of "mere species-being," they argue with Marx in mind and continue to press the idea that mass culture obliterates even the functional difference it prescribes among subjects. Individuals, in other words, are differentiated only in terms of the achievements of the species as a whole. Subjectivity is reduced to individuation, and since forms of individuation are themselves only each other's more or less standardized reproductions, subjectivity passes over to mere "imitation."[55] "Today culture strikes everything with sameness," which, as we now see, means that in the era of mass culture, regardless of the extent to which individuals are yet subjects, nothing, including subjectivity, need any longer remain that is "specific" to human beings except as "an utterly abstract notion."[56]

I suspect that Horkheimer and Adorno are deliberately vague when they argue that the "ruthless unity in the culture industry is evidence of what will happen in politics."[57] Of course, they mean to say that the cultural elimination of difference anticipates the ruthlessness with which Fascist politics treats difference. Since their critique of the culture industry is likewise an indictment of what they understand to be the most advanced stage of American liberalism, however, as I will argue in the chapter that follows, and as it precedes *Dialectic of Enlightenment*'s final essay on Fascism and anti-Semitism ("The Elements of Anti-Semitism"), they are alluding, as well, to a developmental connection between liberalism and Fascism they cannot yet make out distinctly. Perhaps they are saying that what liberalism achieves in one context is not different from what Fascism achieves in another. Or perhaps they mean that liberalism provides the cultural framework for a process that will be duplicated at the political level, suggesting that democratic politics will not be less exempt from the rationality that overwhelms culture, that the ubiquity of formal reason is precisely what defines Fascism, and that as it evolves within the context of liberal democracy the culture industry anticipates the emergence of a Fascist politics not unlike the Fascism contemporaneous with the American culture industry at the time *Dialectic of Enlightenment* is completed (1944). Though the second possibility seems least intended, or least explicit, surely what is common to both the culture industry and Fascism in their estimation is the respective fate assigned to difference in both. In that special regard the culture industry of liberalism anticipates the politics of Fascism and is, in a definite sense, fascistic. Any doubt that this is their position is erased by the examination, in *Dialectic of Enlightenment*'s final essay, of the elements of anti-Semitism that belong to Fascism, while obviously not only to Fascism.

At the heart of Fascism is an intelligence essentially inimical to "difference." Fascism, which "gives full rein to calculation and abides by science as such," they argue, "no longer needs to uphold any [moral or ethical] disciplines."[58] With Fascism, in other words, enlightenment reaches the stage where reason possesses absolutely no standards by which to measure itself other than those of formal rationality. Fascism is the apotheosis of enlightenment, formal reason writ large, an order spontaneously and without question or objection ensuring its self-preservation by transforming all of human being and being into terms that offer no barriers to manipulation and control. All that the world contains becomes a neutralized element in a comprehensive system of formal rationality. Formal reason is the essence of an order that cannot exist without distorting that which it encompasses.

To conceptualize the development of formal reason as it unfolds within Fascism, Horkheimer and Adorno introduce an aesthetic term to illuminate the pathological tendencies of enlightenment. Whereas the concept of "mimesis" refers to an artwork's imitation of an object through an aesthetic orientation to the world that does not identify it with its representations in thought, "false projection," its counterpart, "makes the environment like itself."[59] With the contrast between mimesis and false projection Horkheimer and Adorno highlight the final evolutionary stage of the property of formal reason that historically subdues an aesthetic rationality receptive to difference, the projection of form onto a world whose fathomlessness reason finds threatening. While there is a Kantian sense in which "all perception is projection," whereby reason's formal properties necessarily impart structure to the world so that the world reflects the structure of thought, from the very origins of thought enlightenment unbridles these properties, frees them from those other, mimetic features of thought that enable thinking to distinguish reflectively between an "inner and outer world," the world as thinking constructs it and the world as it may be apart and different from how the subject thinks of it. Eventually overwhelmed in the long course of time by the rule of formal reason's fear of the unknown, thinking slips into a state of "paranoia," the most refined expression of thinking's original fear of the opacity of nature that is embodied in the single-minded obedience to the rule of self-preservation sublimated in formally rationalized social orders. It is this paranoia that defines the Fascist "system of things, the fixed universal order of which science is merely an abstract expression," where the role of subjectivity in thought's ordering and organizing of the world is "overlooked in the schematization," and the system it creates is believed by thought to be "the thing itself" rather than its own mirror image.[60] Fascism is formal reason unable to discern its own reflection in the world it falsely projects. It is a "true madness" that results from the complete loss in thinking of the aesthetic capacity to distinguish between thought of the world and what in the world is different from thought, that results from loss of the ability of thought to participate in what Horkheimer and Adorno refer to as the "negativity in which thought—in contradistinction to fixed judgment—comes into its own."[61] Fascism resembles the madman who makes everything in his universe into his own image, whose madness is so absolute that he becomes the model of the perfectly rational individual the world can never contradict. And formal reason is Fascism's madness.

Far more than its madness, we must add. Formal reason is Fascism's "murderous principle," and it proves the existence of the murderous principle in reason when, as the exclusive principle through which social order is constituted, it inevitably manifests itself as the essential element of Fascist anti-Semitism. "The persecution of the Jews," Horkheimer and Adorno explain, "is *inseparable* from that system of order."[62] Can there be further doubt as to the appropriateness of describing reason as a murderous principle where it is evident that the continuum of domination that began with thought's preanimistic struggle to dispel the unknown culminates in the destruction of the Jews? If this is true, though, must Jews not represent the "difference" to which formal reason throughout the evolution of thought is necessarily antagonistic?

Jewish difference, Horkheimer and Adorno argue, is rooted in Judaism's conception of God and its beliefs about an afterlife. "In Jewish religion," they explain, "the bond between name and being is still recognized in the ban on pronouncing the name of God."[63] By refusing to utter the name of God, in other words, Judaism insists on a "difference" between God as conceived in thought and God as it is, in-itself. The Judaic ban on naming God is an aesthetic recognition of the limits of thought, and not only of the limits of thought in relation to God but in relation to being as such, which God represents. As does aesthetic thinking, it tacitly acknowledges that being always exceeds every thought of being. And it is precisely this excess of being over any concept of being that is the correct "bond" between name and being as Horkheimer and Adorno understand it. "Difference" is being that lies forever outside of thinking, being that is nonidentical with thinking, whose identity, in aesthetic terms, is unknown and unknowable. And the nonidentical character of the Judaic God requires the absence of any thought of an afterlife. Life and death, which without a determination of the nature of God must remain indeterminate and without the possibility of closure, sustain the mystery of the fathomlessness of being. Judaism suffers "no word," they propose, "that would alleviate the despair of all that is mortal."[64] Judaism's faithful pursuit of its prohibition on naming its god and its refusal to entertain the idea of an afterlife determines its own particular difference in this sense. Jews are, like their God, a force unknown, "mana," a latter-day appeasement of magic, as Horkheimer and Adorno put it. As the embodiment of the unknown, Jews consequently pose a threat to formal reason, which in its less "abstract" political form exterminates Jews to rid the world of the terror their difference represents.

With the argument of *Dialectic of Enlightenment* before us, it now can be examined more closely to determine its contribution to a concept of aesthetic individuality.

THREE

Dialectic of Enlightenment as a Genealogy of Reason

RHETORICAL OVERLAY VERSUS LINEAR HISTORICAL NARRATIVE

Is reason's destruction of the Jews the denouement of *Dialectic of Enlightenment*, as it is the denouement of the history of enlightenment as Horkheimer and Adorno have represented it? To be sure, just as reason's destruction of Judaism is the final outcome of the long process of enlightenment, it is the culminating event of *Dialectic of Enlightenment*'s critique of this process, though in both cases in a general narrative sense only. Other events are meant to unfold from a rhetorical inflection concluding their argument. Specifically, the rhetorical inflection is intended to provoke an interpretive reconfiguration of their argument as a genealogical construction that does not then replace, but rather *overlays* the linear historical narrative of an enlightenment of violence stretching from preanimistic thinking to modernity. I return to the thought opening my discussion in the last chapter.

At the conclusion of *Dialectic of Enlightenment* the violence inflicted on the Jews is meant to awaken in our thinking an aesthetic sensibility to the real object of violence, difference, of which the Jew is one representation and the *penultimate* test of the power of formal reason to exterminate difference. In retrospect and for the first time, as it were, we are given to understand that the destruction of the Jews had been present from the beginning of the history of thought. It is an event inscribed deeply in reason's telos to purge the world of difference, stirring embryonically even on the first occasion preanimistic thinking cringed in fear of the fathomless unknown. Our aesthetic sensibility to difference is accompanied by the insights that Fascism is but the political handmaiden of formal rationality gone mad, and that formal reason unleashes Fascism as the irrational potential that lies deep within reason's ancient womb. Contrary to the formal rational thinking *Dialectic of Enlightenment* finds to be characteristic of children of enlightenment, with our sensibility opened aesthetically to the difference formal reason empties from the world, as its argument concludes we are to be again the individuals the process of enlightenment destroyed.

Or we may fail to be. For following the destruction of Judaism, it is the success or failure of *Dialectic of Enlightenment* to awaken our aesthetic sensibility that serves as the *ultimate* test of the power of formal rationality to silence reason's awareness of the violence inflicted upon difference. If formal rationality has achieved an unchallenged hegemony, should our aesthetic sensibility to the genocidal extermination of difference not be as ruined as all reason that has been prepared by enlightenment to accept the "final solution" without further thought? Paradoxically, it seems, Horkheimer and Adorno presume we will be able to engage the argument of *Dialectic of Enlightenment* with that same thoughtfulness its linear historical narrative proposed has vanished. It is at the precise moment their work draws to a close with the destruction of the Jews, symbolizing not only the extinction of all the difference in the world but of all thought sensitive to annihilation on such a scale, that this paradox of the presumption of an intelligence claimed to have disappeared crystallizes. And it is at this same moment that *Dialectic of Enlightenment* is rhetorically inflected, altering the direction of the argument away from the impasse of an enlightenment pursuing an irreversible trajectory of violence of which thinking no longer can become aware. It is as though its argument, by paradoxically presupposing the awakening of an intelligence whose extinction it set out to prove, requires it be turned back against itself to avoid collapsing under its own weight. Whereas the paradox of the argument implicitly divides it against itself, with each level of argument invalidating the other, as *Dialectic of Enlightenment* concludes this schism is made quite explicit, taking a rhetorical form whose effect is to provoke opposition to the linear historical narrative. The opposition works in the following way to allow the text to recognize a reader whose aesthetic sensibility to the violence to difference is being awakened.

In keeping with the logic of the linear historical narrative of enlightenment, Horkheimer and Adorno conclude *Dialectic of Enlightenment* by first writing that the horror of Fascism, as the most fully developed expression of formal reason, is that it "allows of no truth against which it could be measured." No sooner is Fascism construed to be this universal "deception" in which we all are implicated without the possibility of escape, however, than they move to impeach this claim. Given the relentless logic of their narrative, they can do so only hypothetically through a rhetorical appeal to an audience who, from Horkheimer and Adorno's *historical* standpoint, may actually be *imaginary*. Only if we, the "undiscerning," are also "*wholly deprived of the faculty of thought*," they argue rhetorically, can the stunning contradiction between a ubiquitous formal reason and the entire absence of an aesthetic rationality that differs from it escape notice. Since they speak to us of an incapacity we could not possess if they would speak to us at all, at the rhetorical level we are presumed not to be "wholly deprived" of the ability to think. Our attention is consequently focused on the contradiction that cannot now pass by us unnoticed, if ever it had, and the direction of their argument is inflected, leading us away from the impasse to which their linear historical narrative leads. For by working rhetorically to distinguish a public whose sensibility it cannot fail to awaken without penalty of being written for no one, *Dialectic of Enlightenment* is intended for someone. And it is for someone who, now able to recognize the intimate connection between enlightenment and violence to difference, enters the threshold of what Horkheimer and Adorno refer to as "enlightenment in possession of itself." It is for an individual capable of "enlightened self-possession," or "aesthetic individuality," as I refer to it, for thinking that "coming to power can break the bounds of enlightenment" through its aesthetic receptivity to the diversity of differences the world contains, for which these final words of their great work—its rhetorical signature—express hope.

> Though this deception [Fascism] allows of no truth against which it could be measured, the truth appears negatively in [the] very extent of the contradiction; and the undiscerning can be permanently kept from that truth only if they are wholly deprived of the faculty of thought. Enlightenment which is in possession of itself and coming to power can break the bounds of enlightenment.[1]

If *Dialectic of Enlightenment* concludes not merely, let us say, with a rhetorical gesture but with a rhetorical inflection altering its argument in the direction of the aesthetic receptivity to difference belonging to enlightened self-possession, nothing less occurs than that the entirety of Horkheimer and Adorno's linear historical narrative is thrown open to question. Indeed, when we consider that *Dialectic of Enlightenment* virtually *refutes* its historical narrative at the rhetorical level by distinguishing an intelligence engaged by its argument, we realize that by compelling us to recognize its inflection the text possesses a rhetorical strategy that has only begun to unfold. Since at the rhetorical level the linear historical narrative is invalid, the monstrous caricature of the historical process it seemed to be, we are urged on by the rhetorical inflection to retrace our steps through the interior of the narrative to discover there what must have survived earlier in the process of enlightenment if it has survived at its end. What should be discovered in the narrative's interior, if Horkheimer and Adorno's argument is actually inflected, are signs of the intelligence—antecedents of our own intelligence—whose aesthetic sensibility to the violence to difference refutes the linear historical narrative at its conclusion. Once rhetorically provoked to question the correctness of the linear historical narrative, in other words, we are strategically enabled, if not strategically required, to make an interpretive move. As individuals whose aesthetic sensibility to difference is awakened, we are rhetorically situated in opposition to the linear historical logic of enlightenment. Consequently, we find ourselves positioned to reconstruct the linear historical narrative to account reflexively for the individuality—our own aesthetic individuality—that in a greatly abridged form survived the enlightenment's advance of formal reason.

With Horkheimer and Adorno's two-tiered strategy in mind, we now turn to locate a historical moment in the process of enlightenment where thinking first was decisively transformed in the direction of formal rationality, though not *so* decisively that at the end of the process it could not reflect on itself as the intelligence of an aesthetic individuality whose receptivity to difference cannot be completely extinguished. Such a moment is found at the mythological stage of thinking, the stage, as Horkheimer and Adorno explained, that "set off the unending process of enlightenment."[2] For some form of enlightened self-possession could not appear again at a subsequent stage of thought if it could not earlier survive this first conclusive challenge to its integrity at the stage of myth. By locating this earlier form of aesthetic individuality, which I propose is captured in the *Odyssey*'s Sirens episode, our interpretive reconfiguration of the linear historical narrative of enlightenment will have produced evidence, anticipated by *Dialectic of Enlightenment*'s rhetorical inflection, that formal reason does not have an unremitting and unbroken hold over the aesthetic dimension of our thinking, which is thus able to survive the onslaught of enlightenment. Our understanding of the process of enlightenment and our relation to it will have changed. Accordingly, by way of an agonistic reflection designed to investigate and contest the logic of its own history, a remnant of aesthetic individuality, an intelligence whose sensibility is awakened by Horkheimer and Adorno, enters the threshold of enlightened self-possession. Though it has not come to power as a fully developed aesthetic individuality to "break the bounds of enlightenment," this intelligence is at least poised to conceptualize aesthetic individuality as it would appear if it did come to power. And a rhetorically inflected *Dialectic of Enlightenment*, which concludes by directing us to an interpretive reconfiguration that overlays its linear historical narrative and points toward the recollection and recovery of the world-historical loss it chronicles, becomes a genealogy of reason.

INDIVIDUALS IN POSSESSION OF OURSELVES

To recall from the previous chapter, when Odysseus resorts to cunning to outwit Polyphemus by exploiting the play in the similarly sounding "Odysseus" and "*Udeis*" (Nobody), we are presented with one of the earliest examples of how the self is at the same time both sacrificed and preserved through the use of "equivalence."[3] By substituting *Udeis* for his own name, Odysseus employs a formal rational technique that makes out what is different (as Odysseus is different from Nobody) to be the same (as Odysseus sounds the same as *Udeis*). Deceiving Polyphemus into believing his identity to be "Nobody," Odysseus flees the clutches of mythical being. Equivalence secures Odysseus's self-preservation by sacrificing an aesthetically receptive self originally fascinated by the mysteries and wonders of a world essentially different from the disenchanted world in which he safely takes refuge. "Cunning," through which equivalence is strategically adopted, Horkheimer and Adorno conclude, "is the organ by means of which the self, to emerge victorious from adventure, loses itself in order to preserve itself."[4]

A Conflict of the Faculties, Its Hierarchical Resolution, and Identity as Self-Contradiction

In their view, the transition from myth to enlightenment, recapitulated on this and each such occasion Odysseus flees from the supposed dangers of enchantment, represents a catastrophic restructuring of the self, qualitatively distinguishing myth from the demonstrable changes in reason that occurred at the earlier, magical stage of enlightenment. Prior to the traumatic event of self-sacrifice, Odysseus is oriented to the world as an adventuring self, eager to risk encounters with a fathomless world, a world unlike the world he can know. Able to recognize difference, to "think" of difference, he is receptive aesthetically to the diversity of differences that compose the being of this world. Frightened by the unknown's threat of extinction, Odysseus then pursues formal rational calculations to think in ways that suppress his receptivity to difference and that forever alter the self's aesthetic experience of the world. Since it is the sacrifice of an aesthetic mode of thinking and the adoption of a formal rational mode of thought that defines both self-sacrifice and self-preservation within one and the same Odysseus, are Horkheimer and Adorno not saying that originally the self is in conflict with itself? Is there not originally a division within the self characterized as a struggle between two modes of thinking on which the figure of Odysseus focuses our attention? Contrary to my earlier proposal, perhaps Odysseus is less enlightenment's proper metaphor, illuminating decisive stages in the history of enlightenment, the historical forces expressed at each of these stages, the struggles through which these forces play themselves out, and the principles consolidated in the resolution of these struggles, than something else.[5] Perhaps Odysseus is more the symbolic representation of a conflict between two faculties of thought, the formal and the aesthetic, such that the subsequent ascendancy of one over the other, if not literally the sacrifice of the "self," is tantamount to its transformation into another self already contained within it. If so, then when we momentarily turn to his encounter with the Sirens we must think of Odysseus strapped to the mast of his ship as symbolic of the struggle between his aesthetic receptivity to difference and the restraint with which his formal reasoning not only safeguards him from its deadly charms but protects him from *himself*.

Now our orientation to *Dialectic of Enlightenment* noticeably begins to shift. Rather than reading it as a philosophy of history whose eternal antagonists are world-historical principles of reason that either disgorge the world of meaning or recognize and affirm it, we approach Horkheimer and Adorno's work as though it resembles a philosophical anthropology. Although saying this we yet remain at a distance from the final rhetorical reconfiguration of the text, we do move a decisive step nearer to it. Once our focus at the mythical stage of thought is shifted from the world-historical struggle of *abstract principles* of formal and aesthetic reason to a *conflict of the faculties*, or to the formal and aesthetic *modes of thinking within the self*, we can entertain the possibility that the apparent necessity or even lawfulness with which formal reason evolves is somewhat attenuated.[6] Rather than defining a condition antecedent to Odysseus that externally governs his thought and action, the struggle between principles of reason as an internal conflict within the self refers, perhaps, to the ways in which

Odysseus thinks in relation to the conditions in which he finds himself. I do not mean to suggest that Horkheimer and Adorno do not intend their work to be historical. On the contrary, but I am arguing that the rhetorical overlay of *Dialectic of Enlightenment*, which I have argued is forced upon us by a paradox that incites us to recover genealogically what its linear historical narrative proves to have disappeared, redirects its historical inquiry to the recollection of past life as yet living. How, then, does Horkheimer and Adorno's text, as a function of its rhetorical structure, labor to rescue what is gone as what is yet living, instead of using what is past to document an inexorable linear historical logic of domination from which we are unable to escape?

Where they reproduce the world-historical conflict between the formal and aesthetic principles of reason as a conflict between the formal and aesthetic modes of thinking within the self, as they do in Odysseus's encounter with the Sirens, Horkheimer and Adorno describe him as having a certain independence to negotiate solutions to the mythical dangers he confronts, however narrowly his liberty is epically confined. Odysseus, for instance, "does not try to take another route that would enable him to escape sailing past the Sirens. And he does not try, say, to presume on the superiority of his knowledge and to listen freely to the temptresses, imagining that his freedom will be protection enough."[7] While these possibilities for free choice are foreclosed by the determinism of the Homeric epic and Odysseus's ship follows its predestined course, Horkheimer and Adorno stress that he nevertheless discovers an "escape clause in the contract" of mythic foreordination that allows him to "fulfill it while eluding it."[8] Arranging to remain bound to the mast of his ship so that he may hear the Sirens without succumbing to their power, Odysseus escapes the "legal conditions which enclose and threaten him" laid down by myth, and thus "satisfies the sentence of the law *so that it loses power over him*."[9] Although Odysseus's situations are predestined and he is never free, he remains an example of how the "self represents rational universality against the inevitability of fate," Horkheimer and Adorno insist. This can be expressed differently in light of the way they characterize the attitude with which Odysseus negotiates his own destiny. We should say that though Odysseus is not free from fortune, neither is he without opportunities to theorize about his predicaments and to design some sort of praxis, whereby he typically resorts to cunning to cheat the deities while coincidentally ensuring an aesthetic receptivity to the difference in the world the deities represent. By pointing to the success with which he avoids becoming fate's fatality, Horkheimer and Adorno weaken the grip over Odysseus of the lawfulness with which the linear historical process of enlightenment unfolds.

Surely, at the level of the linear historical narrative, *Dialectic of Enlightenment* refuses to accord Odysseus even residual powers that would be at his disposal as a means of ensuring not only his self-preservation but his self-determination as well. Fatefully and unambiguously, self-preservation entails self-sacrifice. Only that self survives that refutes all experience except the experience of survival.

Odysseus may indeed author the dialectical principle behind his actions that spares him, while being aesthetically receptive to a world of difference "throughout the many mortal perils he has had to endure." As Horkheimer and Adorno make clear, however, narratively Odysseus's aesthetic experience of difference is obliterated by the superior confirmation of the unity of his life and of his identity as an individual.[10] By allowing the rhetorical signature concluding the text to guide our understanding of how we are to arrange its arguments, though, we must acknowledge that in his encounter with the Sirens Odysseus's actions reflect a degree of enlightened self-possession or aesthetic individuality. Shortly I will describe it more carefully as a "compromised" form of enlightened self-possession. For the moment I want simply to note that, *rather than obliterated* by, Odysseus's aesthetic receptivity to the difference represented by mythical being, which is certainly tangible, more accurately is *subordinated* to the unity of his life and individual identity that is secured and preserved by the machinations of formal rationality. With this we can say that the world-historical struggle between principles of reason that Horkheimer and Adorno install within the self as a conflict of the faculties is resolved as a *hierarchical ordering* of the formal and aesthetic modes of thinking through which Odysseus and the individuality he represents is oriented toward the world. Consequently, thinking is able to recognize and be receptive to difference if, through such compromised expressions of aesthetic individuality, and however modest the experience of difference as aesthetic receptivity subordinated to self-preservation may be, the self will not be lost as Odysseus—his identity as well as his life—was not lost to the Sirens. Thinking now can be thought of as aesthetically receptive to difference so long as there is one and the same self that is continuous (unified) throughout its internally divided, self-contradictory experience of difference, and whose continuity (identity) is itself the primary, though not exclusive, experience throughout all the discontinuous experiences narratively constituting its life.

Self-Identity and the Triumph of Formal Reason

To this point, by reconstructing *Dialectic of Enlightenment* genealogically we lay claim to one important insight. Odysseus may not be the simple object of formal reason he is construed to be by Horkheimer and Adorno's linear historical narrative. Quite to the contrary, in the Sirens episode he reappears as the subject of a praxis who through tremendous exertion of will would subdue an aesthetically receptive orientation to the world's differences by bringing it under the strict control of formal reason, rather than helplessly *destroying it as a mindless* victim of fate. Once Odysseus's independence is evinced, however precarious it remains, other and related dimensions of their argument move into the foreground that had receded in importance under pressure from the linear force of its narrative structure or that were interpretively conscripted to the narrative theme of historical necessity. Those dimensions of special consequence stand out where Horkheimer and Adorno consistently frame Odysseus's struggle for self-preservation as a struggle to secure self-identity (as he had not struggled by being aesthetically receptive to the Sirens), adventures in which he resists self-contradiction and the threat of dissolution by features internally dividing his self. For their discussion of Odysseus's visit to the underworld and of the dangers collectively threatened by Polyphemus, Circe, Scylla and Charybdis, the cattle of the Sun-god Hyperion, and the Lotus-eaters allows us to understand what *Dialectic of Enlightenment* never explicitly tells us, precisely what is the nature of the self sacrificed through self-preservation. Although this question runs centrally through their work, it surfaces only when an interpretive reconfiguration of their argument points to the contingency of the self, thus recovering it from their linear historical narrative's list of foregone conclusions.

To take Horkheimer and Adorno's interpretations of these episodes together, Odysseus's struggle for self-preservation is read as a struggle to wrest the "unity [of the subject] from the diffuse sagas."[11] Here the formation of Odysseus's personal identity is being compared to the stages through which the process of enlightenment passes. His identity is formed in the same way that the historical identity of reason as formal rationality is constructed in opposition to an aesthetic recognition of the world's fathomlessness and an aesthetic receptivity to difference. Likewise, they offer that Odysseus's "self-realization" will be won only through a consciousness of himself as a unity, where self-consciousness is expressed as an "opposition of the surviving individual ego"—of the I—to "multifarious fate."[12] Again, in this context Odysseus's enlightenment depends upon his self-conscious resistance to a world that at some level of understanding apart from his own need for certainty he consistently experiences aesthetically as meaningful. In all such instances Horkheimer and Adorno are interested in documenting what they refer to importantly as a "unification of intellectual functions" through "the resignation of thought to the rise of unanimity," where *unanimity* is the cognitive successor to the prior *hierarchical ordering* of the formal and aesthetic faculties.[13] Odysseus's identity develops as "a function of the unidentical" through the attempt to bring to an end dissociated experiences of a world of diverse and discontinuous differences, such as his aesthetic receptivity to the Sirens, which presuppose diverse, dissociated, and contradictory modes of formal and aesthetic thought constantly in tension with one another. Horkheimer and Adorno express this perfectly by saying that Odysseus becomes "an entity only in the diversity of that which denies all unity."[14] Thinking's struggle to find coherence in a world that is not in itself coherent is first and foremost a struggle within the self for its own unified identity against thinking that opposes self-identity. Their image is of an agonistic self straining to hold itself together as it labors to integrate qualitatively different forms of thinking in order to produce *one identical world* through the construction of *one identical individual*, an individual whose identity will not itself become different whenever it encounters difference. Odysseus must resist "reversion" and "disintegration" and the "temptation to self-abandonment," Horkheimer and Adorno contend.[15] His identity is a measure of being able to consciously maintain a "perpetual presence of mind," as though thinking possessed properties that would expose it to pressures that force it to disassemble.[16]

In short, throughout his adventures Odysseus represents a self who by virtue of the capacities to think aesthetically and reason formally is able originally to relate receptively to the world as a world of differences as well as to all the differences in the world as not different in the least. *Self-identity*, on the other hand, is a constitutive process that eventually leads to an "inner organization of individuality (*die innerliche Organizationsform von Individualität*)."[17] Here the self's hierarchically subordinated capacity to be receptive to the world aesthetically, as Odysseus experienced the Sirens, finally is sacrificed to an experience and knowledge of the world ruled by formal rational thinking. Yet, not until Odysseus arrives home in Ithaca is his self-identity completely constituted, which for Horkheimer and Adorno coincides with formal reason's imposition on the aesthetic capacity to be receptive to difference and its imposition of identity on difference itself. Before Odysseus reaches his final destination, the world to which he was aesthetically receptive is not lost, nor is his aesthetic capacity for receptivity to difference, though it will take the form of art, as we shall see.

An Ideal Form of Aesthetic Individuality

Reconstructing *Dialectic of Enlightenment* rhetorically, we see, leads us to distinguish an aesthetic form of individuality, although one I have suggested is compromised, from a form of cognitive organization where what at first survives through compromise is finally annulled. A closer study of this compromised, aesthetic form of enlightened self-possession for which Odysseus serves as the model will clarify its features and also enable us to project an ideal form of enlightened individuality *fully* in possession of itself, an ideal form of aesthetic individuality. Let us look again at Odysseus bound willingly to his ship's mast, secure from the danger of the unknown to which he deliberately has opened himself aesthetically, while his oarsmen lead him away on a journey that postpones mastery in favor of retreat from the fathomlessness of being. Of special significance in this adventure, Odysseus refuses to suppress the aesthetic part of his thinking that exposes him receptively to worlds of difference. Unlike the later, postmythological stages of thought where formal reason dominates to the exclusion of aesthetic rationality, and unlike his self-identical state of mind at the end of his odyssey, Odysseus's actions do not entail that "denial of nature in man" whereby the "*telos* of man's own life is distorted (*verwirrt*)."[18]

Odysseus retains an awareness that "he himself is nature" and thus safeguards the "aims for which [man] keeps himself alive," such as "the enhancement (*die Steigerung*)" of his "spiritual powers," aims nullified in the subsequent history of thought when mankind's understanding of itself as nature is discarded.[19] Against this, however, it is equally significant that although Odysseus is aesthetically receptive to mythical being, he does not permit himself to be receptive in ways that would enable his identity to undergo some revision in relation to difference. For according to myth, just as his restraints bind him to the mast, Odysseus, his identity, is bound to an unchanging course, whereas if he were to forgo his restraints his ensuing fate would completely spend his identity and selfhood. With Odysseus as its measure, then, we see that at its mythical stage thinking takes on a certain ambiguity suggesting that his self-possession has struck a *compromise* with enlightenment. As Odysseus is open to the experience of difference, formal reason has sacrificed to self-identity neither aesthetic receptivity to difference nor difference itself. Formal reason has not yet introduced that "distortion" of the ultimate end of human being Horkheimer and Adorno attribute to thought from metaphysics to modernity. At the same time, formal reason's trajectory toward the destruction of difference is not altered in the least by thinking's consciously restrained, self-contradictory encounter with enchantment, just as Odysseus's own course remains unchanged by his aesthetic experience of difference. In view of how this ambiguity of the formal and aesthetic elements of mythical thought plays itself out through Odysseus, it seems evident that aesthetic rationality is not assimilated to thinking in a way that could temper the project of mastering the world through a receptivity to difference that *reconstitutes* formal reason. Rather, the orientation of formal reason to worlds of difference, for the time it briefly permits an aesthetic distraction, is merely suspended.

As is apparent in the Sirens episode, in mythical thought, in contrast to subsequent stages of thought where formal reason completely subdues its aesthetic counterpart in the formation of self-identity, apparently thinking's hierarchically ordered capacities for formal and aesthetic reason coexist with some degree of independence that accounts for thinking's ambiguity. What seems clearly suggested by a rhetorically inflected genealogical reconstruction of *Dialectic of Enlightenment* is that if formal reason were to be reconstituted through an integration of a hierarchically ordered and segregated aesthetic rationality, thinking could avoid the eventual distortion in the telos of the inner nature of thought corresponding to the formation of self-identity. Though a compromised expression of enlightened self-possession, in other words, mythical thinking in its ambiguity nevertheless anticipates an *ideal* form of aesthetic individuality. By integrating aesthetic rationality, individuality in its ideal form would transform reason to itself become different, and through its transformation become aesthetically receptive to difference without loss of identity or the fear of losing its identity that first led to compromise with enlightenment and eventually to the sacrifice of individuality to subjectivity. And by avoiding these distortions in the telos of the inner nature of thinking, this ideal form of aesthetic individuality would prevent the distortion in the ultimate ends *inscribed in* thought, the distortion that results in the telos of the domination of outward nature and the difference it represents. Opposed to the conception of reason's ultimate end underwritten by Horkheimer and Adorno's linear historical narrative, the rhetorically inflected argument enables us to entertain the possibility that reason is not necessarily or inevitably destructive either of individuality's aesthetic nature or of outward nature to which individuality can be aesthetically receptive. Fascism ceases to be the teleological end of life embodied in all forms of life. And Werther's nightmare gives way to a different dream.

Methodological Reflections on the Possibility of Aesthetic Individuality

As a projection based on the compromised form of enlightened self-possession, of course, the ideal form of aesthetic individuality does not represent a real historical possibility. If a rhetorical reconfiguration of *Dialectic of Enlightenment* is to provide insight into the historical possibility for an aesthetically receptive orientation to the world, two tendencies to exaggeration must be avoided. To avoid these tendencies requires that the rhetorical and linear historical levels of interpretation be kept strictly in sight of each other.

Keeping the rhetorical interpretation in view of the historical narrative avoids dangers that arise when *Dialectic of Enlightenment* is approached exclusively in terms of its historicity. Narrowly privileging its historicity has led invariably to a reductionist interpretation of Horkheimer and Adorno's concept of enlightenment, an exaggeration that stresses the irreversible historical development of a formal rationality blind to all values at variance with its own inexorable logic, and foreclosing on the historical possibility of *any* form of aesthetically enlightened self-possession. Against this reduction, though an exaggeration at the other extreme, a rhetorical reconfiguration of *Dialectic of Enlightenment* introduces possibilities for an ideal aesthetic relation to the world not at all overwhelmed by formal reason and that stubbornly reside on the surface of a linear historical narrative beneath which they are meant to vanish. At the same time, though, while these possibilities have not disappeared, neither do they represent real historical possibilities for the (as yet incompletely articulated) normative ideal of aesthetic individuality projected by the rhetorically inspired reconstruction. Conceptualizing historical possibilities that emerge when *Dialectic of Enlightenment* is read against itself by keeping the linear historical narrative in view of the rhetorical reconfiguration disciplines our understanding of these possibilities as arrested with the development of a compromised form of aesthetic individuality. Since in its compromised form aesthetic reason does not escape the historical process of enlightenment, but is implicated deeply in its logic, as a historical possibility aesthetic individuality will remain underdeveloped exactly as it remained underdeveloped in the figure of Odysseus bound to the mast of his ship, as we shall see. What is decisive, however, is that it may be only on the basis of a reconfiguration of *Dialectic of Enlightenment* as a genealogy of reason that the ideal form of aesthetic individuality must be excluded as a real historical possibility that opens up to us. For the value of the ideal projected on the basis of a reconstruction of *Dialectic of Enlightenment* is that it preserves the historical possibilities for aesthetic individuality for which we may be able to find evidence elsewhere.

Since it is the genealogical reading of *Dialectic of Enlightenment* that excludes the ideal form of aesthetic individuality as a real historical possibility, does it not also highlight the risk of exaggerating even the historical possibility for the compromised form of enlightened self-possession? If so, then the reconstruction would depart from the spirit of *Dialectic of Enlightenment* that is expressed when the rhetorical and historical dimensions of its argument are aligned. Perhaps this risk occurs because, distinguished from its "ideal," the compromised form of aesthetic individuality acquires a misplaced historical concreteness. More likely it arises because the reinterpretation of the text proceeds on the basis of first separating a rhetorical from a linear historical approach. Such an analytical distinction may encourage us to think of a rhetorically reconstructed possibility for aesthetic individuality as existing independently of the historical reality to which it is conceptually related. Avoiding both of these errors enables us to broadly imagine enlightenment as a process that does not historically rule over our thinking with the necessity of an iron law. Our understanding of enlightenment is consequently revised, and we are encouraged to entertain the possibility that our aesthetic relationship to the world may exceed, to some extent, the constraints of formal reason. And we understand all the more clearly, as well, that for Horkheimer and Adorno it is history and its narrative that chasten the rhetorical comprehension of possibility and provide the measure for how real such possibilities may be. A genealogical reconstruction of *Dialectic of Enlightenment* does not simply exchange a historical continuum of domination for a range of definite historical possibilities for aesthetic individuality it makes available to us. It permits us to isolate a collection of historical circumstances and their contingencies from the events that followed, as we have with those represented by the wanderings of Odysseus, and to imagine how in their light the future, Odysseus's future and ours, could be different.

With these methodological reflections we appreciate *Dialectic of Enlightenment* as a genealogy of reason that directs us, rhetorically and historically, toward contingent opportunities for thinking of ourselves, in relation to Odysseus, as individuals who are more or less in enlightened possession of ourselves. More or less aesthetically receptive to difference, we are more or less able to introduce our own inflections into and against the historical process of enlightenment, which is to beg the question a genealogy of enlightenment finally enables us to pose. Do we inherit the contingencies belonging to a rhetorically reconstructed image of Odysseus in such a way that we can understand ourselves as individuals who are *more*, or as individuals who are *less*, in possession of ourselves aesthetically than he appears to be?

If we are loyal to the discipline of keeping both levels of interpretation in sight of each other, then we soon recognize that whatever contingencies for an aesthetic receptivity to difference we come to possess from a reconfiguration of *Dialectic of Enlightenment* are not those we discovered were available to Odysseus episodically. As much as we may develop a strong *sense* of our own contingencies from our reconstruction, our actual contingencies are shaped by the linear historical process of enlightenment as it continues to unfold from the ways Odysseus exploits or fails to exploit the contingencies accompanying his adventures. Our actual contingencies, in other words, lie beneath the symbolism of the events of the *Odyssey* in the ways thinking—individuals, cultures, social orders generally—at the mythical stage of thought, which Odysseus only represents, prosecutes the uncertainties of the circumstances in which it finds itself. On certain occasions, we have seen, as in his adventure with the Sirens, Odysseus elects to experience the world as an individual in compromised possession of himself. More often, though, he neglects to author his actions as expressions of aesthetic individuality, and, displaying none of the ambiguity that characterized his self-possessed aesthetic receptivity to mythical being in the Sirens episode, his actions conform to his behavior in Aeaea where he unequivocally "resists the magic of Circe."[20]

Alternating, thus, between an aesthetic experience of the world as a diversity of differences and a uniform experience of a uniform world, Odysseus eventually graduates from a diverse and divided self to a unified identity constituted as the sacrifice of one side of the self to its other. At the culmination of his journey, we realize that in retrospect as much as Odysseus is the victim of a predetermined fate he also is the erstwhile architect of a historical process of enlightenment that acquires a fatelike inertia with each of his failures to exploit contingencies of which he becomes aware. Since Odysseus's fate is none other than the achievement of a unified identity that finally secures his thinking once and for all *against* the flexibility he earlier displayed in relation to mythical being in his aesthetic engagement with the Sirens, then whatever historical relations he represents create a structure of rationality that thins out future contingency. In Horkheimer and Adorno's estimation, for example, because at the end of Odysseus's wanderings the structure of thinking has lost its earlier ambiguous formation, the contingencies available to him at his journey's conclusion are substantially different from those earlier in his odyssey. As a consequence, the contingencies passed down to us from mythical thought are rather thinner than the rhetorical reading of Odysseus's adventures would allow us to believe if it were taken by itself and out of the historical context in which Horkheimer and Adorno situate it. So in answer to the question, whether relative to Odysseus we are individuals more or less in enlightened possession of ourselves, it seems at this point we own less of the self-possession that animated Odysseus's aesthetic receptivity to all the difference in the world. Our enlightened self-possession may amount contingently to nothing more than an opportunity to reconstruct a discourse on the process of enlightenment as a genealogy of reason that grounds the *concept* of aesthetic individuality in its historical and ideal forms.

Modern Subjectivity and Artless Thinking

Some other opportunity for aesthetic individuality could be imagined if *Dialectic of Enlightenment* had offered further evidence of contingency at the stage thinking reaches when Odysseus's travels have drawn to a close. Yet, when Odysseus's wanderings are completed, Horkheimer and Adorno make clear, the possibility for a reversion of thought to an ordering of the faculties bearing some resemblance to "pure natural existence," where aesthetic receptivity is not utterly sacrificed to formal reason, is superseded. No longer will thinking even be tempted by the "rhapsodical" qualities of thought represented by the Cyclops or by the emancipation of a "repressed nature" represented by the animal form of Odysseus's enchanted crew on the island of Circe. Nor can the imagination be drawn to the Lotus flower, whose temptation prods thinking to recall the historical phase of "collecting the fruits of the earth and of the sea," which bears the "promise of a state in which the reproduction of life is independent of conscious self-preservation."[21] Once Odysseus arrives home in Ithaca, in fact, marking the resolution of the struggle between the warring sides of his thinking, or the unification of his identity through the sacrifice of aesthetic to formal reason, the "inner organization of individuality" is a permanent scar on thinking. The self-sacrifice of aesthetic individuality, at first achieved consciously through a series of experiences alternating between aesthetic receptivity to the world and an orientation in which the aesthetic elements have been subdued, from now on is reproduced automatically and without reflection in each and every thought and action. Horkheimer and Adorno describe this petrifaction of thinking as the "transformation of sacrifice into *subjectivity*."[22] "Subjectivity," thinking without nature, without rhapsody, without the Lotus flower. Artless—unaesthetic—thinking.

"Subjectivity," the "unification of identity," the "inner organization of individuality," "self-identity," "formal reason," thinking void of the contingency of aesthetic receptivity to a world of difference, artless thinking, *Reason* as it was called by the Enlightenment, refers to the intellectual achievement that largely defines the individual of modernity. It is an achievement that issues, as for Horkheimer and Adorno modernity issues, from the stage in the process of enlightenment that coincides with the birth of "myth," an event they want us to think of in a quite definite way. Odysseus's return home to Ithaca represents the creation of the modern subject because he subsequently recalls his wanderings as mere "myth," revealing the dominant characteristic of subjectivity to be formal reason, thinking that in its every encounter with difference imposes an identity through which difference appears as something other than it is in-itself. With this we realize the deepest significance of Odysseus's homecoming for the argument of *Dialectic of Enlightenment*. For the designation of individuality's aesthetic receptivity to difference as "mythical prehistory" is what distinguishes modernity and modern subjectivity from earlier forms of thinking that are aesthetically receptive to rather than efface difference. Most importantly, Odysseus's designation of aesthetic receptivity to difference as mere myth anticipates modernity as a history of such conversions in every act of thought. Thinking, as the product of the historical "transformation of sacrifice into subjectivity," becomes a cognitive operation performed by a unified identity—Odysseus's identity at the end of his wanderings, our identity as the subjectivity he already represents. For Horkheimer and Adorno the thinking of the modern subject is now virtually synonymous with "identity."[23]

Tying thinking so intimately to identity, they mean to distinguish the thinking of the modern subject from thinking not ruled by formal reason, from aesthetic thinking. Decisive for their argument is the idea that difference consistently refers to qualities belonging to the object of thought that thinking cannot fully grasp. Difference attaches to those qualities that perpetually exceed the concept. Difference is an in-itself that forever escapes from or is nonidentical with thought. Thinking is always at a loss, so to speak, and where formal rationality does not govern thinking in its aesthetic receptivity to difference, aesthetic thinking knows itself to be at a loss to capture what is unknowable and therefore essentially different from any thought of the unknown. With the modern subject, on the other hand, formal reason dominates thinking to the consistent neglect of the aesthetic recognition of the nonidentical in thought. Thinking abolishes what in its object is different from thought by converting difference into concepts that, without further aesthetic reflection on what is invariably lost to thinking, attribute "identity" to what lies outside the boundaries of thought. For subjectivity, thinking is a process whereby conceptualization represents its object as something knowable, ultimately transparent, possessing an identity that is other than it is in-itself, just as Odysseus's recollection of his adventures as the inventions of mere myth identify the differences he encountered as other than they are.

Throughout its history modernity possesses several aliases for subjectivity that tacitly recognize identity to be at the origin of every thought. Descartes's *cogito*, the "I think," is arguably the first such formulation, certainly the formulation Horkheimer and Adorno understand to be implicit in the modern subject Odysseus arrived at home represents. As thinking's unreflected constant, the "I think" is the identity that infuses meaning and coherence if not life itself into subjectivity. Constituting the meaningfulness of subjectivity as its formal logical proof, the "I think" enables the subject to stand over and against the world whose differences, along with their own essential meanings, in the history of thought will then gradually disappear inside their concepts, the identities thinking imposes on the world. The identity of the "I think" that fades into the identity thinking imposes on the world during its bourgeois capitalist phase is the Cartesian moment of thinking fading into the Kantian. Now occupying a disenchanted world, however, subjectivity knows nothing of the Kantian limits to knowledge rooted in an "in-itself," a supersensible difference forever remaining outside every thought of all the world contains. So the "I think," the Cartesian subject that emerges from Odysseus's "mythic nether world" to become the universal agent of a soon to be formally rationalized modern world, a world without difference, eventually becomes the Kantian "nodal point" of the processes of an industrial world. As a world without difference, in other words, the developed world is related to subjectivity only as the objectification of thinking performed by the subject in its role as the standardized bearer of formal reason. As formal rationality, subjectivity limits our experience of the world by raising the unknown to the level of conceptualization that equalizes all differences through their reduction to the known or knowable. In its "anticipatory identification of the wholly conceived . . . world with truth," explain Horkheimer and Adorno, thinking is unable to reflect on the inadequacy of its grasp of the world. The modern subject is thus secure "against the return of the mythic," free of the "ambiguity of mythical thought as of all meaning altogether."[24] With his identity intact and his capacity for aesthetic receptivity to the world annulled by formal reason, Odysseus's newly born subjectivity thus represents the entire evolution of thought since its mythical stage, becoming the progenitor of an artless world in its relation to an artless subject.

Aesthetic Individuality as Art

Is it not apparent what finally has become of the moment of aesthetic individuality our rhetorically guided reading of *Dialectic of Enlightenment* labored to recover from the linear historical narrative of the process of enlightenment? The aesthetic receptivity to difference animating Odysseus's encounter with the Sirens has survived his homecoming, symbol of the creation of the modern subject and of the winnowing process wherein enlightenment over an expanse of time thins out rather than expands the contingency once belonging to thought, though it has survived as a vastly diminished expression of enlightened self-possession. Having heard the Sirens who "sent their ravishing voices out across the air," Odysseus signals to his crew to release him from his bondage but is ignored and left lashed to his ship's mast.[25] What Odysseus has heard "is without consequence for him," Horkheimer and Adorno conclude, thus insinuating that there was an opportunity when the outcome of his encounter could have been otherwise. Set free, perhaps Odysseus might have taken some meaning from his aesthetic experience of enchantment that then might have buttressed or at least sustained his aesthetic receptivity to the world. Instead, formal reason prevails, now displacing an aesthetic rationality it had subordinated. With Odysseus's bondage unremitted, his mind like his body fixed in place until the Sirens' voices fade and he hears "their song no more, their urgent call," aesthetic individuality's moment as compromised self-possession survives only in a form that is frozen in time with Odysseus before his odyssey is recollected as nothing more than "myth."[26] As he experiences a world of differences through a relationship where time has ceased to pass, Odysseus's aesthetic receptivity to difference takes the timeless form of art. Horkheimer and Adorno argue this precisely where they discern a tragic element in the ambiguity of mythical thought.

> The bonds with which [Odysseus] has irremediably tied himself to practice, also keep the Sirens away from practice: their temptation is neutralized and becomes a mere object of contemplation—becomes art.[27]

As modern subjects, we seem to inherit the compromised form of self-possession only as a historical moment that has been arrested in the sublimated form of art, rather than as the contingent formation through which Odysseus was able aesthetically to engage the Sirens. Looking back over the long history of thought as it appeared to Horkheimer and Adorno before the Enlightenment, in retrospect it now appears justified to have described as *aesthetic* thinking's capacity to recognize and be receptive to difference. For if Odysseus's aesthetic receptivity to difference finds eventual expression in art, then it was reason's *aesthetic* dimension all along that throughout history was locked in a struggle with formal rational thought. Similarly, the individuality represented by Odysseus's receptivity to the Sirens and that only in the form of art will survive the transformation that created the modern subject, whose essential animus toward difference led inevitably to the Holocaust, now appears in hindsight to have been an *aesthetic individuality*. So that from this point onward in our discussion aesthetic individuality may be substituted for all more general references to "enlightened self-possession." And just as the sublimation in art of a receptivity to difference justifies the description of individuality before the Holocaust as aesthetic individuality, art likewise provides evidence for the survival of the aesthetic sensibility to difference that once lay at the heart of Odysseus's individuality. As the form in which aesthetic reason is preserved, art explains the survival of the aesthetic sensibility that, awakened by the narrative of the destruction of the Jews, enables us to recall through a genealogy of reason what is gone as what is yet living, namely the idea, and the ideal, of an aesthetic relation to the world that does not threaten loss of identity through its receptivity to difference.

Yet for Horkheimer and Adorno the aesthetic sensibility to which *Dialectic of Enlightenment* appeals at its end must be quite fragile and virtually indistinguishable from art, in which it finds its predominant form of expression in modernity. Art represents aesthetic individuality at the moment it introduces into our lives a receptivity to difference that make no difference, except as the recovery of an aesthetic relation that has learned of its fate as art. Art is the historical moment where thinking appears to have accepted its compromise with enlightenment as the necessary form that individuality's aesthetic receptivity to difference must assume on an irreversible path to the Enlightenment and its formally rationalized world. Aesthetic individuality and the sensibility that recovered it thus vanishes into art, and in subjectivity we inherit from enlightenment a "deceitful substitution of the stereotype" for individuality that one day, Horkheimer and Adorno promise, "will of itself become unbearable for mankind."[28]

"THE TERRIBLE BASIC TEXT *HOMO NATURA* ... THE ETERNAL BASIC TEXT *HOMO NATURA*"

Through the reconfiguration of *Dialectic of Enlightenment* to which Horkheimer and Adorno lead us rhetorically, the grip of formal reason, which throughout history is imposed on individuality with the blind force of a teleological imperative, has been loosened. A concept of aesthetic individuality is recovered, if only fleetingly for the moment before it takes refuge in art. With this genealogical reconstruction of their argument I have intimated what I believe to be true, that Nietzsche may be the seminal influence on Horkheimer and Adorno. For the most part, thus far such evidence for this connection is circumstantial, pointing only to telling similarities. Nevertheless, if they are there to be found in *Dialectic of Enlightenment*, drawing out its similarities to Nietzsche's genealogical method will be instructive in several ways. It will deepen our understanding of the genealogical framework within which Horkheimer and Adorno reconstruct the evolution of reason as a struggle within thought that climaxes in the inner organization of individuality, the hegemony of formal reason, and the creation of the modern subject. By cultivating a deeper appreciation of its genealogical features, we also will run up against the theoretical limitations of *Dialectic of Enlightenment* as a genealogy of reason and discover the precise point at which Horkheimer and Adorno must turn to Marx for assistance. Finally, by my marking resemblances between *Dialectic of Enlightenment*'s genealogical interests and Nietzsche's genealogical practices, my intention is to encourage a certain openness to the argument that Horkheimer and Adorno's concept of aesthetic individuality has an even deeper Nietzschean connection. It is a connection to *The Birth of Tragedy*, a work earlier than those on which *Dialectic of Enlightenment* as a genealogy may be based. Its parallels to Horkheimer and Adorno's work indicate a more profound connection to Nietzsche than any other we may discover, and they suggest clarifications of the aesthetic features of their concept of individuality that remain less well articulated if the parallels are ignored.

The Task of Translation

In *Beyond Good and Evil* Nietzsche pauses to explain himself.

> For to translate man back into nature; to master the many vain and fanciful interpretations and secondary meanings which have been hitherto scribbled and daubed over that eternal basic text *homo natura* ... may be a strange and extravagant task but it is a *task*.[29]

Dialectic of Enlightenment is just such a translation of the process of enlightenment, a translation of subjectivity back into individuality, of man back into nature, though Horkheimer and Adorno's translation must not be mistaken for a historical record of an *essential* human nature. As they view the Enlightenment as the cultural mirror in which the modern subject sees a self-reflection idealizing and rationalizing its historical conquest of the unknown, the Enlightenment is far less a "fanciful interpretation" than in Horkheimer and Adorno's estimation a "vain interpretation" and "secondary meaning." Specifically, the Enlightenment is modern subjectivity's vain interpretation and secondary meaning of the world-historical struggle between formal and aesthetic reason, the "eternal basic text *homo natura*" into which Horkheimer and Adorno translate the process of enlightenment. Or the struggle between formal and aesthetic reason is the "*terrible* [my italics] basic text *homo natura*" if we drop back but one line further in Nietzsche's aphorism to happen upon a starkly appropriate image of enlightenment as Horkheimer and Adorno translate it.

As an "eternal basic text" Horkheimer and Adorno's translation is as eternal as the history of the process of enlightenment is eternal, defining even what becomes discernible as the origin of thought itself. Accordingly, the struggle and its formal and aesthetic protagonists within thought appear to take on the character of an ontological certainty. In the context of *Dialectic of Enlightenment*, then, Nietzsche's self-explanation may seem to place emphasis on the *nature* of human nature rather than on the *historical text* that is *homo natura*. Horkheimer and Adorno intend no such attribution. Before they can translate the process of enlightenment into the struggle between formal and aesthetic rationality, it first must become established as "the Enlightenment of modern times." Enlightenment must become the historical principle that as the Enlightenment determines what modernity understands to be knowledge as such. Only as such a "vain" and "secondary" historical meaning do Horkheimer and Adorno pursue a translation of enlightenment as a struggle between formal and aesthetic modes of rationality. When the process of enlightenment culminates in the Enlightenment, it becomes available for translation back into the struggle within thought disposed to destroy the world's differences since its beginning in time, back into that terrible, eternal basic text according to which they reconstruct history as a process of enlightenment. Taking as their point of departure its unique historicity as the Enlightenment of modern times, their translation of enlightenment back into "human nature" occupies Nietzsche's genealogical middle ground between mere interpretation and ontological truth.

Equivalence

As a genealogy, of course, *Dialectic of Enlightenment*'s translation of "man back into nature" proceeds at the *conceptual* level at which the process of enlightenment actually evolves through its many historical stages, which again is to follow Nietzsche's lead. At this level there is no concept more pivotal to the evolution of enlightenment than "equivalence," as Horkheimer and Adorno demonstrate. Native in different forms to every stage in the history of thought, equivalence denotes the cognitive operation whereby thinking takes up a position in opposition to itself as a rational response to a world whose darkness appears to threaten self-preservation. Along with the idea of a genealogical reconstruction of enlightenment that reveals subjectivity to be a contingent formation, equivalence, we might say, provides another unique window into thought that helps to expose the struggle of formal reason for a unified identity against aesthetic rationality and its receptive orientation to difference. Equivalence is thought turned inside out, so that its history as the process of enlightenment is the visible trace of the history of thinking from its genesis in diffuse possibilities for aesthetic individuality all the way to its inward collapse into self-identity and subjectivity. Nietzsche, too, we see, underscores the centrality of this concept. Though he does not explicitly relate equivalence to enlightenment, as with Horkheimer and Adorno its importance lies in nothing less that its contribution to the foundations of thinking, as Nietzsche argues clearly in *On the Genealogy of Morals.*

> Setting prices, determining values, contriving *equivalences*, exchanging—these preoccupied the earliest thinking of man to so great an extent that in a certain sense they constitute thinking *as such.* . . . [They are] older even than the beginnings of any kind of social forms of organization and alliances.[30]

Here we also must acknowledge Nietzsche's attention to the ancient forms equivalence assumed, even preceding "social forms of organization," as Horkheimer and Adorno likewise suggested by their discovery of equivalence in thinking as early as the magical stage of thought.

Sublation

Without a doubt Horkheimer and Adorno share Nietzsche's interest in the "entire long hieroglyphic record" of equivalence, as he refers to the distinct lineage belonging to every such concept and traceable genealogically to predecessor concepts and practices for the purpose of recovering its meaning.[31] Hence they construe the "Enlightenment of modern times" as the consummation of a "process of enlightenment," which has a remote origin in a social practice later conceptualized as "equivalence" after it consistently reappears in very different forms and stages of thought. As Horkheimer and Adorno show, from magical thought through modernity equivalence is continually "sublated," just as Nietzsche describes it in his *Genealogy.*[32] Long before the operation of equating differences had its conceptual birth, in other words, equivalence animated ever newer practices by leading a relatively autonomous though increasingly subterranean existence in the different conceptual forms it historically assumes. And Nietzsche's conviction that such sublated principles of reason originate in a visceral "impression that is petrified . . . captured and stamped by means of concepts," or that morality is "a sign language of the emotions," resonates in their claim that equivalence originated out of fear of a fathomless nature. Certainly it is reflected in their claim that the Enlightenment, which in Nietzsche's terms would be a "secondary meaning" of the history of equivalence, "spared no remnant of metaphysics apart from the [collective's] abstract fear [of a frightening nature] from which it arose."[33]

Once these several strands of Nietzsche's method are collected—the task of translation, equivalence, and sublation—we see the elements of genealogy working together in other ways in *Dialectic of Enlightenment* and not only in the argument about equivalence circulating throughout the text as a whole. These same genealogical elements are present at highly concentrated moments when Horkheimer and Adorno's analysis seems to draw especially synoptic insights or conclusions. Early in their text, for example, they propose,

> At the turning points of Western civilization, from the transition to Olympian religion up to the Renaissance, Reformation, and bourgeois atheism, whenever new nations and classes more firmly repressed myth, the fear of uncomprehended, threatening nature, the consequence of its very materialization and objectification, was reduced to animistic superstition, and the subjugation of nature was made the absolute purpose of life within and without.... The essence of enlightenment is the alternative whose ineradicability is that of domination.[34]

Nietzsche's argument that "man can be translated back into nature" from historical "secondary meanings" seems operative in their claim that the "essence of enlightenment" becomes the "absolute purpose of life within and without" expressed as the "ineradicable subjugation and domination of nature." Moreover, variations of Nietzsche's contention that concepts are a "sign language of the emotions" originating in visceral "impressions" that are "petrified, captured, and stamped by means of concepts" appear to underlie several of the arguments contained in this passage. Underlying the argument that "myth [is] the fear of uncomprehended, threatening nature" is the idea that myth is a concept in which the fear of nature is clothed and concealed. Underlying the argument that "myth [is] the consequence of [nature's] very materialization and objectification" is the idea that myth is a concept that purges nature of its substantive qualities so that nature and the fear it instills can be controlled. And Nietzsche's suspicion that emotions are embedded in concepts may also underlie the argument that whenever nations and classes on the path to enlightenment "firmly repressed" myth, "uncomprehended, threatening nature" was being "reduced" to a concept of "animistic superstition." Yet there are far more conclusive elements of genealogy at work here.

Forgetting and the Rise of Enlightenment as a System of Domination

Most importantly, we cannot fail to recognize Nietzsche's thoughts on "forgetting." Because in Nietzsche's view the need to reconstruct the past genealogically arises in the first place when the genesis of an epoch has been forgotten, Horkheimer and Adorno's observations on "repression" may be the strongest evidence yet of a genealogical approach. Whenever "nations and classes more firmly repressed myth" at each of the "turning points of Western civilization," they argued, the memory of our original fear of nature, the memory that nature's terrifying image and our fear of it were our oldest responses to nature's opacity, was locked away ever more securely. As they then explain, the repression of myth as the epochal forgetting of "uncomprehended, threatening nature" is "the consequence of the materialization and objectification of nature," that is, the consequence of "equivalence." Equivalence is revealed to be a mechanism of forgetting. By converting all of nature into matter, equivalence reduces nature to an object having no meaning in relation to us other than as a means for our own ends. Along with the fear and will to mastery an unknowable nature provokes in us, whatever in nature is incomprehensible to thought, whatever is different in nature from our every thought of it, is "repressed" or "forgotten" when nature can be apprehended only as one identical material object of domination.

Nietzsche's voice can be heard here speaking loudly. Does the truth of our practices not depend, Nietzsche had asked in his *Genealogy*, on forgetting the remote historical reasons why they emerged, so that our bad memory is the only guarantee that a destructive habit can appear to the mind transformed into an eternal idea?[35] With the repression of myth, we see now, Horkheimer and Adorno introduce the idea integrating all the genealogical elements Nietzsche places at their disposal. Originating in the visceral impression of fear at an incomprehensible and threatening nature, the cognitive operation much later to be conceptualized as equivalence accedes to the forefront of thinking. There equivalence allows thinking to invent images of a nature that offers no substantive resistance to manipulation and control, images in which what was essential to nature before we as a species were born disappears from thought. Equivalence thus launches a process of enlightenment that progressively conquers nature by "sublating" the practice of mastery in scientific and cultural understandings that reproduce nature only as an object to be dominated. Over time enlightenment's historical stages form a "long hieroglyphic record" of the "turning points of Western civilization" in which our original thought of a terrifying nature is repressed and forgotten, while our original thought of a fathomless nature is preserved in art.

Of course, Nietzsche speaks of our loss of memory so that we will remember. Should we not consider, then, that Horkheimer and Adorno's interest may lie as much in the *recollection* of what has been forgotten through the repression of myth as in the repression of myth itself? When we do so it becomes impossible to exaggerate the importance to *Dialectic of Enlightenment* of Nietzschean forgetting. For whereas the "repression of myth" and the genealogical elements it integrates contribute to reconstructing the process of enlightenment as a genealogy of reason, they also allow for the recollection of what has been repressed in myth to serve as the normative foundation for Horkheimer and Adorno's critique of enlightenment. If, in the wake of the repression of myth and forgetting, the "essence" of enlightenment becomes "the alternative whose ineradicability is that of domination," then locked away with the original fear of nature is the possibility that with historical progress the warrant for the domination of nature could be problematized. If, as a species, in other words, we had not forgotten that our historical justification for the domination of nature lay in its being incomprehensible and threatening, would nature not appear less recondite and terrifying in light of cultural and scientific achievements, and undeserving of its mindless transformation? As the forgotten memory of reason's primordial fear of an unknown nature is thereby recalled through recognition of the repression of myth, a genealogy of enlightenment is what exposes "the absurdity of the state of affairs"

> in which the enforced power of the system over men grows with every step that takes it out of the power of nature, denounces the rationality of the rational society as obsolete. Its necessity is illusive.[36]

When the rationale for enlightenment is recalled, the irrationality of enlightenment is highlighted by cultural and scientific achievements that render the perpetuation of relations of domination unnecessary, and absurd. So long as enlightenment upholds the repression of myth and the memory of reason's fear of nature is recalled only by theory, however, there remains but the logic of either-or, Horkheimer and Adorno stress, merely the inescapable choice between our "subjugation to nature or the subjugation of nature to the Self."[37] *Dialectic of Enlightenment* thus proves that our forgetfulness of history traps us in one of the most fundamental of antinomies, and in one that is identical in its logic to the rigid antinomies of good and evil of which Nietzsche, too, was the first to teach us awareness.

With their thesis of historical forgetting through the epochal "repression of myth," then, Horkheimer and Adorno construct a genealogy of reason that supports the idea of social order as a relatively autonomous "system" of formal rationality. Both the relative autonomy and power of this system are rooted in a formal rational logic that narrowly confines our thinking to a conception of nature that relates us to it in only two ways. Either we must dominate nature or be dominated by nature. Needless to say, this logic of kill or be killed really leaves us with no alternative save the principle of self-preservation. Along with the original fear of nature on which it is based, however, self-preservation is repressed in enlightenment's unreflected commitment to the domination of nature embodied in the concept of equivalence, which universally defines the relationship of social order to all the difference in the world. Responsible for the loss of our original memory of nature, and with it the loss of the explanation for our fear of nature and justification for our will to mastery over nature, equivalence leaps from being a relatively autonomous power over thought and nature to becoming a relatively autonomous power over human being and being. As measured by the development of thought at the "turning points of Western civilization," equivalence evolves from one stage of thinking to another with the rationalization for domination disappearing in the new form thinking adopts at each stage. From the outset of its long history, without any memory of nature as indefinitely exceeding the compass of thought, of nature in its fathomlessness as essentially different from our every thought of it, thinking evolves into a systemic logic that automatically reproduces domination. Though Horkheimer and Adorno's reconstruction of enlightenment recovers repressed and forgotten historical opportunities when our formal rational relationship to nature could have been conceived as a contingent formation, such as at the stage of enlightenment represented by myth, which is an insight bestowed by genealogy, it also proves such opportunities are but fleeting episodes that vanish with the ambiguity of thought and with the rise of enlightenment as a system of domination.

The Autonomy of Formal Reason and Social Order

By now it is unnecessary to point out that Horkheimer and Adorno accent the degree of autonomy with which formal rationality unfolds by distinguishing historical stages in the process of enlightenment as stages in the development of *reason*. Stages of rationality are not differentiated systematically, however, as cultural classifications of the sort with which we are familiar in Hegel's *Philosophy of History*, but rather according to the general genealogical distinctions common to Nietzsche's work, which permits us to see how his influence on *Dialectic of Enlightenment* is extended still further with regard to the autonomy of formal reason.

Nietzsche's comment that genealogy establishes epochal "distinctions between ages, peoples, degrees of rank among individuals" is descriptive of the guidelines Horkheimer and Adorno follow when explaining how social orders differently organize around the need to manipulate nature. In every age, distinguished as "preanimistic," "magical," "mythical," "metaphysical," and "modern" ages of *thought*, social order develops around structures of formal reason that act as the driving force behind enlightenment. From the oldest forms of social organization to those later organized around private property, formal reason engenders enlightenment through processes of production that develop formal reason as they are developed by it, so that formal rationality remains relatively autonomous at every stage of social organization reached. At the "preanimistic" stage of thought social organization is barely distinguishable as it forms around the collective participation of nomadic tribal members in symbolic practices designed to influence nature.[38] When an organized division of labor emerges that in their view is of significance, it corresponds to the "magical" stage of thinking where the responsibility for influencing nature through formal rational symbolism falls to a certain class of specialists, a "rank of individuals," in Nietzsche's terms. In Horkheimer and Adorno's words,

> priests and sorcerers . . . magicians peopled every spot with emanations and made a multiplicity of sacred rights concordant with the variety of sacred places. They expanded their professional knowledge and their influence with the expansion of the spirit world and its characteristics.[39]

It is even at this time that "language enters history" as the technical instrument through which an order of experts can begin the historical process of rationalizing the symbolic structures of formal reason on which their ability to represent and manipulate nature depends.

Social order in all its subsequent stages then evolves as a struggle with nature through a division of labor revolving around the specialized task of rationalizing the means of symbolic manipulation. Serving the dual purposes of collective self-preservation and social reproduction, formal reason enables the division of labor to reproduce the whole of society as a power over the individual, thus propelling the division of labor as a social relation inseparable from relations of domination. As the means for the division of labor's reproduction of social order, formal reason takes on "a fetishistic function." It conceals domination by allowing the rationality of the division of labor in its task of reproducing society as a whole to appear as a universal necessity, though its universality objectively may be a reflection of the particular interests of the class or classes charged with the responsibility for developing the formal rational instruments of social order. From the magical stage of thinking to the Enlightenment of modern times, it is this "unity of the collectivity and domination," as Horkheimer and Adorno put it, "which is expressed in thought forms" through which formal rationality in its identification with the whole increasingly acquires universal validity.[40] By the Enlightenment, nature has been continuously represented as an object to be brought under control by a form of reason that derives its authority from a socially constructed universality that only articulates the universalizing tendencies of reason already present at its birth. The Enlightenment of modern times marks the final victory of formal reason through its recognition of the universal *truth* of equivalency as the criterion for what counts as knowledge as such. As truth, formal reason has completely "repressed" nature's opacity, resolved the struggle within thought with its aesthetic nemesis, and become the light that can banish all darkness by first having banished the darkness of nature.

Genealogy, the Universalization of Formal Reason, and Private Property

As we see, in Horkheimer and Adorno's analysis private property does not enter into consideration as the primary historical determinant of enlightenment at any of its stages. Epochal distinctions drawn genealogically trace a history of sacrifice of aesthetic rationality to a relatively autonomous formal reason, and define the process of enlightenment in precisely these terms. With the culmination of this process in an Enlightenment distinguished by the recognition of equivalence as a universal rational and scientific principle, however, relations of private property have entered into the development of formal rationality in a unique way. The Enlightenment marks the historical point from which the logic of capitalism gradually will become indistinguishable from the progress of formal rationality, and to such an extent, they explain, that the "formalization of reason is only the intellectual expression of mechanized production."[41]

Beginning with the Enlightenment, economic categories, specifically economic stages of capitalist development, displace the genealogical concepts and distinctions with which Horkheimer and Adorno reconstruct the development of formal reason. Whereas the genealogy of a relatively autonomous formal reason served as the groundwork for a history that had produced some evidence for the contingent possibility of aesthetic receptivity, property relations now serve as the basis for a linear historical narrative whereby thinking is drained of all contingency by the inexorable logic of capitalism. Although as a genealogy *Dialectic of Enlightenment* meant to account for the ascendancy of formal reason as the universal principle of knowing, it could not adequately account in genealogical terms for the actual universalization of formal rationality in social and cultural relations that had occurred with and since the Enlightenment. To explain the universalization of formal reason Horkheimer and Adorno turn to Marx, and especially to Lukács's theory of reification. From the Enlightenment through to the period of mass culture, the similarities between *Dialectic of Enlightenment* and Lukács's *History and Class Consciousness* are too obvious to require comment. What should be mentioned, though, is that only an explanation stressing the importance of capitalist relations of production can account for the universalization of formal reason to the point whereby mass culture "strikes everything with sameness" and acquires "control of the individual consciousness." It is not formal reason alone that is "the basis on which technology acquires power over society," Horkheimer and Adorno explain, but rather

> the power of those whose economic hold over society is greatest.... [T]he achievement of standardization and mass production ... is the result not of a law of movement in technology as such but of its function in today's economy.... In our age the objective social tendency is incarnate in the hidden subjective purposes of company directors, the foremost among whom are in the most powerful sectors of industry.[42]

Revisiting one aspect of Horkheimer and Adorno's interpretation of the *Odyssey* may further dispel any confusion about the historical relation between formal reason and property relations in the process of enlightenment with which even close readings of *Dialectic of Enlightenment* could be burdened. When we recall the significance they attach to Odysseus's homecoming, we note that the conversion of an enchanted world into mere myth does more than anticipate the birth of the modern subject through an Enlightenment that secures the hegemony of formal reason and its eclipse of the aesthetic dimension of thought defining individuality. Odysseus's homecoming also represents the stage in the process of enlightenment where formal reason has begun to unfold through relations of private property governed by the logic of capitalism. Pursuing the "unequivocal purposiveness of his own self-preservation," when Odysseus returns to his homeland, Horkheimer and Adorno point out, he likewise returns to his "*fixed estate.*"[43] To the arrival of the Enlightenment and the sacrifice of aesthetic individuality to modern subjectivity, to the ascendancy of formal reason and its imposition through equivalency of identity on worlds of difference, in other words, there corresponds the developmental significance of capitalism. Odysseus's homecoming represents the stage of enlightenment—the Enlightenment of modern times—during which formal reason and private property develop a relationship of reciprocity whereby each ever more closely develops in and through the other to the degree to which they become indistinguishable. As this relationship of reciprocity unfolds, eventually subjectivity will be reduced to that nodal point of technical and cultural processes requiring nothing of it but passive participation. Can we not then understand why they argue so remarkably, "subjectivity (whose fundamental history is presented in the *Odyssey*) . . . "[44]

Even with the introduction of political economy, however, Horkheimer and Adorno never pursue the universalization of formal reason in a way suggesting that their primary concern is with capitalism's development of a structure of rationality that secures the domination of propertied interests. How could this be their concern, of course, since they believe that a propertyless socialism displays the very same allegiance to formal reason as capitalism. "Socialism itself," they simply note without further comment, "prematurely confirmed" that same inability displayed by capitalism to recognize the origin of domination in the nature of thinking when formal reason achieved universalization, as in socialism it had nearly to the same degree as in capitalism.[45] Preoccupied as they are throughout *Dialectic of Enlightenment* with the consequences of formal reason, Horkheimer and Adorno's concern instead is with the destruction of difference entailed by formal reason's increasingly malignant penetration of culture at each of the stages they distinguish in the development of capitalism. Regarding its universalization, then, their interest in formal reason's relationship to private property can be formulated in the following way. If the development of private property is responsible for the universalization of formal rationality, it is because formal reason already was embedded in the concepts that Western capitalism (and later socialism) inherited from a process of enlightenment that created the cultural foundations in thought for capitalism's emergence. And since formal reason's universalization depends upon the development of capitalism, as the vehicle of formal rationality capitalism in its orientation to difference exhibits the same "murderous" characteristics formal reason had exhibited throughout the history of enlightenment. So while the universalization of formal reason would not have entered into their argument as such a formidable historical development if it had not been for capitalism, whose relationship to enlightenment to be understood requires different analytical concepts and categories from those offered by genealogy, their analysis of capitalism is underpinned by the same normative interest in the violent consequences to difference guiding their critique of formal reason throughout.

By underpinning their analysis of capitalism, moreover, Horkheimer and Adorno's normative interest in the violent fate to which formal reason subjects difference appeals to the aesthetic sensibility to the violence to difference awakened at the conclusion of *Dialectic of Enlightenment*. Their analysis of capitalism thus expresses the original intent of their genealogy of reason by provoking a sensibility whose aesthetic orientation relaxes the grip of formal rationality threatening to destroy it. Even when this analysis replaces genealogical with economic concepts and categories, in other words, by appealing to our aesthetic sensibility their normative interest in the violence with which formal reason in capitalism victimizes difference roots their analysis of capitalism in their genealogical approach, which accounted for the existence of this sensibility by tracing its origin to the sublimation of aesthetic reason in art. To the extent of its normative interest, then, their political economy of the development of formal reason in capitalism is no less genealogical than their reconfiguration of the process of enlightenment. At the same time, in addition to this normative connection to the genealogical aspects of their work, their analysis of capitalism draws some further, limited support from the other genealogical elements that inform their reconstruction of enlightenment. Both of these connections to *Dialectic of Enlightenment* as a genealogy of reason are borne out by a more careful inspection of their examination of the stages of capitalist development.

Capitalism and Violence to Difference

Adopting conventional Marxist categories, Horkheimer and Adorno differentiate between a competitive entrepreneurial and a noncompetitive monopoly stage of capitalism. Distinguished as cultural phases belonging to these stages of economic development, "liberalism" and "late liberalism" fall into the stage of competitive capitalism, with the "culture industry" falling into the stage of noncompetitive monopoly capitalism. It would be an error, however, to conclude from this arrangement that they simply construe liberalism to be the ideological handmaiden of market capitalism. As a cultural phase, liberalism does more than facilitate economic competitiveness. More importantly, it allows for the creation of the "new and untried," in a word, for difference. Late liberalism, on the other hand, is a cultural phase that accommodates competition and the production of the new and untried, though only according to somewhat exclusive standards formed on the basis of liberalism's experience with what is and is not successful in the marketplace. Late liberalism, "whose categories and contents derive from liberalism," increasingly narrows the criteria of the market to standardized formulas for cultural production that then dominate as the "culture industry," distinctive for its exclusion of the new and untried on any terms. "And so the culture industry," Horkheimer and Adorno conclude, "proves to be the goal of liberalism."[46]

If there could be any doubt that Horkheimer and Adorno's analysis of capitalism turns poignantly on the issue of its contribution to formal reason's destruction of difference, it is erased by their assessment of the culture industry, expressed unmistakably in their judgment that

> [a]fter the short intermezzo of liberalism, in which the bourgeois kept one another in check, domination appears as archaic terror in a fascistically rationalized form.[47]

At the stage of monopoly capitalism, they are proposing in genealogical terms whose elements are now quite familiar to us, domination appears as the "sublation" of a "repressed" archaic fear of an unfathomable nature in a cultural apparatus whose formal rational structure admits nothing different from rigidly standardized norms. In a similar genealogical vein, they later go on to say, "the totality of the culture industry consists of *repetition*," which alludes to enlightenment's logic of equivalency as the *modus operandi* for the reproduction of the sameness that characterizes mass culture.[48] And from a culture industry shaped by the formal-rational logic of equivalency results the moral antinomy of either-or, where producers and consumers alike are well aware that anyone "who resists can only survive by fitting in." The "only choice is either to join in or to be left behind."[49] One of the most startling demonstrations of their belief that the true significance of capitalism lies in its universalization of formal reason's antagonism to difference is not where they compare the culture industry to a "fascistically rationalized form," but where they point out its explicit similarities to Fascism.

> The ears of corn blowing in the wind at the end of Chaplin's *The Great Dictator* give the lie to the anti-Fascist plea for freedom. They are like the hair of the blond German girl whose camp life is photographed by the Nazi film company in the summer breeze. Nature is viewed by the mechanism of social domination as a healthy contrast to society, and is therefore denatured.[50]

Their point is not that cultural life during the monopoly stage of capitalism proves democracies to be no less fascistic than Fascist states or that capitalist societies carry the seeds of Fascism within, but that there is a third principle that originates with neither and yet is common to both. Although the cultures of anti-Fascism and Fascism similarly produce statements about nature as a healthy contrast to society, nature is perverted in either case by becoming the standard against which both Fascism and anti-Fascism, as the embodiments of nature implied by their cinematic representations, measure their adversaries. Nature's difference is effaced in its assimilation to what anti-Fascism and Fascism have in common: formal reason.

Even though Horkheimer and Adorno's critique of capitalism exhibits that same normative interest in formal reason's violence to difference as their analysis of enlightenment as a whole, unlike the path of enlightenment they traced genealogically through the earlier epochs leading to the Enlightenment, the path of enlightenment through entrepreneurial to monopoly capitalism, liberalism to the culture industry, is from the outset obedient to an irreversible logic. It is important to underscore the linearity of their analysis of capitalism if we are not to misunderstand their attack on liberalism, the cultural phase of capitalism where we might expect reason to be aesthetically receptive to difference, and thus for some contingency in thinking to have subsisted. This is an expectation certainly encouraged by the genealogical dimensions of their approach to enlightenment. Although in their view liberalism supports a culture that at one level is receptive to difference, they show that liberalism inevitably renders aesthetic receptivity to difference pregnable. Because liberalism provides no opportunities for a reflective recognition that the formal rationalization of thought could be a contingent formation, receptivity necessarily collapses under the pressure of rationalization. Struggles between a formal and aesthetic orientation to the world sustained by liberalism are resolved not in the unconstrained proliferation of differences, as is often the image of liberal society. On the contrary, as we have seen, liberalism fosters the development and evolution of common denominators that increasingly narrow the criteria of what is culturally viable to standards that shape competition within the culture industry. Consequently, when we remember that the Enlightenment constituted the foundations for liberalism or, as Horkheimer and Adorno put it, "committed itself to liberalism," we can understand why they argue that for the modern subject "reason is the chemical agent which absorbs the individual substance of things and volatilizes them in the mere autonomy of reason."[51]

By respecting the absolute equality among all differences, of different artistic "styles," for instance, according to the common criteria that different styles meet to varying degrees, liberalism's toleration of difference embodies a principle of equivalence eroding differences among styles, or that "absorbs the individual substance of things." Through liberalism, formal reason achieves an autonomy in the culture industry enabling it to convert what is different and unique into the indistinguishable, so that it can be preserved or discarded by reason of conforming or failing to conform to standards imposed from the outside. By anticipating but also formatively contributing to the end of style finally realized by the culture industry, liberalism appears as an archaic fear whose "sublation" is no less uniformly hostile to difference than is collective fear in its fascistically rationalized form, a conclusion that continues to extend their genealogical critique of formal reason to their analysis of capitalism.

Liberalism also unambiguously subjects difference to the rule of formal reason by undermining its own line of ideological defense for cultural institutions that had emerged within the womb of liberal democracy. As we have learned, Horkheimer and Adorno's view is that from the very beginning of liberalism its logic of equivalence spoiled its intention to encourage cultural freedom and the creativity of difference. Equivalence contributed to the development of the culture industry by serving as the principle of a liberal toleration acting as the proving ground for determining which cultural standards whose proliferation it nurtured would prevail to the exclusion of others. Such a hegemonic cultural formation only succeeds, though, because liberalism permits this same perverse agonism at the cultural level to be reproduced as the conflict of industrial powers that results in the formation of monopolistic interests. It is here, at the level of market forces, that liberalism's principle of equivalence, the legacy of the process of enlightenment genealogically understood, forces into remission the ideological legacy of the Enlightenment contributing to the individual's aesthetic ability to be receptive to difference as well as to be and to become different.

The ideological legacy that recedes under pressure from market forces includes the sovereignty of individual reason to determine its own form of life, the liberal defense of private life, and the precedence of liberty over authority. As monopoly capitalism emerged from market relations defined by liberalism, for example, the institution of the family undergoes a significant structural transformation corresponding to changes in the organization of the economy. Whereas competitive capitalism had provided an economic anchor for patriarchal dominance, the authority of the father in the family declines once his position of economic independence is compromised with the end of entrepreneurial individualism. Monopoly capitalism, Horkheimer and Adorno explain, meant that the

> possibility of becoming a subject in the economy, an entrepreneur or a proprietor, has been completely liquidated. Right down to the humblest shop, the independent enterprise, on the management and inheritance of which the bourgeois family and the position of its head had rested, became hopelessly dependent. Everybody became an employee; and in this civilization of employees the dignity of the father (questionable anyhow) vanishes.[52]

Once the economic floor drops out from beneath patriarchal authority, the psychological dynamics of familial socialization are disrupted. According to the Freudian model of the family to which they subscribe, the imposition of patriarchal authority upon the children of the bourgeois family precipitates an oedipal struggle fostering the development of an individual not only with strong inclinations to conformity but with a tenacious capacity for intellectual resistance to authority as well. Released from the discipline of patriarchal rule, without the antagonistic relation to the father the child no longer develops an independence for thinking that can relate the individual to the world other than through formal rational calculations suppressing aesthetic awareness of difference. "When the big industrial interests incessantly eliminate the economic basis for moral decision," Horkheimer and Adorno explain, "reflective thought must also die out."[53] Neither the family, organized internally by the new relations of production, nor the individual's psyche, weakened internally by the same property relations and vulnerable to invasion by the culture industry, offers the privacy wherein the individual can develop the autonomy basic to reason's reflective recognition of the limits to formal reason's authority.

Among the cultural achievements liberalism undermines by unleashing the powers of formal reason against a world of differences, there is another that is equal if not greater in consequence to the eclipse of the reflective capacity and that likewise follows from the transformation of the bourgeois family. Paternal authority, Horkheimer and Adorno contend, helped to sustain the emotion of love, which in part is awakened by the oppressiveness of patriarchalism, a "thralldom" from which the possibility of love, if only through marriage, promised escape.[54] With the erosion of the father's authority, the yearning for freedom from the family through the ideal of love is diminished. Love that has been diminished as an expression of freedom and means for independence gives way to other gratifications as love is postponed, a postponement that finds economic support in the newly found opportunities for employment in large corporations that supplant the independent entrepreneur. Although love had been the "human emotion proper" through which "enjoyment was coupled with a deification of man," once it becomes anachronistic the intense emotions experienced through love are released from its sublimations of pleasure.[55]

Separated, love and pleasure meet with different fates. At one extreme, love without pleasure finds its need for satisfaction fulfilled in "romance." "Love downgraded to romance" finds models for its experience in the stereotypical romantic relationships mass-produced by the culture industry. At the other extreme, Sade's Juliette, as we saw, is the figure symbolizing the consequences of love's separation from pleasure, which is pleasure taken in the instrumental treatment of lovers. More to Horkheimer and Adorno's point, then, the pursuit of pleasure separated from love is oriented to sadomasochism. Recalling Juliette's practices, Horkheimer and Adorno conclude that

> [p]leasure is joined not with tenderness but with cruelty, and sexual love becomes what, according to Nietzsche, it always was: "in means, war; and, basically, the deadly hatred of the sexes."[56]

Moreover, the conversion of pleasure into cruelty draws up another similarity of capitalism to Fascism. The rebellious bourgeois Juliette justifies her cruelties through an ethic of human superiority extolling the virtues of practices she believes oppose the norms of an anti-individualistic, moralistic bourgeois capitalism. Ironically, Juliette's opposition only projects an image of the bourgeois's own future when the structural tendencies of capitalism have completely unfolded. "That fatal love which Sade highlights," they decide, "cruelty as greatness, when imagined in play or fancy, deals as harshly with men as German Fascism does in reality."[57]

At last they remind us, however, again affirming the normative interest in formal reason's violence to difference that awakens our aesthetic sensibility and roots their analysis of capitalism in their genealogy of reason, that the instrumental rationality that frames human relationships when pleasure is separated from love is not primarily the result of capitalism or of its tendencies toward Fascism, or of the logic of property relations through which the former would ascend to the latter. Our instrumental orientation is, on the contrary, first and foremost a singular expression of enlightenment and its relatively autonomous formal rationality, which "denounced as metaphysics . . . every kind of universal love, for reason displaces all love."[58] Hence, appreciated genealogically, the separation of love and pleasure that unfetters cruelty finally retires what had remained, through love's care for being, of reason's aesthetic receptivity to a world of differences that formal reason will next destroy in time. It finally retires what is left of reason's aesthetic receptivity to all that is inherently and objectively meaningful, to what enchants us or ought to enchant us.

FOUR

Aesthetic Individuality by Analogy: *Dialectic of Enlightenment* and the Birth and Death of Tragedy

"SPREAD OVER POSTERITY LIKE A SHADOW THAT KEEPS GROWING IN THE EVENING SUN"

Insofar as we discover telling resemblances between Nietzsche's genealogical tactics and Horkheimer and Adorno's critique of enlightenment, the larger purpose served by this examination comes into view. Laying bare the genealogical dimensions of their work concentrates our interest on their original translation of "man back into nature," of subjectivity back into individuality. For by way of this translation all the arguments of *Dialectic of Enlightenment* proceed from a common point of departure. Individuality is the normative point of departure for an argument that reconstructs the evolution of reason as a struggle within thought that culminates in a defining historical event. An aesthetic form of individuality, whose promise shone brightly though evanescently through the narrow window of contingency circumscribed by the ambiguity of mythical thought framing Odysseus's adventures, is sacrificed to the inner organization of individuality. In Odysseus's sacrifice of individuality's aesthetic features, Horkheimer and Adorno offer us a metaphorical representation of the creation of the modern subject coinciding with the Enlightenment of modern times, through which formal reason becomes objectified in structures enabling it to achieve universality. Aesthetic reason, which had oriented individuality receptively to a world of fathomless differences, is confined to sublimated expressions in art and to the aesthetic sensibility preserved by art. Against this catastrophic historical event, which launches the modern subject on a trajectory leading to the Holocaust, we are encouraged through their Nietzschean translation to conceptualize individuality as originally oriented to the world aesthetically, an orientation receptive to the world as in some profound way different from our every thought of it. Aesthetic individuality is thinking's recognition of the opacity and mystery of being, thinking's intuition that the darkness of the world may conceal some fathomless meaning lying forever beyond the boundaries of thought. Aesthetic individuality is perhaps nothing less than thinking's reflection of the limits of thought, though it also is a great deal more.

Even if, despite the methodological parallels, we cautiously refrain from inferring an indebtedness to Nietzsche, what genealogical habits Horkheimer and Adorno at least share with him lead us to identify aesthetic individuality as the idea on which their reconstruction and critique of enlightenment are balanced. If the weight of my examination is consequently shifted toward the idea of aesthetic individuality to which Horkheimer and Adorno are led genealogically, the extent to which *Dialectic of Enlightenment* reproduces Nietzsche's genealogical practices invites comparison between his idea of individuality and theirs. Rather than continuing to pursue those later works of Nietzsche's that have served as the basis of my methodological comparison and are well known for their idea of individuality as well as for their genealogical structure, I find that *The Birth of Tragedy* possesses a concept of individuality unambiguously resembling its aesthetic concept in *Dialectic of Enlightenment*. Indeed, while Nietzsche's *On the Genealogy of Morals* and *Beyond Good and Evil* contain the genealogical design *Dialectic of Enlightenment* resembles, the concept of individuality these works possess is wholly at odds with that belonging to Horkheimer and Adorno, as I will argue at a more appropriate time.[1] As in my earlier discussion, my intention in introducing *The Birth of Tragedy* here is not to prove that Horkheimer and Adorno actually are influenced by Nietzsche. Though I believe that to be true, and to an extent that we only have begun to surmise, adopting a less controversial path and one less likely to stall the discussion precisely at the point it becomes most interesting, I want to show that the similarities of *The Birth of Tragedy* to *Dialectic of Enlightenment* are so remarkable as to deepen our understanding of the concept of aesthetic individuality at the heart of Horkheimer and Adorno's critique of the process of enlightenment.[2]

The Birth of Tragedy and the Concept of Aesthetic Individuality

Nietzsche famously begins the first section of *The Birth of Tragedy* by proposing that it would be of benefit to the science of aesthetics to learn how "the continuous development of art is bound up with the *Apollinian* and *Dionysian* duality."[3] Of fascination to Nietzsche is the presence of a fundamental conflict between two aesthetic principles within the history of Greek art, present more generally within the history of art, and finally more generally still within the history of thought. At each of these levels historical development unfolds dynamically through a "tremendous opposition" between the Apollinian and the Dionysian, two different historical "tendencies" that despite both being "art-states of nature," are distinguished by different aims. Running "parallel to each other, for the most part openly at variance," the Apollinian and the Dionysian are embodied in distinct forms of art that represent one principle more or less than the other at various stages of Hellenic cultural evolution. Eventually the two principles "appear coupled with each other, and through this coupling ultimately generate an equally Dionysian and Apollinian form of art—Attic tragedy."[4] Attic tragedy, the most powerful of the artistic offspring to which these antagonistic forces give birth (before the music of Richard Wagner), is eclipsed by a subsequent development in the dramatic arts. Importantly, this development is indicative of a deeper tendency in thought that will extend itself into modernity.

Without penetrating very far into Nietzsche's work, already we see traces of an argument echoed in Dialectic of Enlightenment—if it does not, in fact, establish its very basis. Whereas for Nietzsche a struggle between two forces determines the history of art and ultimately the history of thought, for Horkheimer and Adorno a struggle between two forces defines the process of enlightenment. For Nietzsche as for Horkheimer and Adorno, both forces are forces of "nature," or seem so, as even when they express themselves independently of each other they always are found together in the history of art and the history of thought, authoring such different forms of art and thought that they each appear to be entirely unique principles. And although there is no *actual* coupling of formal and aesthetic rationality in the history of enlightenment that is a counterpart to the coupling of the Apollinian and the Dionysian in Attic tragedy, the *ideal* of aesthetic rationality we earlier inferred from its compromised form of aesthetic individuality (or enlightened self-possession) is this counterpart exactly. Attic tragedy, I will argue, is not merely the art form Nietzsche believed expressed the ideal relationship between the Apollinian and the Dionysian art-states of nature. Attic tragedy is also the model for the relationship between formal and aesthetic reason that constitutes the ideal of aesthetic individuality, the normative ideal that remains in the shadows while animating and driving Horkheimer and Adorno's critique of enlightenment. For all these analogies to hold, however, upon closer study formal and aesthetic rationality and the historical struggle between them must be completely prefigured by Nietzsche's understanding of the Apollinian and the Dionysian and how their "continuous development" is bound up with their duality. We pursue these analogies by first inquiring after the nature of each of these "art deities" and why they must struggle at all. Nietzsche appears to have these questions in mind as he considers each principle apart from the other according to their own analogies with dream states and intoxication. Dreams and intoxication, he suggests, "present a contrast analogous to that existing between the Apollinian and Dionysian."[5] Imitating Nietzsche's method of elucidation, the Apollinian and the Dionysian, I will argue, present a contrast analogous to formal and aesthetic reason leading to further analogies in turn.

Analogy from the Apollinian and the Dionysian: Art Deities and Forms of Thought

Through the "beautiful illusion of the dream worlds, in the creation of which every man is truly an artist," Nietzsche proposes, each of us is protected from a "pathological effect" were our dream life to be lived. Substituting the "reality of dreams for the reality of existence," the "mere appearance" of reality for reality itself, as Nietzsche also puts it, we receive dreams "with profound delight and joyous necessity."[6] Nietzsche is describing a familiar experience, yet he is easily misunderstood nevertheless. It is not that any imagined reality, with its pleasures or horrors, can appear in a dream, permitting a dreamer to indulge in some elusive happiness or to escape some contemplated pain, yet leaving waking reality unchanged. It is that reality is dreamt and known through dreams that keep reality itself at bay.

Apollo, "the sculptor god," "god of plastic energies," Nietzsche argues, embodies the "joyous necessity of the dream experience," because the Apollinian "art of sculpture" expresses the force through which in art and in thought we represent what is living by "images" that mediate our experience of life. As do dreams, Apollinian images afford an "interpretation of life."[7] Any and all ideas we have of life are infinitely exceeded by life itself, because that which is interpreted always exceeds its interpretations, as Nietzsche will stress often by drawing our attention to the intrinsic difference between images or concepts of being and being itself, thus affirming that being is essentially unknowable. Illusion, appearance, image, beauty as the illusion and appearance of life, image as the interpretation of life, though, are but manifestations of the Apollinian's essential characteristic—the "principle of individuation." Possessing Apollinian powers of illusion, appearance, and image, individuals maintain a dividing line between reality and what thought would make of reality that is comparable to the "delicate boundary which the dream image must not overstep."[8] Indeed, individuation *is* that Apollinian dividing line between image and reality, for if the division between appearance and reality were lost the individual, too, would be lost, as in dreams individuals would be lost to the pathology of realities from which they are spared by the illusion of dream worlds. Indistinguishable from individuation—for in Nietzsche's view, "we might call Apollo himself the glorious divine image of the *principium individuationis*"—the Apollinian fully emerges as the principle according to which identity is maintained through the capacity to form representations that mediate an individual's every experience of the world.[9] By means of dreams, then, we are to learn that the Apollinian alienates the individual from the world and through alienation preserves identity from the dissolution of its boundaries.

Dreams are thus the perfect analogy for what Nietzsche labors to say about the Apollinian. Through the dreamlike qualities of illusion, appearance, image, and interpretation, the Apollinian sets art and thought over and against that which is real. Dreams stress that the Apollinian is always "of a mind," we might say, that defends the identity of the individual against threats to its integrity, specifically the threat to individuation that flows from the indivisibility of individual and world before there is any image or, in short, before there is any thought of the world. Through dreams the Apollinian is formed as representation, identity, opposition to the world, and alienation from the world, the meanings of which become virtually interchangeable.

Just as certainly as the Apollinian protects identity and individuation, were its powers to fail the individual as they do when the Dionysian prevails, "everything subjective," Nietzsche insists, would vanish into "self-forgetfulness."[10] Falling victim to self-forgetfulness would be as though the individual were under the intoxicating influence of a "narcotic draught," or as though moved "in song and dance" to wild expressions. As is suggested by the disappearance of subjectivity in the context of an analogy between narcotics and song and dance, the "Dionysian art of music" stands in the same relationship to "intoxication" as the Apollinian art of sculpture stands in relation to dreams. Whereas the Apollinian constitutes identity through individuation, representation, opposition, and alienation, the Dionysian effects the collapse of individuation and the dissolution of identity. Our Apollinian remoteness from the world is summarily violated where the Dionysian compromises the individual's power to form images that separate us from the world in response to the Apollinian fear of crossing the line between art, or thought, and reality. The point of the analogy, then, between intoxication and the "nonimagistic" Dionysian art of music, as Nietzsche refers to what he considers to be music's most important aesthetic quality, is to depict a condition whereby there would be no self or subject to conceive of itself as distinct from the surrounding world.

With this loss of self we encounter the decisive feature belonging to the Dionysian collapse of individuation, the return of the individual to the "primordial unity." Nietzsche explains by saying,

> Under the charm of the Dionysian not only is the union between man and man reaffirmed, but nature which has become alienated, hostile, or subjugated, celebrates once more her reconciliation with her lost son, man.[11]

Union among men, reconciliation with nature, the "primordial" clearly is a comprehensive philosophical term for Nietzsche encompassing nothing less than "being itself," which is evident as we read through *The Birth of Tragedy* to its latter parts. Through the art of the Dionysian, Nietzsche poeticizes in section 17, "[we] are really for a brief moment primordial being itself," and in the section immediately prior he sings again and even more poetically that when "the spell of individuation is broken" through the Dionysian "the way lies open to the Mothers of Being."[12] Bringing an end to the separation between human being and human being, human being and nature, the Dionysian ends the fundamental separation between human being and being, thus restoring the oneness of being that characterized being at its origin. The Dionysian relationship to being ending the separation between human being and being entails an aesthetic receptivity toward being, about which Nietzsche is quite clear. "Under the charm of the Dionysian," Nietzsche declares, the individual is enchanted, his "very gestures express enchantment."[13] Enchanted, the individual recognizes in being what is lost to individuation, recognizes what identity excludes, what the image omits. No longer, Nietzsche concludes, is the individual an Apollinian artist, locked away from the world by his representations. Enchanted, he has become a "work of art," one and the same being as art's object.

Just as Nietzsche explicated the Apollinian and the Dionysian through an analogy with dreams and intoxication, we arrive at a more complete formulation of formal and aesthetic reason by drawing out their analogous relationship to the Apollinian and the Dionysian. By converting the diversity of nature's differences into the commonly held property of "matter" in order to render nature susceptible to mastery, formal reason establishes an Apollinian connection between thinking and identity that reproduces each of the dimensions of this connection as Nietzsche understands it. Reducing nature to matter, formal reason creates an opposition between human being and being, an Apollinian subject related instrumentally to nature conceived as an object. Formal reason's Apollinian "image" of nature as matter excludes from thought the Dionysian aesthetic receptivity to qualities that belong to being intrinsically. Narrowly circumscribing the boundaries of what we can think about nature, our Apollinian experience of the world is abridged, while the source of this estrangement between human being and being that formal reason installs in thought is tied intimately to the constitution of identity, as it is with the Apollinian. And as we shortly shall see when we take up the origins of Apollinian culture, the source of Apollinian estrangement from being is little different from the source of formal reason's alienation from nature in its need to protect the individual from what in nature is unknown. Interpreted as terrifying and threatening to self-preservation, the unknown is formal rational thinking's initial provocation for its conversion of nature's differences into matter, reconstituting nature in terms that render it everywhere familiar and that allow the individual's own identity to survive a terrain whose opacity makes it appear alien and terrifying.

It is this symmetry among thinking, identity, opposition, and alienation shared between formal reason and the Apollinian that both aesthetic rationality and the Dionysian endanger, as is now evident when we recall Horkheimer and Adorno's interpretation of the *Odyssey*. Tempted to relinquish his uncertain control over nature and to lose himself to the allurements of mythical being, Odysseus must resist "the temptation to self-abandonment."[14] Where Horkheimer and Adorno speak of "self-abandonment (*Selbstpreisgabe*)," it is worthwhile to note, Nietzsche speaks similarly of "self-forgetfulness (*Selbstvergessenheit*)" and "self-abnegation (*Selbstentausserung*)."[15] Through his aesthetic receptivity to nature, of which self-abandonment would be the extreme, pathological form, Odysseus's identity is revealed to be torn within, precarious in a way that becomes evident in his encounter with the Sirens. There the "tremendous opposition" within Odysseus between the "duality" of a formal and aesthetic orientation to the world is "*openly* at variance," as Nietzsche describes the Apollinian and Dionysian conflict occurring during that same period in Greece, we should remind ourselves, in which Homer composed the *Odyssey*.[16] Odysseus borders on self-abandonment, his identity verging on collapse and his selfhood about to vanish with the end of his estrangement from the world and all that it contains. Enchanted by the being of the world that as "subject" he would be unable to recognize, Odysseus exchanges an Apollinian formal rational orientation to the world for an aesthetic receptivity resembling the Dionysian. Indeed, captured by the Sirens' music, and "nonimagistic" in a way not unlike the special sense in which

Nietzsche argues that the "Dionysian art of music" is nonimagistic, Odysseus's aesthetic receptivity to nature is neither exclusive of being nor of the idea that being may be different from his thought of it. In the figure of Odysseus, aesthetic rationality opens to the Dionysian idea that there is a world that lies beyond the horizons of Apollinian thought and that is forever lost to it, thereby overcoming our estrangement from being by dismantling the model of one identical and qualitatively undifferentiated world throughout that safeguards the enlightenment ideal of one identical individual. If for Odysseus there is a thought to which being is not lost, then, it is only of the *difference from thought that is being*, a Dionysian thought to which Horkheimer and Adorno's aesthetic concept of individuality returns us. This is the thought that underpins the conceptual division within identity between formal and aesthetic reason, just as the division between the Apollinian and the Dionysian, the division between the image of being and being itself, is the thought that arises from an understanding of being that is already aesthetic. This is Nietzsche's understanding, as it is Horkheimer and Adorno's.

Up to this point, the analogies we find between *The Birth of Tragedy* and *Dialectic of Enlightenment* help to illuminate the aesthetic dimensions of the principle of rationality that Horkheimer and Adorno oppose to formal reason. They assist, further, in demonstrating that an individuality oriented receptively to the world in a way outlined by these features is aesthetic. Until there is clarification of the relationship between these opposing principles when aesthetic rationality is neither hierarchically subordinated to formal reason in a compromised form of aesthetic individuality nor sacrificed to formal rationality in the form of subjectivity, however, we will have an incomplete picture of the concept of aesthetic individuality that animates their work. Such clarification becomes possible as we turn from Nietzsche's analogy of the Apollinian and the Dionysian with dream states and intoxication, where he considered each art deity as it "burst forth from nature herself, *without the mediation of the human artist*," to an examination of their corresponding forms of art, where Nietzsche elaborates upon features of the Apollinian and the Dionysian he first revealed by analogy.[17] As our further comparison of these two sets of terms now will permit us to see, Nietzsche's understanding of the "continuous development" of Greek art presents a parallel to the process of enlightenment as it is described by Horkheimer and Adorno. It is a parallel sufficiently well defined to allow us to recognize in Nietzsche's argument counterparts to the two distinct forms of aesthetic individuality contained in their work. Specifically, Nietzsche's discussion of Greece's encounter with the Dionysian is analogous to the compromised form of aesthetic individuality reflected in Horkheimer and Adorno's notion of the "ambiguity" of mythical thought, which subsequently gives way to the inner organization of individuality and the sublimation of aesthetic reason in art. And his discussion of Attic tragedy offers an analogous model of the ideal of aesthetic individuality from which we can infer a more precise formulation of what until now is only implicit in *Dialectic of Enlightenment*.

Analogy from the Greek Dionysian Festival: Aesthetic Form and Forms of Thought

At the time the Dionysian first appears in Greece as an art form, Nietzsche maintains, the Apollinian already is well established aesthetically and is nobly embodied by Homer's epics and other art forms of the Olympian culture of Homeric Greece. En route from Dionysian festivals celebrated in parts of the world the Greeks considered to be barbarian, the world "from Rome to Babylon," in Nietzsche's words, the Dionysian enters Greece through the Greek festival, where "nature for the first time attains her artistic jubilee."[18] Apollinian culture, Nietzsche stresses, had been hostile to the Dionysian because the barbarian festivals had centered in "extravagant sexual licentiousness, whose waves overwhelmed all family life and its venerable traditions," unleashing "the most savage natural instincts."[19] In the Greek Dionysian festival, however, when "the destruction of the *principium individuationis* for the first time becomes an artistic phenomenon," the broader sociopathic manifestations of the barbarian Dionysian celebrations were avoided.[20] Once the Greeks confined the Dionysian to the festival as an *artistic* phenomenon, supposedly freeing the Apollinian Hellenes from the Dionysian dangers to identity plaguing the barbarian world, for those who participate in the arts of the festival the Dionysian is experienced in a direct and unmediated ("nonimagistic") way. Through the art of the Dionysian dithyramb, "something new and unheard-of in the Homeric Greek world," the individual experiences a unity with nature expressed through the "entire symbolism of the body," the "whole pantomime of dancing," which calls into play other symbolic powers, especially those of music. Such a "collective release of all the symbolic powers" means that the individual's Dionysian experience enabled him aesthetically to fleetingly experience that deindividuated "height of self-abnegation" that seeks expression in "a new world of [artistic] symbols."[21] While the Hellenes escape its impact on the barbarian world, the Dionysian is yet such a traumatic event for the Greeks that it leaves Apollinian culture dramatically though unevenly changed, as becomes evident when we consider Nietzsche's description of its history and cultural characteristics.

Apollinian culture had been erected to enable the Greeks to cope with the afflictions of the preceding Titanic Age, when the horror that the Titans and the fearful powers of nature together wreaked upon the Hellenes nurtured in them the "keenest susceptibility to suffering" and a depressiveness imperiling their survival. To endure these terrors, Nietzsche determines, the Greek "had to interpose between himself and life the radiant dreambirth of the Olympians."[22] In the gods of the Olympian universe born out of that "same impulse [to individual self-preservation] that embodied itself in Apollo," the Greeks created a "*middle world* of art" that "deified" all of life's values, good as well as evil, idealizing and affirming life, "seducing one to a continuation of life."[23] The "artistic structure of the Apollinian culture . . . the glorious Olympian figures of the Gods . . . [t]heir deeds, pictured in brilliant reliefs, adorn[ing] its friezes," offered a "transfiguring mirror" that reflected an illusion of beauty suppressing the horrors of the world and combating the ill effects of Greek sensitivity. Borrowing Schiller's conception of the "naive" to describe art that through the illusion of beauty triumphs "over an abysmal and terrifying view of the world," Nietzsche finds the naive to be the "highest effect of Apollinian culture" and attributes the "complete victory of Apollinian illusion" over the Titanic Age to Homeric naiveté. If by means of an aesthetically naive genius Hellenic culture preserves the Greek from the terrors and torments of existence, Nietzsche submits, then the Apollinian is obedient to "but one law—the individual, i.e., the delimiting of the boundaries of the individual, measure in the Hellenic sense." And in the Apollinian sphere, Nietzsche adds, the individual's self-identity can be preserved only through "self-knowledge," which means that Apollinian culture places "side by side with the aesthetic necessity for beauty . . . the demands 'know thyself' and 'nothing in excess.'"[24] For only an individual certain of his identity knows what he may open himself up to without endangering his individuation and what is different and threatening and must be excluded.

Immunized to world sorrows by this culture of illusion and self-discipline, the Apollinian Greek was shocked by the "titanic" experience of the Greek Dionysian festival, and at the same time was reminded by it that he was "inwardly related" to the overthrown Titanic Age out of which his Olympian culture originated. No longer, Nietzsche explains, could the Apollinian Greek suppress what the Dionysian experience revealed and forced him to acknowledge, that regardless of the beauty and moderation that sustained his identity his life rested upon a reality hidden from view. Beneath the seen and known world lay the "essence of nature" or the "mysterious ground of our being" or the "truly existent primordial unity," all terms Nietzsche invokes to describe the unseen and unknown Dionysian world composed of pleasures and pains, of joys and sufferings, of all of life's polarities that being integrates into one "eternal contradictory." With the Dionysian festival, Nietzsche concludes, the Apollinian now

> paled before an art that, in its intoxication, spoke the truth. . . . The individual, with all his restraint and proportion, succumbed to the self-oblivion of the Dionysian states, forgetting the precepts of Apollo. *Excess* revealed itself as truth.[25]

Nietzsche concludes this part (sections 1–4) of his extraordinary narrative by speculating that as a consequence of the shocks it introduced into Greece, the Apollinian-Dionysian covenant of the aesthetic form of the festival forged during late Homeric culture dissolved into two distinct cultural tendencies, each then finding its way into different areas of the Hellenic world. "[W]herever the Dionysian prevailed," he advises, "the Apollinian was checked and destroyed," whereas wherever the "Dionysian onslaught was successfully withstood" the

Apollinian "exhibited itself as more rigid and menacing than ever." [26] Nietzsche thus documents the consequences of the stages into which his reconstruction has arranged the history of Homeric Greece up to the birth of Attic tragedy. Out of its instinct for self-preservation Apollinian culture emerged to suppress the disturbing elements of the earlier Titanic period and the terrors threatened by nature. Cultural powers are developed through which the Apollinian Greek, Nietzsche explains with the aid of the dream analogy, "completely lost sight of the [terrifying] waking reality" and is "compelled to consider this illusion ... as empirical reality." [27] Tenaciously resisting Dionysian pressures to become divided against itself, a Homeric culture obedient to Apollinian principles strains to repel what appears to threaten its existence. Forced to relent to what seems inevitable, Apollinian culture manages to contain the divisive Dionysian element in the aesthetic form of the Dionysian festival, in this pacified form believed to threaten neither the self-identity of the Greek nor the identity of Hellenic culture as a whole. Opening the Greek to the intoxicating experience of being in all of its diversity, the power of the Dionysian art form nevertheless causes the strategy of aesthetic pacification to fail throughout Greece. Finally, as the Hellenic world falls victim to the division it had hoped to forestall, its Apollinian heritage is embodied dramatically in the evolution of Doric art, the Doric worldview, and Sparta, the Doric state, which Nietzsche describes as the "permanent military encampment of the Apollinian." Let us now take Nietzsche's reconstruction of how the Hellenic world came to be divided, and the image of the Greek world as a whole where he left the older Hellenic history before moving beyond it to the birth of Attic tragedy, and examine them against Horkheimer and Adorno's interpretation of Homer's *Odyssey*.

At the outset we should recall Nietzsche's interest in the historical path the Dionysian followed to Greece. Aside from its historical value, which has been controversial, Nietzsche most likely locates the first appearance of the Dionysian in the barbarian world to allow himself the opportunity to distinguish the Dionysian in its *nonaesthetic* (barbarian) form, from its *aesthetic* (Greek) form. Though Greece had been insulated geographically from the Dionysian infection of the ancient world, when knowledge of the Dionysian finally reaches Greece, Apollinian culture staves off the barbarian invasion only by means of an aesthetic rapprochement through the Dionysian festival that disarms its "powerful antagonist" of "destructive weapons." [28] Clearly, Nietzsche is calling attention to the singularity of the aesthetic achievement, as do Horkheimer and Adorno in their analysis of the *Odyssey*'s Sirens episode. With Odysseus no less than the Apollinian Greeks, reason devoted to self-preservation agrees to open itself to nature on the condition that being inevitably will appear only as an *art form*. Just as Horkheimer and Adorno write that the "temptation" the Sirens hold out to Odysseus bound to his ship's mast is eventually "neutralized and becomes a mere object of contemplation—becomes art," Nietzsche surmises that the Greeks imagined the Dionysian would be rendered harmless through its confinement to the art forms of the Greek festival. What Horkheimer and Adorno share with Nietzsche analogously is suggestive on two levels.

First, where individuality's aesthetic receptivity to nature is finally limited to art, its original ability to experience the world aesthetically has been displaced, which suggests that our experience of the world through art is not the *primary* aesthetic experience of which thinking is capable. Rather, experiencing the world through art may be the result of a prior compromise within thought through which aesthetic reason's pursuit of a direct, receptive experience of nature is tempered by being made to coexist with formal rationality, as Horkheimer and Adorno's analysis of the Sirens episode proves. Bound to his ship's mast so that his crew can safely guide it past the danger posed, Odysseus directly experiences the Sirens by means of a compromise through which he comes to represent the ambiguity of mythical thought. Though direct, the aesthetically receptive quality of his experience is pacified through subordination to the formal rational goal of survival. Analogously, Nietzsche views the Greek Dionysian festival precisely as the achievement of a "seasonally affected reconciliation" between two art impulses of nature, wherein Dionysian receptivity to nature is pacified through subordination to the Apollinian principle of individuation just as for Horkheimer and Adorno aesthetic reason is pacified through subordination to formal rationality. Reconciliation appears as compromise insofar as the conflict between the art impulses that lie at its base is not erased, as Nietzsche assures us it is not. "At bottom" of the reconciled impulses on which the art of the Greek Dionysian festival rests, he explains, "the chasm was not bridged over."[29] Whatever else art may be, we are being told by Horkheimer and Adorno and Nietzsche, art springs from an arrangement in thought that displaces what forms of reason or impulses we originally possess to be aesthetically receptive to the world.

Second, their arguments are only in part weighted toward the recollection of an aesthetic receptivity to the world that is forced into a compromise prefiguring art. To an equal extent they commonly focus on the subsequent development of art as imprisoning aesthetic reason and rendering it powerless outside of its own narrow domain. Nietzsche's image of Greek culture during "the last attained period, the period of Doric art," when in the wake of their broken covenant the Apollinian seizes up against an irrepressible Dionysian challenge, portrays the two art impulses as each having conquered separate domains of the Hellenic world. "And so," to recall Nietzsche's words, "wherever the Dionysian prevailed, the Apollinian was checked and destroyed.... [I]t is equally certain that, wherever the first Dionysian onslaught was successfully withstood, the authority and majesty of the Delphic god exhibited itself as more rigid and menacing than ever," as in the "military encampment" of the Spartan state.[30] Divided as a whole within, Greek culture reproduces all the features of the "ambiguity of mythical thought" Horkheimer and Adorno flesh out in the *Odyssey*. Just as do formal and aesthetic reason within thought as a whole, as in thinking's ambiguous orientation toward the Sirens, Apollinian and Dionysian forces each stake out their opposing territories but together nevertheless fitfully coexist as factions internally dividing Hellenic culture. And if the analogy between the arguments regarding the confinement of aesthetic reason to art is not yet perfectly established, it can be extended still further. After his encounter with the Sirens Odysseus's signal to be released from his restraints is ignored by his men. A compromise with formal reason ensuring selfhood and self-preservation and allowing for aesthetic receptivity to nature then turns to the aesthetic contemplation of art as, unheeded, Odysseus with his identity intact is forced to look on passively at the mysterious world of being that thinking undisciplined by the art form could abide only fleetingly. Now compare Nietzsche, who in *The Birth of Tragedy* remarkably invokes a virtually identical metaphor to illustrate the superior strength of the Apollinian when it is engaged aesthetically by the Dionysian vision of being—the individual, "sunk in contemplation of it, sit[s] quietly in his tossing bark, amid the waves."[31]

Just before introducing evidence for the "mysterious union" of the Apollinian and the Dionysian in Attic tragedy, we see, Nietzsche leaves these dual orientations to nature in a relationship that is mirrored in Horkheimer and Adorno's interpretation of the *Odyssey*'s Sirens episode. A new art form originates with the Greek Dionysian festival, which emerges as the power of self-preservation harnesses an opposing form of reason that unbridled would shatter all Apollinian illusions suppressing the aesthetic recognition of being. From this artistic representation of the conciliation between its two cultural principles, we learn that at this time the identity of the Homeric world had stood in an ambiguous relationship to itself and to the world. Divided against itself, it is this ambiguity in Homeric thinking that orients myth to the world ambiguously. Nietzsche thus portrays late Homeric Greece as an image of a compromised form of aesthetic individuality. For Nietzsche, it springs from an aesthetic receptivity to the world subordinated to an identity ruled by the principle of individuation, and trapped in the art form of the Dionysian festival without hope of realizing the original promise of forging a harmonious relation with Apollo, whose self-discipline and self-denial predominate. So too has Odysseus's aesthetic receptivity to the world been subordinated to his selfhood and become trapped in art with formal reason as fearful of an aesthetic receptivity to being as Nietzsche's Spartan encampment. For Horkheimer and Adorno, the Sirens episode represents the world-historical turning point where aesthetic rationality becomes frozen timelessly as art. Art is the final form aesthetic receptivity to nature will assume before aesthetic reason in the interest of enlightenment is sacrificed to the "inner organization of individuality," to the dominion of formal reason through the construction of the subject.

For Nietzsche, on the other hand, "after many and long precursory struggles" the Apollinian and the Dionysian reach a "common goal," a "glorious consummation" in the birth of Attic tragedy, where the two impulses of nature work together to comprehend the being of the world. Studied against the background of the analogous relationships established between the Apollinian and the Dionysian and aesthetic and formal reason, Attic tragedy represents the ideal form of an aesthetic individuality that would have emerged historically if not suppressed by the process of enlightenment. As the Apollinian and the Dionysian relate to each other within it, Attic tragedy sketches a relation between formal and aesthetic rationality that functions implicitly in *Dialectic of Enlightenment* as the normative ideal with which Horkheimer and Adorno formulate their critique of enlightenment. And as we shall see as well, when Attic tragedy is eclipsed by further developments in drama, the forces Nietzsche believes cause its demise closely resemble those Horkheimer and Adorno hold responsible for the sacrifice of aesthetic reason before it could achieve the ideal of aesthetic individuality represented by Attic tragedy. With Nietzsche's "death" of tragedy, if you will, and Horkheimer and Adorno's sacrifice of the aesthetic features of individuality, the parallel between *The Birth of Tragedy* and *Dialectic of Enlightenment* is complete.

Analogy from Attic Tragedy: The Ideal of Aesthetic Individuality

To clarify the relationship between the Apollinian and the Dionysian, imagistic and nonimagistic elements of Attic tragedy, Nietzsche first examines lyric poetry and then a historically earlier form of tragedy, "tragedy as chorus only," which I will consider briefly as he takes each in turn. At once both Apollinian and Dionysian, words and music, lyric poetry's inspiration is nevertheless Dionysian and its foundation musical. What the lyric expresses in images through language, Nietzsche explains, draws its lifeblood from all the agitations of passion that first require the musical qualities of poetry for their adequate expression. By virtue of its musical qualities, in other words, lyric poetry presents Nietzsche with the opportunity to elaborate upon the relationship of music to the Dionysian, which he does with great piquancy and beauty, so that we might also understand why lyric poetry is "dependent on the spirit of music."[32]

Standing in a primary symbolic relation to the "primordial contradiction" at the "heart of the primal unity," symbolizing "a sphere which is beyond and prior to all phenomena," music is an imageless "repetition and a recast" of the world, of what lies at "the heart of the world," of being's "vast universality and absoluteness."[33] Leaving nothing out, music is the expression of everything that is in "urgent and active motion," the veritable expression of the will of the world, of life and the will to life. Music enables the lyrist to achieve that state of Dionysian "self-abnegation and oneness," a "surrendering of subjectivity" out of which the "lyrical poem," the linguistic, Apollinian element of the lyric art form, can spontaneously flow as the natural extension of one continuous aesthetic experience. Accordingly, poetic language and its images, symbols, and concepts are entirely dependent for their representational power upon music in its primary relation to the world. Only when music allows the lyric poet to become the "moving center" of experience at the "basis of things," through which he encounters being and himself in his difference as part of being, can he become "conscious of a world of images and symbols" that enable him to conceptualize being and his relation to being. Essentially, lyric poetry is the Apollinian image of the lyric poet's aesthetic immersion in the being of the world, an image through which the poet—his identity—persists despite his self-abnegation, and through which the being of the world itself is redeemed, visibly come to life in defiance of our ordinary blindness to it. As a sounding "from the depths of his being," Nietzsche insists, the Apollinian image of the poet's identity teaches him of his relation to the world, elevating his aesthetic receptivity to a cognitive level of apprehension.

In Nietzsche's view lyric poetry thus possesses two all-important features. Though lyric poetry is born from an aesthetic receptivity to being, the Apollinian representation of being in images, symbols, and concepts prohibits the Dionysian from destroying the poet's identity, while at the same time the preservation of identity does not obstruct its representation of the Dionysian experience of being. For the first time in the history of art, if not in thought, Nietzsche seems to propose, we have identity and difference integrated into one form of representation, where identity need not exclude and lose the world for fear of losing itself to the world. Yet, lyric poetry cannot fully realize this aesthetic achievement, because "all the eloquence of lyric poetry," Nietzsche reminds us, "cannot bring the deepest significance of [music] one step nearer to us" than music itself.[34] No matter how explosively it is born from music—and at one point Nietzsche creates the spectacular image of the lyric poem as the "imitative fulguration (*die nachahmende Effulgaration*)" or *flash of lightning* of music in images and concepts—lyric poetry cannot adequately articulate what is expressed musically. Nietzsche is not attributing the abridgment of expression to the Apollinian as such, however. Rather, it is through the lyrical image that the poet finally "rests in the calm sea of Apollinian contemplation," intellectually detached from being and the primordial contradiction, or life's pleasures and its pains, that embodies the diversity of being. Nietzsche attributes the inadequacies of conceptualization to this particular form of the Apollinian, to lyric poetry specifically, thus establishing a still higher standard of aesthetic representation to be met by another art form.

Just as the aesthetics of the poet's experience with being is foreshortened by the Apollinian element in its lyric form, Nietzsche points to a similar relationship between the two art impulses in "tragedy as chorus only," the historical antecedent of Attic tragedy. Speaking of the satyric chorus within religiously sanctioned practices of Hellenic society, originally, Nietzsche stresses, "*tragedy arose from the tragic chorus*," in actuality was the "chorus and nothing but chorus," the "chorus as such, without the stage—the primitive form of tragedy," the "real protodrama."[35] What Nietzsche means to accentuate through repeated references to the origin of tragedy in chorus, of course, is the origin of tragedy in music and the primacy of music in tragedy, because tragedy derives its effects from the music belonging to the satyric chorus of "magically enchanted Dionysians." Of the effects produced by early tragedy, most are Dionysian, leading Nietzsche to describe "tragedy as chorus only" as *Dionysian tragedy*, and among these effects some elaborate upon Nietzsche's already robust concept of the aesthetics of the Dionysian experience. As we would expect, through Dionysian tragedy identity collapses, and in this context Nietzsche prefers the term "nullified (*aufgehoben*)" to explain the consequences for subjectivity of an "overwhelming feeling of unity leading back to the very heart of nature."[36] With its intimate relation to nullification, Nietzsche introduces tragedy's "*lethargic* element," through which the Greek becomes oblivious to his personal history and through self-forgetfulness is able to open or "surrender his individuality (*ein Aufgeben des Individuums*)" to an experience exceeding the limits and boundaries of his existence.[37] Finally, "metaphysical comfort," no doubt the best known of the effects Nietzsche culls from Dionysian tragedy, leaves the Dionysian chorist with the sense that "life is at the bottom of things, despite all the changes of appearances, indestructible and powerful," thus tempering the Greek's unique susceptibility to the "tenderest and deepest suffering," which we learned is fostered by the Dionysian.[38]

Importantly, each of these effects is experienced beneath a conscious and explicit level of cognitive awareness and understanding, which appears to undermine the final cognitive achievement of early tragedy. Even "metaphysical comfort," among all the effects of tragedy seeming on the face of it to be its most highly developed cognitive act, appears in "incarnate clarity," Nietzsche makes a special point of saying, as a bodily revelation of the pleasures taken from tragedy. Proceeding from a transfiguration the Greek undergoes in response to the symbolism of the satyric chorus, by which he becomes "fused" with the dramatic images and sees himself changed, as by magic, into a "satyr," tragedy's effects occur through a "vision" and remain at an "unconscious" level of understanding.[39] Indeed, Nietzsche's entire argument is that the satyric chorus of primitive tragedy offered the Greeks an apprehension of nature "as yet unchanged by knowledge, with the bolts of culture still unbroken," offering an experience of the world, we might say, as it was before we as a species were born.[40] "Tragedy as chorus," in other words, is for its greatest part nonconceptual, bottom-heavy with Dionysian elements. Only when the Apollinian element finally emerges out of the Dionysian transfiguration, as it does spontaneously in the manner of lyric poetry, as a *second vision* from the first, does the Dionysian Greek who has taken himself for a satyr through his metamorphosis then "*see the god*" Dionysus. With this new vision of Dionysus, the Greek beholds the "Apollinian complement of his own state" and, Nietzsche concludes, "the drama is complete."[41]

It is apparent from Nietzsche's presentation of the "real protodrama" of early tragedy that its Apollinian and Dionysian elements do not work together differently than they do in lyric poetry. Again we find identity and difference integrated into a single form of representation, with the Dionysian experience of being through tragedy embodied in an image, a vision of the god Dionysus, that raises to a conscious and explicit level of understanding what previously had been unconscious and tacit. What misapprehension and fear of the world the Apollinian displayed as a Homeric cultural formation prior to its marriage to the Dionysian in lyric poetry and early tragedy have dissolved. Through their receptivity to nature and being, both lyric poetry and early tragedy raise their aesthetic engagement with the world to a new level of insight and understanding and pose no threat to identity. Lyric poetry and early tragedy, I am proposing, clearly exhibit features of the ideal of aesthetic individuality for which Horkheimer and Adorno always appear to reach and that will emerge fully from Nietzsche's concept of Attic tragedy. Aesthetic individuality appears in both art forms as an aesthetic receptivity to being that redefines the limits of identity through new, albeit imperfectly conceptualized, understandings to which the self can surrender without loss of self. This we now understand the Homeric view of the world portended for Nietzsche no less than for Horkheimer and Adorno in the Sirens episode of the *Odyssey*.

Yet, although both art forms anticipate the ideal of aesthetic individuality, early tragedy as well as lyric poetry each fall short in one decisive respect. Whereas lyric poetry's inadequately developed Apollinian dimension underrepresented the aesthetic experience of its Dionysian moment, early tragedy privileges the Dionysian at the expense of the Apollinian, as Nietzsche certainly intimates by referring to it as *Dionysian* tragedy. Nietzsche is careful to explain, as we have seen, that the Apollinian element of tragedy as chorus appears in a "vision," a second vision outside the Dionysian reveler but otherwise not less of a vision than that which first occurs as his imaginary transfiguration into a satyr. Nietzsche similarly draws attention to the visceral, noncognitive features of Dionysian tragedy by describing it as the "womb that gave birth to the whole of the *so-called* dialogue," thus accenting the diminished significance of Apollinian linguistic representation in relation to the immediacy of the Dionysian experience.[42] With his examination of lyric poetry and early tragedy, then, neither of which produce a symmetrical relationship between the dual art impulses of nature, the way is prepared to consider Attic tragedy, its remedy for the imbalance between the Apollinian and Dionysian, and its contribution as an ideal of art to an ideal of thought, to an ideal of aesthetic individuality.

Once Nietzsche ends his discussion of Dionysian tragedy, he appears satisfied that in the course of his presentation he has described all the elements also belonging to Attic tragedy but one, which will produce its own original effects. Whereas early tragedy produced its Apollinian element as one continuous sphere of expression that grew spontaneously out of the Dionysian experience of transfiguration, Attic tragedy divides the protodrama into "two utterly different spheres of expression."[43] Instead of appearing in a vision and not actually present, as in Dionysian tragedy, the god Dionysus is played by an actor, making the Apollinian moment of tragedy an element that is structurally distinct from the Dionysian. With this change "tragedy as chorus only" evolves into a theatrical performance, and Attic tragedy, drama in the "narrower sense," as Nietzsche puts it, is born. Now the chorus is charged with the task of exciting not only its own members but an audience as well, all of whom achieve a state of Dionysian rapture and transfiguration through which the actor playing the role of the god appears to them to be a "visionary figure."[44] Of greatest consequence, the effects of Attic tragedy are "no longer merely felt (*nicht mehr jene nur empfundenen*)," as they are in Dionysian tragedy. Attic tragedy's Dionysian effects continue to be registered at a visceral level of understanding through the Dionysian moment of the drama, but are then "condensed" into Apollinian images through dialogue belonging to the tragedian symbolizing his god.[45] Attic tragedy is now poised to achieve nothing less than a qualitatively new aesthetic form.

To grasp in what way Attic tragedy is created from these developments as a new art form, we must be absolutely faithful to Nietzsche's conception of the relationship between its Apollinian and Dionysian elements. "Everything that comes to the surface in the Apollinian part of Greek tragedy," Nietzsche judges, everything Dionysian expressed through dialogue, that is, "looks simple, transparent, and beautiful," "Homeric" in character for its "clarity and firmness," "lucidity" and "precision."[46] Undoubtedly, in Nietzsche's estimation Attic tragedy is unique for its ability to raise an aesthetic receptivity to being to an aesthetically unprecedented degree of insight and understanding, and it appears to do so as a consequence of the cognitive position the Apollinian occupies in relation to the Dionysian. In the aesthetic form of Attic tragedy there is no compromise between the Apollinian and Dionysian, as there was with the Dionysian Greek festival, according to which the art and thought of Homeric culture appeared to relate to the world ambiguously. Nor is there the utter sacrifice of the Dionysian to the Apollinian, as we will see occur with the death of Attic tragedy. With Dionysus played by a tragedian speaking and acting the part, the nonimagistic Dionysian is at the outset of the drama *already present* in an imagistic, Apollinian form, joining the Apollinian and Dionysian together in a symbiotic relationship. The Apollinian is not representational in any conventional semiotic sense, let us say, as a signifier standing in abstractly for its referent, the visionary god Dionysus. In the symbiotic manner in which it is joined with the Dionysian, I am arguing, the Apollinian's representational capacity is *itself transformed* in relation to the Dionysian transfiguration that occurs through music. This double metamorphosis is suggested by Nietzsche's contention that when Attic tragedy made the attempt "to show the god as real," it was able to "represent the visionary figure *together with its transfiguring frame*."[47]

Nietzsche is inviting us to imagine the Apollinian representation of a Dionysian transfiguration, or the way in which identity, the images and concepts it produces, is *itself transformed* through aesthetic receptivity to nature. Identity ceases to be inadequately representative of being, as it was in lyric poetry and the earlier Dionysian form of tragedy. And as a result identity ceases to be related to nature as a subject in opposition to an object, as a self fearing for its preservation against hostile forces surrounding it. For at the moment their Dionysian transfiguration provides all those present, who in an enraptured state believe the tragedian representing the god to be the figure of Dionysus, with a glimpse into "the inside and terrors of nature," the aesthetic experience produces an explosion of "bright image projections."[48] "Bright image projections" are insights that redeem the Dionysian experience by healing the Hellene of the fear of a terrifying nature. In Nietzsche's words, they are "luminous spots to cure eyes damaged by gruesome night." Representation has crystallized in the cognitive space lying between the two extremes, on the one side, of Apollinian images as they would be if they were uninformed by the aesthetic receptivity to nature provided by the Dionysian, and, on the other, a Dionysian experience entirely void of representation, as it would be if it were direct and unmediated by the Apollinian principle of individuation.

Within this cognitive middle ground, as I would call it, neither is there a purely conceptual apprehension of the sort associated with formal reason, where nature in its essence is presumed to be known or knowable, nor is there a purely visceral awareness of nature that never rises to a conceptual level. Rather, as Nietzsche explains, what the Apollinian knows through the Dionysian, what thinking through its bright image projections knows of nature, in other words, "is in the last analysis nothing but a bright image projected on a dark wall, which means appearance through and through." By providing an appearance of nature as it is in-itself, Attic tragedy pushes the Apollinian beyond the mere constructions of nature it invents in response to the terrors nature is believed to threaten, though it does not then capture the essence of nature as it exists prior to all representation. Or if we put it in the terms in which Adorno later will express it in his *Aesthetic Theory* when, like Nietzsche, he formulates the relationship between art and nature, Attic tragedy represents the "appearance" of an "essence."[49] Attic tragedy provides for a form of representation that recognizes that the innermost ground of being is unknown and fathomless, the province of appearance only. Recognizing that nature is essentially different from its image in art and in thought, and not the terror the Apollinian had with certainty previously taken it to be, the Apollinian is freed of its fear of nature and thinking is freed of the need to impose on nature a form representing it as other than it is.

Enlightenment is now aesthetic. By means of the collaboration between the Apollinian and the Dionysian, Attic tragedy teaches that identity can overreach the limits of individuation to become receptive to nature without fear that identity and individuation would be lost to the world. Through art, individuals whose identities rest upon illusions built on the image of a terrifying nature have an experience of being, a Dionysian transfiguration, which suspends the limits of their identities by means of a "*symbolic intuition* of Dionysian universality," of being's "countless forms of existence."[50] Identity now is oriented inclusively to the diversity of differences that constitute being's universality, which previously it had concealed beneath the Apollinian forms it had imposed upon nature. At the same time, the very emergence of this Apollinian intuition into the universality of being proves that the identity through which the intuition is expressed symbolically in "images and concepts" is not contrary to an experience of the world exceeding the limits of individuation. Aesthetically transfigured, no longer would the Hellene be disciplined by an Apollinian identity creating illusions alienating him from his own aesthetic nature as from nature, illusions whose false image of nature he was "completely wrapped up in" and "composed of" and compelled to accept as "waking reality."[51] Out of its recognition of the unknown, that nature is essentially different from any way in which it appears to art or to thought, an insight unavailable to the purely formal reasoning of Apollinian thought unaided by the Dionysian, Attic tragedy thus banishes the Hellene's fear of a terrifying nature by integrating an aesthetic rationality that Homeric culture earlier had hierarchically subordinated to a dominant Apollinian ethos. Attic tragedy demonstrates that Nietzsche's interest lies in an aesthetic relation to the world that would abolish our alienation from nature through an individuality whose receptivity to being would reconstitute while preserving identity, allowing the self to be in possession of itself while being enlightened.[52] With this in mind, we see that it is correct to speak of Attic tragedy as a model of an ideal form of aesthetic individuality, or, precisely speaking, of an openness to the world through which identity can become different without either loss of individuation or sacrifice to the inner organization of individuality of its aesthetic receptivity.

In essence, Nietzsche demonstrates that by integrating the Apollinian and Dionysian into a single art form, Attic tragedy accomplishes for art what at an implicit level of analysis Horkheimer and Adorno accomplish for thought. Perhaps we would do well to appreciate the similarity of these accomplishments by paraphrasing Horkheimer and Adorno's observation that ending enlightenment's "denial of nature in man" will end the "distortion" in the "telos of man's own life" and the "distortion" in the "telos of the outer control of nature." For Nietzsche, Attic tragedy similarly ends Homeric culture's denial of an aesthetic receptivity to being in order to avoid the "distortion" in the "inner nature of art" and the distorted image of a threatening nature, from which the Apollinian impulse to mastery arose in the Homeric period to be expressed in the birth of the Olympians. Now turning this analogy around, we infer that by avoiding the subordination to self-identity of an aesthetic receptivity to being, Attic tragedy serves as a model of an ideal form of rationality able to avoid the distortion in the inner nature of thought by integrating formal and aesthetic reason, which Horkheimer and Adorno's concept of aesthetic individuality requires. And as a model of an ideal of aesthetic rationality, Attic tragedy likewise serves as a model for how reason might eliminate the distortion in the outward domination of nature resulting from the inner hegemony of formal reason. Surely, from the analogies thus far uncovered, it seems as though Horkheimer and Adorno had in mind a concept of aesthetic individuality that corresponds to the concept of an aesthetic receptivity to being, of aesthetic enlightenment, that Nietzsche discovers in Attic tragedy. And it does not appear less certain that Horkheimer and Adorno's concept of aesthetic individuality stands in the same relation to enlightenment and modernity as Nietzsche's concept of art stands in relationship to the culture of Homeric Greece. Though not only to Homeric Greece, as we will now see.

If the analogies between *The Birth of Tragedy* and *Dialectic of Enlightenment* were at this point exhausted, I believe there could be little if any doubt that Horkheimer and Adorno conceptualize individuality aesthetically. What question yet remains may be dispelled by looking to Nietzsche's text for an analogy that, while continuing to clarify the aesthetic dimensions of their concept of individuality, further establishes its role as a normative model and ideal that deepens our understanding of the process of enlightenment's catastrophic path. Such an analogy also produces a more complete picture of the extent to which the aesthetics of Attic tragedy flesh out the conceptual dimensions of aesthetic individuality and the way they circulate critically at an implicit level of analysis throughout the entirety of Horkheimer and Adorno's argument.

Analogy from "Aesthetic Socratism:" Socratic Reason and Enlightenment as "Murderous Principles"

With the plays of Euripides, Nietzsche charges, the ideal epoch of Attic tragedy that appeared fleetingly through the dramas of Sophocles and Aeschylus is summarily ended. As though his intention were to return to the aesthetics of late Homeric Greece when the Apollinian and the Dionysian were opposing forces, Euripides attempts to base tragedy exclusively on the Apollinian, albeit unsuccessfully, Nietzsche adds. Tragedy was hollowed out, reconstructed on the foundation of an "un-Dionysian art," meaning that music was eliminated from drama along with its Dionysian effects. Yet, purging the Dionysian elements of tragedy, Nietzsche explains, only makes it impossible for Euripides "to attain the Apollinian effect of the epos."[53] Alienated "as much as possible" from the Dionysian, the Apollinian cannot emerge as "bright image projections" of our experience of nature. Without an aesthetic receptivity to nature, without an aesthetic transfiguration at the Dionysian level, there can be no comparable Apollinian transformation that produces enlightened conceptual understandings of our relationship to being. For Nietzsche's purposes, Euripides' plays appear to be less important than the deeper, more disturbing cultural tendencies his work expresses.

Tragedy's real nemesis is what Nietzsche refers to as "aesthetic Socratism," an ironic term he invents to convey his impression of the Socratic influence on

Euripides' plays, which he holds responsible for the aesthetic principle at work in Euripidean tragedy. Following the principle "'to be beautiful everything must be intelligible,'" as the poet of *"aesthetic Socratism"* Euripides compensates for the loss of the Dionysian by allowing the subjectivity of the individual's own emotions to replace its transfiguring effects.[54] And he subverts tragedy's Apollinian enlightenment by introducing a dramatic "prologue" that converts the drama at its outset into a reflection of what the dramatist already knows subjectively to be true prior to any further aesthetic experience offered by the play. Once the familiarity of the individual's own emotions substitutes for the Dionysian transfiguration, and the prologue answers all questions in advance of the possibility of new insights and understandings, "beauty as intelligibility" leaves identity unchallenged and individuation intact. In the light of Nietzsche's analysis, the aesthetics of tragedy under the impact of Socratic reason begin to resemble Horkheimer and Adorno's concept of formal rationality when it has completely subdued an aesthetic receptivity to nature through the inner organization of individuality. As aesthetic Socratism formal rationality appears in the guise of art, affirming the primacy of the subject by privileging subjectivity's emotions and understandings exactly as art and reason finds them. Subjectivity is the first and also final standpoint from which the world and our relationship to it is interpreted, so that through identity's imposition on the world the world can be nothing different from our thought of it.

It is entirely in keeping with the intent of Nietzsche's critique of tragedy to draw out this initial similarity to Horkheimer and Adorno's critique of enlightenment. For as Nietzsche continues it becomes evident that his interest in aesthetic Socratism turns more precisely toward Socratic reason as the un-Dionysian worldview responsible for the death of Hellenic culture's aesthetic receptivity to nature and being, of which Attic tragedy is but one victim. Indeed, for Nietzsche Socratic reason is not different in its essential elements from those Horkheimer and Adorno discovered in formal reason at the metaphysical stage of the historical development of thought. Nietzsche attacks the "conceit of knowledge," the "profound illusion that first saw the light of the world in the person of Socrates," that "unshakable faith that thought, using the *thread of logic*, can penetrate the deepest abysses of being" and "is capable not only of *knowing being* but even of *correcting* it."[55] Nietzsche's claim recalls Horkheimer and Adorno's argument that enlightenment knows nature by making the world *known* through a *logic of equivalency* that converts the diversity of nature's differences into a uniform material throughout susceptible to *mastery*.

Not until Nietzsche draws our attention to Socratic reason's missing reflective capacity, however, do we truly recognize how closely it resembles enlightenment rationality as it is presented in *Dialectic of Enlightenment*. Nor until we reach this point do we fully understand the extent to which Nietzsche's position on this issue perfectly clarifies Horkheimer and Adorno's interest in enlightenment as well. The "logical urge that became manifest in Socrates,"

Nietzsche insists, "was absolutely prevented from turning against itself."⁵⁶ Once the Dionysian is expelled from tragedy by aesthetic Socratism, the Apollinian is forced into a Socratic "cocoon of logical schematism," preventing Euripides from attaining "the Apollinian effect of the epos." All the changes accruing to tragedy by virtue of aesthetic Socratism, in other words, have undermined the possibility of an aesthetic reflection that by representing being as appearance leaves it unknown and fathomless. Offering an aesthetically enlightened comprehension of nature, we saw, Attic tragedy's "bright image projections" register the essential opacity of world and nature and being in the space that emerges between the Apollinian and the Dionysian when neither aesthetic impulse prevails over the other in the least. Without an aesthetic reflection on the difference between thought and being teaching that being exceeds and is necessarily different from our every thought of it, Socratic reason cannot but pursue its project of mastery—of "correcting" being—unchecked by an understanding that contradicts its mistaken belief that the meaning of being "can be fathomed."⁵⁷

Death of tragedy by aesthetic Socratism is thus symptomatic of "the enormous driving-wheel of logical Socratism . . . in motion, as it were, *behind* Socrates," and which "must be viewed through Socrates as through a shadow."⁵⁸ What Nietzsche has done, then, is to uncover a process of enlightenment that having sacrificed its aesthetic dimension and become unreceptive to the diversity of the world's differences, in his words, though Horkheimer and Adorno could have been speaking, can "spread over posterity like a shadow that keeps growing in the evening sun."⁵⁹ What began as a critique of Homeric Greece ends as a critique of modernity. "[N]ever again," Nietzsche reflects, though Horkheimer and Adorno could have been speaking here as well, will we "find any stimulus toward existence more violent than the craving to complete this conquest and to weave the net impenetrably tight."⁶⁰ Hence Nietzsche describes reason bereft of an aesthetic receptivity to being—the Apollinian "withdrawn into the cocoon of logical schematism," reason divorced from the "heart of the world," from the "innermost heart of things," "formal reason" in the words of Horkheimer and Adorno—as a "murderous principle."⁶¹

RECONCILIATION AND THE ALLIANCE BETWEEN KANT AND HEGEL, OR HEGEL WITHOUT THE ABSOLUTE, KANT WITHOUT THE SUPERSENSIBLE

Among the many ways in which *The Birth of Tragedy* clarifies Horkheimer and Adorno's critique of enlightenment, at this point the most important contribution we take away from our discussion is a more complete understanding of their concept of aesthetic individuality. As we read *Dialectic of Enlightenment* through the conceptual framework of Nietzsche's work, it seems evident that for Horkheimer and Adorno the distinction between individuality and subjectivity rests upon the presence or absence of an aesthetic dimension in thought. Attic tragedy and individuality, "bright image projections" and "enlightenment in possession of itself breaking the bounds of enlightenment," secure an aesthetic receptivity to nature and being, in a word, to a "world" (as I will now speak of nature and being) whose meaning is fathomless and in its fathomlessness exceeds every thought of it and infinitely so. Aesthetic individuality illuminates what enlightenment, formal reason, and subjectivity conceal, a great divide between the known world and the unknown world, a chasm that is, as Nietzsche's aesthetic demands, at bottom unbridgeable, and that for Horkheimer and Adorno as well as Nietzsche is the presupposition of the individual's aesthetic receptivity to the world. As a bottomless reservoir of meaning that lies always beyond the boundaries of art and thought, this chasm becomes individuality's impulse for an aesthetic recognition of the world and all the world contains as necessarily different from its appearance to which art and thought are confined. Everything the world contains that is encountered by individuality aesthetically becomes as fathomless as the world and thus a world unto itself, so that aesthetic individuality is receptive to fathomless worlds in their diversity rather than to one world. Yet, however certainly his thoughts resemble Horkheimer and Adorno's idea of an aesthetic form of individuality whose enlightened self-possession can break the bounds of enlightenment, Nietzsche appears to betray their conception in a decisive respect.

Nietzsche argues, we recall, that Attic tragedy produces Apollinian images that "condense" the Dionysian experience of being. As condensations, regardless of their luminosity, "precise" and "lucid" representations of the "essence of the world" never reproduce what art, through music, conveys that lies beneath the level of appearance on which conceptual representations are formed. Unique among the arts, music is able to provoke the deeper, nonsymbolic understandings that accompany tragedy "by representing *what is metaphysical*, the thing-in-itself (*das Ding an sich darstellt*)."[62] This "inmost" Kantian "kernel" that the Dionysian art of music reveals "*precedes all forms*," Nietzsche declares, and he illustrates his claim wonderfully by appealing to our own musical experiences, saying,

> whoever gives himself up entirely to the impression of a symphony, seems to see all the possible events of life and the world take place in himself; yet if he reflects, he can find no likeness between the music and the things that passed before his mind.[63]

Nietzsche hardly could be clearer. The difference between the world as it appears and the world as it is essentially is measured aesthetically by the cognitive distance between an understanding constructed in images, symbols, and concepts, that is, in thoughts, and one formed in the depths below this representational surface.

Despite his obvious clarity on this matter, Nietzsche still may be read as attributing to the Dionysian experience provoked by music a level of understanding typically associated with concepts by the Socratic standpoint he attacks. Occasionally Nietzsche encourages such misreading where he speaks, for example, about the Dionysian in tragedy as offering a "fundamental *knowledge (die Grunderkenntnis)* of the oneness of everything existent."[64] Or he may do so when he unwittingly embellishes the cognitive dimension of the Dionysian when suggesting, as in his discussion of lyric poetry, that it overcomes the unbridgeable divide between appearance and reality by enabling the lyric artist to become "at once subject and object."[65] Perhaps anticipating such interpretations of his work, Nietzsche seems more disposed to describe the Dionysian in noncognitive terms, speaking often of a "primordial relationship" forged by art between the "thing-in-itself" and "appearance" or of a "unification (*Einswerden*) with primal being."[66] Nevertheless, the cognitive status of the Dionysian experience is surrounded by sufficient ambiguity that Nietzsche's philosophically important remark that under its charm nature "celebrates once more her *reconciliation* with her lost son, man," may be taken to mean reconciliation that entails *conceptual* knowledge of essences.[67] To be sure, for Horkheimer and Adorno aesthetic reason does not reconcile individuality to the world in this ideal sense, and is opposed to such an ideal of reconciliation. Proceeding from the idea that being is fathomless, aesthetic rationality affirms the divide between the world as it appears and the world as it is, in-itself, through it sustaining a receptivity to being that would be foreclosed if reason knew the world essentially, as though at some point the world could be no different from our thought of it, which is formal reason's presupposition and arrogance.

When Horkheimer and Adorno distinguish their notion of aesthetic individuality from a receptivity to being that entails the ideal of reconciliation, it takes the form of their discussion of the "concept," an important argument that like others that serve as scaffolding for *Dialectic of Enlightenment* is woven through their text like a *leitmotiv*.[68] Reconciliation is problematized indirectly in their work through this discussion, and the parallels between *The Birth of Tragedy* and *Dialectic of Enlightenment* already drawn do not discourage speculation that their discussion of the "concept" in part may be a response to the way reconciliation is negotiated by Nietzsche. At the least, the relationship between reason and reconciliation in Nietzsche's text has established the context for their discussion of the "concept," which revolves around Kant and Hegel and completes their work on aesthetic individuality. By taking up their discussion of the "concept" in relationship to the notion of reconciliation we arrive at the sharpest articulation of the "concept" and of conceptual thinking's contribution to an understanding of individuality's aesthetic dimensions.

Beginning with Horkheimer and Adorno's simplest formulation, "concepts" are the products of thinking that is based on a "divisive function," one that enables thought to separate an idea from its object.[69] Throughout *Dialectic of Enlightenment* this principle is returned to often and expressed in a variety of ways. Perhaps they best capture its meaning where they compare the "concept" to the tool, which "is held on to in different situations as the same thing, and hence divides the world as the chaotic, manysided, and disparate from the known, one, and identical."⁷⁰ Conceptual divisiveness, in other words, introduces into thinking the understanding that the identity of what is being thought, how it is known or what it is called, does not correspond to what it really is. Horkheimer and Adorno's seemingly extravagant choice of the words "chaotic, manysided, and disparate" is their attempt to stress the utter simplicity of the "concept" in relation to the infinite diversity of the world it divides from thought. For all the divisiveness of conceptual thinking, which represents the world separated from thought at a distance from what as a whole it really is, the "concept" also is related to the world intimately. Through mimesis the division between thought and world is partially overcome and the object of thought is present in thinking in part as what it really is. Ultimately the mimetic property of thought must defer to thinking's divisive function, which is to say that by its nature the "concept" reflexively installs into thinking a separation from the world that thought is unable to transcend. To deny the divisiveness of thought is to adopt the position of formal reason and to disavow reflection. It is to expect that the world as it is in-itself can be known completely, and in the fulfillment of this expectation to pursue an illusion of reconciliation through which the world believed to be well known is simply the identity of the little known *projected* upon the unknown. Whatever in the world is different from and nonidentical with any thought of it takes on the identity imposed upon it. By maintaining a consistently divisive sense of the world as different from thought, and orienting thinking aesthetically toward the world as composed of a diversity of differences whose difference is tacitly recognized in any "concept," conceptual thinking is contrary to reconciliation, which in contrast appears as an expression of formal thinking's impulse to mastery.

Although the foundation for Horkheimer and Adorno's idea of the "concept," this formulation as it stands too strictly distinguishes conceptual from nonconceptual thought, aesthetic from formal reason. "In a certain sense," Horkheimer and Adorno add, "*all* perception is projection."⁷¹ All thought contains formal elements that make thinking the cognitive work of an individual who is able to "bridge the gulf" between the "undisputed data of the senses" and the "true object" (the object of thought as it really is), "between within and without."⁷² "Unconsciously conceptual elements," as Horkheimer and Adorno refer to thinking's formal elements, organize the data of perception and enable the individual to create "the world outside himself from the traces which it leaves in his senses."⁷³ Kant's notion of transcendental apperception is thus introduced to suggest that the unity of consciousness through which knowledge of the world becomes possible deprives the "concept" of any innocence of imposing form on the world, and in fact recognizes that very function as belonging to the "concept" intrinsically. At the same time, however, their Kantian formulation of the "concept" restores its divisive function by recognizing that in conceptual thinking there is a distinction made by the individual, who has the external world in its own consciousness and yet recognizes it as something other. Therefore reflection, the life of reason, takes place as *conscious* projection.[74]

Both of the earlier described mimetic and divisive properties of conceptual thinking are now incorporated into Horkheimer and Adorno's notion of "conscious projection," their term for Kant's understanding of reflection.[75] Mimesis is embodied in the way thinking relates intimately to the world in the form of conceptual projections that unify and identify the perceptual "traces" apprehension lifts from all that the world contains. Divisiveness appears in the way thinking distinguishes the conceptual records of traces of the world from the world itself, so that in this enlightened self-consciousness of thinking's projections there always will be thought of more world and thus of an unknown world apart from the world's tracings imprinted in its conceptual outline. Through Kant, Horkheimer and Adorno's "concept" emerges as the tragic element in thought, and in a way not unlike Nietzsche's idea of tragedy. In the act of reflection thinking reestablishes our connection to nature while aesthetically affirming our *irreconcilable separation* from nature at the same moment. To think conceptually means individuality's aesthetic relation to nature is our nature. To be a part of nature is to be apart from nature.

What philosophical support for the "concept" Horkheimer and Adorno marshal from Kant in their estimation does not appear to be entirely adequate to the task of orienting thinking to the world aesthetically.[76] Although they do not argue the point explicitly, it seems that the idea of reflection they cull from Kant's work is precariously balanced on an epistemology that lends itself too readily to an instrumentalist theory of cognition. Where cognition forms its object through "concepts," it may not press beyond abstract representations of the world and conceptual thinking would be arrested. While this line of criticism would follow from their critique of the development of formal reason during the Enlightenment, it is established obliquely when Horkheimer and Adorno remark that the "task of cognition does not consist in mere apprehension, classification, and calculation."[77] Where it is reduced to formal reason (mere apprehension), thinking ceases to be reflective and conscious projection (a conscious awareness of the difference between thought of the world and the world itself) disappears along with the disappearance of reflective thought upon which it depended. Conscious projection now becomes "false projection"—the world collapses into the unreflected projections of the world in thought, the unknown world is equated with the world as it is known, what is nonidentical with thought is equated with the identities thought projects upon it. Drawing out the consequences of false projection by substituting the "concept" of an object for the object itself, Horkheimer and Adorno write, objectifying thought "contains the despotism of the subjective purpose which is hostile to the thing and forgets the thing itself, thus committing the mental act of violence which is later put into practice."[78] And taking their critique of the pathology of formal reason one final step, they argue that in its despotic and violent imposition of the "concept" of an object on the object itself false projection resembles paranoia. Like paranoia, false projection takes root in that "abyss of uncertainty" that stretches between our thought of the world and the world as it really is, in the abyss that opens up in the great divide between the known and the unknown world that formal reason finds terrifying and that aesthetic, reflective thought acknowledges without attempting to cross. False projection is the thought of the paranoiac who "makes everything in his own image."[79] "Paranoia," Horkheimer and Adorno determine, is but "the dark side of cognition."[80]

So that reason neither will slip into the formalism of mere apprehension nor descend further into the pathological expressions of formal reason, Horkheimer and Adorno's Kantian formulation of the "concept" is corrected by means of Hegel's dialectic. This revision is anticipated early in *Dialectic of Enlightenment* and long before they enter into a discussion of Kant's "concept," when they recall that with "the notion of determinate negativity, Hegel revealed an element that distinguishes the Enlightenment from the positivist degeneracy to which he attributes it."[81] Determinate negativity, the activity of thought through which the self divides itself reflexively into subject and object, enables subjectivity to comprehend that self and other reciprocally constitute each other's identities, such that the boundaries of individual and world are each determined by the other. By producing a self-conscious understanding of how self and other are constituted in relation to each other, negativity ensures the division between self and world and the self-understanding that self-identity and self-development are relative to the differentiated forms self and other assume. For Horkheimer and Adorno, in other words, negativity enables individuality to affirm the existence of a *difference* between individual and world, and to understand that difference determines the identity of every "concept" in relation to every object, the identity of every self in relation to every other.

It is interesting that their discussion of determinate negativity appears within the context of a broader philosophical understanding of the history of thinking. As Horkheimer and Adorno at one point put it, for example, the

> concept, which some would see as the sign unit for whatever is comprised under it, has from the beginning been instead the product of dialectical thinking in which everything is always that which it is, only because it becomes that which it is not.[82]

Their phrase "from the beginning" should not be passed over in haste, because it implies a certain understanding of the history of thought consistent with their analysis of thinking from its preanimistic through metaphysical stage. From the beginning of thought the original form of thinking separated "concept" and thing, and is the "same form which is already far advanced in the Homeric epic and confounds itself in modern positivist science."[83] Dividing the individual from the world from its beginning, constituting the individual as what it is through a consciousness of what it is not, originally thinking negatively orients individuality to the world as that which exceeds every thought of it. What then exceeds thought becomes the essential property of an individuality whose own creative self-determinations depend upon such an aesthetic orientation to the world. Horkheimer and Adorno's specific mention of conceptual thought in the Homeric epic, where thinking's negative relation to the world finally is "neutralized and becomes art," supposes that conceptual thought along with individuality forms an aesthetic relation to the world that eventually is suspended while preserved in the work of art.

While Hegel offers Horkheimer and Adorno a formulation of the "concept" that improves upon Kant's by relating individuality to the world aesthetically in a way less hospitable to the incursions of formal reason, Hegel's "concept" is not unproblematic. Though determinate negativity is intended to rescue the Enlightenment from the degeneracy of positivism by grounding conceptual thought, by "ultimately making the conscious result of the whole process of negation—totality in system and in history—into an absolute," they argue, Hegel "contravened the prohibition" against reducing enlightenment to formal rationality.[84] "Absolute Knowing," Reason that recollects *in themselves* all the substantive forms that Reason assumed historically, as Hegel in the closing pages of his *Phenomenology of Spirit* explains, in Horkheimer and Adorno's estimation vitiates determinate negativity by anticipating the reconciliation of thought and world.[85] Individuality would be subdued by a subjectivity burdened with concepts mistakenly believed to render nature and world and being transparent. Although Hegel is guilty of reconciliation, he is so at best, while at worst his absolute suppression of negativity may be symptomatic of false projection and paranoia, though in the final analysis for Horkheimer and Adorno there may be no difference between what is best and what is worst. Each seems to be implied equally of Hegel's absolute by their analogy between "Hegel's idealism" and the "hallucinatory power" of thinking where the "subjective is blindly transferred . . . into the apparent obviousness of the object."[86]

Taking Kant and Hegel together, then, Horkheimer and Adorno further elaborate the idea of an individuality oriented to the world aesthetically by assembling philosophical arguments that revolve around the notion of the "concept." Through Hegel, Horkheimer and Adorno restore the element of thought that had receded in Kant's philosophy, a capacity for reflective awareness that recognizes an essential difference between individual and world that is necessarily reproduced in a division between every "concept" of the world and the world itself. With Kant, on the other hand, the idea of a world that is unknown and, irreconcilable with thought, finally unknowable, is secured against the cognitive imperialism of Hegel's absolute. Nevertheless, if through the alliance they forge between Kant and Hegel Horkheimer and Adorno amplify the position that there is a world beyond our every thought of it that is fathomless, and thus with which thought can never achieve reconciliation except as the illusion of formal reason, why do they not explicitly endorse the Kantian notion of the "thing-in-itself," which they adopt implicitly in the idea of the unknown?

Perhaps Hegel's rejection of Kant's supersensible realm may offer some insight on this matter. Hegel famously begins the Introduction to the *Phenomenology of Spirit* with a critique of Kant's epistemology where he concludes that the approach to cognition that it entails "certainly does not let [what truly is] be what it is for itself."[87] Kant's understanding of how we can know what we know, Hegel is arguing, does not relate truth to us in any meaningful way, but rather makes it "absurd" to believe that consciousness can secure for cognition what is true by persuading us that there is a "boundary" between knowing and truth. In my own argument, it is clear, I have tried to make the case in a variety of ways that Horkheimer and Adorno accept Kant's idea of a boundary between every thought of the world and the world that exceeds every thought of it. At the same time, I have argued that this great divide is at the very heart of their idea of an individuality that is related to the world aesthetically. What lies unknown and unknowable on the other side of this divide is thus not for Horkheimer and Adorno an inert or dead truth, as Hegel implies of Kant's supersensible realm. Unlike the thing-in-itself, Horkheimer and Adorno's Kantian-like "unknown" relates individuality to the world meaningfully, as to a meaningful world whose opacity conceals fathomless meaning that with all its depth opposes formal reason's illusions of transparency and mastery. To whatever extent formal reason knows the world, the unknown constitutes not so much a limit as an ultimate limit to formal rationality that does not hinder but fosters the ideal of maturity with which Kant defined enlightenment, and to which his own concept of the supersensible he did not take to be inimical.[88]

In view of their discussion of the "concept" we can understand more easily why Horkheimer and Adorno argue that individuality is transformed into subjectivity under the pressures of enlightenment. Individuality's aesthetic dimensions orient it toward the world in precisely the way conceptual thought is oriented toward the world, an orientation that is incompatible with mastery, the telos of enlightenment. Accordingly, like the "suspension of the concept," as Horkheimer and Adorno refer to the Enlightenment's positivist assault on thinking, the "inner organization of individuality" that coincides with the birth of the modern subject is only another cultural expression of the ascendancy of formal reason. Modernity's marriage to "technical civilization" has nurtured the universalization of formal rationality, which has overwhelmingly favored in individuality the suppression of the aesthetic receptivity to the fathomlessness of the world it also annuls in conceptual thought. As Horkheimer and Adorno put it, the "tendency to false projection," to the morbid, pathological expression of formal reason, "is so *fatefully present in the mind (dem Geiste)* that this isolated pattern of self-preservation [embodied in technical civilization] threatens to dominate everything which extends beyond it: all culture."[89] So in the aftermath of the Enlightenment of modern times not only has aesthetic individuality been utterly sacrificed to subjectivity, but there appears to be no form of conceptual thought that can survive the attack waged upon it by formal reason. Horkheimer and Adorno find historical evidence for this thesis in the destruction of the Jews.

AESTHETIC INDIVIDUALITY AND THE DESTRUCTION OF THE JEWS

Surely one of the most compelling arguments of *Dialectic of Enlightenment*, Horkheimer and Adorno tie the fate of aesthetic rationality to the fate of Judaism in their analysis of Judaism's relationship to reconciliation. "In the Jewish religion," they explain, "the connection (*das Band*) between name and being is still recognized in the ban on pronouncing the name of God."[90] All the elements of thought associated with the "concept" are contained in Judaism. As the Judaic God is being as such, the prohibition on naming God moves God beyond the reach of thought and into the unknown, and through God moves being into the unknown as well. With the opacity of being a reflection of an imageless God extending beyond the horizon of thought, the essential division between thinking and being, the nonidentity of being, is affirmed. Moreover, the idea of being as the unknown represented by an unknown God is reinforced through the absence in Judaism of any thought of an afterlife, as Horkheimer and Adorno argue by saying that "Jewish religion allows of no word that would alleviate the despair of all that is mortal."[91] For Judaism, the "entire meaning" of reconciliation is "expectation," which means not that messianic salvation is guaranteed at some time in the future, however indefinite. Rather, as an event that is endlessly deferred but always waited upon, salvation installs an unbridgeable distance between the finite and infinite that encourages discontent with finite existence while orienting us toward possibilities for its amelioration without any hope of complete fulfillment, without hope for reconciliation, that is. For Horkheimer and Adorno, Judaism orients thinking toward the idea of being as a continually unfinished project unfolding within a space of time that traces into the infinity of the unknown the diversity of forms being can assume. Judaism consequently embodies the aesthetic elements of individuality and conceptual thought they shield from formal reason through their alliance between Kant and Hegel.

Judaism's embodiment of all that is unknown, or nonidentical and irreconcilable with thought, is placed into sharp relief when viewed in the context of Horkheimer and Adorno's critique of Christianity, which is distinguished from Judaism in a way that provides a key to the religious origins of anti-Semitism and the destruction of the Jews. In the image of Jesus Christianity endows God with a human face and calls God by a human name, and through Jesus Christ God dies a human death—"progress over Judaism is purchased with the claim that the man Jesus has become God," Horkheimer and Adorno argue. By allowing the individual to "find his own reflection in the deity," Christianity replaces the imageless God of the Jews to contrive a "*reconciliation* of civilization with nature" that erases thinking's "horror" of the unknown symbolized by the Judaic God and on which Jewish difference comes to rest.[92] As the unknown, Jewish difference represents the threat to self-preservation that unknown nature poses, and it is the fear of Jewish difference in this sense in which Christian anti-Semitism is rooted, a conclusion Horkheimer and Adorno draw by saying, with the German Christians in mind, that "the adherents of the religion of the Father are hated by those who support the religion of the Son."[93]

Fascism is similarly related to the image of Jewish difference as the representation of the unknown. In Horkheimer and Adorno's words, to the Fascist the Jew is the "negative principle as such."[94] Whatever else drives Fascism, then, its destruction of the Jews must be understood as an expression of the same impulse toward nature that animates the historical process of enlightenment, the impulse to "false projection" that eliminates what is different from thought by making "the environment like itself."[95] Fascism emerges as a necessary expression of formal reason, the child of enlightenment. Indeed, so fatefully is the extermination of the Jews a historical expression of enlightenment's single-minded annihilation of difference, and inscribed in every stage of enlightenment that extends the dominion of formal reason, that Horkheimer and Adorno interpret the "Jewish Question" as the "turning point of history."

> By overcoming that sickness of mind which thrives on the ground of self-assertion untainted by reflective thought, mankind would develop from a set of opposing races to the species which, even as nature, is more than mere nature.[96]

"Overcoming that sickness of mind" would abolish the "Jewish Question," which as they conceptualize it here as the "turning point of history" becomes the "question of difference." "Overcoming that sickness of mind" would rid the world of the holocaust of difference by overcoming reason as a "murderous principle"—overcoming "subjectivity," the "unification of identity," the "inner organization of individuality," "formal reason," thinking void of an aesthetic dimension, unreflective, nonconceptual thinking, Reason, "false projection," "paranoia," in a word, *enlightenment*. To rid the world of holocaust would first be to "liberate thought from domination," Horkheimer and Adorno are saying, *to liberate individuality's aesthetic receptivity to difference* that historically has been dominated by the formal elements in thought. Still, to liberate thought from domination supposes an "enlightenment which is in possession of itself and coming to power can break the bounds of enlightenment."

In the wake of the destruction of the Jews, Horkheimer and Adorno find in modernity neither signs of an aesthetic individuality that is able to mount resistance to formal reason nor sources for its coming to power. With the Enlightenment of modern times, Odysseus has arrived home in Ithaca and what contingent possibilities existed for aesthetic receptivity to the world have long since disappeared. All that remains in the present as a reminder of the past are the possibilities defended abstractly by the mere *idea* of the "concept," which anchors the "intransigence of theory in the face of the insensibility with which society allows thought to ossify," and an aesthetic sensibility preserved by art through which we are able to recollect the violent history of its own making to which it is not yet inured.[97] If the Jews could be "wiped from the face of the earth," who by virtue of their imageless, unknown God, other than the "intransigence of theory," represented the most obstinate source of resistance to domination by calling into question everything for which enlightenment stood, then the struggle within thought is ended and formal reason goes uncontested.[98] Even liberal democracy, which in its early stages at least, according to the terms of their analysis, Horkheimer and Adorno might have construed to hold some promise of resistance to enlightenment, only displays an ambiguity in the rationality of its practices that in every instance is resolved in favor of the logic of formal reason. Blind to what promise in democracy there may have been for an aesthetic receptivity to the world, an intransigent theory is left only with the concept of aesthetic individuality confined to art. Odysseus, unafraid, is enchanted by the unknown, receptive to being in a way he believes endangers his way of being. Bound to the mast of his ship to experience the Sirens' song, Odysseus signals to his men to release him. He is ignored, the moment passes "without consequence for him," and his temptation "is neutralized and becomes a mere object of contemplation—becomes art." With its aesthetic receptivity to the world having taken the form of art before it could develop further, perhaps to resemble more fully its ideal aesthetic form, individuality becomes the province of aesthetic theory, from which the philosophical basis for the concept of aesthetic individuality now must be recovered.

FIVE

RECOVERING AESTHETIC INDIVIDUALITY FROM ART: AESTHETIC REASON IN ADORNO'S AESTHETIC THEORY

In *Dialectic of Enlightenment*, the "progress" for which modernity is indebted to formal reason becomes its fate, a fate that is unaltered by the defeat of Fascism. As enlightenment, progress weaves the fate of the modern world out of the fabric of a social order whose logic over time has become indistinguishable from formal reason. Fate is moored deeply in a modern social order that is erected through the process of enlightenment to quell thinking's original fear of the unknown, from which the threat to self-preservation and the imperative of formal rational order first arose to infringe on individuality's aesthetic nature. Modernity emerges as the historical realization of a principle of formal reason that always had been so "fatefully present in the mind," as Horkheimer and Adorno wrote. Modernity is that culture of self-preservation in which enlightenment culminated, enabling formal reason to dominate: through formal reason modernity becomes fated as a culture of domination.

Whatever kind of civilization modernity may be, then, before everything else it is a civilization of certainty whose rationality is wholly absorbed in the illusion of reconciliation flowing from the belief that the world ultimately is transparent to thought. And the knowledge of the unknown sought after with ruthless single-mindedness by the civilization of certainty is guaranteed by a logic of equivalency that knows the world not as it is, in-itself, but in terms of identities that reason projects upon it, which are the illusory images formal reason consistently substitutes for the essence of the world it pursues but that lies forever beyond its reach. At best, the illusory identities formal reason projects convert the world into an object of mastery. At worst, the world in its infinite diversity of differences becomes a victim of the cruelty, violence, and barbarism that inheres deeply in thought. To modernity's cultural illusion of reconciliation, which as it is created and sustained by formal reason subdues the world through the false projections of "identifying thought (*identifizierendem Denken*)" or "identitarian thinking (*Identitätsdenken*)," Horkheimer and Adorno oppose another principle of reason.[1] Timelessly preserved as art in Horkheimer and Adorno's interpretation of Odysseus's encounter with the Sirens, and fleshed out conceptually by uncovering analogies between *Dialectic of Enlightenment* and *The Birth of Tragedy*, aesthetic rationality reappears in Adorno's *Negative Dialectics* as thinking that can do justice to the world only "negatively." The world *is* what it is *not* thought to be. It is essentially what is essentially different from thought.

To judge from his critique, Habermas is most acutely aware of the global threat that the work that followed from Adorno's collaboration with Horkheimer presents to social and political thought. Negative dialectics, Habermas complains, the only remaining theoretical approach that Adorno's critique of reason leaves open, is "a path that cannot be traversed discursively." If theoretical discourse is mired in the formal rational thinking of the modern subject, as Adorno alleges, theory could not hope to rationally redeem the objective standards of judgment needed to answer Habermas's question "How can we explicate the idea of reconciliation (*Versöhnung*)?"[2] Reconciliation, disguising a universal will to domination for Adorno, becomes a utopian goal, but one to which reason in good faith no longer can aspire.[3]

Were it Adorno's intention to undermine not merely this utopian element in thought but theoretical discourse itself, Habermas could not be faulted. Theoretical discourse, as well as the concept of reconciliation, would be endangered, as he suggests. Habermas, however, is only partly correct. As with Hegel, for Adorno philosophical thought begins when the world is divided. Unlike Hegel, and Habermas, Adorno does not look to reason to heal a divided world. It is Adorno's unique contribution to want to emancipate thought from all such missionary undertakings as are represented by the idealism of Hegel's absolute and Habermas's theory of communicative action. To free thought of the obligation to envision reconciliation would be to free those who are divided within and from the world of the identities imposed upon them by the images and ideals conceived to reconcile different forms of life, different forms of being. In particular, it is the world of Jewish difference that Adorno seeks to protect from the representations of identifying thought, because Jewish difference is the last line of defense against formal reason's will to the extinction of all difference. If formal reason can extinguish the "negative principle as such," which Judaism embodies, no form of difference can withstand the onslaught of formal rationality. Adorno would emancipate the Jew not, however, as does Marx in "On the Jewish Question," from the need for political emancipation so that a complete, *human* emancipation would be won.[4] For such an emancipation abolishes the difference distinguishing Judaism. Rather, Adorno would emancipate Jew and non-Jew alike from identity as such, from all that within thought suppresses the identity of each. For Adorno, the "Jewish Question," which in *Dialectic of Enlightenment*, I proposed, becomes the "question of difference," the question of the "identity of difference," would "prove in fact to be the turning point of history."[5] It would mark the end, *not of theoretical discourse*, as Habermas fears, but of the violence in all thinking that pursues the illusion of reconciliation.

Negative dialectics, then, leaves us with but one way to contend with the problem of reconciliation. For the violence its solutions may entail, "explicating the idea of reconciliation" is a problematic negative dialectics forbids us to conceptualize. From this we can see why Habermas takes Adorno to be waging war on theoretical discourse.⁶ Since negative dialectics is concerned with what we must *not* want to know, the reconciliatory impulse in every cognitive act, knowing an object as it is, in-itself, seems to invite the hostility of negative dialectics toward all discursive thought. Refusing to abandon the project of enlightenment, determined to salvage the rational content of modernity, Habermas's strategy is to lay negative dialectics to waste by ensnaring Adorno's argument in an epistemological paradox. If reason has become inescapably identitarian, as Adorno insists, and negative dialectics disproves not the more limited possibility of discovering solutions to a problem that masks a will to power but the entire possibility of theoretical discourse, as Habermas contends, then Adorno cannot rely upon philosophical discourse to ground his critique of reason. To do so would implicate Adorno in what Habermas describes as a "self-referential" or "totalizing" critique that attacks the very basis—reason—of its own validity. Either Adorno's claim against reason must remain ungrounded, and consequently one of the "subjectivistic premises" from which Habermas wants to sever rationality, or were it to be rationally grounded it ironically would prove reason innocent of Adorno's charges. In either event, Habermas insists, without philosophical foundations negative dialectics "renounces its theoretical claim while operating within the means of theory."⁷

As Adorno stressed in *Negative Dialectics*, although this work implies a critique of the concept of foundations, negative dialectics undermines neither theoretical discourse nor its own discursive justification. To the contrary, "what *would be* the foundation, according to the governing conception of philosophy," Adorno promises, "will be developed long after the author has discussed things of which that view assumes that they grow out of a foundation."⁸ Adorno alludes dismissively to the preoccupation with foundations as a "game" he refuses "to play." He will not be forced back into the mode of thought that the entirety of his work is meant to indict. He would not permit the validity of his argument to rest on whether it can avoid a paradox, as though, like Oedipus, he cannot find his way without first solving riddles. Adorno knows, too, that foundations only untrouble thought about its deeper implications, specifically those exposed by a critique of formal reason's interest in reconciliation.

Adorno formally provides justification for negative dialectics, to be "developed long after" the work by that name, in his *Aesthetic Theory*.⁹ Another of his works, *Philosophy of Modern Music*, contributes as well, though, and must be considered in any attempt to arrive at a complete understanding of Adorno's aesthetics. Adorno thinks of art as the embodiment of reason, as its "objectification (*vergegenstandlichten Geistes*)." By this he means that art is representational precisely because every work of art is mediated by reason through aesthetic form. With this formulation art and aesthetic theory can be related as a series of "reflections." An embodiment of reason, art holds up a mirror that reflects an image of reason. As such a reflection, reason can be studied through the study of works of art. The study of reason as the study of art is precisely what Adorno holds aesthetic theory to be.[10] Through theoretical and philosophical concepts the image of reason in art, reason in its *aesthetic* form, is then mediated "by reflection a second time (*von der Reflexion ein zweites Mal*)"—aesthetic theory is the reflection of a reflection.[11] Reflecting how reason functions *within* the artwork during the process of aesthetic representation, aesthetic theory, like art, stands *outside* of formal rational, identifying thought, enabling reason to be "traversed discursively," to recall Habermas's terms, justifying the totalizing critique of reason without attacking the presuppositions of its own argument. Aesthetic theory is a discursive reflection on aesthetic reason and its representational vicissitudes. It is a reflection that beginning again where the failures of reconciliation leave off, returns through art to teach each of us separately or together how to think and act in relation to the world, and all the worlds within it, that our reason would take as its object. Adorno's aesthetic theory clarifies what it means to be receptive to the world aesthetically. It clarifies the meaning of aesthetic reason, the philosophical basis for the concept of aesthetic individuality to be developed in the chapters that follow, which will further develop the features belonging to the concept of aesthetic individuality formulated in the previous chapters.

THE AESTHETICS OF DARKNESS

Into the Unknown is a remarkable sculpture by Hermon MacNeil that sits in Brookgreen Gardens, Murrell Inlet, South Carolina, among four hundred other works by nineteenth- and twentieth-century American sculptors. Surrounded by twenty-three acres seamlessly blending art and nature, it depicts a female seraph on bended knee, a chisel held tightly in her raised left hand, its sharp end pressed firmly against a marble slab, as is her left arm and the entire left side of her body, to provide a brace for the blow she is poised to strike with her right hand. Her right hand grips a hammer that is dropped below her waist and behind her back, positioned to be swept upward in an arclike motion and then forward, driving the chisel into the stone. We await not only an artistic creation but creation, for the sculpture is an epiphany, the divine is present. And it is "being" that the divine creates, or, what is the same for the creator, the *vision* or *image* representing being, a point that is made emphatically by the mere fact that the creation of being is represented both *in* a work of art and *as* a work of art—a sculpture of a "sculpture." *Into the Unknown* brings us to that moment when being-in-itself will be presented as it is represented for the first time, when that which is unknown will be known and reconciled with the identity it will be given. Yet, the sculpture urges us only toward the *expectation* of reconciliation, in the sense in which Horkheimer and Adorno conceptualize expectation, as we notice that the face of our divine sculptress is flush with the stone.[12] Cruelly, she is made to look eternally into darkness and is denied a vision of being-in-itself, now inaccessible to representation and to remain forever fathomless, "different" from our every thought of how being could have been created. Taking itself as

Into the Unknown, Hermon Atkins MacNeil

its object, art thus sees that it cannot see, knows that it cannot know. It teaches that the idea of reconciliation is an illusion. And what follows from this most important lesson, the sculptor's tools that would present being as it is, in-itself, through its representation, are forever suspended—nature, world, and being, "difference" is left alone. It is as though *Into the Unknown* stands guard, a sentry posted to divert our attention from nature and whose charge it is to teach us how to see the world in which art is situated. Art is a missionary from a world of darkness unseen and unknown.

It is this uniquely reflexive capacity of art that Adorno believes distinguishes it from all thought in modernity, where reason has been reduced to formal reason. Art's superiority to every kind of cognitive expression lies in its power to teach that the idea of reconciliation is an illusion. In every instance thought and speech ineluctably entail the imposition of form, of identity, on difference that suffers violence through cognitive acts necessarily inadequate to the task of representation. Thought cannot escape what Adorno, with a tragic sense, describes as a "universal delusive context"—the prison that *all* thought constructs and carries with it in every attempt to move beyond its limitations. As Adorno concludes in *Negative Dialectics*, critical thought must turn even against *itself*. By *denying* the possibility of reconciliation, we learn from Adorno's work on aesthetics, art turns against thought, against critique. In the modern world, art alone breaks the spell of enlightenment by grounding an aesthetic rationality constraining subject and object, human being and being, to live in benign coexistence. How is it that art accomplishes what thought can only imagine?

Beauty and the Unknown

This question leads us directly to Adorno's understanding of art's relationship to nature. Nature is opaque to art. But what of beauty? Does art not portray the beauty of nature and in so doing represent, if not nature, then one of nature's most essential qualities? Through the portrayal of the beautiful in nature as the quality of loveliness or as other qualities that bring pleasure to the senses or exalt the human spirit, art envelops nature in a mystique. This mystique is not nature's beauty, as though beauty were a property belonging objectively to nature. It is, rather, one way in which art captures nature's foreignness, strangeness, unknownness. Beauty, as Adorno conceives of it, is one possible way that art intimates the "nonidentity (*Nichtidentischen*)" of nature. Deciphering art's power to articulate nature's nonidentity is the most serious challenge posed by Adorno's aesthetics, one that can be met by examining his conception of beauty, as well as his concepts of trace, rationality and mimesis, spirit, and expression, each of which will be taken up shortly. For now, we acknowledge this power to articulate nature's nonidentity as art's advantage over words. Words, Adorno insists by comparison, "may glance off nature and betray its language to one that is qualitatively different from its own."[13] Nature cannot be said to *be* beautiful, except, perhaps, in an inchoate and ephemeral way, meaning that we cannot deny there are sunny days in southern countries waiting to be taken notice of. Adorno does not deny our ordinary pleasures, only that they can be justified as pleasures taken in a nature presumed to be knowable.

By nonidentity, Adorno does not mean that nature or being has no identity. Such an argument would leave us stranded, without any reference point to fix our relationship to nature. Rather, Adorno consistently uses nonidentity to refer to nature, being, or the world and all it contains as having identities that cannot be known, because identity is always different from the ways it can be represented by thought. Since beauty, to return to our first example, alludes to nature as nonidentical, as unknowable, as with other representations of being it offers us no principles, save one, through which to regulate our interactions with nature. So long as we do not know what nature is in-itself, and this we can never know, we cannot be reconciled to nature. We can live with nature on its own terms, coexist with nature, if we leave nature be, that is, forbear from inquiring into what those essential terms are.

Art is not simply a language denying the possibility of reconciliation. It is also a language of domination, even having an affinity with death. By imposing an ideal form of beauty on aesthetic objects outside the artwork, which Adorno refers to all inclusively as the "living manifold," "art 'works on' things, it represses them." Art's idealization of this living manifold subjects it to its own laws, proving fatal for aesthetic objects, since Adorno considers such representation to be a violent effacement of being. With this Adorno distinguishes his "nonidentical" conception of beauty from that of classical German aesthetics, notably of Kant and Schiller. The latter concept, which he describes as an illusory, unblemished (*ungetrübten*) beauty, creates the impression that the absolute is present in art. To put it differently, and this goes to the experience each of us has had with great art during especially rapturous moments, art seems to provide knowledge of the essence of aesthetic objects, of things as they are in-themselves. Beauty taken as the illumination of being-in-itself thus evokes a false, illusory sense of reconciliation, as though reconciliation as it is imagined through art actually could be achieved in light of some moral or ethical ideal. We have only to think of the reconciliation of those dissonant chords harmony imposes in the "Choral" movement of Beethoven's Ninth Symphony, and how the beauty of its melodic lines manifests the ideal of an already achieved brotherhood of mankind in a fragmented world, to understand Adorno's indictment of beauty as the illusion of reconciliation. We have only to recall, then, why Thomas Mann, in *Doctor Faustus*, asked that the Ninth Symphony be revoked. Art lies, Mann warned, though as we will discover, for Adorno the greatest art, which would include Beethoven's masterpiece, finally is unable to lie.[14]

Art is ambiguous. As the image of reconciliation, art creates an illusion. As the subtle articulation of the nonidentity of being, however, art also exposes the illusion and reveals an insurmountable barrier to reconciliation and to the violence to nature and difference meted out by the quest for reconciliation. Aesthetic expressions of nonidentity reconcile us to difference only in the sense, as it were in Eden, that without knowledge of being we are unable to determine nature's meaning or value. Although in Adorno's estimation there are far fewer examples where art's critique of reconciliation as illusion prevails over its masking of illusion, the history of art as a whole resolves the ambiguity of art in favor of critique. As each new aesthetic form challenges the representational powers of its predecessors, the historical continuity of art consists less in one artwork being taken as a model for another than in works of art as mortal enemies. The "unity of the history of art," Adorno maintains, "is the dialectical figure of determinate negation. Only in this way does art serve its idea of reconciliation."[15] Paradoxically, Adorno is saying, art "achieves reconciliation," provides an idea of what nature is and our relation to nature ought to be, only by showing through the history of artworks that every image of reconciliation is a lie.

Trace and the Unknown

Adorno's concept of art as "trace" elaborates upon the argument that art insinuates the nonidentity of nature as it does through its portrayal of beauty. I want to recommend an example I believe well illustrates what Adorno means by this concept, which otherwise remains quite abstract in *Aesthetic Theory*. Between 1892 and 1895 Claude Monet produced a series of paintings of the Rouen Cathedral that represented its various facades during different times of the day. Viewing these paintings is not unlike taking a long morning or afternoon to gaze through your window at a garden that appears differently as sunlight and shadow vary with the passing of the day. There may come a moment when we realize that it is not the garden that we see but the outline or trace of the garden as it appears throughout the duration of time. Likewise, Monet's series of the Cathedral at Rouen teaches that we can never capture an object as it is. The "being" of the cathedral is elusive, and indefinitely so as we study, or as Monet paints, painting after painting that come to reflect not upon the cathedral represented, but upon what it means to represent the cathedral. Taken in its entirety, the series represents representation. Representation is represented as identifying nature, but identifying nature incompletely. Yet, Monet's paintings represent the representation of an identity that, although unknown, is not nothing or nonbeing or nonexistent. Nature has a prerepresentational life that is expressed through art, but only as a "discontinuous and intermittent kind of life," as Adorno puts it, as one revealed in the ephemeral glimpses through which art traces the nonidentity of being.

There is no doubt that Adorno's approach to art does not take the aesthetic experience of the spectator, of an audience, as its point of departure. Adorno begins with the work of art. His break with subjectivist aesthetics is consistent with his critique of the subject in *Dialectic of Enlightenment* and *Negative Dialectics*. Since every act of thinking imposes identity on objects whose particularity is transfigured and denied in the process, an audience's grasp of art would be constrained by identitarian thought, or it would be misled by the illusory images of reconciliation imposed by aesthetic form. Unable to transcend the principle of identity, the limiting condition of all thought, even critical reflection is unable to free us from this solipsism. Critique itself, Adorno laments in *Negative Dialectics*, "against its own tendency, must remain within the medium of the concept.

It destroys the claim of identity, while honoring it through critical analysis (*prüfend*). Therefore, it can reach only as far as that claim."[16]

Though in *Aesthetic Theory* Adorno focuses on the work of art in a way that permits him to clarify its relation to the aesthetic object of the artwork, the work of art cannot be cleanly distinguished from the subject, for it includes subjectivity within it, as we may suspect from Adorno's discussion of beauty as in part the (identitarian) illusion of reconciliation. Indeed, Adorno seems to argue that the more art is permeated with subjectivity, the more subjective reason legislates formal principles and aesthetic rules and the more hostile the artwork becomes to all that is objectively given. There is violence in artwork that perfects illusion by arranging and composing every detail. As we have seen, though, there also are features of art that belie aesthetic formalism in their oblique representation of nonidentity. These allow Adorno to construe art as a language that can expose reconciliation as illusion, as a language of domination in its representation of illusion. Adorno's argument seems to be that art is empowered to depict difference in a way unintended by the subject, and being is depicted faithfully the more subjectivity and its intentions are purged from the artwork. This will be clearer when later we take up Adorno's fascination with Schoenberg, whose music achieves the level of objectivity that permits all the insight into being, nature and difference possible for art or thought. At this point, it is useful to examine the aesthetics constituting the ambiguity of art if we are to discover the limitations of aesthetic objectivity and the way in which art communicates within these limitations.

Rationality, Mimesis, and the Unknown

Through the concepts of beauty and trace, Adorno presses the argument that art is unique because it is the only form of thought able to convey the nonrepresentational character of nature, nature's nonidentity, and to expose the illusion of any aesthetic impersonation of being. What is it that permits art this exception? This question returns us to Adorno's view of the subject. Though identitarian in every form its reason takes, subjectivity also possesses a mimetic capacity that enlightenment drove underground and that took refuge in art. For Adorno, art remains proof of our capacity for a mimetic mode of behavior. Unlike reason, which in whole or part re-forms the world to correspond to an identity conceived by the subject, mimesis is the expression of a nonconceptual affinity for an objective difference that the subject displays through art. Mimetic behavior is the assimilation of the subject to the object, of identity to difference, an orientation leaving intact and unharmed the being of the object. "[A]rtworks," Adorno argues, "take it upon themselves to fulfill [this mimetic assimilation]."[17] The more art can be released from the formal rationality of subjective interests by being structured along objective lines, the more would the mimetic capacity be set free and the more articulately would art become a nonconceptual language, a language of reconciliation. Adorno goes so far as to say that if such an objective aesthetic form could be constructed, at the extreme aesthetic objectivity could speak in a language that may be the same in which "the Book of Nature" is written.

Can such extreme objectivity be reached? Trace and beauty, falling considerably short of this ideal of objectivity, are among the best aesthetic achievements for which we can hope. Both denote art as a medium through which objects pass discontinuously and that unmasks as illusion any image disguised to be more than their fleeting impression or imperfect glimpse. But where art acts as such a medium it offers hints of its subterranean powers, of a deeper meaning contributed by mimesis. As a medium of discontinuity the traces art leaves imply the presence of nature stirring just beneath and about to break through to be disclosed as the identity of nonidentity. Stirring beneath what? About to break through what? The answers are, stirring beneath form; about to break through form. Form, the aesthetic representation of reason, collides with the mimetic capacity to prevent the breakthrough of nature and to produce art. Through form mimesis is made to share in rationality. Adorno describes a "dialectic of rationality and mimesis" that explains how works of art can represent a stance toward reality that is qualitatively different from the violent opposition of subject to object, identity to nonidentity, form to content that produces the illusion of reconciliation. It is here, as we will see, that, among other great aesthetic achievements, the genius of Schoenberg's twelve-tone music lies. Form need not reproduce reason's conceptual ordering of the world and the violence it entails. Though the mimetic capacity of art cannot displace aesthetic form because without a "form" of representation being would remain inarticulate, form can work dialectically to illuminate subjective interests and hostile intentions. Form can be constructed to conform, not to the aesthetic object, but to the *objective aspiration* of the mimetic capacity of art, which is to represent difference in a way that expresses the wish to spare it the violence inflicted by aesthetic form.

Ordinarily, though, the collision between rationality and mimesis has no dialectical form. Throughout the history of art, nature or being or difference has experienced the violence of an aesthetic metamorphosis that creates and perpetuates the illusion of reconciliation. Nature is lost in every such artwork that represents it as eternally other than it is. This "death and transfiguration" is portrayed by Strauss's piece of that name, which combines musical and visual images to create an illusion of beauty that pacifies the violent history of art even in its efforts to represent nature truthfully.

At one extreme, then, aesthetic form can be distinguished from its power to create illusion. As form, aesthetic rationality need not impose identity on the object it represents, which would distinguish art from mere appearance, from the illusion produced by most art. At the other extreme, aesthetic form can be distinguished from mimesis, the assimilation of form to the object so as to move aesthetic representation beyond illusion. If art were assimilation of form to difference, the object could not be represented or known in any form. Art without form is the end of art. To distinguish aesthetic form from mimesis is to distinguish art from essence. Neither appearance nor essence, what then is art? As the "representation" of the nonidentity of being, of the unknown and impenetrable mystery that is nature, art must be the way in which *essence appears*, the appearance of an essence, which is precisely what Adorno argues.

> [I]n artworks . . . essence must appear, and its appearance is that of essence. . . . Accordingly, no work of art, regardless what its maker thinks of it, is directed toward an observer. . . . No artwork is to be described or explained in terms of categories of communication.[18]

We will have occasion to clarify the last part of this statement, for Adorno does not wish that art be left in silence. While he warns us not to try to capture art's representation of essence through appearance in terms of categories of communication, the outer and inner limits of communication can be defined in terms of his aesthetics.

Spirit and the Unknown

Beauty, trace, rationality, mimesis, and form are the principles that perform the delicate work of preserving the nonidentity of being in its representations. Adorno scrupulously avoids language that threatens to dissolve this paradox, which is the very center not only of his aesthetic theory but of his critical theory. Sustaining this paradox, which he has so painstakingly formulated, is itself an aesthetic achievement. As with art the language of paradox must consistently represent in a way that *negates* representation. All other representation is misrepresentation. The care Adorno exercises is likewise reflected in his concept of "spirit," which he introduces to describe what more there is in art or about art that enables it to "represent" nonidentity. On his part this move is something of a theoretical risk, as identity can be attributed to spirit in the form of the soul or some other animating principle. It is a necessary risk, though, because the language of beauty, trace, and so forth, through which art reveals reconciliation to be an illusion, represents nonidentity, "the appearance of an essence," only by intimating or insinuating or alluding to the nonidentity of being. By comparison, spirit is demonstrative. Spirit represents nonidentity by actually summoning that dividing line which conceals the world from us. The spirit of great art, in particular, situates us on that line so that we look into the darkness of the unknown. Spirit leads us into darkness and then enlightens by failing to illuminate what the darkness contains, thus marking the presence of the unknown.

The uncanny work that spirit performs becomes intelligible by our thinking of it in this way. As Adorno describes it, spirit seems to turn an artwork into an apparition. We cannot hear or look at an artwork without seeing through it at something, though at what we do not know. Spirit grants access to another realm beyond what is immediately before us. It is this excess or surplus that, along with the content (substance) of an artwork explicitly represented through aesthetic form, constitutes a work of art. We can appreciate Adorno's conception of an artwork when we consider the visual or programmatic dimension of a work in relation to its spirit, the real inner strength of a work of art.

To illustrate Adorno's concept of spirit, consider Beethoven's *Pastoral* Symphony, Mendelsohn's *Hebrides* Overture, and Schubert's *Wintereise*. Each may be considered as far less the image of nature it is taken to be than a spiritualized attempt to overcome our separation from nature. The aesthetic form, for example, of the well-articulated counterpoint of the third movement of Beethoven's *Pastoral* Symphony individuates the forces (or voices) of nature—wind, rain, thunder and lightning—that mount a summer storm. But the overall effect of the individual voices, the aesthetic whole greater than the sum of its parts, expresses the real fury of nature as an irrational moment of art that threatens to break through its aesthetic form to dissolve the work of art. As nature's elements through music combine to overwhelm us, for an instant we anticipate a glimpse of nature. Nature is near. Of course, form asserts itself against nature by rationalizing this irrational moment in the form of art. There is no storm; only its visual image in sound. Yet, nature's *spirit* has broken through aesthetic form even though *nature has not*.[19] Nature is depicted as unknowable—less than an essence. But nature has been present in spirit, and is thus more than an illusory appearance. Through spirit, art becomes the vehicle through which the essence of nature appears vividly. As the *appearance* of an essence, as the appearance of nature as unknown and fathomless, art infers nature's presence through an aesthetic that finally conveys only nature's remoteness. Spirit seeks to disabuse us of the belief that we can learn nature's identity, which as the visual images produced by the artwork—wind and rain, thunder and lightning—and represented by form, is eroded (negated) by spirit. The greater the spirit of an artwork, the greater the erosion of what the work's form represents. When in art nature appears as more than a collection of elemental forces, nature's spirit is appearing as more than the formal elements that make it possible.

We can say then that nature's nonidentity is conveyed through the spiritualization of an artwork. Spiritualization does justice to nature, to being, by setting it free from representation. Through spiritualization art is "a vision," Adorno declares, "of the nonvisual." Accordingly, no great work of art is ever what it appears to be about, and where the meaning of a work of art is nothing but its ostensible meaning, it is not art. Without spirit, works of art do not exist.

Expression and the Unknown

Spirit is the means through which art achieves expression and requires that we relinquish our customary way of thinking of artistic expression. For Adorno, artistic expression contradicts the romanticized view that art expresses sadness or sorrow or joy in ways words cannot express. Art does not, as the romantic idea of expression implies, and as we so often hear, express the inexpressible. To deny this would be to suggest that image and sound achieve what words fail to achieve. Art would simply share in the illusion created by words—that the being of the world with which we seek reconciliation can be objectively represented. The belief that art can render being as it is is precisely what Adorno rejects. Regarding artistic expression, he makes this same point differently by saying that art's "expression is the antithesis of expressing something."[20] If we are perplexed at trying to imagine how there can be expression that is not expression but only the negation of expression, there is a positive way to construe Adorno's notion of expression without compromising the meaning of his argument. Is he not saying that art expresses the inexpressibility of the inexpressible? Turning a phrase that so consistently expresses nature's inexpressibility defines the position Adorno seeks to place us in in relationship to being, nature, and difference. Expression is the moment where nature seeps most deeply into art, where what there is to know about being is known, which, of course, is that difference remains forever unknown. Perhaps, Adorno may be encouraging us to believe, the sadness that art expresses is the grief that we can love nature only in its absence.

Can it be the entire purpose of aesthetic rationality to be expressive in this way? Posed in response to his idea of expression, our question is formed in the context of our own experience of art and nature. We can only conclude from his argument that it recommends an ascetic discipline to our era that, as a consequence of its brutality toward nature, must now learn to love nature in its absence. Those living in this era who seek justification for such asceticism may take pleasure in discovering that aesthetic expression unveils the violence to nature contained in our every thought and action. But for others it is painful to realize that art disavows insight other than this into who we are and what we can do, which historically has been thought of as the truest pleasure, the truth that art bestows. Adorno's aesthetics thus annihilates the two polar dimensions of aesthetic experience. It mounts an attack on the knowing and perceiving and feeling subject; artistic form rises up against the illusory images of reconciliation. And by so doing art rebels against the promise of mimesis—nature, or difference, or being remain hidden from us. Art is neither seeing nor the seen. Art does justice to nature, Adorno confides, only by "probing in the darkness."[21] "[D]arkness (*das Finstere*)," the unknown, "has become the representative (*Statthalter*) of [art's] Utopia."[22] Adorno leaves us with an aesthetically grounded asceticism that underwrites only thought and action that can be derived from its categorical imperative—because it is unknown, *we must leave nature be*. Does this mean that reason must abolish itself? Or does Adorno's aesthetics allow for one final move. Can reason learn to see in the darkness?

It is not only Adorno who has brought us to these questions. Theory today is not innocent of the view that we must find a way to live without the violence of which reason is suspected to be a transcendental cause. When we turn to Adorno for an answer to this question it is because we know that the critique that leads us to where it can be asked has eliminated the possibility that any theory could be sufficiently reflexive about the violence inherent in the forms of life that it endorses. Yet, Adorno disappoints us to the verge of despair. To avoid the violence formal rational thought inflicts on nature it seems that we must avoid thought or at least any relation with nature that thinking may propose. This is the standpoint aesthetic theory appears initially to recommend.

Art does break with enlightenment, though not so unequivocally as when we mistakenly view art from the standpoint urging that we look to art to free us from reason. From that standpoint, we look to art because it appears to be the opposite of reason. This misreading of Adorno's aesthetic theory, likewise peculiar to those who, such as Habermas, accuse Adorno of aestheticizing critical theory, is not unreasonable. Adorno's aesthetic theory appears to support a framework of mutually exclusive extremes. At the one end there is art, at the other, reason, and because art can escape identity and the violence identity entails, reason seems to be put in the position of envying art. But that misreading is the standpoint of reason believing it can overcome itself. It is reason wanting to become art.

But Adorno's aesthetic theory is neither constructed nor to be interpreted from the standpoint of reason. Rather, Adorno develops aesthetic theory from the vantage point of art. From that vantage point reason cannot overcome itself, because art is graced with powers of reflection unavailable to reason. Aesthetic theory does not oblige thought to become art, however, but to adopt the perspective of art in order to grasp whatever possibilities it may convey for a renewal of reason. Importantly, this does not require that reason become art or (at first) even a theory of art, as though reason were continuously viewing art from the outside. Aesthetic theory requires that reason view itself as *internal* to an artwork, view art as the *first reflection* (my term) or objectification of reason. Reason can do this without becoming art because art includes reason within it, as aesthetic form. Aesthetic theory, the *second reflection* (Adorno's term), the reflection of how reason functions within the artwork during the process of aesthetic representation, originates within an aesthetic dimension wherein reason acquires a uniquely reflexive view of itself. It is only from within the artwork that reason can learn whether it can see in the darkness.

REASON AND DARKNESS

Why does art create the illusion of reconciliation? Rationality, in Adorno's words, is the "unity-constitutive moment of art." Put differently, reconciliation is the achievement of aesthetic form. Through form reason fulfills its promise of happiness by ending the antagonism between subject and object, human being and human being, being, nature, and difference. Art also unmasks this illusion of reconciliation. It is from within the artwork, then, that reason discovers its self-deceptions—the identities art constitutes through the rationality of aesthetic form are canceled, and nature's identity remains beyond the reach of reason or, what is but the same thing, beyond the reach of aesthetic form. This is what Adorno means when he argues that art "is rationality that criticizes rationality without [being able to] evade it (*ohne ihr sich entziehen*)."[23] Within art reason learns what as a consequence of the process of enlightenment it cannot learn on its own, that it is not within its power to achieve reconciliation, that its images of reconciliation are projections of a reason that puts itself in the place of the worlds it sets out to discover. Art amends conceptual knowledge, Adorno is proposing, in that thought learns through art what it fails to discover when it represents objects in ways other than through art, that no perfectly objective quality discloses itself through subjective effort.

Adorno's proposition refers to but one of the lessons that art teaches reason by providing it with a uniquely reflexive view of itself. There is a second, decisive lesson. When art takes reason to task for its lies, it does not intend the end of reason. Without reason, without aesthetic form, there can be no art. In its rejection of illusory images of reconciliation, art requires that reason (form) refrain from lying. Accordingly, the history of art appears as a history of discrete efforts that, taken together, attempt to reach beyond every artwork's allegiance to the ideal of reconciliation. As each new work of art is yet one more representation of the ideal, the history of new works proves every image of reconciliation to be only another in a succession of illusions. The critique of identity is sustained through the history of art, and relentlessly so. Through the history of art, reason discovers that it is obliged, not to abolish itself, but to be productive of ever new forms (of life), forms (of life) no longer based on the presumption of knowing nature, or difference, or being-in-itself. Consequently, for Adorno's aesthetics art not only shields the unknown from the invasions of reason. It *releases and protects*, as well, the *contingency and indeterminacy of thought* that reason extinguishes in its pursuit of the ideal of reconciliation, so that no longer bound by the foundations for thought that the illusion of objectivity provides, aesthetic creativity explodes. Art unfetters creativity by substituting darkness wherever the ideal appears. "Nature," Adorno confides, "can only be seen blindly (*nur blind sehen*)."[24] Art blinds reason to restore its vision. With the world hidden from sight, with reason's eyes turned away from nature, which had serviced reason's projects and served as its foundations, reason's vision is restored by being thrown back upon itself. The opacity of being is tied inseparably to the contingency and indeterminacy of reason. There is Reason by first admitting the darkness. Through art reason learns that it can see in the darkness, and only in the dark. What, then, can reason see?

Adorno does not confine the aesthetic education of reason to lessons taught within the aesthetic dimension, as though the issue were what is left for art to do once the rationality of aesthetic forms refrains from lying. Reason is only truly instructed where art serves as the original text, or first reflection, for what finally is conveyed by words. Perhaps we should be surprised by this turn? After all, if art denies the authenticity of all images of reconciliation, is there anything remaining for the word to say? Adorno does not condemn art to silence; to do so would turn art into the opposite of language, invoking words through their absence. By shadowing art, silence would allow artworks to mean anything other than what Adorno believes they ought to mean. Rather than condemn art to silence, the aesthetic dimension sets limits to what we can say, say about art or expect art to say. Aesthetic experience must become "philosophy." Otherwise, Adorno warns, it will not be "genuine experience."[25]

Since Adorno intends the aesthetic dimension to establish the limits to what we can say, within these limits should we not be able to think and act purposely in ways that, to put it as harshly as Adorno's critique of identity often seems to require, leave us with less of nature's blood on our hands? Within these limits, in other words, is there an outline of a praxis? That there is becomes apparent where Adorno turns to the aesthetic dimension to support claims against the hegemony of technical reason. Putting an end to the technological exploitation of nature, Adorno contends, would require "a reorientation of technical forces of production that would direct these forces not only according to desired aims but equally according to the nature that is to be technically formed."[26] This passage is striking, for it constitutes a revision of *Dialectic of Enlightenment* and *Negative Dialectics*. Departing from the earlier works, for all *practical* intents and purposes it ceases to reduce reason in modernity to formal rationality. Formal reason is identified with technological rationality, removing the tremendous pressure imposed on the subject by Adorno's critique of enlightenment to monitor, and even to abstain from, each and every thought for the damage it inflicts on being. Adorno's aesthetic theory forgives knowledge its original sin. Subjectivity need not bear the guilt attached to that tragic sensibility toward nature made painfully known to us by Adorno's attacks on reason. Freed from its indenture to formal reason, nature would be acknowledged as the unknown art proves it to be, to become the standard according to which reason would take nature as its object. Formal reason thus would be displaced as the *raison d'être* of modernity.

Yet, it is not only nature but subjectivity as well that is the benefactor of the pacification of formal reason. Here the implications of Adorno's aesthetic theory for a theory of aesthetic individuality move nearer to the surface. Adorno intends his aesthetics to succeed where Hegel had failed to define the "experience of the nonidentical as the *telos* and emancipation of the aesthetic subject."[27] Subjectivity's relinquishment of its mastery over nature would be akin to the rationality of aesthetic form renouncing as illusory its images of reconciliation in the face of art's nonidentical representation of being. For subjectivity, reason, like art, would recognize that its every re-creation or representation of the world contains a "creative," constructed element the world does not possess, and that its representations are, perhaps for the most part, though not entirely, constructions rather than depictions of things-in-themselves. Reason's creativity, like the creativity of art, would no longer be fettered by a formal rational interest in producing images of reconciliation that capture an object essentially. Reason, like art, could "see," or know, the worlds it forms creatively from its own imagination, while remaining blind to worlds outside its creative imagination it acknowledges to be opaque to representation. Worlds other than those reason and art create would inspire both. As they are unknown, though, fathomless worlds would no longer serve as models for subjectivity's aesthetic creativity.

Adorno's aesthetic theory has led him to a separate peace with enlightenment. Aesthetic theory makes the mystery and fathomlessness of being that is revealed by art the axis around which individual and collective thought and action are to revolve. Thought is to amalgamate itself with art so that it can imitate art in a subtle sense. Reason must abandon any practice, such as that of technological mastery, that presupposes the transparency of nature. Nature would be left alone to flourish as it would in a world before we as a species were born. Reason then can open thought to the same contingency and indeterminacy of form that becomes available to art when aesthetic rationality relinquishes its representational interest in the objectivity of being. Neither forms of art nor forms of life would any longer reach beyond the representations that resemble, not nature or being or difference, but the constructions that are our own thoughts. While nature continues to be "draped in black," as Adorno puts it, art does allow our reason to see in the dark, to think and act and speak in the dark, though what reason can see, and *knows* that it can see, are different reflections of itself.

NO TRESPASSING

Metaphor will help clarify these philosophical reflections, for although Adorno speaks in words he thinks in images, or his thought opens to images or forces us to think in images. The possibilities his aesthetic theory offers us come to an end on a horizon where light meets darkness. Looking out to meet this horizon, our eyes travel an expanse of possibilities for individual creativity. This expanse measures as far as we can see—but *only* as far as we can see; not beyond the horizon into the darkness. The position from which we look out to the horizon is our world and the worlds within our world; the distance to the horizon circumscribes the possibilities for how our world and individuals within it can be aesthetically transformed. Indeterminacy and contingency, promissories that without moral or ontological fault each can be anything other than whatever she or he has become, emerge from Adorno's aesthetic demonstration of nonidentity with darkness as a limiting condition. It is a condition that distinguishes the meaning of indeterminacy in Adorno's aesthetic theory from its conventional philosophical meaning as infinite possibility, and thus distinguishes Adorno from thinkers for whom indeterminacy includes the reconciliation of subject and object, the trespass into darkness.

We can now think of this limiting condition as a version of the Edenic myth. Adorno's aesthetic theory permits us to become anything except creatures who have knowledge of difference, of being-in-itself, and who create ourselves and our worlds in accordance with such knowledge. While nature, difference, and being connote for Adorno an essential realm, it is a realm of truth that lies always beyond our horizons and in the darkness, though the representational traces left by great art may offer intimations, precious though forever imperfect glimpses of it. Denying us *only* this knowledge, Adorno allows us all possibilities but one. We are forbidden to negotiate, morally or ethically, individually or collectively, for space within our protean forms of life for the identity of being-in-itself that knowledge is thought incorrectly to disclose. Relations between identity and difference must pass beyond all identifications of difference, beyond treating difference violently, to the far simpler togetherness of differences. Passing beyond the identity of difference to the togetherness of differences, difference would be spared the misrepresentations that social and political forms of such spatial negotiations ineradicably entail.

Adorno's aesthetically grounded limiting condition does not cause us to be less productive of diversity, nor to wonder at the diversity of being any the less. Are we not potentially more productive for having been emancipated from the interest in forbidding or restricting or cultivating ways of life in obedience to standards and possibilities that are justified by nature or being or difference thought to be objectively intelligible? Differences may originate with subjects, with individuals alone or with groups, or with structures reputed to "speak" subjects, with languages or cultures and their idiosyncrasies. But these are not differences that can be *known* in themselves by anyone other than the subjects (individuals, groups, cultures) to whom they belong, and even then are known only in part. It is a diversity of differences that remains, even as it flourishes, mysterious and unknown in each of the differences of which it is constituted. With aesthetics Adorno has erected a barrier between "subjects" and "objects" in all their relations—among individuals, groups, and cultures, between human beings and being, nature, and difference. On the subject's side of the barrier that it is forbidden to trespass lies a present and future whose possibilities are unencumbered by the claims of formal rational thought, which then ceases to be a threat to differences on the side of the barrier belonging to the "object."

It is evident that Adorno's aesthetics aggressively distinguishes his theory of reconciliation from that of several thinkers, notably Kant, Hegel, Nietzsche, and

Heidegger. Centrally important are his differences with Nietzsche, to be taken up shortly. To lay the groundwork for that discussion, what should be first mentioned is that Nietzsche, from whom Adorno surely learned of identity as the will to power and whose position we can be certain he had in mind when formulating his own, nevertheless is guilty of trespassing the barrier to darkness. Nietzsche fails Adorno just at that moment when his aesthetic idealism achieves its loveliest and most eloquent expression. In *Beyond Good and Evil*, Nietzsche dreams of what I will describe as "a music that touches all shores," an aesthetic reconciliation of all differences,

> a supra-German music which does not fade, turn yellow, turn pale at the sight of the blue voluptuous sea and the luminous sky of the Mediterranean . . . a supra-European music which holds its own even before the brown sunsets of the desert, whose soul is kindred to the palm-tree and knows how to roam and be at home among great beautiful solitary beasts of prey . . . a music whose rarest magic would consist in this, that it no longer knew anything of good and evil, except that perhaps some sailor's homesickness, some golden shadow and delicate weakness would now and then flit across it: an art that would see fleeing towards it from a great distance the colors of a declining, now almost incomprehensible *moral* world, and would be hospitable and deep enough to receive such late fugitives.[28]

As sublime as is this image of reconciliation, particularly for its closing forgiveness of the moral will that punishes difference by converting it to otherness, Adorno nevertheless would see it as the very expression of that will to power it is meant to overcome. Art must shatter the illusion of reconciliation. Philosophy must not idealize it.

THE GREAT DIVIDE

The distance between Adorno and those whose shoulders he may stand upon in other ways, particularly Nietzsche, at the very least is a measure of how radical is his concept of nonidentity. Adorno's conception of nonidentity, of difference as an unfathomable void, which he once referred to as "a thesis secretly implied by Kant," forces a great ontological divide between all subjects and their objects, between human beings and being in all its diversity of difference. It is this divide and the question of whether it can be bridged around which turns the issue of the possibility of reconciliation. How can Adorno be so certain that this divide cannot be crossed, that difference is unknowable, that the attempt to cross the great divide is trespassing?

In *Aesthetic Theory*, Adorno's categories, even "spirit," can only somewhat more than "trace," to borrow his own word, what it is about art that teaches that being is always different from every thought of it and beyond its reach. At the outset of this extraordinary work (in his "Draft Introduction" to *Aesthetic*

Theory), Adorno appears to remind himself that the properties enabling art to be uniquely reflexive also undermine confidence in aesthetic theory's ability to explain the philosophical reflections art can produce. "The dilemma of aesthetics," he says, "appears immanently in the fact that it can be constituted neither from above nor from below, neither from concepts nor from aconceptual experience (*der begriffslosen Erfahrung*)."[29] Adorno's theoretical self-consciousness is appropriate, though he runs the risk of being taken literally. Believing conceptualization suppresses the difference it means to express, Adorno's dilemma is that he ought to work without concepts. Without concepts, however, there is only pure experience and no words to explain what by default remains inarticulate. Does Adorno seek this impasse?

According to Adorno's aesthetic theory, art is nonconceptual *yet* communicative. Art is uniquely equipped to represent the nonidentity of difference, its fathomlessness, nonrepressively. Aesthetic theory conceptualizes the unknown communicated by art. It expresses, as it were, the presence of an absence. Aesthetic concepts are self-reflexive—they refer to something, and at the same time to something the concept leaves out. The more aesthetic theory conceptualizes art's representation of difference, the more are the limits to conceptualization dramatized. The presence of that which the concept leaves out, the presence of the absence, is more intensely felt. In this way aesthetics "puts into words" what art reveals about difference. In effect, aesthetic theory escapes identitarianism by providing a (second) reflection of art's refusal to disclose difference. Why, then, the dilemma, if the deficiencies of concepts seem to be avoided conceptually? Because Adorno encounters the dilemma at a level deeper than that indicated by either the insolvency of concepts or of pure experience. Aesthetic theory provides no answer to the question whether the fathomlessness of difference whose presence art reveals cannot be known because aesthetic theory is inadequate, or whether aesthetic theory truly reflects art's ability to convey the nonidentity of difference. Aesthetic theory, in other words, appears unable to say with any certainty how it "knows" the nonidentical is unknowable.

Is the best for which we then can hope from Adorno's aesthetic theory only the intimations and inferences of a great, irreconcilable, ontological divide communicated by art? To be sure, this is no minor lesson. His aesthetic theory underwrites critical perspectives otherwise unavailable to political and social theory. When, for example, he argues in *Negative Dialectics* that subjectivity, even in its most transcendentally reflective forms, is actually constitutive of the world it seeks to know and be reconciled with, he has not based this indictment on an immanent critique of the subject's philosophizing about its being and the world that it invents. On the contrary, Adorno's argument only could result from the reflections peculiar to art conceptualized by aesthetic theory. If Adorno were not aesthetically positioned, he could not have so fundamentally challenged conceptual thought. It is only after the second reflections of aesthetic theory revealed the ontological need for a home inherent in all thought that Adorno could proceed to illustrate the presence of that need in ontology itself. Despite aesthetic theory's teachings, though, if art's intimations and inferences of the great divide are the best for which we can hope, would it not be to act in bad faith to require aesthetic theory to take on the burden of proof? Adorno knows that it would. He knows, too, that it would suggest that he may have arbitrarily adopted an aesthetic standpoint from which to critically approach enlightenment. On both counts he would cheat himself of hard-won insights and risk impasse. For these reasons Adorno must not have intended his dilemma of being unable to constitute aesthetics from either concepts or aconceptual experience to erode confidence in aesthetic theory until its solution could be found. Rather, *art* must already have proved to Adorno that nature or being is unknowable, and he posed his dilemma only to demonstrate the reflexive form that aesthetic theory must take if it is to maintain consistently the fathomless meaning of difference. This does seem to me the developmental path of Adorno's aesthetic theory. Assuming it may be, we can return to the original question. How could art have communicated not simply aesthetic theory's intimations and inferences that difference is unfathomable but evidence it is forever so?

Let us follow Nietzsche's lead in imagining an art form that can be brought to bear on such questions relating to reconciliation. Returning to the earlier discussion of Adorno's concept of trace, I suggested that Monet's series of the Rouen Cathedral leaves the being of the cathedral elusive while registering its impressions. Suppose now, though, we imagine Monet did not paint a series of Rouen portraits from which he selected only twenty for display, but that he devoted his entire life to producing an *infinite* series of these paintings. Through such a series the being of the Rouen Cathedral would not simply be traced but perhaps be fully known. Any difference omitted by one painting or collection of paintings of the cathedral may eventually find its way onto a canvas. Such a hypothetically perfect mimetic art form as an unending series of paintings of an aesthetic object would contain within it all possible forms of expressing its being. The cathedral's indeterminacy and contingency could be fully revealed. And the secret of art's existence would be revealed as well. Art either would disclose being fully, overcoming the distance and reconciling the difference between subject and object or, failing this, would affirm that there is a "difference," a cathedral, that is left out and remains beyond what art and its aesthetic identities represent. Art would say for certain if and how it knows whether difference is unknowable. Yet this hypothetical endless series is a chimerical concept and belies our efforts to imagine how painting could so demystify art. Pursuing Nietzsche's lead more closely, we should consider the art form that can achieve what for other arts would simply be fantastic.

"A MUSIC WHOSE SOUL KNOWS HOW TO ROAM AND BE AT HOME AMONG GREAT BEAUTIFUL SOLITARY BEASTS OF PREY"

Nietzsche dreamt of a music that is not strange to any people, a music that would express the singularity of each way of life and make it known to every other way without injury to it or sacrifice of its meaning or value. Nietzsche imagined different ways of living for those who became weary or skeptical of their own way of life and who wished to be different, or who out of temptation or curiosity or compassion or justice or the simple need for diversion sought to create a place for difference and to welcome it into their lives. Nietzsche's vision of a new music is a vision of aesthetic reconciliation. It is an identity held in common by those who share identities and their nonidentical others who bear no resemblance and, excluded, remain outside. It is an identity of identity and nonidentity that pulls everything outside inside, and pushes everything inside outside, that makes everything the same different, and everything different the same. Like Nietzsche, Adorno, too, looks to music for an image of reconciliation. Unlike Nietzsche, for Adorno there is no doubt that the image is illusory. Music can sustain neither the idea of reconciliation nor its promise. How is it that Adorno could lay to rest the matter of whether music *ever* could achieve the reconciliation that Nietzsche imagined? To answer this question, and to bring us nearer to understanding how Adorno could know difference to be unknowable, we must first ask how Nietzsche could envision music affirming the possibility of reconciliation.

Nietzsche's dream of reconciliation, I propose, very likely was inspired by *Tristan und Isolde*, an opera with which Nietzsche became intimately familiar a full quarter of a century before the publication of *Beyond Good and Evil*, his work describing what I have referred to as a music that could touch all shores. I say intimately because in 1862, joined by two adolescent companions with whom he founded the society Germania, Nietzsche studied and worked out on the piano the score of Wagner's music drama from an arrangement first available in that year. Much later, perhaps as a direct result of his experience with the piano transcription, though more likely as a consequence of hearing the opera performed, Nietzsche may have come to realize how philosophically profound were the extraordinary chromatic inventions Wagner introduced into *Tristan und Isolde*.

Until that work, there never had been a musical composition that so completely undermined diatonic relationships through a chromatic writing that exchanged tonic resolution for a "sense" of nonresolution, the agonizingly uncertain impression of nonresolution conveyed by the contrapuntal relationship among chromatically articulated voices. Expressing Wagner's achievement in simpler terms, what this meant is that the organizational device, the so-called tonic key, that throughout the history of Western music achieved resolution (e.g., harmony) within musical composition by subordinating all musical ideas to a dominate idea, was—*for all intents and purposes*—annihilated. I say "for all intents and purposes" because Wagner does not actually destroy the dominant key. Rather, the "sense" of a missing dominant tonal organization is created by Wagner through his deployment of ideas (chromatic chords) that cannot be related to a tonal center or central idea harmonizing all other ideas. In effect, not having to defer to an alien identity imposed upon them, the meaning and value of every chromatically articulated musical idea in the work, essentially their own identities, are expressed without reference to any leading voice. Every theme and musical idea, each phrase, motif, chord, each tone of which they are formed, is known in-itself, not re-presented through a superordinate musical relationship that establishes a (dominant and dominating) "tone" through which all other tones are to be interpreted. As different as they are, and in *Tristan* each musical idea is virtually as different from others as it can be, musical ideas appear to be reconciled, not harmonized, each to all and to the work as a whole. In view of its mimetic implications, could Wagner's chromaticism have been taken by Nietzsche for the musical promise of reconciliation belonging to what I have described hypothetically as Monet's infinite series? Certainly, *Tristan und Isolde* could have suggested to Nietzsche the "supra-German music" of reconciliation he later imagined, though at the beginning of his intellectual life it ironically launched that small society that in its artistic tastes and aspirations was German through and through.

While I believe Nietzsche's dream to have been inspired in the way I have described, Wagner's extreme chromaticism cannot sustain unequivocally the image of reconciliation Nietzsche envisioned. Listening to *Tristan und Isolde* one can discern that by virtue of some technical or thematic quality belonging to the complex (contrapuntal) fabric of voices, there is a voice the composer intended to be dominant and that is meant to disclose the key that determines the final meaning of all other "keys" (chords, ideas). This tonal centricity to *Tristan*, a musical idea resolving in one direction the values and meanings peculiar to all other ideas, deprives Nietzsche's vision of its power. It renders the Wagnerian image of reconciliation illusory and lowers its sight to "fatherlands," for which music is composed, Nietzsche insists, until it can touch all shores.[30] On Nietzsche's side, however, the tonal center cannot be recognized with certainty *by the ear*. As it cannot be *heard* with certainty, debates can emerge about the identity of the dominant key. And, it can be argued, debates about the identity of the tonal center are actually debates over whether a tonal center is present at all! Knowledge of the dominant key would be available only by consulting the score. Nietzsche's vision no doubt was based on the imaginings provoked by the ear, not by the eye. To this explanation of Nietzsche's dream, though, it is worthwhile adding that Nietzsche, if his sister is to be believed, when learning to play the piano score of *Tristan und Isolde* was unable to make the melody (associated with a dominant key, subject, or theme) stand out from the rich harmonic background.[31] What Nietzsche's sister anecdotally reports as her brother's difficulties with Wagner's score speaks implicitly to how utterly the organizational principles of the opera are hidden within the seams of the composition, and hence even from the eye. This doubles the possibility that *Tristan und Isolde* could go far toward inspiring Nietzsche's dream, though technically Wagner's creation cannot produce definitively the image of reconciliation it seems to promise.

Since Wagner's score misleads the ear and frustrates the eye as to its underlying structure, if Nietzsche were inspired, as I propose, he would not in any unqualified sense be wrong about *Tristan*'s tonality. His vision consequently would offer instruction. Implicit in Nietzsche's vision, and more important than the quarrel over whether the Wagnerian image of reconciliation is or is not illusory, would be the insight that Wagner had taken a decisive step toward emancipating music from rules that impose limits on musical expression. Nietzsche would have recognized in *Tristan* an aesthetic form making it possible to compose without conventions. He would have learned from *Tristan* that the organizational principles of music are artificial, external to the musical material itself, arbitrarily selected by the composer to achieve certain musical ends and to avoid others. With his vision of a supra-German, supra-European music Nietzsche would have tacitly begged the larger question. Could music's emancipation from convention mean its mimetic potential could be released from subservience to form, released even from what Adorno later called dialectical form, form's "dialectic of rationality and mimesis"? Nietzsche's dream would be truly prescient. It anticipates the future of music, specifically Schoenberg, and invites Adorno's philosophy of a new music, which recognized in Schoenberg's achievements an answer to the question Nietzsche had begged. Through music, can being become fathomable, difference transparent, and reconciliation reality?

Nietzsche's farsightedness is borne out by the evolution of Schoenberg's compositions. In their employment of chromatic and contrapuntal writing to subvert their tonal and harmonic bases, Schoenberg's early compositions are comparable to *Tristan* and, in retrospect, a prelude to his abandoning tonality altogether. Wagner, in other words, makes Schoenberg possible. *Erwartung* (literally "awaiting," figuratively "expectation"), an opera in one act, is one of Schoenberg's earliest (1909) and best known atonal compositions. It is certainly his most extreme atonal piece for its uncompromising avoidance of key centers and a central harmony (the tonic triad), and for his musical presentation of all chromatic elements as essentially equal. These innovations, in turn, contributed to destabilizing other time-honored conventions, such as meter, tempo, and melody. Abolished are the conventions that construct identities to which all ideas within a composition are forced to become assimilated. *Erwartung* appears to such an extent to open the way for music to express the aesthetic object in-itself that we cannot be surprised when in his *Philosophy of Modern Music* we find Adorno looking to *Erwartung* for a determination of whether the being of an aesthetic object can be known.[32]

Erwartung's aesthetic object is the "expressive subject," at the symbolic level the solitary individual searching for meaning in a strange world where it is cut adrift from its past. At the dramatic level the subject is a woman, painfully alone and horribly anxious at the possible loss of her lover through death or desertion. Searching for him in the darkness of a wood, she emerges, exhausted, into a clearing illuminated by a full moon and collapses as she stumbles upon what appears to be his dead body, a moment of horror that is left ambiguous as to whether it actually occurs or is the hallucination of a woman terrified at its prospect. *Erwartung* possesses two qualities that recommend it as a test of music's capacity to achieve reconciliation. Its atonality realizes the structural aspirations of Wagner's efforts to suppress tonality within a tonal system. And the expressive subject to be revealed in its objectivity possesses an urgency and insistence, a dramaturgical presence that is perfectly suited to permit the being of human expression to be disclosed, if it can be disclosed by art at all. What is Adorno's estimation of these musical tendencies? With *Erwartung* in mind, Adorno captures both of these qualities exactly in his description of Schoenberg's first atonal works.

> The actual revolutionary moment for him is the change in function of musical expression. Passions are no longer simulated, but rather genuine emotions of the unconscious—of shock, of trauma—are registered without disguise through the medium of music. These emotions attack the taboos of form because these taboos subject such emotions to their own censure, rationalizing them and transforming them into images. Schoenberg's formal innovations were closely related to the change in the content of expression. These innovations serve the breakthrough of the reality of this content.[33]

Schoenberg's expressionism, Adorno is arguing, strives to present the "pure here-and-now," to overcome the representational distance of art, introduced by form, from the immediacy of life.

Erwartung fails, however, precisely where it succeeds. With its "seismographic registration of traumatic shock," its self-evident display of terror, hatred, jealousy, desire, forgiveness, profound sadness, *Erwartung* becomes, Adorno explains, a "case-study" of expression. *Erwartung* studies and problematizes expression; it literally interprets expression as a principle to be explicated. As a case study in expression, Adorno concludes, *Erwartung* "is no longer 'expressive.' . . . With its expressive outbursts the dream of subjectivity explodes. . . . [Its] chords invalidate their unique expressive function. What they portray as their object . . . [is] the same subjectivity whose magic dissolves before the exactness of the penetrating eye cast upon it by the work."[34] Objectifying rather than revealing the objectivity of expression, *Erwartung* imposes identity on expression, all the more as it tries to move ever closer to immediacy. *Erwartung* "officially denies" the claim to reconciliation, which is proved to be illusory, nature, being, and difference remain opaque, and music tends toward breaking the bounds of enlightenment.

Erwartung's atonality, however, cannot finally prove that music is unable to achieve reconciliation. To have offered such a proof, atonality must completely liberate music from the constraints of conventional tonal forms and must remain free of formal properties that substitute, for expurgated conventions, new fetters on atonality's mimetic potential. *Erwartung* did succeed in escaping the limitations of tonality. But its atonal structure, though serving every expressive purpose, turned around on itself to reveal, rather than a spontaneously expressive subject (the solitary individual), a subject (the composer, the composition) that unwittingly took expression as its object. Once free of convention, it seems, atonality was amorphous and episodic. To establish continuity and coherence among musical ideas, compositions either were brief or, as with *Erwartung*, relied upon written texts to furnish the missing coherence by programmatically structuring the score. This was true without exception for all of Schoenberg's free atonal compositions. In other words, although atonality released the mimetic capacity of music from convention, it was newly confined to compositional forms that were either narrowly measured or bound together textually, substituting other limits for the conventional restrictions they replaced. There were no compositional forms sufficiently complex to complement atonal music's mimetic possibilities.

Schoenberg required a form of composition that, like the system of tonality, made possible complex and coherent large-scale works but maintained its freedom from tonal conventions. Such a compositional form could offer a vehicle for the mimetic potential of the new music, though Schoenberg did not think of it in this way. The aesthetics of this vehicle could offer Adorno the means to definitively answer the question whether there could be a music that touched all shores.[35]

Schoenberg's twelve-tone music, so named to differentiate it from the free atonality of his earlier creations, was a system of composition he designed to overcome the limitations of both tonality and atonality. What is decisive for our purposes, it also preserves the possibilities of tonal composition (length, complexity, coherence) for the mimetic potentialities of atonality. Still atonal, twelve-tone music exiles the disciplines of key centers and their conventional supports. In their place it introduces a system of variation that begins with a unique though arbitrary arrangement of the twelve tones into a basic row or series. This "model," as it is referred to, is the foundation for a compositional structure *derived* from the row, as are derived what once were tonal ordering devices, elements such as counterpoint, melody, and harmony. Adorno puts this well when, thinking of the fixed melodic statement that acts as the thematic basis for tonal works, he points out that in a twelve-tone score the "concept of the *theme* itself has been absorbed by the concept of the row."[36] He means that the theme, along with musical elements now all contained *within* it, evolves as the logic of the twelve-tone series. Because there is no melodic theme that from the outset of the work has a special office protected by a compositional development through these elements, there are no differentiated melodic lines (or voices) appearing in relationships that are fleshed out by counterpoint. Adorno, in fact, prefers to think of voice as identical to the twelve-tone work as a whole. While this figuratively describes a twelve-tone piece, he intends to press home the idea that all musical functions are derived from, because they are synonymous with, the twelve-tone row. Without the differentiation of melodic voices structurally prejudicing the meaning of a work, considerations of harmony, inseparable from counterpoint, cannot be said to assume an independent organizational role in the composition. And if the melodic theme along with the developmental techniques of counterpoint and harmony are integrated into the row, the twelve-tone system "contradicts," to borrow from Adorno, other such formal devices as dynamics and transition. Since melodic lines are no longer thematically privileged, dynamics loses its function as a means of articulating and developing themes and the subordination of music material is no longer required to form transitions between thematic passages conventionally assigned greater weight in a work.

So fundamental is the row in the determination of the composition, that there is no technical element or device that can emerge to externally unify the work or to order any of its partial moments in relation to the rest. Every tone in the row is the equal of every other; no tone, its meaning and value, can be trumped by the identity of any other tone and the meaning and value it bears. However, does not the row now become the predominant organizational device of the tones within the composition? Does the row not undermine the mimetic achievement of reconciliation toward which twelve-tone music strives?

Twelve-tone composition represents a qualitative leap over free atonality in eliminating obstacles to the mimetic potential of music. Compositional development ceases to occur through organizational devices that, in tonality as well as free atonality, were imported into the music from the outside to make possible large-scale, coherent, and continuous compositions and to structure relationships determining how the music is to be interpreted. Development now takes place through *variation*, twelve-tone music's key compositional procedure whereby a system of combination and permutation creates inexhaustible, virtually limitless possibilities for the rearrangement of the basic row. Variation vitiates any hegemony the original row, at the outset of the composition, seems to possess in relation to its inclusive tones. In its potentially infinite forms each variation of the row becomes a new thematic idea known and equal to every other variation (row, idea) in meaning and value. In their equality these musical ideas are "indifferent to one another." None dominate. To view twelve-tone compositions from the inside out, then, just as within the row no tone can dominate any other tone, within the composition no row as musical idea can dominate any other row as musical idea. The twelve-tone system of variation is thus clearly unrelated to tonality's own system of development, where a melodic idea along with its organizational supports creates a center of gravity not indifferent to but determining the weight of all other musical dimensions through which they evolve. Built into the music as a system with a logic of its own, variation also reduces the contribution of the composer to the organization of the basic row. Variation, as Adorno puts it, becomes "absolute." Whatever the music reveals is revealed, it can be said, without subjectivity intervening. As a form of instruction, twelve-tone music, unlike any music preceding it, is objective. What does music's objectivity teach us?

Adorno wants us to view the theme of a twelve-tone composition, which is synonymous with the variations of a row and the structural elements of the composition derived from a row, as an identity. Yet, since it is the identity of a twelve-tone *composition*, the identity of the theme does not exist in itself but is secured only through variation. The identity of the theme exists, in other words, both as the row *and* as that (variation) which is different from or not identical to the original row. Thematically, the identity of the row and its nonidentical variations are thus the same identity in their difference, which is precisely what makes each variation equally known, equally meaningful, equally valuable. And since identity and nonidentity, sameness and its difference develop virtually without limit, the identity of a twelve-tone composition leaves no difference (variation) outside. Indeed, Adorno prefers to discard the idea of a twelve-tone composition as a "work" that entails closure. Because the twelve-tone system constrains the composer to compose to the virtually infinite objective possibilities of the row, in theory a work finished is a work never really completed. Finished though incomplete, twelve-tone compositions are consequently less interesting as works than for what their objectivity teaches about the developmental tendencies of the row. What, then, are the developmental tendencies of the row?

If the row and its variations, identity and its nonidentity, sameness and its difference can develop potentially limitless forms, leaving no difference (variation) outside the composition to be expressed, does a twelve-tone composition not resemble Monet's endless series? Are not the developmental tendencies of the row toward knowledge of difference; toward permitting difference to be articulated as it is, in-itself; toward including what has been excluded so that both difference and the identities whose construction and preservation had required its repression could each be enriched by the meaning and value embodied by the other? Are not the developmental tendencies of the row toward the identity of identity and nonidentity—toward reconciliation?

NIETZSCHE'S DREAM, ADORNO'S NIGHTMARE

That nothing different remains that is not absorbed into the endless continuum of the row does not mean that the meaning and value of what finally is included are known and that identity and difference are reconciled. On the contrary, through the absoluteness of a system of variation strictly governing the developmental possibilities of the row, twelve-tone composition achieves the "rational *total* organization of the *total* musical material."[37] This "musical domination of nature," as Adorno describes it, "objectively makes music into a picture of repressive society" and even "approaches the *ideal* of mastery as domination."[38] Just when we thought music was about to escape order once and for all, "it flees forward into order," to which meaning and value are subdued. Twelve-tone composition "enchains music by liberating it." But unlike tonality—and this is decisive—which is concerned with how musical meaning can be organized, twelve-tone technique shows how its nightmare of musical organization can become meaningful. Speaking quite remarkably, as though he had in mind Nietzsche's aesthetic idealism, Adorno recalls that twelve-tone music "strives for that which once arose more freely . . . out of the decay of tonality."[39] In the "sphere of past memories" twelve-tone music finds its original aspiration, Adorno says, though Nietzsche could have been speaking, "a new will to expression," the "dream-image of the future"—a will to reconciliation. "Faced by the gravity of this dream," however, Adorno continues,

> the constructivism of twelve-tone technique reveals its constructive weakness. This constructivism is capable only of ordering the moments, without revealing their essence in any penetrating way to each other. The newness *prevented* thereby is . . . nothing but the reconciliation of those moments which twelve-tone constructivism has failed to achieve.[40]

The only music that truly can bring the idea of reconciliation within reach, twelve-tone music strives for reconciliation only to demonstrate it is unattainable. "All of its beauty," Adorno asserts, "is in denying itself the illusion of beauty" that constitutes art.[41] Twelve-tone music proves the opacity of being and by so doing takes "upon itself all the darkness and guilt of the world" so that the artwork of the future can avoid striving for an ideal that allied it with domination. Like the new music, art must become blind and admit the opacity and fathomlessness of difference. For it is only by admitting the darkness of being that art can be free of the illusion that the difference between "subject" and "object" can be overcome.[42]

THE MARRIAGE OF LIGHT AND DARK

From Adorno's aesthetic theory we recover an aesthetic form of rationality that had been trapped in art when the Sirens who had enchanted Odysseus became an object of mere contemplation. Though eventually lost to art, aesthetic reason's receptivity to the world that historically had defined individuality and that had been represented metaphorically in myth is now clarified through a theory of the artwork. An individuality whose rationality is aesthetic recognizes that the world is unknown and unknowable, forever different from its every thought of it. To be oriented receptively to the world in its fathomless diversity of differences becomes aesthetic individuality's first principle. It is the basis on which aesthetic individuality must be developed if it is to rid the world of formal reason's violence to difference, in which the individual for want of aesthetic receptivity would be implicated. Aesthetic individuality, enlightenment in possession of itself and coming to power, can break the bounds of enlightenment by affirming the darkness in which the world is shrouded. Aesthetic individuality will prove to be the marriage of light and dark.

PART II

SURFACES

"Flaunt of the sunshine I need not your bask—lie over!
You light surfaces only, I force surfaces and depths also."

Walt Whitman,
"Song of Myself"

"Through poems . . . to form individuals."

Walt Whitman,
"By Blue Ontario's Shore"

SIX

An Ethic of Appearances

UP FROM THE DEPTHS, ONTO THE SURFACES OF THE WORLD

If it were possible to summarize Adorno's achievement in his *Aesthetic Theory*, perhaps we could say that he disenchants art to reenchant the world, and by so doing reveals a deep ethical impulse within art. Whenever art seemed to disclose meanings underlying our existence, or to celebrate nature's beauty as a promise of happiness, or to intimate that those who are different from us live out possibilities in ways that also could belong to us, art turns around on itself to betray the illusory qualities of these images. Art deprives us of the belief that our world can be known in such ways, by uncovering a great divide that separates us from what lies unknown on the other side and is forever different from what we know it to be. Unforgivingly and uniquely reflexive, as art's recognition of the unknown establishes limits to what can be learned from art it establishes limits to reason as well, and it is precisely in the limits to enlightenment installed by the unknown that art's ethical impulse lies. Reenchanting the world by finding it always different from our every thought of it, art releases reason from the interest in mastery inherent in its need to universalize itself, from its mission to find itself, its principles and its laws and the world to which they pertain, everywhere and always the same. Art sustains a notion of aesthetic rationality, which through the artwork encourages a sensibility to the harm inflicted on difference in every attempt to cross the divide and make the unknown known as though the world conformed to its representations. Affirming the unknown by recognizing the difference between our thought of the world and the world itself, illuminating the violence that accompanies the attempt, in every representation of difference, to cross the divide between thinking and being, art implores us to leave difference be. Through art all the difference in the world opaque to reason takes refuge in a depth beneath the divide separating the unknown world from the known.

Art thus denies to us the identity of difference in relation to which our individuality would constitute the identity belonging to each of us. Art forces individuality up from the depths onto the surfaces of the world, to which individuality now is oriented receptively and creatively in its construction of identity. Art recasts the relation between identity and difference as a relation between surfaces and depths, so that our individuality would create our own identities in relation to surfaces that rest on depths unavailable to us as sources of the self. Oriented *receptively* to the surfaces of the world means we conceive of our possibilities for becoming as lying on the surface, which is to be thought of as the vehicle for our creativity. Depths are spaces for nature, being, and difference that remain beneath these surfaces and are exempted as sites for identity's ontology of becoming. The creative possibilities for becoming of which our identities can avail themselves are virtually indeterminate and only exclude identities that look into the depths for differences from which to distinguish themselves or through which to establish their own self-certainty.

Beyond the compelling though undeveloped idea that an aesthetically receptive individuality has at its disposal for the creation of identity all the forms in which we find surfaces formed, however, the aesthetics of surfaces and depths to which Adorno leads us conveys little of *how* individuality can orient itself creatively to surfaces as the sites for its own becoming. So while Adorno's aesthetics forces us up from the depths, returning us to the surface from where we began the long journey of enlightenment to make known what is deep and unknown, and orients individuality receptively and creatively to the surfaces of worlds about it so that their depths are left alone, the idea of aesthetic individuality to which his aesthetics gives birth is incomplete. Having relinquished any interest in a knowledge of the world that would regulate its relationship to it, individuality cannot imagine what form its creativity can assume when it is receptive to the surfaces of the world in their multiplicity of forms. Creativity is without an aesthetic form in which it can be oriented receptively to the surface forms in which the world appears.

NIETZSCHE'S PURE SURFACES

Here, Nietzsche will be of help to Adorno, as he has been so often, for he finds us on the surface of the world where we began and always have remained, a surface with depths—with meaning and value—that are our own creation and come into being only as we *will* depths by imposing form on the surface.[1] For Nietzsche, it is our "vision" of how a surface can be formed, our idea of its meaning and value we embody in our own creations, that is reflected on the surface as its depth. In *Thus Spake Zarathustra*, Nietzsche speaks of the powerful soul "to which the high body appertaineth, the handsome, triumphing, refreshing body, around which everything becometh a mirror."[2] A mirror, the world is but a reflecting surface, with "no above and no below," as Zarathustra with "avian wisdom" later sings in Nietzsche's poem. As a surface that mirrors, *as its depths*, our image of how its meaning and value can be formed, *originally* the world and each world within it—for all that the world contains is itself a world and a surface—are "pure" surfaces, surfaces without meaning and value, without depths, at least as Adorno understands depths as belonging to the surface of a world from its beginning, prior to any creative act. Nietzsche gives us to understand that only thought of as mirrors do surfaces have depths, that depths are first created as the reflection of our image of the world mirrored on its surface. Once we grasp Nietzsche's aesthetics of surfaces and depths we become the "pure, smooth mirrors" for Zarathustra's teachings.[3] We reflect as the depths of Zarathustra's creativity our ability to see on the world's surfaces reflections of what the meaning and value of worlds in their depths can become through our own creativity.

As does Adorno, Nietzsche relates us aesthetically to the surfaces of the world, though there are important differences in what they mean by an aesthetic relation. While it is clear that for both Adorno and Nietzsche an aesthetic relation entails aesthetic receptivity to the surface, differences between them lie in Nietzsche's idea of the "pure" surface to which we can be receptive, and in his idea of the relation between surfaces and depths, which will be developed shortly but already may be somewhat apparent from the way he conceives of the creation of depth on a pure surface. Moreover, when we consider Nietzsche's "will to power," we find evidence for an idea of creativity that distinguishes his concept of an aesthetic relation from Adorno's, which revolves around receptivity largely to the exclusion of any more robust idea of what form creativity can take when individuality is receptive to the surface. For Nietzsche, a will to power underlies our every vision of how we can form a world, underlies our every image, our every creation of value and meaning reflected on its surface as its depths. Consequently, a will to power "in all events ... is operating," as Nietzsche explains in *On the Genealogy of Morals*.[4] In all events "the intrinsic will to power which is precisely the will of life," Nietzsche stresses in *Beyond Good and Evil*, is "*essentially* . . . imposition of one's own forms."[5] This form-giving impulse expressing a will to power as a will to life transforms things until they "*mirror*" our power, Nietzsche writes in *Twilight of the Idols*.[6] And when the world mirrors our will to power, has exhausted our powers for imposing form on the surface of a world, then our power to "transform" the world has achieved "perfection"—it has become "art."[7]

Nietzsche is urging us to envisage "the aesthetic problem from the point of view of the artist."[8] Just as the artist creates the world from his own image, we are to relate to the world aesthetically by creating the world as the reflection of our own image, as Nietzsche makes clear by placing "creator" parenthetically adjacent to "artist." We must envisage "the aesthetic problem from the point of view of the artist (the creator)."[9] Or as he expresses it in *The Will to Power*, the artist "is only a preliminary stage" that prefigures our own aesthetic relation to the world.[10] We are to think of the "world as a work of art" in which its inhabitants originate images of the world to become its creators.[11] At the extreme, Nietzsche is saying, there is no world before the surface of the world mirrors our creation of the world's meanings and values. Or to put it even more emphatically, a world that precedes our image of a world mirrored on its surface is no world at all. Through the creativity of the artistic will to power, a world comes into being as depths that are the reflections of meanings and values created on its surface. As man's "world grows deeper," Nietzsche remarks in *Beyond Good and Evil*, "ever new stars ... come into view."[12]

In the figure of Zarathustra, Nietzsche develops an image of an individuality oriented aesthetically to surfaces and depths from the point of view of the artist.

Zarathustra adopts, and recommends that others adopt, poetic forms to be used by the creative will to form the self in its depths as a world of differences from others. Poetic forms likewise are to be adopted by the will as the media that structure the relations of the self to the world's own diversity of differences and to the worlds of differences who are others. The self is a surface formed linguistically through poetic forms whose poetic devices, such as simile, provide "hints" of the fathomless meanings that are constructed through a poetics that creates the depths of the self that make it different from other selves. Early in his journey Zarathustra advises a company of followers who call themselves his disciples,

> [s]imiles, are all names of good and evil; they do not speak out, they only hint. A fool [is it] who seeketh knowledge from them! Give heed, my brethern, to every hour when your spirit would speak in similes: there is the origin of your virtue. 13

Appearing aesthetically to others as a surface reflecting fathomless depths, Zarathustra's depths mark off his differences in the uniqueness of the meanings and values he creatively attaches to the world, so much so that he describes the self so constructed as a separate world. "To each soul belongeth another world," Zarathustra counsels. "I teach you the friend in whom the world standeth complete," by which he means that others as well, though not all others, can be thought of and should think of themselves as different worlds in precisely this way.14 As Zarathustra explains, "My brother, when thou hast a virtue, and it is thine own virtue, thou has it in common with no one.... Ineffable is it, and nameless.... Let thy virtue be too high for the familiarity of names." 15

So "every surface is a cloak," as Nietzsche asserts in *Beyond Good and Evil*, behind which one ensures self-concealment by adopting speech for "silence," as he demonstrates with the use of simile to surround Zarathustra with layers of images whose depths intimate qualities that cannot be determined from their surface meanings. If simile connotes depths and differences that are concealed, then each world in relation to every other world can be no more than a surface on which its depths and differences are reflected as that which is mysterious, inscrutable. Reflecting depths that are mysterious, surfaces importantly determine that our receptivity to the differences of the world and of others' worlds will be as though they, too, are mysterious, as Zarathustra makes clear by cautioning us to refrain from the folly of seeking out knowledge of depths. Nietzsche makes this same point more directly in *Beyond Good and Evil* where he speaks of the hermit who out of his own solitude and separation has begun to be receptive to the world by making a distinction between its surfaces and their unfathomable depths. The hermit comes to "doubt whether a philosopher *could* have any 'final and real' opinions at all, whether behind each of his caves there does not and must not lie another, deeper cave—a stranger, more comprehensive world beyond the surface." 16

When considering Nietzsche's idea of the aesthetics of individuality from the point of view of the artist receptive to surfaces as the media through which creativity unfolds, individuality's creativity and originality must not be obscured by an image of it situated in the darkness and opacity of the depths it creates. Individuality's will to power is a will to the creation of meanings and values that, whether more or less new as interpretations, additions, interpolations, or poeticizing of existing valuations, are each *different*.[17] More or less new, all meanings and valuations are different from those created last and next, which Zarathustra conveys by invoking difference through images of depth.

> [T]hen came to me the day ... Surprised and pale doth it stand—before the rosy dawn! For already she cometh, the glowing one,—*her* love to the earth cometh! Innocence, and creative desire, is all solar love! See there, how she cometh impatiently over the sea! Do ye not feel the thirst and the hot breath of her love? At the sea would she suck, and drink its depths to her height: now riseth the desire of the sea with its thousand breasts. Kissed and sucked *would* it be by the thirst of the sun; vapour *would* it become, and height, and path of light, and light itself! Verily, like the sun do I love life, and all deep seas. And this meaneth to *me* knowledge: all that is deep shall ascend—to my height.[18]

Nietzsche's spectacular imagery captures the creation of meaning and value as the illumination born with the dawn of a radiant new day, a measure of time within which we live anew. As a new dawn illumines the sea, its light *differently* reflects on the surface values creating its depths by the light of yesterdays' dawns. The new dawn's different reflections deepen seas by creating depths that tomorrow will be mirrored differently again on the surface of the sea as the source of a new valuation, a new morning of the world. Each new dawn, each new creative act of valuation, through its creativity empties the sea of yesterdays' meanings and values and of more or less of yesterdays' fathomless other depths, and reflects depths deeper than the dawns that had come before. Each new dawn's creativity thus redeems the dawns before it by transforming yesterday's "It was," as Nietzsche puts it, into today's "Thus would I have it."[19] Each new dawn's valuations are the creative will's ever varying depths, depths whose fathomless, indeterminate meanings are reflected on the surface of the sea differently from dawn to dawn, valuation to valuation, whose every value is differently valued as a darkness that the will makes its guiding light.

Throughout the span of time what depths are reflected on the surface of the sea become the measure of a creative will's height; there is nothing in its world that is not such a measure. The heavens and heights far above are the will's creations and valuations and mirrored on the sea's surface are reflected as the sea's depths, or as Nietzsche expresses it far more eloquently, "O heaven above me, thou pure deep heaven! ... Up to thy height to toss myself—that is *my* depth."[20] Throughout eternity there is no valuation that is not willed, no value formed by the will that will not be formed differently in an eternity of redemptions, so that eternity is endless creation and re-creation, an eternal becoming of value, and time a surface reflecting the infinite depth of eternity's different creations. "Joys want the eternity of *all* things," Nietzsche concludes the "drunken song,'" "they *want deep, profound eternity!*"[21] In an eternity of valuations eternally redeemed, where no depth reflected through eternity will not be reflected ever more differently and deeply on the surface, no darkness that in an eternity is not made the will's guiding light, then as Nietzsche's final words in *Beyond Good and Evil* tell, time is at last a marriage of light and dark. Now "friend *Zarathustra* has come, the guest of guests! Now . . . the wedding day has come for light and darkness."[22]

Up to now I have proposed that Nietzsche conceives of an aesthetic relation to the world as a receptive and creative orientation to its surfaces. Through our aesthetic receptivity to the surface, surfaces become the media for our creativity. How the world is deep and different for each of us appears as a reflection on its surface that mirrors our image of how we will the world to be formed. Our images achieve the status of art when the world is transformed until its surface becomes a mirror of our creativity's powers. To another the depths and differences that our aesthetic creativity wills appear as a fathomless image on a world's surface, which can become the source for another's creativity and the mirror for another's image of its depths. Finally, I have suggested that this aesthetic relation constitutes Nietzsche's idea of individuality, as exemplified by the figure of Zarathustra. Certainly these features of an aesthetic relation to the world do not exhaust Nietzsche's conception of individuality. They are, though, indispensable elements of its composition and together emerge from a consideration of "the aesthetic problem from the point of view of the artist (the creator)." I have focused only on these particular elements of aesthetic individuality in Nietzsche's thought to supplement Adorno's, though very shortly it will become evident that their conceptions of individuality cannot simply be integrated. Rather, a concept of aesthetic individuality that draws from Nietzsche and Adorno must partially revise each thinker's conception in terms of the other, and then develop this third idea in a way that would not be possible if we confined our interest to both together without further reflection.

The point of view of the artist, then, in Nietzsche's view is didactic, as it teaches what in an aesthetic sense it means to be receptive to the world and creative. To be sure, Nietzsche's interest is not in aesthetics *per se*, but in creativity, which is meaningful to him only in an aesthetic sense. And those who understand the meaning of creativity in its aesthetic sense are "noble." With this the decisive feature of Nietzsche's idea of an aesthetic individuality is highlighted. To be noble is to be the "determiner of values," to be one who "*creates values*" as an artist creates a work of art, on the surface of a world that reflects the artist's image of a world as its depths.[23] Yet, it is neither primarily in actions, which are "always ambiguous, always unfathomable," nor even through "works" that nobility is defined. With respect to what is noble, Nietzsche argues, it is only "*faith* which is decisive here, which determines the order of rank here . . . some fundamental certainty which a noble soul possesses in regard to itself."[24] As

Nietzsche answers the question "What is noble?", in other words, we learn that a surface's reflection of an image created by the artist-creator and mirrored as the depth of a world is prior to and in spite of actions and works. In essence, the reflection of the creator's image of the world is, first and foremost, the reflection on some sort of surface of the creator's *idea* of what values the world *ought necessarily to* reflect as its depths. Either the world is a surface that actually mirrors nobility's creativity, as it would if it were the scene of nobility's works, or nobility's creativity is mirrored by the surface of its eye, as nobility envisions the world, by the surface of its ear, as nobility believes the world ought to sound, or by the surface of its mind, as nobility conceives the world. It seems evident that the identity of what is noble, that "fundamental certainty which a noble soul possesses in regard to itself," is always the image of nobility's creation of value reflected on the *surface* (of the world, of the mind, of the eye, of the ear) as its depth, and the product of an aesthetic receptivity to surfaces as the vehicles of its creativity.

Nietzsche's idea of an aesthetic relation to the surface of the world thus leads to an understanding of how identity is created for the noble type, how identity is formed for an individuality whose orientation to the world is aesthetic. What Nietzsche's argument about the interrelationship between aesthetics, surfaces, and nobility suggests is that identity can be created without regard to the depths of another world, that is, without entailing the representation of what Adorno understood to be nonidentity or difference. Indeed, Nietzsche's idea of an aesthetic relation to the surface of the world bears a striking resemblance to the concept at which Adorno arrives in *Negative Dialectics* and that is anticipated in *Aesthetic Theory*. This is Adorno's utopian conception of identity "beyond identity and beyond contradiction (*über der Identität und über dem Widerspruch*)," that is, of identity no longer constituted through a relation of contradiction to nonidentity and difference.[25] Presented at a high level of abstraction in Adorno's work, this concept is illustrated clearly by Nietzsche in *On the Genealogy of Morals* and, in fact, is introduced at precisely the moment he discusses the nature of the relation through which the identity of nobility is constituted.

> While every noble morality develops from a triumphant affirmation of itself, slave morality from the outset says No to what is "outside," what is "different," what is "not itself"; and *this* No is its creative deed. This inversion of the value-positing eye—this *need* to direct one's view outward instead of back to oneself—is of the essence of *ressentiment*.[26]

> [The] noble man . . . conceives the basic concept "good" in advance and spontaneously out of himself and only then creates for himself an idea of "bad"! This "bad" of noble origin and that "evil" out of the cauldron of unsatisfied hatred—the former an after-production, a side issue, a contrasting shade, the latter on the contrary the original thing, the beginning, the distinctive *deed* in the conception of a slave morality.[27]

Later, when in *Twilight of the Idols* Nietzsche thinks back to this argument in his *Genealogy*, he recalls it by saying, "Of the antithetical concepts of a *noble* morality and a *ressentiment* morality," it is only the latter that derives "from a *denial* of the former."[28] And in *Thus Spake Zarathustra* Nietzsche had argued that "[n]o people could live without first valuing; if a people will maintain itself, however, it must not value as its neighbor valueth. Much that passed for good with one people was regarded with scorn and contempt by another."[29] What Nietzsche in each of his works rejects consistently is the logic that Adorno rejects, the logic that individual or group "identity requires difference in order to be."[30] If Nietzsche had not rejected this logic of contradiction, we then could easily describe Zarathustra's beliefs and values, the beliefs and values of the noblest type, for they would have been constructed within the context of a relation of contradiction between identity and difference and thus appear as the negation of that morality that Zarathustra opposes. In that case, Zarathustra's beliefs and values, his "creative deed," would be a "No" to whatever lies "outside" and is "different" and formed no differently from the creativity and morality of the slave. As we found, though, Zarathustra's identity is an unfathomable depth created on a surface through an aesthetics that "cloaks" his depths and differences and whose creation does not rely upon a logic that negates the depths and differences of others.

For Nietzsche, identity consequently is formed through an aesthetic receptivity to the surface. Identity need not be created as the moral identity of the slave is constituted, through the representation and denial of difference belonging to others. Identity need not be constituted through a dialectical process of enlightenment, by which the depths and differences of one's own identity are created through the contradiction of what deep and different in the identity of another is falsely presumed to be known. If identities could not be conceived from the point of view of the artist, through an aesthetic receptivity to surfaces whereby differences are newly created, rather than serving as preexisting characteristics to be negated, then Zarathustra could not be "beyond" good and evil. Zarathustra's creativity would be restricted to values and meanings ordered by disciplinary practices shaped by the logic of a framework of contradiction, the mechanics of slave morality that confine identity to the duality of good and evil and its variations. Zarathustra's identity is rather a difference created aesthetically outside the logic of such a framework, as is the identity of every individuality created as a depth on the surface of a world. By conceiving of identity as the creation of depth through an aesthetic receptivity to surfaces on which creativity occurs, Nietzsche appears to respond to Adorno's concerns about the violence intrinsic to thinking throughout the history of enlightenment. Since aesthetic individuality does not require the representation of difference to be, it can create difference as an unfathomable depth beyond the identitarian thinking peculiar to the representational logic of contradiction. As had Adorno's, Nietzsche's idea of an aesthetic receptivity to surfaces on which creativity takes place seems to enable the difference belonging to oneself or to another or to the world to disappear into the darkness beyond the horizon that separates the unknown from the known, the fathomless depth from the surface it lies beneath.

Or does it? It initially appeared that, like Adorno, Nietzsche orients individuality receptively to the surfaces of a world so that identity's difference, either the depth as which individuality creates itself on a surface or the depths belonging to another, would be situated in the realm of the unknown and sealed off from the violence in the representations of thought. It was Nietzsche, we should recall, who challenged the rationality of the Enlightenment's self-understanding with the terrifying idea, though Adorno could have been speaking, that "in all desire to know there is already a drop of cruelty."[31] By concealing differences within fathomless depths, differences whose identities would be "beyond identity and beyond contradiction," Nietzsche seemed to aspire to that same utopia to which Adorno aspires, the "togetherness of differences (*ein Miteinander des Verschiedenen*)," a togetherness of individuals or groups whose differences lie beyond one another's encroach.[32] Yet, there is a fundamental difference between Adorno and Nietzsche's formulations of the relation between surfaces and depths, a difference that undermines the aesthetics of Nietzsche's idea of individuality by drawing it into the orbit of formal reason. For Adorno, depth resides *beneath* the surface. For Nietzsche, depth appears as the reflection of creativity *on* the surface. While in the preceding chapters I have tried to account for Adorno's view, to discover the basis of Nietzsche's understanding of the aesthetics of surfaces and depths we must turn back briefly to the concept of the will to power to consider the assumptions that underlie his notion of an aesthetic orientation to the world. Doing so will permit us to better determine the meaning assigned to depth and difference when it becomes an "aesthetic problem from the point of view of the artist (the creator)."

THE CREATIVE WILL AND ITS DESTRUCTION OF DEPTH

Since the world acquires depth only as the mirror image of the heights the will creates on a world's surface, as Zarathustra's stunning parable of creativity's solar love of the sea attests, what becomes of depths antecedent to the creative act and lying beneath the surface on which the will imposes its forms? Let us ask this question supposing, in other words, that a world possesses depths as being-in-itself, as we learn from Adorno, depths whose meaning would be ineligible for recognition as depths by a will to power who sees depth only as the reflection of its own creations. To a will heedless of such depths and their difference from the surface, depths become indistinguishable from the surface, in theory and practice are taken for a part of the surface, and thus the differences such depths embody would be represented by the creative will's aesthetic activity on the surface of a world. As surfaces, Adorno's antecedent depths would be transformed into the mirror images of forms imposed upon surfaces by others. The meaning of Adorno's depths would be obscured, effaced, or otherwise violated as they are reflected as depths whose meaning has been created by another, so that depths taken for part of the surface become perpetually other than they are. Nietzsche eagerly concedes this where he has Zarathustra proclaim while explaining the nature of the will to his disciples: "[B]eing" shall "accommodate and bend itself to you! So willeth your will. Smooth shall [being] become and subject to the spirit, as its mirror and reflection. That is your entire will . . . as a Will to Power."[33]

Clearly, the aesthetics of the will to power implicitly entails the disenchantment of being (which as Nietzsche also argues explicitly and often is simply "an empty fiction"), and it entails the rejection of being's corresponding property of the in-itself (which he denounces no less frequently and emphatically).[34] Without some version of being-in-itself, moreover (and it need not be Kant's), nature, like being, becomes meaningless in any terms other than those the creative will imposes on it. Nature becomes a "difference" compelled to submit to what Adorno referred to as morbid projection.[35] Nature becomes just another "depth" to be taken as part of a surface, as Nietzsche insists by saying, "in nature there is no *sound*, it is mute; no color; no form either, for form is the result of a reflection of the surface in the eye."[36] Adorno, of course, opens the way to conceive of being-in-itself and nature and difference, in a word, of *depths*, as the unknown, as that which is nonidentical with thought, for which he finds support in aesthetic theory and in arguments about thinking drawn from Kant and Hegel (and perhaps from the early Nietzsche).[37] As the unknown inaccessible to thinking, the depth of being, nature, and difference is shielded from identitarian thought by orienting reason receptively to surfaces in a way that leaves differences in their depths alone. Against this backdrop of Adorno's position, based on a rejection of being and the in-itself Nietzsche's depths now prove to be based on the rejection of depths, and not only on the rejection of depths rooted in being-in-itself and nature but on the rejection of the depth of difference as well. For when depths are simply mirror images of an aesthetic activity on a surface, as mere surface reflections depths *are not different from surfaces*, which is to say that the difference that Nietzsche's depths represent is not a real difference, as it is a depth that is not a real depth but a mere reflection. Consequently, the rejection of depths that accompanies Nietzsche's rejection of being and the in-itself secures a surface to which depths are converted, and within which the depth of difference vanishes.

Converted to surfaces, then, Adorno's antecedent depths become the surface to which Nietzsche's will relates as an expression of *formal reason*. Depths that lay beneath a world, defining its difference and acting as the rich background of creations on its surface, become instead the plastic foreground on which the will imposes its forms. Even Nietzsche's depths, first coming into existence only as they originate on the surface, as the foreground of the will's subsequent creativity relinquish any value they acquired as the creations of an aesthetic point of view that is supposedly "*affirmation, blessing, deification of existence.*"[38] Converted to surfaces, depths are subject to the will's explosion of creative powers, through which whatever appears on the surface of a world undergoes violent metamorphosis. As Nietzsche argues in The Gay Science, although "all aesthetic values" may be variously distinguished from one another, the question as to whether

> the desire to fix, to immortalize, the desire for *being* prompted creation, or the desire for destruction, for change, for future, for *becoming* . . . [,]

is resolved further into a "main distinction," according to which he then asks "in every instance: 'is it hunger or superabundance that has here become creative?'"[39] Underlying this more fundamental distinction, Nietzsche continues, the creativity of hunger and the creativity of superabundance have in common the "desire for destruction, change, becoming," which

> *can* be the expression of an overfull power pregnant with the future . . . but it can also be the hatred of the ill-constituted, disinherited, underprivileged, which destroys, *has* to destroy, because what exists, indeed existence itself, all being itself, enrages and provokes it.[40]

So the desire for destruction is the ultimate source of creativity. The desire for becoming is the expression of the will to power's artistic desire for the destruction of what exists, of all existence, all being, an expression of what Nietzsche elsewhere refers to as the "artists' violence."[41] "Cruelty," in other words, is a principal element of the creative will's artistic transfigurations, as Nietzsche explains.[42] Cruelty enables art to achieve "perfection," to transform the surface of the world into a mirror of the creative will's powers. While in fairness to Nietzsche we must recall that his aesthetics of surfaces is committed to the *redemption* of depths, it nevertheless is clear that redemption occurs through the extinction of depth and its difference by a will eternally sacrificing existing depths for different depths, in an eternity of creative acts reproducing the identitarianism of formal reason. As Nietzsche says bluntly through Zarathustra, "only where there are graves are there resurrections."[43]

Now that we have learned the fate of depths beneath the surface on which the will imposes its forms, which is the fate of Nietzsche's depths reflected on the surface as well, let us ask a different question of Nietzsche, one that brings his relationship to Adorno regarding the matter of depth into sharper focus, namely, why must depths and their differences be the object of the will's destructive power? Indirectly, of course, an answer to this question already has been provided as we recognized that Nietzsche's interest in aesthetics was the expression of his interest in creativity, in individuality. Nietzsche does not destroy depths for the sake of destruction, in other words, but for the sake of creativity, though depth is related to creativity in a dual sense. From what we have learned of the aesthetics of Nietzsche's will to power, we should suspect that there is a concept of depth that poses an obstacle to creativity as Nietzsche understands it, a depth that is being destroyed in every act of the will also creative of depth. At the same time, since the will is as creative of depth as it is destructive, the idea of depth obviously is not one that Nietzsche chooses to dispense with. There are no doubt important reasons why he retains the language of depth despite the obstacles it poses.

Nietzsche's idea of depth originates in his critique of the distinction between appearance and reality. "The 'apparent' world," Nietzsche argues in *Twilight of the Idols*, "is the only one: the 'real' world has only been *lyingly added*. . . ."[44] As the realm in which "being" is situated, the "real" world is likewise the realm of truth, such that Nietzsche's indictment of the concept of the real world is rooted, in turn, in his critique of the belief that there can be a truth known about being. In Zarathustra's words,

> "Will to Truth" do ye call it, ye wiseth ones, that which impelleth you and maketh you ardent? Will for the thinkableness of all being: thus do *I* call your will! All being would ye *make* thinkable: for ye doubt with good reason whether it be already thinkable.[45]

Here Nietzsche describes the will to truth as a form of the will to power—its inversion. In its form as the will to truth, the will to power has been overwhelmed by the need to erase uncertainty about the impermanence and indeterminacy of the world of "appearance," the doubt whether there is any objectivity at all to being beneath or behind or beyond the world of appearance. As it is conceptualized through the will to truth, the image of "being" formed by the will to power, which is but one of its images of the world, is transformed into an immutable "real" world of universal value against which the value of all other forms of existence are to be measured. The will to truth valorizes being over becoming, a symptom of the creative will's decay.

Confined to a standard outside of itself, a standard of truth it has set up over itself, for the creative will also "wants to be master within itself and around itself and to feel itself master," as a will to truth the will to power's creativity is paralyzed by its own creations.[46] It were as though the will's limitless desire for creativity that finds expression in its power to form its world had been deadened by the belief that the meaning and value of the world lay in its own unaffected being, not in being a work of art, a created work. It were as though the world could be appreciated only through an "*immaculate* perception of all things," as Zarathustra says sarcastically, that wants "nothing else from them, but to be allowed to lie before them as a mirror with a hundred facets."[47] Nietzsche is describing the wish to allow the world to be reflected *as it is essentially*, the wish to enable the world to gainsay its appearances and to speak in its own terms, terms that establish standards to which all that appears or could appear in the world should conform. He is describing the wish for the world of appearances, the world created by the will to power, to be reconciled to the in-itself of the world, to its innermost depths. If there is to be the *creation* of value, however, value valued for its *difference* from rather than correspondence to a known value, something other than a "real world lyingly added" to the apparent world must be willed. Or as Zarathustra declares, "[S]omething higher than all reconciliation must the Will will which is the Will to Power."[48]

By disavowing the depth of a "real" world, then, Nietzsche emancipates the will to power from inversions of the will that subdue its creativity by holding it accountable to forms that have achieved mastery over its creative drive. Yet, Nietzsche's intention is not simply to rid us of the concept of the real world but of the dichotomy "real" and "apparent," because the antinomy "appearance-reality" continues to impose itself on the creativity of the will to power. As Nietzsche explains in the context of critically reappropriating artistic creativity,

> to divide the world into a "real" and "apparent" world . . . is only a suggestion of *decadence*—a symptom of declining life. . . . That the artist places a higher value on appearance than on reality constitutes no objection to this proposition. For "appearance" here signifies reality *once more*, only selected, strengthened, corrected.[49]

If the artistic will creating appearances (forms, images) is thought of as a will creating and re-creating, or selecting, strengthening, and correcting "reality," appearances then constitute reality and acquire the value accorded reality.[50] According appearance the same value as reality, the artist appears to perpetuate the antinomy appearance-reality and the devaluation of appearances it entails, though only in part. Although the aesthetic point of view of the artist initially falls within the conventional frame "appearance-reality," it does so in a way that eventually allows artistic creativity to escape the devaluation the antinomy attaches to artistic "appearances" and forces the abolition of the antinomy itself. With appearances valued as reality, the normative distinction between appearance and reality finally collapses, so that appearances no longer are devalued against the real world and the antinomy itself also begins to dissolve. When appearances become reality, the "real" world disappears, which Nietzsche concludes ingeniously by saying that once "we have abolished the real world: what world is left? The apparent world perhaps? . . . But no! *With the real world we have also abolished the apparent world.*"[51]

Hence, by "envisaging the aesthetic problem from the point of view of the artist (the creator)," Nietzsche transcends (in the inclusive sense of "negates") the antinomy "appearance and reality," for which he substitutes the distinction between "surfaces and depths." Surfaces and depths permit appearances (surfaces) to acquire the value of reality (depths), but to acquire it in a way that immeasurably increases their value as a reflection of what depths the will to power creates on a surface. For as value is the depth of creations newly formed and reflected on a surface composed of past valuations, what the will to power differently creates redeems values earlier created, creating a depth whose value becomes as deep as an eternity of valuations, as a reflection of depths that extends into infinity. To put it differently, if the value of depth is incomparably more valuable than the value of what was "real," it is because Nietzsche replaces a depth that weighs down the creativity of the will to power by a depth that reflected by the light on the surface, makes the will light, that is, allows the will to be creative without proscription.

Now taking Adorno and Nietzsche's aesthetics together, without knowing its origin we could easily attribute to Adorno Nietzsche's extraordinary remark in *The Will to Power* that "We possess *art* lest we *perish from the truth*."[52] For Adorno, art preserves a receptivity to the world at the core of individuality that distinguishes an aesthetic form of individuality from the modern subject. As ancient as Odysseus though sharing with individuality roots far older, the modern subject is disciplined by a pursuit of truth, enlightenment, grounded in a primordial fear of the unknown, and its ideal of truth, the Enlightenment, is the abolition of the unknown. In opposition to e/Enlightenment's pursuit and ideal of truth, art recognizes the unknown as that from which thinking is ineluctably divided. Art teaches that the abolition of the unknown is not, as e/Enlightenment supposes, knowing the unknown but the violent transformation of the unknown into a form that is no longer strange to thought, so that abolishing the unknown is actually the extinction of the unknown, of what in nature and being is different from thought. From Adorno's aesthetics of the artwork aesthetic individuality is recovered as a receptivity to the world opposed to the extinction of the unknown. As is art, aesthetic individuality is premised on the recognition of the great divide between thinking and being, nature, and difference, so that oriented to the world as art is oriented aesthetic individuality would let be what is different from thought lest it perish from the truth. As is art, aesthetic individuality is receptive to the surface of the world beneath which it permits the unknown to lie as an unfathomable depth protected from the incursions of formal reason.

Yet, on the basis of Adorno's understanding of art aesthetic individuality finds itself little more than receptive to the world's surface as to a barrier to the violation of what depths possess. While aesthetic individuality finds the surface mysterious and in mystery perhaps the inspiration for its creativity, its creativity remains undeveloped beyond the concept of aesthetic receptivity that individuality has at its disposal as a way of imagining its relation to the surface. Nevertheless, though Adorno leaves the creativity of individuality undeveloped beyond an aesthetic receptivity to surfaces, his idea of the depth beneath the surface is indispensable to an individuality whose ethic cultivates, out of its respect for difference, an acute, aesthetic sensibility to the violence to difference in thought. It is individuality's aesthetic sensibility to violence that is at the very heart of Horkheimer and Adorno's *critique of enlightenment*.

Nietzsche contributes to the conceptual development of the aesthetic dimensions of individuality precisely where Adorno's contribution leaves off. Individuals appear wonderfully as surfaces and depths and are receptive to others and to the world as to worlds composed of surfaces and depths. Depths are reflected on the surface as individuality's fathomless creations of meaning and value, the immeasurable measure of its differences from others. Differences reflected as the depths of surfaces constitute individuality's identity, an identity that does not require the fathomless differences belonging to others to serve as representations in contradiction to which individuality creates and identifies itself. When individuality creates its identity it takes both the differences with which it forms itself as a world and the differences forming the worlds of others to lie beyond representation as depths concealed by a surface. At all times for Nietzsche, individuality's creativity remains on the surface, an identity "beyond identity and beyond contradiction," an identity beyond identity as it is constituted through the representation and negation of differences belonging to others. Nietzsche's aesthetics of surfaces and depths recognizes that from the point of view of the artist, difference can be the *product* of a relation to the world through which individuality creates its identity aesthetically. Difference need not be the requirement, the *precondition* of a relation through which identity is created according to the logic of the morality of the slave.

Nietzsche's aesthetic creativity on surfaces consequently opposes truth on his terms and on Adorno's terms as well. Envisaging the aesthetic problem from the point of view of the artist, the problem of creation from the perspective of what the creator envisions upon a surface, the will creates depths and differences and then deeper depths from the depths it earlier created. No depth may set a standard for creativity. Unencumbered by depth the will is able to create its own good and evil, becoming "light," a "bird" defying the "spirit of gravity," as Nietzsche speaks of the will creating on the surface rather than from the depths of the world, as do "the mole and the dwarf, who say, 'Good for all, evil for all.'"⁵³ Envisioning every new depth to be different from the last depth created on a surface, Nietzsche seems to likewise affirm Adorno's view that depth is always deeper and different than we know, that there is no depth with which thought, no difference with which identity, is ever reconciled. Nietzsche's aesthetics thus seems to anticipate a concept of individuality whose creativity would not reproduce the violence that Adorno attributes to thinking that denies the difference between a thought of a world and the world itself.

By conceiving of depths only as reflections of creations on the surface, though, Nietzsche assimilates to the surface on which creativity occurs other and unknown depths that may lie below, antecedent depths of which he is heedless. Nietzsche's aesthetic achievement finally comes at the expense of depths and their differences by converting all depths into the surfaces on which individuality's will represents its creations. Although by envisaging the aesthetic problem from the point of view of the artist he orients individuality receptively to the surfaces of the world, freeing creativity from the limitations imposed by depths presumed to be known or knowable, Nietzsche's aesthetic achievement ultimately fails to meet the criteria belonging to our concept of aesthetic individuality. Nietzsche's aesthetics wants for an idea of depth that acknowledges the unknown and unknowable depths through which Adorno's aesthetics establishes the philosophical basis for individuality's aesthetic receptivity to the surfaces of the world. This particular philosophical deficit compromises an individuality that not only is creative but through a recognition of the unknown attempts to cultivate an aesthetic sensibility to the violence in its creativity that shields differences in their depths from the violence of representation. Like the depths imagined by Nietzsche, Adorno's unknown depths do not limit individuality's creativity as do the "fathomable" depths that ground truths and other universals and ideals creativity must obey, to which in the interest of creativity Nietzsche rightly opposes his concept of depth. Without a concept of antecedent, unknown depth comparable to Adorno's, Nietzsche's aesthetics may even threaten to diminish individuality by imagining its creations as possessing depths indistinguishable from the way they appear on the surface. Individuality would be productive of depths without difference.

An aesthetic individuality whose ethic equally values creativity and the cultivation of a sensibility to the violence in the representation of difference revolves around the possibility of marrying aesthetic creativity on the surfaces of the world, along Nietzsche's lines, to an aesthetic sensibility to the depths of the world, along Adorno's. Surely one path to such a conceptual marriage would be through work that can be brought to bear on individuality as an aesthetic problem. This is the path that opens to us only if we do not neglect the centrality of the role played by Adorno's aesthetics of the artwork and by Nietzsche's efforts to envisage the aesthetic problem from the point of view of the artist. Given the philosophical requirements Adorno and Nietzsche compel art and artist to meet, it might be impossible to imagine such a marriage of artwork and artist if it were not for the work of Walt Whitman, whose poetry so seamlessly weaves both together that they are nearly indistinguishable. With an uncanny precision bearing all the marks of an imaginary collaboration between Nietzsche and Adorno, Whitman in two extraordinary poetic lines distills his thoughts about individuality into an image that weds the aesthetic point of view of the artist who orients us creatively to the surfaces of a world to an aesthetics of the artwork protective of its depths by encouraging a sensibility to the violence in creativity. As Whitman writes in "Song of Myself,"[54]

> Flaunt of the sunshine I need not your bask—lie over!
> You light surfaces only, I force surfaces and depths also. (987–88)

In the discussion completing this chapter we shall see how as an artist (the creator), Whitman is creative of value, of an "ethic of appearances," as I call it, in artwork through which he affirms a great divide between the known and the unknown, appearance and reality, in poetry that traces the depths of a world unavailable to an aesthetic individuality whose creativity is confined receptively to its surfaces. When in the following chapter we next have the opportunity to recall these lines, we will be in the process of discovering how from the point of view of the artist Whitman's ethic reflects as its own depths the idea of an aesthetic individuality creative of limitless depths on the limitless surfaces of limitless worlds.

INTO THE UNKNOWN

In "A Song of the Rolling Earth," Whitman encourages us to adopt a counterintuitive attitude toward art, one very nearly resembling that recommended by Adorno's aesthetics.[55]

> A song of the rolling earth, and of words according,
> Were you thinking that those were the words, those upright lines?
> > those curves, angles, dots?
> No, those are not the words, the substantial words are in the
> > ground and sea,
> They are in the air, they are in you. (1–4)

> The workmanship of souls is by those inaudible words of the earth,
> The masters know the earth's words and use them more than
> > audible words. (15–16)

> I swear I begin to see little or nothing in audible words. (98)

As he opens his poem by thematizing the inadequacy of language, Whitman's ostensible interest is preliminary to a deeper concern. Although Whitman highlights the connection between the limitations of language and what it is that language excludes, his poem draws our attention away from the insufficiencies of language and toward a line that divides us from a world of meaning inaccessible to language. The fault appears to lie less with the poverty of language than with the remoteness of worlds—the ground, the sea, the air, and each of us—whose meaning is thus remote, or "inaudible," as he says. Poets, "masters," do not bring the inaudible within reach of language. Contrary to our sense of the aesthetics of poetry, poetry's art is not the expression of the inexpressible, a claim that Adorno makes with regard to all art. For Whitman as for Adorno it is a matter of confirming boundaries, rather than an aesthetic dissolution of boundaries normally separating us from the world, as though art could allow us to see or hear what could not be seen or heard without the work of art. Using "inaudible words," as Whitman formulates it paradoxically, words that neither can be written nor spoken, poets convey silence. Poetry reveals as the inadequacy of language an absence that marks the presence of worlds that have no voice. It is a silence Whitman intends for us to hear. "I speak not," Whitman explains, "yet if you hear me not of what avail am I to you?" (26). Where speech is inarticulate appear the "words of the *eloquent dumb* great mother" earth (41; my italics), as do appear all words that cannot be spoken, and are thus heard.

Nonidentity and the Unknown

Whitman's conception of language is dialectical, though in the unfamiliar sense in which Adorno speaks of a "negative dialectic." Far more important than its representational features are language's aesthetic capacities for nonidentity. In fact, as will become evident shortly, the capacity of language to identify, or to represent, becomes of use to us ethically as speakers or hearers, as seers or actors, only when we develop an aesthetic awareness through poetry that language alludes to something necessarily outside of it. It is this ineradicable "outside," an identity that escapes representation (or identification), that is unknown and remains unknown, which Adorno introduced as the "nonidentical." Typically, though, poetry appears to privilege representation. "Upright lines, curves, angles and dots," all the resources of language, to paraphrase Whitman, seem to identify what is outside, to discover and express its meaning. Poetic reflection on the nonidentical, then, on that which is "untransmissible by print" (23), in Whitman's words, is a self-conscious recognition by the poet, to whom Whitman in his poem refers, of that which evades language.

Straining to illustrate this lesson in "A Song of the Rolling Earth," Whitman resorts to making it explicit ("The masters know the earth's words and use them more than audible words"), perhaps not trusting our sensitivity to a poetry that reflects on its own aesthetic practices. To be sure, poetic reflection on the nonidentical does not appear for Whitman to be a natural or inevitable turn that poetry takes. It is more an angle of aesthetic reflection implicit in the artwork of poetic representation that poetic language by its own insufficiencies pressures the poet to adopt. From this angle Whitman views language from what lies beyond it and installs into poetry an aesthetic recognition of what it is unable to represent. Through such aesthetic recognition poetry offers Whitman a consistent sense of nonidentity, a sense of a meaningful world that is unknown. As Whitman admits in "Song of Myself," and as he elsewhere explains in various ways, "My voice goes after what my eyes cannot reach. . . . Speech is the twin of my vision, it is unequal to measure itself" (564, 566). "Unequal to *measure* itself" (my italics)—poetry is unable to represent, to identify, to speak what words it makes heard. Taking language into the unknown, Whitman finds the same tragic dimension in the capacity of poetic language to trace images of worlds it leaves out that Adorno later discovers in art.

Poetry's "negative dialectic," to now draw Whitman even more securely into Adorno's orbit, indirectly proves the fathomless objectivity of the world. Occasionally Whitman abandons such subtlety, as he does in "A Song of the Rolling Earth" when, establishing the meaningfulness of an otherwise unknown world, and implying the Kantian thesis underlying it, he describes our earth as "latent in itself from the jump," wherein its "truths . . . continually wait" (19, 22). Meaning lies "Underneath the ostensible," in "possessing words that never fail" (38, 40). No less declarative in "Song of Myself," Whitman there reports that "All truths wait in all things" (648). Similarly in *Democratic Vistas* Whitman refers to the "purport of objective Nature . . . doubtless folded, hidden somewhere here," the motif circulating throughout his work that permits him, as we see in "Song of the Redwood-Tree," to attribute identity to worlds-in-themselves that in any more substantial way must remain opaque with an "untold life" (24).[56] But whether he relies upon a negative dialectic to project the nonidentity of surrounding worlds or, perhaps being somewhat didactic, invokes the identity of meaningful worlds-in-themselves only to insist on their anonymity, Whitman is adamant in his refusal to decipher or interpret the unknown. Perhaps warding off interest in the secrets we might hope or expect his poetry to reveal, in "A Song of the Rolling Earth" Whitman admonishes,

> I swear I see what is better than to tell the best,
> It is always to leave the best untold. (102–3)
>
> The best of the earth cannot be told anyhow . . . (108)
>
> I swear I will henceforth never have to do with the faith that tells
>   the best,
> I will have to do only with that faith that leaves the best untold. (119–20)

Whitman is careful to distinguish the unknown from what can be known. Each of us is a world known to himself or herself only, a conviction Whitman expresses more or less emphatically. Self-knowing, moreover, often entails other restrictions on the possibility of our knowing any other world. Whitman sometimes suggests, for instance, that knowing oneself or about oneself sets limits to whatever else I can know, as he does in "Song of Myself" by observing that "One world is aware and by far the largest to me, and that is myself" (416). More often he simply instructs us to modest considerations of what we can know of another, as when he concludes without wistfulness in "A Song of the Rolling Earth" that,

> The song is to the singer, and comes back most to him,
> The teaching is to the teacher, and comes back most to him,
> The murder is to the murderer, and comes back most to him,
> The theft is to the thief, and comes back most to him,
> The love is to the lover, and comes back most to him,
> The gift is to the giver, and comes back most to him—it cannot
>   fail,
> The oration is to the orator, the acting is to the actor and actress
>   not to the audience,
> And no man understands any greatness or goodness but his own,
>   or the indication of his own. (82–89)

What is Whitman's inspiration? In part, the impulse to limit what we can know of worlds outside each of us originates in an acute aesthetic sensibility to difference. Whitman's determination to trace an ontological divide between the known and unknown requires that every "I" be recognized aesthetically by every other "I" as a unique world of difference whose being lies in darkness. We must be distrustful of thinking that we know another, Whitman insists in "Are You the New Person Drawn toward Me?"[57] "To begin with take warning, I am surely far different from what you suppose," Whitman assures us, as only one could who knew that his appearance and our image of him may be "all maya, illusion" (2, 9). Whitman rarely abridges this distance. He allows there may be one "Among the Multitude," as he entitles his wish for a perfect lover, who through Whitman's "faint indirections" (6) discovers the difference distinguishing him from others.[58] Knowledge of another, though, is finally the privilege of dreams. Boundaries denying access to another vanish where "I dream in my dream all the dreams of the other dreamers, And I become the other dreamers.... Only from me can they hide nothing," Whitman imagines in "The Sleepers" (30–31, 37).[59] Here reconciliation, as the possibility of knowing another, becomes possible only as a dream.

It is not only our own appearances that do not reveal to others what is different about each of us. Appearances resist disclosure universally. "The skies of day and night, colors, densities, forms," Whitman speculates in "Of the Terrible Doubt of Appearances," "may-be these are (as doubtless they are) only apparitions, and the real something has yet to be known ... (How often I think neither I know, nor any man knows, aught of them)" (6, 8).[60] So Whitman does not mean to channel the distrust of appearances he encourages into a search for the real something yet to be known. He is stressing that from appearances we can know nothing of worlds that appearances identify. And since "identity" (representation, appearance) is the "only entrance to all facts," as he puts it in *Democratic Vistas*, if we can know nothing real from appearances we can know nothing real at all. Appearances act rather like language. It is their peculiarity to intimate a presence that eludes grasp. How often Whitman tells us that no sooner does something catch his eye than it immediately brings into view what cannot be seen. "Oxen that rattle the yoke and chain or halt in the leafy shade, what is that you express in your eyes?" Whitman asks in "Song of Myself." "It seems to me more than all the print I have read in my life" (235–36).

Whitman consistently installs paradox into our lives. What is true of oxen is true of all worlds. Each world exceeds what can be sensed, spoken, written, and represented of it. And perhaps infinitely so, we cannot be certain, which is a consequence of the fundamental uncertainty belonging to the unknown. What "certainty" we do own is the presence of worlds established largely through their absence. Inquiring about the world, Whitman thus leaves us with an interpretive darkness, as he does here in "Song of Myself."

A child said *What is the grass?* fetching it to me with full hands;
How could I answer the child? I do not know what it is any more
    than he.

> I guess it must be the flag of my disposition, out of hopeful green
>   stuff woven.
> Or I guess it is the handkerchief of the Lord,
> A scented gift and remembrancer designedly dropt,
> Bearing the owner's name someway in the corners, that we may see
>   and remark, and say *Whose?*
> Or I guess the grass is itself a child, the produced babe of the
>   vegetation.
> Or I guess it is a uniform hieroglyphic . . . (99–106)

Uniform hieroglyphics, leaves of grass stand, if they stand for anything, for what *resists* interpretation. Does not Whitman conclude this inquiry with lines that complete a metaphysical journey from puzzlement to interpretive indeterminacy to an interpretive darkness that is heard even while it is unspoken?

> This grass is very dark to be from the white heads of old mothers,
> Darker than the colorless beards of old men,
> Dark to come from under the faint red roofs of mouths. (116–18)

Leaves of grass are dark, too dark to be white, too dark to be colorless, too dark to be colored. Resisting identification by way of comparison, they stand outside of conceptualization, the dark turning into darkness. Whitman leaves behind what is familiar as the means of discovering what is different. He catches himself in a web of comparisons, but he accepts his predicament not as an incitement to know what is different but as compelling him to choose between assimilating worlds to worlds comparatively known and accepting the darkness of the unknown. Whitman accepts the darkness, as he assures us again in his "Song of the Open Road."[61]

> You road I enter upon and look around, I believe you are not all
>   that is here,
> I believe that much unseen is also here. (16–17)
>
> I believe you are latent with unseen existences . . . (29)

Perspectivism and the Unknown

Nonidentity is but one of two angles of aesthetic reflection through which Whitman grounds the unknown. He proposes, as well, that in ways we are unaware of we are naturally perspectival. Objects perceived, Whitman cautions in "Of the Terrible Doubt of Appearances," "Maybe seeming to me what they are (as doubtless they indeed but seem), as from my present point of view, and might prove (as of course they would) nought of what they appear, or nought anyhow, from entirely changed points of view" (9). Not one "seeming" being more real than another seeming, Whitman's perspectivism confines us receptively to appearances and does not for a moment entertain a connection between appearance and an underlying reality. His perspectivism may go further. Does Whitman's perspectivism not also undermine the very idea of "semblance" (seeming, appearance) by implying that what is perceived, though a representation, as mere perspective is disconnected from what it identifies and consequently is no representation at all? This seems to be Whitman's more radical intention, especially as it appears to be implied by his figurative gesture "*or nought anyhow, from entirely changed points of view*" (my italics). Disconnected from what is real of worlds, appearances do not constitute a denial that there is an objectively meaningful dimension to which they allude. It is only that there ceases to be a meaningful sense, an interpretive sense, in which appearances are representational. What is striking here is that by weakening the representational alliance between appearance and reality, Whitman's perspectivism breaks with the normative convention that has framed our relationship to the world since the Enlightenment.

What Whitman's perspectivism importantly accomplishes can be brought into sharper focus when considered alongside Adorno's concept of identitarianism, from which it is barely distinguishable. The resemblance is highlighted where Whitman speaks directly to the extent to which our ideas impose form upon the world, as he does in "A Song for Occupations."62

> All architecture is what you do to it when you look upon it,
> (Did you think it was in the white or gray stone? or the lines of the arches
>   and cornices?)
> All music is what awakes from you when you are reminded by the
>   instruments,
> It is not the violins and cornets, it is not the oboe nor the
>   beating drums, nor the score of the baritone singer singing
>   his sweet romanza, nor that of the men's chorus, nor that
>   of the women's chorus,
> It is nearer and farther than they. (93–97)

As it appears before us, when we "look upon it," as Whitman says, the world becomes what we make of it, or "do to it," a projection behind which its objectivity vanishes. Like the architecture we see and the music we hear, all perceptions are in the first yet also final analysis preconceptions. Hence worlds are "nearer" than our perceptions suggest, because perceptions are also preconceptions, though also farther than we realize, because whatever is "perceived" lies more outside the perception than in its path. Capturing the identitarian tendencies of what Adorno understood to be entailed by thinking, Whitman's perspectivism takes the world-in-itself to be concealed by the identities (representations) foisted upon it. And as with Adorno's critique of identitarianism, Whitman's perspectivism does not permit us to confuse the identity of the world as it is in-itself with these imposed identities (representations), the unknown reality of the world with its appearances. By disconnecting the appearances of the world from its reality, Whitman ensures that the world of difference and its identity concealed behind appearances will remain concealed and unknown, that the world as an in-itself will be left alone. At the risk of getting ahead of myself, already we see a striking resemblance to Adorno. As does Adorno's, Whitman's idea of the unknown orients us away from the "depths" and receptively toward the "surfaces" of a world.

Whitman's two angles of aesthetic reflection—poetic language's intimations of the nonidentical, and the perspectival divorce of the world as an in-itself from its representations—bear a heavy philosophical burden. By hiding the reality of the world from view, by protecting worlds of difference from representation, by shattering the identification of the world with its appearances, we are aesthetically receptive to the realm of appearance. Appearance no longer is to be thought of as a form, likeness or semblance, representation or identity of what is higher or more perfect or perfect. The authority of appearance is not to be derived from what is prior or fundamental. Its authority is intrinsic to it, as is the ontologically distinct authority of the world in-itself protected behind or beneath it. With this new authority attributed to appearance Whitman alters its ethical value decisively, and with it the world as we know it on its surface and may live in it. To appreciate just how decisively the status of appearances has been altered, the question concerning the position that God occupies in the revised relationship of appearance and reality is necessarily foregrounded. For if appearance and reality are no longer connected, does not God, too, lose all connection with worlds of appearances?

God and the Unknown

If the relationship between appearance and reality has been revised by Whitman along the lines I have described, should we not expect that he also would conceive differently of the relationship of God to our world? After all, where what is real of worlds cannot be otherwise than unknown, when what is essential ceases to be an object of representation and appearance at best can be thought of as offering only intimations, highly imperfect representations of worlds-in-themselves, and where appearances would have an authority no longer indebted to what is believed to be real, then God would cease to infuse reality with the spiritual light to become known and appearance (representation, identity) with the spiritual power to represent it. With these revisions, in other words, all designed to create an unbridgeable divide between appearance and reality, God once believed not only to define but to be embodied by what is real would cease to be connected to the world of appearance. With God's connection to the world severed, appearance could no longer provide ways to bring a remote God within reach. Appearance would lose its power to represent the world as an expression of the power to know God.

Our expectations are met without hesitation. Whitman revokes all possibility of learning God's identity. "O Thou transcendent, *Nameless* . . ." Whitman cries in "Passage to India" (194–95, my italics),[63] and this after honoring all gods and confessing to a certain devotion to beliefs with which they are associated, as he does in "Song of Myself" (verse 43). As we are unable to identify or represent God, in "Passage to India" Whitman holds that God becomes a mystery with which "we dare not dally," though he also professes a belief in God even greater "than any priest" (186, 185). But the decisive move is where Whitman brings his unknown God into alignment with the discontinuity he inserts between appearance and reality. As he prescribes in "Song of Myself," in what surely are some of the most poignant and provocative lines in Whitman's poetry, and with a tone recalling Nietzsche's Zarathustra,

> And I say to mankind, Be not curious about God,
> For I who am curious about each am not curious about God ... (1278–79)
>
> Why should I wish to see God better than this day? (1283)

Whitman's powerful affirmation of life—for if God cannot, can anything lure away our interest in life?—springs from the opacity he attributes to God. To observe a nameless God would be to fail to observe life. Our need to be close to an unknown God ought not interfere with our absorption in the world. The insoluble mystery of God should not distract our attention from living and from what is living. Yet, although providing reason to live our lives without reference to God, God's opacity is also a measure of his distance from the world, if not his apparent then his real distance. For even though he is able to "hear and behold God in every object," Whitman "understand[s] God not in the least," and cannot "understand who there can be more wonderful than myself" ("Song of Myself," 1281–82). Nothing about us or around us serves as a sign of God. We are not to orient ourselves to worlds as though they contain clues to the unfathomable mystery that is God. So emphatically does Whitman remove God from our lives, for all of our own intents and purposes, for purposes belonging to the world, to nature, in short, to being, God does not exist. Not even death and the afterlife should make a difference to life. Like God, the afterlife is that "unknown region," "all a blank before us," an "inaccessible land," even "undream'd of" and unknown by the soul, Whitman confesses in "Darest Thou Now O Soul" (2, 8, 9).[64] And death, the "unknown shores" (178), as Whitman puts it in "Passage to India," "I cannot define," he admits in "To Think of Time" (110).[65] Death becomes known only when it is upon us, only when it "loosen[s]" our ties to "darkness," one of the existential, not eternal, "bounds bounding us," concealing death and rendering it unknown, he explains in "Darest Thou Now O Soul" (10, 12).

Taken together, God, death and afterlife, the "supernatural," as Whitman summarily describes the unknown in "Song of Myself," are "of no account" (1050). So it is not that Whitman dissolves the appearance-reality distinction, though at times he may appear to do so, as we shall see. It may be that as he newly conceptualizes an aesthetic receptivity to appearances, Whitman intends the relationship between appearance and reality to now serve weakly, at best, as an exemplar of faith. But what we can be certain of is that what we believe to be real Whitman so far removes from appearances, makes so inaccessible and so protected, that appearances, though not reality, become *our* reality.

AN ETHIC OF APPEARANCES

If Whitman means to inspire a revaluation of the world as it appears before us, why does he not simply discard the distinction between appearance and reality? Why does he not take that next step taken by Nietzsche? After all, it is clear from the direction in which Whitman takes us that his valorization of appearances dispenses with the philosophical privileges previously accorded to reality. Reality no longer can serve as a foundation for an ethic that enables or constrains our thought and action in the world of appearances. And if the power to represent the in-itself beneath appearances is lost, so is the strongest ethical claim for privileging some appearances, some identities (representations), over others. Would it not then be appropriate for Whitman to abandon altogether thought that invokes older philosophical obligations and adopt language reflecting new commitments to an ethic of appearances, an ethic that values appearances overall?

As we shall see, especially in the following chapter, not only does Whitman propose language to stand in for the distinction between appearance and reality, it is astonishing that the terms he chooses—"surfaces and depths"—correspond to the ways in which Nietzsche and Adorno encourage us to think about the world and our relation to it. Whitman adopts surface and depth contingently, though, as is evident by the regularity in his work with which poetic images suggesting either appearance and reality or surface and depth are each used often and interchangeably. His strategy seems to be to weight an important ethical tendency in his thinking without definitively replacing appearance and reality. Whitman's reliance upon both pairs of concepts indicates no ambiguity in his thinking regarding his revision of the relation between appearance and reality and its philosophical implications.

Of course, although on the strength of the work that nonidentity and perspectivism jointly perform Whitman could abolish the distinction between appearance and reality and introduce surfaces and depths to permanently substitute, it is Whitman's belief in God that constrains him from doing so. No matter how "clear and sweet is all that is not my soul" (52), Whitman reminds us in "Song of Myself," our absorption in the world as it appears to us requires that we at least acknowledge another world beneath or behind it. The "unseen is proved by the seen" (53), Whitman maintains. Figuratively speaking, to discard the unseen world is to risk our own disappearance. "Lack one lacks both" (53), Whitman lectures bluntly, ironically agreeing with Nietzsche that "once we have abolished the real world . . . we have also abolished the apparent world." To Whitman's mind, however, although the seen entails the unseen, appearance entails reality, and God provides the transcendental warrant for this entanglement, the inscrutable mystery of God relieves us of the obligation to spend our curiosity deciphering either the meaning of God or of God's world. God, and the reality and identity of the world, what is essential about it, what is different from the ways in which it appears and what is different from the ways in which we identify and represent it, are simply unknown. It is in this spirit that we should understand Whitman's instruction "Be not curious about God" and take him at his word when he says, "For I who am curious about each am not curious about God." To take Whitman at his word means to understand that it is to the world as it appears before him to which his considerable creative powers are to be aesthetically receptive, and it is to the world as it appears before us to which Whitman means for our powers of creativity to be aesthetically receptive. As the ethic of appearances in Whitman's poetry requires, we begin to see, aesthetic receptivity means more than it had for either Adorno or Nietzsche taken alone. More, in other words, than either individuality's receptivity to surfaces following its recognition of the unknown or its receptivity to surfaces on which creativity occurs from the point of view of the artist.

Mystery, Wonder, and Delight in Appearances

"I and this mystery here we stand." With this matter-of-fact reflection early in "Song of Myself" (51), Whitman signals he has reached a new starting point, a point where he will begin again to relate to the world out of an experience with mystery that has been such an incitement to do so. His reflection conveys more than that the world is filled with mystery, however. It is not as though the world were more or less transparent in some parts while in others enigmatic. The world is mystery. There is nothing in the world or about the world that is an exception to its darkness. Opacity is the world's most fundamental quality. As Whitman continues further on, for instance, "I cannot tell how my ankles bend, nor whence the cause of my faintest wish, Nor the cause of the friendship I emit, nor the cause of the friendship I take again" (546–47). Whitman is not denying the possibility of explanation. Rather, he is insisting that any explanation for what the world is or for what is in the world leaves its mystery, its meaning, untouched. Its "facts are useful, and yet they are not my dwelling," he remarks about modern science. "I but enter by them to an area of my dwelling. Less the reminders of properties told by words, and more the reminders they of life untold" ("Song of Myself," 491–94). "Reminders they of life untold," reminders of the world as mystery, our every encounter with the world conveys it as the "puzzle of puzzles, And that we call Being" (609–10).

Whitman's reflection "I and this mystery here we stand" is meant to summarize his experience with worlds, the world that is Whitman, the world that is each one of us, and the surrounding world, and to change our position in relation to worlds through mystery we discover to be unknown. Beginning again, we must be aesthetically receptive to mystery and to the wonder with which mystery fills the world and all the worlds within, an attitude of aesthetic receptivity displayed in all of its breadth as Whitman, in deliberately reflexive thoughts that open "Salut au Monde!" appears to rearrange himself physically in full frontal view of the world.[66]

> O take my hand Walt Whitman!
> Such gliding wonders! such sights and sounds! (1–2)

Everything in the world is wonder-filled, an insight celebrated throughout Whitman's poetry and prose. So intense are Whitman's celebrations that they situate us in such a way that we are unable to view the world from other positions. In one brief verse alone (31) in "Song of Myself," Whitman imagines that

> a leaf of grass is no less than the journey-work of the stars,
> And the pismire is equally perfect, and a grain of sand, and the egg
>   of the wren ... (663–64)
>
> And the running blackberry would adorn the parlors of heaven,
> And the narrowest hinge in my hand puts to scorn all machinery. (666–67)

And in a later verse (41) he considers "a curl of smoke or a hair on the back of my hand just as curious as any revelation," "the bull and the bug never worshipp'd half enough, Dung and dirt more admirable than was dream'd" (1039, 1048–49). Whitman's aesthetic receptivity to wonder leaves nothing without wonder and leaves no wonder out, resetting parameters that further install wonder into the world.

It could be said, and not without justification as this verse proves, that Whitman's aesthetic receptivity to the world is ecstatic and that he encourages the like in us. Yet, Whitman does not mean the world to overwhelm us, transport us. Rather than subdue reason, our receptivity to wonder is to provoke reflection on the world.

> Immense have been the preparations for me ... (1157)
>
> All forces have been steadily employ'd to complete and delight me ... (1167)

Stepping back to examine his reflection on a wonder-filled world, Whitman interprets delight as inevitable, as necessary as the immense forces and preparations—as the wonder—that produces it, or "completes" us, as he puts it. Whitman's aim seems twofold. By construing it to issue from our aesthetic receptivity to wonder, Whitman privileges delight as the attitude to be cultivated in relation to an unknown world. Once the world has revealed itself through mystery to be unknown and wonder-filled, which he believes it cannot fail to do, our delight in the world is a response that ensures well-being if we take delight to mean the experience of well-being from the pleasures experienced through encounters with mysterious, unknown, and wonder-filled worlds.

Although it is through delight that wonder enters reflectively into our experience with the world, wonder enters more profoundly than is suggested by either the pleasure or sense of well-being that delight brings. Should not wonder lead us to estimate the world's value, Whitman asks in "A Song for Occupations"?

> The wonder every one sees in everyone else he sees, and the
>   wonders that fill each minute of time forever,
> What have you reckon'd them for, camerado? (61–62)

Wonder cannot be valued for trades or profits or even for leisure, Whitman's verse replies (63–64), though replies rhetorically so that the *question* of value continues to prevail over any possible answer. Wonder is thus sustained interrogatively, compelling reflection on the world and its value only to return us time and again to its mystery. Wonder ensnares us in a series of further reflections that begin and end in the same place, revealing the world to be known only as the unknown, as a world of appearances. Whitman often traces our receptivity to a wonder-filled world as this very circuity. As we are trapped by wonder into reflections that return us to our point of departure so that we must begin our reflections again, a relation to the world that is nonreflective appears in relief. Returning us reflexively to mystery and the unknown, in other words, our aesthetic receptivity to wonder produces reflections that undermine any hope of bending the world to our will. Whitman's capture of this intellectual odyssey in "Song of Myself" deserves to be cited at length.

> To behold the day-break!
> The little light fades the immense and diaphanous shadows,
> The air tastes good to my palate.
>
> Hefts of the moving world at innocent gambols silently rising,
>   freshly exuding,
> Scooting obliquely high and low.
>
> Something I cannot see puts upward libidinous prongs,
> Seas of bright juice suffuse heaven.
>
> The earth by the sky staid with, the daily close of their junction,
> The heav'd challenge from the east that moment over my head,
> The mocking taunt, See then whether you shall be master! (550–59)

Images explode from these lines. Whitman is stunned by the rebirth of horizon, the division of earth and sky brought with the twilight of the new day by the rays of a sun as yet hidden within the night as it slowly breaks into dawn. It is a division dividing the seen from the unseen, appearance from reality, the known from the unknown. It is a division ridiculing our pretense to mastery over nature that reproaches and erects barriers to formal reason.

It would be mistaken to conclude from Whitman's enthusiasm for mystery and wonder that he intends to enlist us in an anti-Enlightenment crusade. Whitman is certainly no enemy of the Enlightenment, as his admiration for the spirit of progress and invention in such works as "Song of the Exposition" clearly demonstrates.[67] The yoke of reflection that our receptivity to mystery and wonder impose upon us, from which Whitman does not believe we can be free, is meant to chasten modernity's instinct for domination. No matter how objective the attitude we adopt toward the world, and Whitman selects the attitude of mastery for its allegiance to a paradigmatic objectivity, wonder disturbs our practices, moral, scientific, and aesthetic, of framing the world as an object of thought. By returning us to the fundamental opacity of the world, mystery and wonder express the world's resistance to representation, encouraging an aesthetic receptivity that interrupts thought in its formal rational quest to make the world out to be knowable and known in ways that obscure its diversity of differences. Mystery and wonder urge us to relate to the world receptively *just as it appears before us*, to the diversity of different appearances as ends in themselves, as surfaces rather than as the means that inhere instrumentally in thinking that necessarily represents the world as other than it is. As Whitman expresses it unequivocally in his preface to the 1855 edition of *Leaves of Grass*, "Men and women and the earth and all upon it are simply to be taken as they are."[68]

No matter how powerfully and seductively mystery and wonder draw us toward appearances, because aesthetic receptivity to appearances entails repudiation of the possibility of knowing any underlying, universal principles that would exclude all but certain relations to the world, our receptivity to the world as it appears on the surface is available to us only as a contingency. An aesthetically receptive orientation to appearances is but one ethical orientation among all others. Whitman argues this precisely in his 1855 preface by saying that though "[g]reat is the faith of the flush of knowledge and of the investigation of the depths of qualities and things," as the "depths are fathomless and therefore calm . . . innocence and nakedness are resumed . . . [and] are neither modest nor immodest."[69] By relativizing our relations to the world, aesthetic receptivity thus chastens, but does not forbid, an interest in mastery and domination. At most, our aesthetic receptivity to appearances can justify the constraints of an ethic rather than the prohibitions of a moral imperative, and cannot warrantee in any absolute sense the care for the world by which an ethic valuing appearances overall is distinguished. Without the prohibitions of a moral imperative, perhaps Whitman relies upon our delight in mysterious and wonder-filled worlds, and upon the yoke of reflection they impose, to steady our aesthetic receptivity to the world as it appears before us, the decisive ethical feature of an orientation to the world that disrupts representational thought.

Appearance and Difference

I do not doubt that Whitman does rely upon mystery and wonder to encourage us to be aesthetically receptive to the world as it appears on the surface. Nor do I doubt that he relies equally on the effects of aesthetic receptivity upon us, notably its disruption of representational thought, to undermine the contingency of an ethic of appearances in order to secure its influence over the ways in which we relate to the world, an influence we can regard in another way. In its opposition to formal rational thinking, an ethic of appearances necessarily articulates a special relationship to difference that is cultivated through our aesthetic receptivity to the world as it appears before us. Difference is spared the fate to which it is subjected in identitarian thought. Because aesthetic receptivity is confined to the appearances of the world, what is different about the world that sets it apart from its representations ceases to be the concern of thought. Thinking is absolved of the responsibility for representing the identity of a world as it is, in-itself. Out of sight, what difference is, is out of mind. But what in a world is out of mind is not, by its absence, excluded from thinking. Difference is excluded only where thought fosters the illusion that nothing different from our representation of the world has escaped identification. In effect, aesthetic receptivity to appearances tacitly acknowledges an irreconcilable divide between concept and object, identity (representation) and the identity of difference as it is, in-itself, and thus reproduces the quality of "divisiveness" Horkheimer and Adorno argue distinguishes reflective thought from formal reason.[70] With this acknowledgment built into it, an ethic of appearances aspires to deliver all the difference in the world from the deception that what difference is really or essentially, its identity or truth, and the identity and truth of the world to which it belongs, can be represented. Difference is rescued from the violence of being represented by an identity that is other than it is.

Both the absolution of thought from the obligation to represent difference and the ransom of difference from harm are explicated by poems in Whitman's "Calamus" collection. In "Earth, My Likeness," Whitman says he, too, like the surface of the earth, will appear "impassive," protecting from view what he "dare not tell ... in words, not even in these songs," concealing within something volcanic, "fierce and terrible in me eligible to burst forth" (2, 7, 6).[71] Here Whitman enlists us to take him as he appears, as he "is," to paraphrase his recommendation in the 1855 preface to simply take men and women and the earth and all upon it as they are. Whitman wants only to allude to an unseen and unspoken sexuality, his unseen and unspoken reality, while allowing his appearance, like the earth, his likeness, to be filled with the mystery of what must remain forever unknown. And why must his sexual identity remain unknown? "I dream'd in a dream," Whitman reports in the very next poem by that name in his "Calamus" series, "I saw a city invincible to the attacks of the whole of the rest of the earth, I dream'd that was the new city of Friends" (1-2).[72] Back to back, then, Whitman's songs register his fear of violence, the threat of exclusion, his awareness of a difference that, unable to disappear within a "new city of Friends," where the identity of one particular difference could become no difference at all, must disappear beneath an appearance that conceals it from view, rendering it unavailable for representation and shielding it from assault.

We must be clear about what Whitman is doing. He is not hiding from the world, nor is he advocating that others hide. Rather, as "In Paths Untrodden," the first of the "Calamus" poems, explains, Whitman is very boldly drawing our attention to the identity of a difference that already has long been hidden. Speaking to us from a "secluded spot," having "Escaped from the life that exhibits itself," Whitman is "Resolv'd to sing no songs to-day but those of manly attachment" (10, 3, 12).[73] Whitman gives away his position. He tells us that we can find him outside the boundaries of normalized existence. But despite his avowal (in his second "Calamus" entry, "Scented Herbage of My Breast"[74]) to "unbare this broad breast of mine, I have long enough stifled and choked" (21), as the "Calamus" poems unfold he is increasingly indirect and finally elusive about what it is precisely he wants us to know about "the life that does not exhibit itself" (11), as "In Paths Untrodden" refers to it. We see then that Whitman neither hides nor reveals himself. We learn only that there is a "secluded spot," a "life that does not exhibit itself" ("In Paths Untrodden," 10, 11), an "underneath," a "conceal'd heart," a "down there so ashamed," a "real reality," a "behind the mask of materials" ("Scented Herbage of My Breast," 8, 18, 20, 33, 34), a *difference* to which he denies identity (representation). Whitman leads us into the unknown so that we can discover that the unknown must remain unknown. As he warns us in "Whoever You Are Holding Me Now in Hand," his third "Calamus" entry,[75]

> But these leaves conning you con at peril,
> For these leaves and me you will not understand,
> They will elude you at first and still more afterward, I will
>   certainly elude you,
> Even while you should think you had unquestionably caught me,
>   behold!
> Already you see I have escaped from you. (27–31)

Is it not plain what Whitman expects of us? Does this work not trace the relationship to difference prescribed by an ethic of appearances that marks the identity of difference as the unknown and beyond our reach? As Whitman concludes "Whoever You Are Holding Me Now in Hand,"

> For all is useless without that which you may guess at many times
>   and not hit, that which I hinted at;
> Therefore release me and depart on your way. (37–38)

Since we cannot fathom what, in Whitman's estimation, constitutes his difference, which is the lesson we are to learn by working through the paradox of receiving only "hints" about a reality we were promised he would "unbare," we are to relinquish hope for reconciliation, for mutual understandings where deeply personal thoughts and feelings are not only shared but grasped on their own terms. We are to go our own way, to "depart," letting his way be. Is this not the very rule that Whitman follows in his own aesthetic receptivity to appearances? In "On Journeys through the States," at each stop Whitman says he will "Dwell a while and pass on" (12).[76] And of the sights and sounds, events and myriad individuals and their lives with whom he reports contact in "Song of Myself," he comments, "I mind them or the show or resonance of them—I come and I depart" (166). Whitman "minds the show," observes appearances or the qualities the ostensible emits, and pursues no relationship of reconciliation. Whitman remains in his "place," he points out in "Song of Myself" (351), for when the "universe is duly in order, every thing is in its place," as he elaborates in "The Sleepers" (155).

The Sufficiency, Equality, and Uniqueness of Appearances

As we see, Whitman quite deliberately orients himself receptively to the world as it appears before him. Scrupulous in his observations of appearances, he is particularly scrupulous to observe a distance from whatever reality is believed to belong to the appearance it lies beneath. Of all those appearances he encounters, for instance, described tenderly in "Song of Myself" as "letters from God dropt in the street," Whitman reports, "I leave them where they are" (1286, 1287). Or earlier in that great song, when marking differences between our world and the world of animals, of the latter Whitman comments, "I stand and look at them long and long. . . . So they show their relations to me and I accept them" (685, 692). Whitman first observes appearances, then accepts their differences. Making no further inquiries, he leaves what is fathomless unfathomed.

By orienting us receptively to appearances to the exclusion of "deeper" sources of meaning, certainly the artwork of poetry permits Whitman to be the world's advocate. Both the aesthetic sensibility at the heart of this receptivity to appearances and the desire to privilege its ethical standing among his other powers are embodied and nurtured by poetry but do not originate with it. It originates with Whitman, with the point of view of the artist (the creator), therefore with each of us (though to a lesser extent, it is surely needless to say). As Whitman makes clear, poetry is only the last, and at least for that reason perhaps the most perfect, expression of his love for the way the world appears before him. Looking back on the journey that brought his aesthetic sensibility to the heights of poetic expression, Whitman says in one of his more arcadian verses,[77]

> Beginning my studies the first step pleas'd me so much,
> The mere fact consciousness, these forms, the power of motion,

The least insect or animal, the senses, eyesight, love,
The first step I say awed me and pleas'd me so much,
I have hardly gone and hardly wished to go any farther,
But stop and loiter all the time to sing it in ecstatic songs. (1–6)

Is Whitman not saying that "these forms," these *appearances*—for no more than appearances can be apprehended by bare consciousness—are sufficient, that whatever we may look for in being, or whatever questions concerning being we may pose, we need look no further nor question more deeply than appearances require? "The earth, that is sufficient," Whitman declares in "Song of the Open Road," "I do not want the constellations any nearer" (8–9). To find meaning, we are to find it in the world as it presents itself on the surface, distancing ourselves from thoughts that distract us from what is nearest and from what the life at hand cannot reflect. Our minds ought never wander from what we see or what we hear, from what our senses prove, which without exception is what will be always and simply before us. And whatever is yet to be, Whitman says in "Song of Myself," "will in its turn prove sufficient, and cannot fail" (1122). Lives we lead, worlds as they appear and disappear, are forever ends, never means, the ethical standard according to which Whitman takes his own measure, or implores us to take his measure, in "One Hour to Madness and Joy." "To have the gag remov'd from one's mouth," to appear as he is, would permit Whitman "To have the feeling to-day or any day I am sufficient as I am" (14–15).[78]

By declaring the *sufficiency* of appearances, Whitman directs our attention to features that are precious to an ethic of appearances and that further elaborate a "surface" composed of appearances. The idea of "sufficiency" is rooted in Whitman's original forfeit of a basis for judging appearances that is believed to lie beneath, behind, or beyond appearances, as nature, reality, being, God, and similar transcendental principles are said to lie. It offers an ethical justification for appearances, and for aesthetic receptivity to appearances, that provides no grounds for discriminating among appearances. If appearances are sufficient then all appearances are equally sufficient, that is, all appearances are of equal value and have equally realized their value. Throughout his work Whitman provides generous and unequivocal reminders of both of these dimensions of equality, but his appreciation of their importance is never more eloquently summarized than in "To Think of Time," where he sings, "What will be will be well, for what is is well," and "What is called good is perfect, and what is called bad is just as perfect" (64, 114). Here we come to understand why Whitman believes that "the greatest poet does not moralize or make applications of morals," as he proposes in his 1855 preface to *Leaves of Grass*.[79] Nor need the greatest poet redeem immorality. By the argument from the sufficiency of appearances, if everything appearing is equally good and every good equally perfect, Whitman's ethic of appearances should allow for the transvaluation of moral necessity. So we ought not be surprised when we discover Whitman, in "Song of Myself," speaking of

> forbidden voices,
> Voices of sexes and lusts, voices veil'd and I remove the veil,
> Voices indecent by me clarified and transfigur'd . . . (516–18)

and, in "Starting from Paumanok," announcing, "there is in fact no evil" (100).[80]

At the same time as the sufficiency of appearances pertains importantly to the ethical value of appearances, it pertains as much to the identity (representation) of appearances. We should expect this of an ethic that cultivates a special relationship to difference. Here, though only for the purpose of clarifying the direction and sensibility of Whitman's artwork, I want to point out a utopian moment in his thinking that agrees with the most important dimension of Adorno's thought, namely, his preoccupation with the essential inadequacies of conceptual thought, which I have examined in the previous chapters. Forfeiting a standard outside of appearances for assessing their value, the sufficiency of appearances likewise surrenders concepts according to which appearances are identified. Despite even the greatest similarity among them, as the identity of each in-itself is unknown all appearances are unique. Of the "manifold objects" Whitman has perused, we learn in "Song of Myself," there are "no two alike" (134). An ethic of appearances suddenly multiplies the diversity of the world exponentially. As the appearance of a difference, every appearance has its own identity, an identity that is unknown at any level deeper than appearance. The world becomes as diverse and mysterious, then, not as there are types, or categories, or concepts, or universals, or as any identity (representation) allows us to believe. It is as diverse and mysterious as there are "objects," to repeat Whitman's word, or as we might say, as there are people, places, and things, already to casually efface through concepts the particularities of the infinite diversity of different appearances—of differences—he means to convey. If to put a noble idea in its simplest possible terms is sometimes to capture its elegance and to bring its sublimity and beauty nearer our reach, there is little or nothing in Whitman's work that retreats from this view—just as the world contains every thing, so too is every thing a world, a world whose uniqueness is lost to the generality of language and its concepts.

By way of précis, recognizing that mystery and wonder convey the fathomlessness of the world, an ethic of appearances respects the dividing line between the known and unknown by orienting us receptively to the appearances of the world. Through its aesthetic receptivity to appearances, an ethic of appearances protects the difference of the world from the invasions of thought, letting difference be. It affirms the sufficiency of appearances, acknowledging the equal value and common perfection among the diversity of appearances and the uniqueness belonging to each, a uniqueness residing in the fact that every appearance is also the appearance of a difference. At this point a certain suspicion may arise, however. In its vigilance to place all the difference in the world out of harm's way, insulating as well as the difference that makes each of us a world the differences that constitute the worlds surrounding us, is there perhaps a way an ethic of appearances becomes its own undoing? Does not an ethic of appearances, through the barriers and distances it places between differences, convert our receptivity to appearances into a merely formal orientation? And if our relationships with worlds of difference were to become merely formal, would we not then lose our appreciation for the mystery and wonder originally orienting us receptively to appearances and ensuring our respect and affection for the world? And over time would there not be increasingly less substance to our inspired respect and extravagant affection for worlds whose differences retain their mystery and wonder, uniqueness and integrity through an undisturbed solitude?

An Intimacy with Appearances

Though an ethic of appearances presupposes the opacity and extraterritoriality of differences concealed beneath the surfaces of worlds to which we orient ourselves receptively, our aesthetic relationship to appearances is in no sense merely formal. To the contrary, though it sounds paradoxical, or at least somewhat unusual in light of what we customarily understand intimacy to mean, an ethic of appearances encourages a certain "intimacy with appearances." By displaying an unwavering respect for the seclusiveness, the *privacy* of levels of being whose identity and meaning exceed our grasp, an ethic of appearances valorizes our acquaintance with appearances when we recall that every appearance is also the appearance of a difference. Once our attention is oriented receptively to appearances, in other words, the uniqueness of differences can stand out rather than appear swallowed up in the representation of some deeper reality, as it invariably is when we are oriented to appearances in terms of commonalities among them. Forgoing the depth of the world, we become *intimately acquainted with its sheer breadth*. Whitman forgoes depth when he says, in "Crossing Brooklyn Ferry," "Appearances, now or henceforth, indicate what you are," and then concludes, "We fathom you not" (120, 130).[81] His conclusion enables us to understand his image of the "knoll," the high ground Whitman seizes to take in the greatest expanse of the world as it appears broadly before him. We are treated to this image in "Song of Myself," where he says,

> But each man and each woman of you I lead upon a knoll,
> My left hand hooking you round the waist,
> My right hand pointing to landscapes of continents and the public
>   road [,] (1207–9)

and again, in "Our Old Feuillage," as though corroborating such an all-encompassing perspective, Whitman imagines himself a "scout riding on horseback over the plains west of the Mississippi," where "he ascends a knoll and sweeps his eyes around" (44).[82]

Nor is anything that appears in this great expanse omitted, or without relevance. "I lean and loafe at my ease," muses Whitman famously in "Song of Myself," "observing a spear of summer grass" (5), thus introducing in the most insignificant object the symbol of a poetry, of a *Leaves of Grass*, that like the world it seeks to encompass contains everything and leaves nothing out. Nothing appears uninteresting, no detail is without fascination, Whitman assures us in "Song of Myself." "If you would understand me," he advises, "go to the heights or water-shore, The nearest gnat is an explanation, and a drop or motion of waves a key" (1252–53). And no appearance, no matter how ordinary, is without its seductions, unloved, or finally resistible. Passionately Whitman says,

> The atmosphere is not a perfume, it has no taste of the distillation,
>   it is odorless,
> It is for my mouth forever, I am in love with it,
> I will go to the bank by the wood and become undisguised and
>   naked,
> I am mad for it to be in contact with me. (17–20)

With the value of nothing ever lost on us, it is also a simple matter to understand why, once we are aesthetically receptive to all the world's appearances, our experience of the world can never be exhaustive. It is appropriate that Whitman draws this conclusion in "Crossing Brooklyn Ferry," where he speaks of fathomless appearances as though they can be appreciated for what they are only after their meaning is acknowledged to be a secret silently kept.

> You have waited, you always wait, you dumb, beautiful ministers,
> We receive you with free sense at last, and are insatiate hence forward. (126–27)

Finally, if our aesthetic receptivity to the breadth of appearances of the world omits no detail and finds nothing uninteresting, without its fascinations or seductions, unworthy of love or resistible, and promises experiences that each are inexhaustible, can we not readily see that an intimacy with appearances allows us to recognize intimacy in our experiences where it typically goes unnoticed or is believed to be absent? Whitman captures this point, precisely, in "Song of Myself," where he sings,

> I have instant conductors all over me whether I pass or stop,
> They seize every object and lead it harmlessly through me.
> I merely stir, press, feel with my fingers, and am hungry,
> To touch my person to some one else's is about as much as I can stand. (615–18)

SEVEN

Individuality as a Poetic Form of Life

Working with a concept of depth quite like Adorno's, Whitman elaborates an ethic of appearances resting on the same philosophical assumptions and meeting the same philosophical requirements. Although at times we find him to be less explicit, or on those occasions perhaps more subtle, throughout his verse Whitman lays out clearly principles that support an aesthetic receptivity to the world according to the way in which it appears. And Whitman leaves little question as to the meaning of these principles. He is never vague about what it means to relate aesthetically to appearances or why such an exclusive orientation is justified, nor is he vague about qualities belonging to appearances. No mystery is made of the mystery and wonder of unfathomable worlds, or of the feelings of delight and well-being wonder occasions. Nor does Whitman mystify the fathomless darkness that leaves us with what lies ostensibly before us, or falsely illuminate either the opacity that sets worlds apart from us as worlds of difference or the darkness of each world that makes it different from the rest. Whitman is convinced and makes plain his conviction that nothing before us is without wonder and that no wonder, on that account, should be left out of account or can be given a complete account, and that every account only returns us reflexively to the mystery and wonder that provoked it. Whitman does not doubt or permit us to doubt that the appearances he revalues are each unique and of equal value and sufficient when taken as they are. Nor does he appear the least uncertain that difference suffers injury when represented as being anything other than it appears to be and that it can be protected by letting it be, a tolerance providing the *raison d'être* of an ethic of appearances. Surely Whitman's aesthetic sensibilities are especially, and often enough painfully, acute, with regard to his concern about the safety of difference, as in his "Calamus" poems. And Whitman unselfconsciously parades the most effusive attachment for the appearances of the world, as though cultivating a genuine intimacy meant having but the intense sense of a world of wondrous though inaccessible privacies.

Always undisguised though constantly changing forms and contexts, these ideas circulate together throughout Whitman's work at the level of appearances where they can be taken as they are. Yet, can the purpose for which Whitman poeticizes worlds—the world of each "I myself" or "Me myself," as he puts it in "Eidolons" (80)[1] and "Song of Myself" (74),[2] the worlds that are others and other things, and the world that all worlds within the world share—be to set out unmistakably an ethic simply orienting us receptively to the appearances of a world, so that in relation to his poetry we also are confined interpretively to the level of appearances? It is surely his purpose, though to formulate it in this way is not to capture his purpose entirely. With the respect due the complexity of Whitman's thought we might say that insofar as he explicates an ethic of appearances at the *surface* of his work, his purpose is to compose songs that also direct us to their *depth*, to the deeper meaning and intention of an ethic of appearances.

Why would Whitman write as though what he means and intends without question on the surface, however, entails a second and deeper level of understanding? What Whitman composes on poetic surfaces creates a depth, a deeper level of argument, designed to draw us into an interpretive relationship with his work so that we might also be compelled to fathom its deeper meaning, and then attempt to do so. That Whitman draws us into an interpretive engagement does not adequately answer the question, though, why he should want us to dig beneath the surface at all when he appears determined to orient us receptively to its appearance. Just as we have seen Whitman adopt an idea of an unknowable depth quite like Adorno's, here we shall see how, after Nietzsche's fashion, he creates deeper layers on the surface of an argument that obliges us to remain at the level of appearances. Like Nietzsche, Whitman adopts the point of view of the artist (the creator), who creates depths on the surfaces of the world. Unlike Nietzsche, Whitman's creativity will not violate the depths originally antecedent to the surface that he and Adorno also find below.[3]

A POETIC FORM OF LIFE

Whitman knows we are inveterate burrowers, Nietzsche's moles and dwarfs. He knows that no matter what he leaves on the surface of his work for us to find, we will not hesitate to seek deeper meanings. Indeed, we barely cross the threshold of "Song of Myself" before Whitman problematizes our interpretive interests. "Have you practis'd so long to learn to read," Whitman asks us, "Have you felt so proud to get at the meaning of poems?" (31–32). At which point he proposes,

> Stop this day and night with me and you shall possess the origin
>   of all poems,
> You shall possess the good of the earth and sun, (there are millions
>   of suns left,)
> You shall no longer take things at second or third hand, nor look
>   through the eyes of the dead, nor feed on the spectres in books,
> You shall not look through my eyes either, nor take things from me,
> You shall listen to all sides and filter them from your self. (33–37)

"Stopping" with him, Whitman is promising, provides us with the resources to have an experience of the world that is underived, originating and original with each of us, born of a new relationship with the world. For as our experience will resemble the experience of the world from which poetry springs, an experience that is the "origin of all poems," Whitman would enable each of us to form a relationship with the world as the poet forms a relationship with the world, to form our thoughts as poetic thoughts, our actions as poetic actions, our relations to the world and to all the worlds within it as poetic relations. At a level deeper than the poetic surface on which an ethic of appearances appears, we are to become aesthetically receptive and creative as poet and poetry are aesthetically receptive and creative. Inviting us to stop with him, Whitman implicates each of us in a relationship to the world where poetic form, the form of Whitman's relationship to the world as it is shaped by the form of his poetry, is to become the form of our own relationship to the world. Remarkably, if we stop with Whitman to engage his poetry at its deeper level, to answer our earlier question, poetic form becomes our form of life, a form of life forming an individuality that can belong to each one of us. And relating us to the world through poetic form as Whitman is related to the world, then our individuality will relate us to the world aesthetically from the point of view of the artist (the creator).

In what sense, though, may poetic form as individuality's form of life be spoken of as the deeper level of Whitman's poetry? Let us now think of the ethic of appearances created by Whitman poetically as his creation of meaning and value, in the sense in which Nietzsche wants us to think of the creation of meaning and value. According to Nietzsche, whenever the surface of the world is formed aesthetically, its depth is reflected on the surface as the meaning and value attached by the artist (the creator) to the new form in which the world appears. In these terms, Whitman's poetic form possesses depth in the meaning and value reflected on the surface of the world as it is formed into images poetically. Stopping with Whitman to possess the "origin of all poems" is to possess his poetry at its deepest level. It is to possess its poetic form in the meaning and value it creates.

Configuring the depth of Whitman's achievement in Nietzsche's terms seems especially appropriate, because Whitman deliberately relates poetry to the world as an *aesthetic form* of relationship that reflects an ethic of appearances. In the discussion that follows, all of the extraordinary images we will find formed by Whitman poetically, then, should be thought of as Nietzsche asks us to think of the aesthetic form of the world. The images Whitman creates poetically on the surface of the world, on the surface of his mind, the surface of his eye, of his ear, on the surface of his every sense, possess depth precisely in the meaning and value reflected by their forms. And since the meaning and value of poetic form lie in the depths beneath the surface of Whitman's poetry, the form of his poetry should offer insight into the relations between surfaces and depths, and into how Nietzsche's depths, which are the reflections of the meaning and value created on the surface, can be brought to respect the integrity and well-being of Adorno's depths and differences below.

When we now stop with Whitman to relate to the world aesthetically from the point of view of the artist (the creator), so that the form of his poetry becomes our individuality's form of life, as it is surely the form of his life, the ethics of the form of his relation to the appearances of the world is also reflected by the form of individuality's own relation to the world's appearances. As the form of individuality's relation to the world, for us the form of Whitman's poetry does not, then, merely reflect certain meanings and values, but also is an important angle of reflection on what at its deepest level individuality's form of life may become as a poetic, aesthetic form. What may we then hope to learn from this angle of poetic reflection? Examining the form of Whitman's poetry, essentially his relationship to the world, now to become the form of our own individuality's relationship to the world, we will see an image of what it means for individuality to be oriented aesthetically—receptively and creatively—to the world just as it appears. As a reflection of an aesthetically receptive and creative orientation to the world at the "origin of all poems," an image of the form that each individual life must take when the individuality belonging to it is oriented aesthetically to the appearances of the world will crystallize. This will lead us in turn to an image of the form of life that all lives living together according to such an aesthetic orientation can share, which will be taken up in the chapter that follows.

EVERY EXISTENCE HAS ITS IDIOM

Speaking of the work of the poet in "Song of the Answerer," Whitman remarks, "Every existence has its idiom, everything has an idiom and tongue." It is the poet who "resolves all tongues into his own and bestows it among men"(31–32).[4] Whitman could not construe "existence" more broadly. It includes any existence each of us might lead, racial, ethnic, and religious, our sexual existence and existence as genders, and all more personalized experiences that set apart the existence of each individual from the existences of the rest, as well as every existing thing the world contains. Each having its own "idiom and tongue," each existence Whitman has in mind is the existence of a difference. The privilege Whitman accords poetry implies that were it not for the creativity of poetic verse, the difference that is peculiar to every existence and that constitutes an unbridgeable divide among our identities would remain shut up within its own idiomatic structure. Difference finds a second form, a poetic form, which "resolves" what is idiomatic into language that allows difference to become articulate and recognizable. To what extent as well as in what way poetry grants difference voice and renders difference recognizable, though, is no small philosophical matter. For while Whitman commits poetry to relieving difference of its solitude, it has been his view all along that difference is unknown and remains in darkness despite our best efforts (which are always more or less injurious), to overcome the intransigence of difference to reason and representation. Is the solitude of which Whitman now relieves difference the ontological solitude he has so carefully protected?

Whitman is not reluctant to contradict himself, of course, as we recall from his famous comment in "Song of Myself," "Do I contradict myself? Very well then I contradict myself, (I am large, I contain multitudes.)" (1324–26). Not meaning to be haughty, he holds as a characteristic of sound thinking the willingness and ability not only to entertain but also to show allegiance to contradictory beliefs and understandings. And he believes that a life well lived is characterized by the desire to take from a deep appreciation of diversity and difference the ability to live, as well as to think, discontinuously. On this fundamental issue in his work, however, we do not find him at odds with himself. While poetry creates a common "form" through which every existence in its idiomatic uniqueness can be articulated, it is not a "common" form that effaces difference by translating the difference that distinguishes each existence into the same and alien form. On the contrary, Whitman continues to insulate difference from such harm by forming the surface of an existence into poetic images so that difference appears in a recognizable form while remaining concealed beneath its surface. But it is to simplify Whitman's achievement if what we would understand by this is that it is only the surface of an existence that through poetry appears recognizably to us, and that what is different about it does not enter into Whitman's compositions. It would be to neglect Whitman's all-important point that every existence, having its own idiom and tongue, is the existence of a difference, an existence that manifests difference, and that it is precisely its difference that distinguishes each existence from every other and earns it the representational interest of art.

Following Whitman's lead by foregrounding difference, we should rather say that the surface of an existence appears through poetry as the *appearance of a difference*, to further develop a term I introduced in the previous chapter.[5] This formulation recalls Adorno's claim in his *Aesthetic Theory* that through aesthetic form difference appears as the *appearance of an essence*. Attributing similarly creative powers to aesthetic form, Whitman and Adorno agree that in its representation of difference, difference both appears through aesthetic form and disappears beneath it. Difference is represented, but in such a way as to spare it injury.

Both of these moments can be distinguished in Whitman's work. Whitman represents an existence in such a way that the form to which it is adapted poetically allows verse to represent it as a surface as though its idiomatic intransigence has been overcome. In "Song of the Answerer" Whitman associates poetic form with the power to represent a particular existence in a way that enables it, in its difference, to become recognizable, by saying that the "Answerer"—the poet—"puts things in their attitudes" (1, 18). As evidence of poetic representation's creative capacity to acquaint us with what is strange, he suggests that no existence represented as such a recognizable surface should fail to recognize its *own* idiomatic existence when it is reflected in a poetic looking glass. When the poet succeeds in representing an idiom and tongue, Whitman proposes,

> Then the mechanics take him for a mechanic,
> And the soldiers suppose him to be a soldier, and the sailors that he
>   has follow'd the sea,

> And the authors take him for an author, and the artists for an artist . . . (39–41)
>
> The English believe he comes of their English stock,
> A Jew to the Jew he seems, a Russ to the Russ, usual and near,
>   removed from none. (45–46)

And what does it mean that the Jew, let us say, put into his "attitude," sees his reflection? It means, I believe, that at the same time as the power of aesthetic form to represent the surface of Jewish difference is confirmed by the Jew seeing his image reflected poetically, neither does the Jew appear to himself or others as other than a Jew or as a Jew in some form of otherness. While the Jew appears on the surface as he is, all the difference distinguishing the Jew not represented on the surface escapes representation. Difference is left alone. What difference appears on the surface does not appear as an identity imposed by others from without. Difference is spared both the rod and the rule of representation. Does Whitman not explain in "Song of the Answerer" that the poet "puts things in their attitudes . . . so that the rest never shame them afterward, nor assume to command them," and that "The maker of poems settles justice" (18, 20, 58)? Taking these moments together, we can summarize Whitman's achievement in this way. Beneath the aesthetic representation of idiomatic Jewish existence, beneath the poetic appearance of a Jewish "as it is," disappears the difference of a Jewish "as it is, in-itself." This seems to me to be precisely what Whitman means when he says, to return again to the words of his preface to the 1855 edition of *Leaves of Grass*, "men and women and the earth and all upon it are simply to be taken as they are." As the form through which existences, "differences," are "taken as they are," poetic representation illuminates their surfaces and leaves their depths in darkness, adding nothing, subtracting nothing, changing nothing of the unseen being seen, leaving what cannot be seen unseen. Or as Whitman with immense poignancy speaks of his poetry in his 1855 preface,

> What I experience or portray shall go from my composition without a shred of my composition. You shall stand by my side and look in the mirror with me.[6]

Even before taking up the form of Whitman's poetry directly, we learn from his own account of poet and poetry in "Song of the Answerer" that the creativity of poetic form embodies an ethic of appearances by positioning us receptively in relation to worlds as to surfaces that are recognizably and depths that are mysteriously different. At one and the same time, he explains, poetic form's creativity receptively orients the individuality belonging to each of us to existences as to differences that become in part recognizable and remain in other part mysterious. Poetic form aesthetically orients our individuality to the appearances of the world in this way so that the diversity of the world's differences might merely be taken together as they are and left alone. From here, what should follow is a consideration of how the form of Whitman's poetry actually orients individuality creatively and receptively to the world in precisely this way, how poetic form leads us to aesthetically envision a particular form of life for each of us as individuals and for all of us together. Before taking this next step, I want to explore briefly another of Whitman's verses because of the preliminary bearing it has on our discussion of poetic form as a form of life. "Song of the Answerer" is but one of Whitman's poems offering encouragements that point in the direction of poetic form as a clue to how individuality might be creatively and receptively oriented to the world according to an ethic of appearances. Another is Whitman's great "Passage to India." Devoted in part to celebrating the world-historical importance of poetic creation, in this context Whitman adopts language of biblical proportions to present an idea that quite visibly and remarkably resembles the conception of an aesthetic orientation to the world as it crystallized around Adorno's critique of reconciliation. Discovering in Whitman's poetry an idea that is nothing less than the virtual twin of the concept playing so vital a philosophical role in Adorno's aesthetics, the concept of the "togetherness of differences," provides further measure of the great divide Whitman recognizes among diverse and different forms of life and of the philosophical burdens to be borne by his verse.

The Distant Brought Near

When Whitman oriented us receptively to the surfaces of worlds so that we may be respectful of their depths, he met Adorno's strictest criterion for how art is to be related to an unfathomable world, and how aesthetic form and an aesthetic relationship to the world are to be understood. Consistent with this aesthetic receptivity to appearances, by endorsing a counterpart to Adorno's "togetherness of differences" in "Passage to India" Whitman again forswears the possibility that individuals can be reconciled to worlds taken either as objects of art or as objects of other relationships, however they may be conceived. Believing like Adorno that individuals are unable to know one another, unable to know worlds of difference, nature, or being as they are, in-themselves, Whitman has been led by his rejection of the idea of reconciliation to pursue, instead, Adorno's far more limited ethical aspiration that different forms of life, though culturally fathomless to one another, can coexist peacefully within the same social and political space.

Modernity is particularly distinguished for Whitman by a solitary scientific achievement, a wonder, as he puts it in "Passage to India," that has the "antique ponderous Seven outvied" (4).[7] Technological advances in exploration, travel, and communication enable the discovery of difference and draw differences within range of one another so that their new proximity might breed an acquaintance of each difference with every other. Perhaps, Whitman implies by encouraging the thought of these geographical ties as marriages, invention relates differences to one another as though they come to share with a certain degree of intimacy some form of a common life, or at least Whitman's language suggests as much. "Lands found and nations born" (78), Whitman writes enthusiastically,

> Thou rondure of the world at last accomplish'd ... (80)
>
> [T]he marriage of continents ... lands, geographies ... (118, 122)
>
> The races, neighbors, to marry and be given in marriage ... (33)
>
> Europe to Asia, Africa join'd, and they to the New World ... (121)
>
> As brides and bridegrooms hand in hand. (123)

And "The Past—that dark unfathom'd retrospect!" (10) and whatever *has* a past, "literatures, tremendous epics, religions, castes" (134), are "brought forward" (127) out of their anonymity. In no respect, though, does what is historically, culturally, ethnically, and religiously different and remote become *known*. Rather, the strange, the mysterious, the wondrous, the different, Whitman is careful to explain, is only "the distant brought near" (34).

Bringing what is distant and different near, an achievement unique to modernity, is only a prelude, in Whitman's estimation, to a far greater, more necessary task. "[S]ome hidden prophetic intention" (86), Whitman adds, a "first intent," present from time's beginning or from the time of our own beginning, "remains, and shall be carried out" (99). From the way Whitman is speaking, it seems that modernity fails to raise itself to a level of self-understanding where it has grasped this "first intent," the broader historical, perhaps even teleological, meaning of its own accomplishments. Such insight becomes available, Whitman argues explicitly, "after" the revolutionary transformations introduced by modern science have prepared the cultural conditions for just such a self-reflection. Whitman appears to anticipate later critiques of modernity that focus on its want of interpretive insight into its own world-historical purpose, and that tie this failure to the absence of normative reflection accompanying enlightenment's commitment to formal reason. Who will reveal the meaning of modernity, or as Whitman poses the issue, "Who justify these restless explorations?" (94). This is the question to which modernity has brought us, a question that, once answered, will reveal the purpose for which the modern world exists. And once Whitman asks who shall reveal the "first intent," who shall decipher the telos of modernity, he answers without hesitation. It is the poet who arrives in modernity's stead to justify its deeds.

Whitman lays the groundwork for this poetic justification of modernity by reconstructing a biblical narrative.

> Down from the gardens of Asia descending radiating,
> Adam and Eve appear, then their myriad progeny after them,
> Wandering, yearning, curious, with restless explorations,

> With questionings, baffled, formless, feverish, with never-happy
>   hearts ... (88–91)

Not wanting to be taken literally, of course, Whitman is not arguing playfully or gratuitously either, but telling a story to set the stage for his argument. He is preparing to situate poetry, his own poetry and idea of poetry, in relation to modernity, essentially to take the position that modernity's self-image, captive to the achievements of scientific progress, must be elevated to an aesthetic self-understanding. "Descending" and "radiating," Whitman says, spreading out over the surface of the earth, we are divided amongst ourselves and from nature, estrangements obliging "restless explorations," "questionings," "never happy-hearts" that call forth "modern wonders" (4), as he describes enlightenment, that bring near what has become distant. "Finally," Whitman proclaims, in the wake of modernity's "the distant brought near,"

> After the seas are all cross'd, (as they seem already cross'd,)
> After the great captains and engineers have accomplish'd their
>   work,
> After the noble inventors, after the scientists, the chemist, the
>   geologist, ethnologist, (101–3)

"shall come the poet worthy that name" (104).

What must the poet "worthy that name" accomplish that these modern thinkers fail to accomplish? What challenge must a poet meet to be worthy of being called a poet? "All these separations and gaps," Whitman continues, which remain as cultural divisions after the distant is brought near, "shall be taken up and hook'd and link'd together" (109). Turning a phrase, the poet, we might say, is to bring together those whom God has put asunder. Hooking and linking together what is separated, poetry will prove that the distant that has been brought *near together* can now *be together*. For when the separations and gaps are taken up and hooked and linked together, Whitman promises, "All these hearts as of fretted children shall be sooth'd" and "All affection shall be fully responded to" (107–8). And it is not only the togetherness of those who have been brought near together with whom Whitman is concerned, but the togetherness of man and nature as well, which "shall be disjoin'd and diffused no more" (114).

As Whitman writes of the poet's responsibilities to the modern world, he offers some indication that the aesthetic task he has in view may not be entirely unlike a "reconciliation." Since the reconciliation of man to God was, according to Jesus, one reason for his incarnation, when Whitman refers to "the poet worthy that name" as "The true son of God [who] shall come singing his songs" (104–5), he may be thinking of his challenge to the poet as a challenge to reconcile man to God by reconciling man to man and man to nature. Certainly we cannot ignore Whitman's reference, or pass it off as hyperbole, because he refers to the poet as the "true son of God" no less than three times and on the second occasion invokes the specter of reconciliation again by saying that the "Trinitas divine shall be gloriously accomplish'd and compacted by the true son of God, the poet" (111). If Whitman is not thinking of reconciliation specifically, what more could he be saying about the poet and poetry by speaking of them in this way?

At the least, he is arguing that by meeting the challenge to link cultural "separations and gaps" that were left behind by modernity after "the distant brought near," the poet achieves reconciliation by another name, though a name that alters its meaning and intent essentially. Whitman is precise. Separations and gaps are hooked and linked. He does not say they are overcome. He means that the great divide between what was distant remains when the distant is brought near, because the distant is not only physically, or spatially, distant. To Whitman's mind, what is distant is also different! Separations and gaps, and the differences they distinguish, are hooked and linked together as a "togetherness of differences." If Whitman is arguing more than this, it could be no more than that the trinity gloriously restored by the poet is the "reconciliation" of the human and the divine, but reconciliation in the sense that the form linking together all human differences would be a divine form and a divine achievement. It is as though Whitman were thinking that modernity culminates in an achievement where all the difference in the world need wait no longer upon an afterlife as the only home where all differences can be together.

The question "Passage to India" leaves with us is an interesting variation of the question left by the "Song of the Answerer." "Song of the Answerer" brought us to the point where we asked how the form of Whitman's poetry orients individuality receptively to the appearances of the world so that each of us can creatively envision forms of life where the diversity of the world's differences would be taken together as they are and left alone. "Passage to India" encourages us to ask how the poet through poetic form can creatively transform modernity's "distant brought near" into a "togetherness of differences." Whitman's aim may be to make modernity into the subject of a discourse through which poetry might define the form of modernity's future as an aesthetic form.

REPRESENTING A WORLD

An ethic of appearances can be no more deeply embedded in the form of Whitman's poetry that in its heart, and the heart of poetic form is representation. In this respect, of course, poetry is no different than any other form of thought. In Adorno's words, "[t]o think means to identify," or in terms more familiar to an era of deconstruction, to think means to represent.[8] For Adorno, art teaches that the distance between our representations of the world and the world as it is, in-itself, cannot be abolished, that our efforts to bridge this great divide wreak havoc upon the world, and that thinking should struggle to live within the limitations prescribed by a world that resists all attempts to know it. For Whitman, too, art, poetry, teaches this lesson and a second as well. Poetry not only teaches that there is a great ontological divide between a world and its representations, and that through our individuality we must struggle to live within the limitations this divide entails, but also teaches a way to live creatively with worlds with which we cannot be reconciled. From the point of view of Whitman, the artist (the creator), poetry's lessons have to do with aesthetic representation, with how through individuality we can creatively represent a world we cannot know, with how through individuality representation can be oriented receptively to the surfaces of the world so that, obedient to an ethic of appearances, representation frees our relations with the world of formal reason. Among the ways Whitman's poetry teaches these lessons is at the level of poetic form, as though if there were any truth at all to an ethic of appearances it would have to rest upon the way in which poetry itself creatively and receptively represents the world. Poetry becomes a powerful exemplar for individuality of an ethic of appearances where its own aesthetic relationship to the world assumes a form through which we can learn to be together in our differences without hope for reconciliation. How, then, does poetic form creatively and receptively represent the world? More precisely, from Whitman's aesthetic point of view, the point of view of the artist (the creator), how does poetic form form the world?

Representing Surfaces Descriptively

A bare seven lines of verse, "A Paumanok Picture" is a refined illustration of a form of poetic representation that Whitman relies upon extensively throughout his poetry.[9]

> Two boats with nets lying off the sea-beach, quite still,
> Ten fishermen waiting—they discover a thick school of mossbonkers—
>   they drop the join'd seine-ends in the water,
> The boats separate and row off, each on its rounding course to the
>   beach, enclosing the mossbonkers,
> The net is drawn in by a windlass by those who stop ashore,
> Some of the fishermen lounge in their boats, others stand ankle-
>   deep in the water, pois'd on strong legs,
> The boats partly drawn up, the water slapping against them,
> Strew'd on the sand in heaps and windrows, well out from the
>   water, the green-back'd spotted mossbonkers.

One of the most striking characteristics of Whitman's poetry, its use of description, or "descriptive representation," as I will call it, conveys a deliberate effort by the poet to take men and women and the earth and all upon it simply as they are. His aesthetic strategy is obvious and unmistakable, as we see here. Through his use of description, Whitman wants us to notice that his verse is free of an interest in interpretation, that there is another and superior representational interest that is being formally represented. Poetry's creative interest is to describe the world and to distinguish representation that relates our individuality to what it is that poetry describes. Description is being represented and at the same time recommended for orienting individuality receptively to the appearances of the world.

"I am afoot with my vision," Whitman says in "Song of Myself" (716). He then devotes nearly all of the sixty lines that immediately follow in verse 33 to describing what he sees as he—his sight—travels. If we jump from one line to another we receive a distinct impression of a special connection being formed between peripatetic observation (movement and seeing) and describing.

> By the city's quadrangular houses—in log huts, camping with lumbermen ... (717)

> Where the panther walks to and fro on a limb overhead, where the buck turns furiously at the hunter ... (722)

> Where the brook puts out of the roots of the old tree and flows to the meadow ... (735)

> Under Niagara, the cataract falling like a veil over my countenance ... (749)

> Where sun-down shadows lengthen over the limitless and lonesome prairie ... (760)

> Through the gymnasium, through the curtain'd saloon, through the office or public hall ... (773)

Whitman positions himself in relation to the world as its peripatetic viewer and reporter so that he can fuse observation with description. Moving from place to place, sight rests momentarily at each stop. Of course, vision may not rest "momentarily" in any precise sense. It may stay a moment or linger an hour. We are not told. It is the impression of vision's momentary taking something in, which accompanies the description of sight's simple movement from place to place and to yet another place, that conveys both simple observation and simply observation. Whatever Whitman sees he will describe. Description creatively orients us to appearances, to simple observation. But the peripatetic observation that enables description at the same time enables it to remain conscientiously attentive *only* to what can be seen at a glance, a relation that is simply observation. The connection between moving and seeing and describing, we should say, permits the creativity of descriptive language to orient individuality receptively to appearances as to the surfaces of the world.

Consequently, when Whitman writes elsewhere, as he does in "Song of the Answerer," such verse as "To the cities and farms I sing *as they spread in the sunshine before me*" (2; italics added), he is intimating that language, or thinking, or representation need have creative access to nothing more than the appearances directly before us. Whitman forces description and observation to collaborate aesthetically through representation to confine meaning receptively to the surface and to foreclose interpretive intervention into the world. Representation becomes a barrier to seeking to know about the world what cannot be known, a barrier to the pursuit of meaning lying in the depths. Affirming the ontological divide between the known and the unknown, the creativity of poetic form entails an aesthetic form of receptivity to the appearances of the world, an aesthetic form of regard and respect for the world just as it is.

Through this use of poetic form, Whitman develops a rather extraordinary idea. As an aesthetic practice that lets every world be by taking every existence receptively simply as it is on its surface, poetic form is aesthetically *indifferent* to the difference that distinguishes every form of life. The way in which every world is a difference in-itself that differentiates it essentially from every other world is to play no part in how it is to be creatively represented. Representation—identity—does not require difference in order to be. Descriptive representation thus moves toward the emancipation of thinking from the formal reason Adorno believed to be inherent in all thought that seeks to represent difference in-itself. According to Adorno's critique of identitarianism, every identity that requires difference in order to be imposes form and inflicts injury on difference. Where identity requires difference in order to be, difference loses any claim to an identity of its own outside of its relation to the identity being constituted, a relation from which the meaning of identity and difference is derived. Identity and difference are reduced to contrasts, to terms that stand in contradiction to one another, so that what identity and difference each becomes is merely that which the other is not. With Whitman, however, poetic form takes a decisive step toward the realization of Adorno's "utopia . . . beyond identity and beyond contradiction," a utopia that expresses Nietzsche's desideratum of creativity as well. Receptive to differences just as they appear, letting differences be, the creativity of Whitman's descriptive form of representation opposes the creation of identity in a relation where difference becomes known, in whole or in part, as a contrast to identity. Poetic form ends this relation of identity and difference, and with it the harm difference suffers in every identity that requires difference in order to be.

What Whitman intends for poetry's relationship to the world he also intends for the relationship to the world in which individuality is placed through his poetry. This is nowhere more evident than when he describes not only the world but his descriptive representations of the world. Consider Whitman's conclusion to the eighth stanza of "Song of Myself." After devoting the entirety of its verse to a reverie of virtually random descriptions of this variety,

> The little one sleeps in its cradle . . . (148)
>
> The suicide sprawls on the bloody floor of the bedroom . . . (152)
>
> The hurrahs for popular favorites, the fury of rous'd mobs . . . (157)
>
> What exclamations of women taken suddenly who hurry home and give birth to babes . . . (163)
>
> Arrests of criminals, slights, adulterous offers made, acceptances, rejections with convex lips . . . (165)

Whitman says matter of factly, "I mind them or the show or resonance of them—I come and I depart" (166). Once again Whitman is drawing our attention to his use of descriptive representation, though on this occasion rather more explicitly than when he intimates that representation is a relation to the world as "it spreads in the sunshine before [him]." Descriptive representation is turned reflexively on itself. Whitman's descriptions—the little one sleeping, the suicide sprawling, the mob in its fury and women exclaiming and hurrying and giving birth—are first represented as forms of "minding." At the least, as forms of minding, Whitman's descriptions are not less than creative expressions of individuality's awareness of the world, and may even exhibit individuality's protective care for the being of the world, as though the world were our individuality's child to "mind." Representation is then reflected a second time, however, in order to further objectify the creative orientation toward the world that representation as minding entails. To mind the world, to be aware of the world creatively, to care for it protectively, Whitman is explaining, is "to come and depart," to forgo intervention in the world just as he omits any term intervening between coming and departing that would represent acting upon the world in yet another way. Minding, coming, and departing display an aesthetic receptivity to the being of the world as it is when we first become aware of the world, and coax us to review the language of the preceding descriptions as representations that create a relationship with the world free of our intervention. Perhaps the harmlessness that descriptive language intends toward the world, together with the harmlessness it intends for individuality's relation with a world whose surfaces it compels us to prize receptively above all, is expressed wherever Whitman represents not just the world but his descriptions of the world. For is he not again teaching, here in "Song of Myself," to cite one more example, how individuality is to orient each of us creatively and receptively to our world when, poeticizing a mere butcher-boy, Whitman says of his aesthetic relation to this world he now descriptively represents, "I loiter enjoying his repartee and his shuffle and break-down" (218)? Is Whitman not recommending that we, too, loiter, delaying and remaining aimless, without reason?

By affirming the divide between what can be known and what remains unknown, by confining individuality's interpretive interest in the world to what meaning rests on its surface, so that all meaning in a world different from what appears as a surface can lie undisturbed in its depths, by orienting individuality receptively to the world as it appears before it, in other words, the creativity of descriptive representation also is meant to prove the "sufficiency" of appearances discussed earlier.[10] Why, though, we should ask, does representing the world descriptively, representing the world as a surface, establish its sufficiency? Could it not rather be likely that describing the world might merely be an expression of Whitman's trust that men and women and the world and all those upon it, simply taken as they are, will hold our fascination, and that we, too, will want to "loiter enjoying . . . "? Our suspicion only begs a second question. Why would Whitman place his trust in the sufficiency of appearances and imagine that the appearances of the world will hold our interest as they hold his? The answer to this question will answer the first as well.

For Whitman, aesthetic representation is a natural extension of aesthetic perception. Representation and perception are so tightly intermingled, in fact, to Whitman they may not be different at all, as he seems to believe when he says, in "Song of Myself," that "Speech [representation] is the twin of my vision [perception]" (566). In view of this remark, we can develop the relationship between representation and perception by saying that as Whitman speaks of the world descriptively he *sees* the world descriptively as well. Since Whitman represents the world descriptively as a surface, he must also see the world as a surface, as he does tell us often enough. We are reminded immediately of the line in "Song of the Answerer,"

> To the cities and farms I sing as they spread in the sunshine
> before me . . . (2)

where Whitman explains that the world he describes (speaks of, sings of) is its image as it appears exactly before him, as a surface, a connection for which he laid the groundwork in "Song of Myself" by observing that "sunshine . . . You light surfaces only" (987–88). And we are reminded of the verse in "Song of Myself,"

> But each man and each woman of you I lead upon a knoll,
> My left hand hooking you round the waist,
> My right hand pointing to landscapes of continents and the public
> road [,] (1207–9)

where Whitman explains again that he will represent—"lead" each one of us to—the world as he sees it as a surface, in outline, as a landscape. Such examples proliferate in Whitman's work. Each one is a relatively self-contained argument that representation is no different from perception, that the creativity of describing the world as a surface means to have seen the world as a surface, to have been receptive to the world as he creates it through a descriptive form of representation.

Once the world appears receptively to Whitman as an object of description, as a surface it assumes all the features of the unknown. Fathomless, mysterious, and wonderful, all that appears as the surface of the world is proved sufficient, and what can the sufficiency of appearances be if not that which inspires the artist's creativity? When we find Whitman singing, in "Song of Myself," for example,

> The Yankee clipper is under her sky-sails, she cuts the sparkle and
> scud,

> My eyes settle the land, I bend at her prow or shout joyously from
> the deck [,] (180–81)

he wants us to understand, first, that "settling" on the land, his eyes are resting on the world as on a surface, and, second, that it is because the world comes into view as a surface that it appears to him as mysterious and wonder-filled, as sufficient to earn his attention and delight, to *inspire* shouts of joy. And precisely as the world appears in sight (receptively) before him, he now represents the world (descriptively). The "twin of [his] vision," it is through the creativity of descriptive representation that poetry itself now "settles the land," through description that speech represents the world receptively as a surface that appears wonder-filled and sufficient to earn the representational interest of the artist. From Whitman's aesthetic point of view, the interest of the artist (the creator) is to creatively convey the world's wonder by limiting representation to a description of the world as it appears on the surface, to a description of the Yankee clipper under her sky-sails cutting the sparkle and scud on the surface of the sea.

To *prove* the sufficiency of appearances, though, the creativity and receptivity of aesthetic representation does more than bear witness to the wonder of the world by describing its surfaces. While it would be difficult to estimate the precise extent to which Whitman uses a descriptive form of representation, it is by far his poetic form of choice. So extensively does Whitman rely upon description, it seems that if time and space allowed, his poetry would describe the world and all the worlds the world contains. Indeed, so often and so strenuously does his poetry adopt the creative task of describing worlds to which it is receptive that his poems seem themselves like worlds, in that each aspires to contain everything. (Is a world not that which contains everything?) At the very least, the predominance of description relays Whitman's intention to display, as far as any aesthetic form can allow, the complete diversity of the being of the world.

If we take this achievement together with his representation of the world as mysterious and wonder-filled, it becomes evident that Whitman's creative ambition is to represent every world, and to represent each as wonderful and sufficient to warrant individuality's attention. Mystery and wonder then appear as the defining *gestalt*, the definitive value of the being of the world. By reflecting the diversity of being in this way, through descriptive representation Whitman abstains from privileging any particular form of being, from representing some forms of existence as being more or less wonder-filled, more or less valuable than others. Rather, the value of the diversity of being is inscribed in the mere appearance of every world mirrored descriptively by poetic form as a surface that is fathomless. As Whitman puts it decisively in "A Song for Occupations," "I send no agent or medium, offer no representative of value, but offer the value itself" (43).[11] Through the creativity of descriptive representation, Whitman once again exemplifies the element of indifference in the aesthetic receptivity to appearances that his work recommends throughout. Aesthetic receptivity to appearances confines value as well as meaning to the surfaces of the world, allowing representation to be further indifferent to the difference that distinguishes each form of life at its depths. Where the value of a world is inscribed in its mere appearance and the mere appearance of a world is what poetic form values, the creativity of such aesthetic representation spoils the valuation of difference as a determination to be made in relation to the identity of another world. Orienting individuality receptively to the surface of the world, poetic form teaches that through individuality we may be able individually and collectively to subdue our interest in creating our identity in relation to the value of difference. Where the value of every difference on its surface is equal to every other, and where identity becomes aesthetically indifferent to difference's intrinsic meaning and value concealed at a depth, representation insulates every difference from all relations through which the identity of difference is constituted instrumentally.

It might be objected, of course, that ultimately Whitman cannot hope to represent the entire world descriptively, that from his aesthetic point of view creativity cannot avoid privileging forms of being that are represented and discriminating against those excluded from representation. Failing to contain the world, at the extreme, representation by default must value some forms of difference differently from others. Representation cannot but fail to realize that indifference to difference that spares it both the insult and the injury of being known through contradiction as the mere shadow of identity. Poetic form would then be an agent, medium, or representative of value rather than offer the value itself, as Whitman argued so exactly. Such an objection, though, does not appreciate the creative spirit of the aesthetic point of view from which Whitman poeticizes the world. Although no art, as we learned from Adorno, can form itself (mimetically) into a world, no art, that is, can represent everything belonging to any particular world, it is clearly Whitman's *aspiration* to poeticize in ways that do so, as revealed by the sheer extent to which he represents the world descriptively. Descriptive representation makes us aware of his aspiration as the democratic intent of his poetry. As demonstrable efforts to be representative of everyone and everything the world contains, Whitman's verse encourages our *anticipation* of what it next may include. It makes us aware that there is *always* something left out of the poetic frame, though left out only for a time, so that the anticipation of representation Whitman encourages becomes the way that what is left out of verse is not, by its omission, excluded. Whitman's efforts to be all-inclusive mark the presence of what is always left out but not to be excluded. So when Whitman remarks, in his 1855 preface, that "[m]en and women and the earth and all upon it are simply to be taken as they are," we must be careful to place equal stress on the word "taken" and the phrase "as they are," or else with misplaced emphasis we slight the creativity of his intention to *take in everything*. From Whitman's point of view, the aesthetic point of view of the artist (the creator), individuality is to be receptive to every world, as it is. Individuality's receptivity thus takes every world to be identical in meaning and value to every other, which earns it the indifference of representation that protects difference from the vicissitudes of formal reason.

Representing Surfaces Metaphorically

While through his descriptive form of representation Whitman aspires to a creativity and receptivity that is all inclusive of the world, I do not mean to suggest that he confuses the aspiration to be all-inclusive with the possibility of actually being so. To the contrary, descriptive representation consistently implies that there is something left out. What is represented always refers to a not-yet-represented, what is identified to a not-yet-identified. Whitman's poetic form consistently affirms the nonidentity of the world, that the world is representationally inexhaustible. But by aesthetically maintaining this tight, ontological relation between the identity of the world and its nonidentity, Whitman creates the impression that the world forever out of reach is also just within reach. It is right here, in the extraordinary ways in which nonidentity and difference are the spiritual familiars of identity (representation), that the equal meaning and value of all differences, the indifference of representation, and the emancipation of difference from formal reason are rooted. If, from his aesthetic point of view, Whitman's description of the world and all the worlds it contains sometimes seems endless, it is because he wants to acquaint us with the world on its surface, with each of its details, and because he wants us through our own individuality to similarly acquaint *ourselves* with the world so that we will share an intimacy with the world that in its mere appearance is to appear to us sufficient. Whitman creates a modern form to justify the modern world, an aesthetic form that, like modernity, brings the distant near. How near? How intimate? Whitman's deepest affections for the world are formed descriptively, as in this passage from "Song of Myself."

> Smile O voluptuous cool-breath'd earth!
> Earth of the slumbering and liquid trees!
> *Earth of the departed sunset*—earth of the mountains misty-topt!
> Earth of the vitreous pour of the full moon just tinged with blue!
> Earth of the shine and dark mottling the tide of the river!
> Earth of the limpid gray of clouds brighter and clearer for my
>   sake!
> Far-swooping elbow'd earth—rich apple-blossom'd earth!
> Smile, for your lover comes. (438–45)

Whitman's love for the appearances of the world is meant to entice, to arouse our love for the appearances of the world, and thus to draw us ever nearer to the surface of the world. How can we resist Whitman's inspiration? (Surely I cannot.) The beauty of his world of appearances is transcendent. It appears other-worldly.

Now we have troubling questions. If we admit that from his aesthetic point of view Whitman's world of appearances appears other-worldly, do we not allow that the world described is not described only, or perhaps at all? Other-worldly is the world not transformed wholly or in part through imagery attaching meanings that make it a different world, perhaps a personified world, at least other than the very worldly "earth" to which he refers? Is the world being represented not for the sake of the world but for "my sake," as he says? Though Whitman loves the world and encourages love of the world in us, does his verse cast doubt that his poetic form creatively represents the world with the gentle receptivity of an ethic of appearances? Does Whitman then turn the world into a victim of formal reason?

To portray the earth's sunset as departed, the mountains as misty-topt, its days and nights, light and shadow varying the color of the river, and its moon tinged of blue is to adopt language that is descriptive, though ambiguously so. The denotative features of descriptive language are forced to recede within a context Whitman makes vividly connotative. Voluptuous and cool-breath'd, slumbering and liquid, the earth and trees take on a meaning that is figuratively constructed and that applies pressure to the more straightforwardly descriptive language that follows to suggest figurative meanings as well. With its allurements the earth cuts the figure of a lover, a lover to whom we come as lover, too. Can there be any doubt that the creativity and receptivity of descriptive representation slide precariously toward an interpretive language that leaves the surfaces of the world for its depths, to find there what according to an ethic of appearances should be inaccessible to representation?

While our initial impression that Whitman's verse is composed in a descriptive form of representation is not incorrect, it mistakenly favors a somewhat literal interpretation of Whitman's figurations by conscripting the above passage to a meaning that nullifies its interpretive range. Connotative as well as denotative, figurative as well as literal, the lines of Whitman's verse form an alliance that shifts the weight of the entire passage from a descriptive to a metaphorical form of representation. Yet this shift in creative form does not necessarily betoken a corresponding shift from a receptivity to the appearances of the world to an interest in what these appearances "really" mean. There are at least three reasons why this shift in creative form is not at odds with Whitman's ethic of appearances.

When from his aesthetic point of view Whitman first oriented individuality receptively to the appearances of a world fathomless beneath its surfaces, he enchanted the world again, or recognized the world's enchantment, its unknown and unknowable, mysterious and wonder-filled being. By then confining the creativity of aesthetic representation descriptively to surfaces, Whitman's poetic form reflected the enchantment of the world through its respect for the remoteness of the difference, the meaning and value, that distinguished each form of life in its depths, and through its concern for the fate that difference suffered in every effort to identify it. Since description incorporates the idea that the world is always different beneath its surface, it likewise presumes its meaning and value to be far more inaccessible than accessible to representation, to exceed its grasp so that the meaning and value of the world are not identical to its representations. What is decisive is that by systematically acknowledging that the world is nonidentical, in effect, that *everything is always something else*, all of Whitman's poetic language, even the most pristinely descriptive poetic representation, "the green-back'd spotted mossbonkers" of "A Paumanok Picture," can be approached figuratively and metaphorically. Rather than a shift from a receptivity to the surfaces of the world to an invasion of its depths, from an ethic of appearances to the instrumentalism of formal reason, the shift in creative form from descriptive to metaphorical representation introduces another poetic form to affirm the nonidentity of the world. Ethically, in terms of the intent to represent, to identify, to think about the world from his aesthetic point of view, by affirming a consistent sense of nonidentity Whitman's use of metaphorical representation entails no shift at all away from the ethics of descriptive representation.

Next, metaphorical representation acquaints individuality with the world's indeterminacy. By affirming the nonidentity of an unknowable world, by affirming that the being of the world can be something or anything more than what it appears to be on its surface, from Whitman's aesthetic point of view poetic form encourages us to consider that the possibilities for being are not only indefinite but perhaps infinitely so. Recall Whitman saying in "Song of Myself" that the grass, the meaning of which eludes him, must be a "uniform hieroglyphic" (106), a sign or token, not just of something else but of *everything* else (and of Whitman's strategy to let nothing be less mysterious or more provocative than anything else). And it is precisely its opacity, preventing us from saying what it is for certain, which makes each world into a sign that compels individuality to entertain the thought that it could be anything or everything. Metaphor undermines the authority arrogated to every aesthetic representation of the identity of a world.

Finally, as intimately acquainted with the world as Whitman becomes through descriptions representing the rich diversity of its differences, metaphorical representation reaches new heights of intimacy by permitting him to imagine the resplendent particularities—which Whitman calls "idiocrasies"—of an unseen world. Because metaphor expresses the world's indeterminacy, though, Whitman's poetic fantasies, for instance, that the world's allurements confer upon him the figure of its lover, do not identify the being of the world. Where the world is fathomless, metaphors are more abstractions than approximations of the world as it is, in-itself. Representation brings individuality into touch intimately with a world whose familiarity metaphor enables Whitman to invent, while allowing whatever the real identity of the world may be to remain hidden behind the great divide measured by every metaphorical representation. Individuality's receptivity to the appearances of the world, its confinement to the world's surfaces, is assured as metaphor implicates the creativity of representation in a paradox. From Whitman's aesthetic point of view, poetic form closes the figurative distance between the world and its representations through a metaphorical intimacy that traces the unbridgeable distance between appearance and reality, surfaces and depths. Metaphorical representation establishes the world's separateness by imagining what it may be like if, through individuality, our distance from the world were ever overcome. Whitman's paradoxical use of poetic form is perhaps no more clearly illustrated than when he speaks in "Song of Myself" of "the dark suns I cannot see" (353). Even that within a world which we cannot see and cannot feel, he is saying, is bright and warm and life-giving, the being of every being around which all other beings revolve, the intense light burning within that appears only as darkness from without.

Whitman represents individuality, his own and the individuality belonging to each of us, as an ethical form of life through the creativity of descriptive and metaphorical forms of poetic representation. Incorporating the ethic of his aesthetic point of view, poetic form forms individuality's relationship to the world according to an ethic of appearances. So faithfully do Whitman's poetic forms orient individuality receptively to the appearances of the world, poetic form mirrors an ethic of appearances. Poetic form appears as the form in which the world, created from an aesthetic point of view, reflects the value, the ethic, that is born of individuality's creativity and that forms the "origin of all poems." As we think of Whitman's aesthetic point of view as Nietzsche thinks of the aesthetic point of view of the artist, the intimate relationship between ethics and aesthetics in Whitman's poetry is not accidental. In Whitman's verse, ethics and aesthetics can no more be distinguished than Nietzsche distinguished between the artistic creativity of the artist and the ethical creativity of the creator when he spoke of "the artist (the creator)," by which he understands value to be the creation of the artist and art to be the value of creativity.

To appreciate Whitman's achievement, the relationship between the ethics and aesthetics of appearances can be expressed in another way. If in our every relation with the world we orient our individuality receptively to its surfaces, as for Whitman poetic form is oriented, we would do no less than represent the worlds about us creatively from an aesthetic point of view. And if there were truly no difference between ethics and aesthetics in Whitman's poetry, we would not only find in his work what it means for our individuality's creativity to represent worlds ethically, to ourselves, from an aesthetic point of view, but discover that there are, as well, ways for our individuality to represent itself ethically, to others, from an aesthetic point of view. We would learn from Whitman's poetry how individuality can create, or *present*, the world that is each of us to others as his aesthetic point of view has taught us how individuality can create, or represent, every other world. An ethic of appearances would be as deeply embedded in his poetry's aesthetics of self-creativity as in its aesthetics of creating the world in images, in individuality's aesthetic form of presentation as in individuality's aesthetic form of representation.

PRESENTING A WORLD

There is a moment in *Democratic Vistas* when Whitman thinks aloud of the philosophical background for the ideas of identity and individuality that appear in his work. It is a moment both rare and remarkable for his willingness to conceptualize explicitly what in his poetry and prose is regularly spoken of only circuitously. Whitman writes, there is

> in sanest hours, a consciousness, a thought that rises, independent, lifted out from all else, calm, like the stars, shining eternal. This is the thought of identity—yours for you, whoever you are, as mine for me. Miracle of miracles, beyond statement, most spiritual and vaguest of earth's dreams, yet hardest basic fact, and only entrance to all facts.[12]

What strikes Whitman as miraculous is that identity is a certain "quality of BEING, in the object's self," as he puts it metaphysically. Identity is that "central idea and purpose," he goes on to explain, possessed by each and from which each one develops in kind, "growing therefrom and thereto," permitting each of us to distinguish ourselves as individuals.[13] Either it is a quality belonging to the being-in-itself of every individual, or, individuals also being in part social constructions, as Whitman acknowledges, it is a quality of being that in the time portioned to each life at the very least takes on the characteristics of the supersensible. Whitman does not let on if he believes identity could be accounted for with Kantian categories, nor do I believe he would concern himself with such a problem. Such an inquiry simply would be part of the "supernatural of no account" he warns should not distract us from living life.[14] Either by nature we possess the quality of being through which each of us becomes who we are, or nature, following its own course out of necessity and unassisted, exemplifies how we may originate and nurture it. These two possibilities Whitman leaves equally open by suggesting that the miracle of identity is the "lesson of Nature."[15] That identity is a quality of being that urges us, individually, to create ourselves as centers of meaning through which we then, having "entrance to all facts," discover that meaning also is everywhere removed at distances from our centers, is surely inevitable though enigmatic, Whitman is saying. Whitman's concerns run, too, to identity's endangerment. He expresses anxiety about the eclipse of individuality "amid this more and more complex, more and more artificialized state of society," wherein the expropriated and alien European culture of modernity transplanted to American soil spoils the "precious idiocrasy and special nativity" peculiar to each one of us.[16]

Describing identity as the "miracle of miracles," anchoring identity as a central idea and purpose in a quality of being-in-itself, Whitman inscribes mystery so deeply within identity that it becomes an intrinsic source of wonder pervading each life, essential to its self-creativity. It is, Whitman seems to say, because our identities are mysterious to us that we are forced to engage an existence that offers us insight into ourselves, into what are our identity is, what our own central idea and purpose may be. Identity is the mystery through which we become known to ourselves by creating ourselves gradually though always incompletely, making us less mysterious to ourselves though never so well known that the mystery that incites self-discovery and self-creativity is banished. By inciting self-discovery and self-creativity, in other words, the mystery in identity inspires in each of us an individuality that preserves the mystery in identity while discovering and developing identity's "own central idea and purpose," so that it "grow[s] therefrom and thereto." Present at the point of our every new departure, identity is the mystery that compels individuality to emerge and press us into being, as it were, in the expectation, ever defeated yet ever renewed, that the mystery in identity might become transparent. Precisely because identity is tied securely to mystery, our individuality is vulnerable to cultural influences. Where the terms of the public world, with as well as without our compliance, shape individuality's development, the mystery in identity dissipates. Mystery in identity, in the being of individuality itself, is disenchanted. As a product of a public world already known to us, our identity assumes a degree of transparency mystery denies it. And the odyssey through which each individuality develops, discovers, and lays claim to the "precious idiocrasy and special nativity" of one's own identity is arrested.

When Whitman announces, in the first line of the first poem of those collected as "Inscriptions" in *Leaves of Grass*, that it is to "One's-Self I sing, a simple separate person," he does more than dedicate his great work.[17] He introduces the subject to whom his work is dedicated as the personification of the metaphysics of individuality that along with mystery is inscribed into identity. By "separate" Whitman proposes to consider individuality as a response to the mystery that incites being, individuals as they escape or resist or remain free and independent of powers threatening identity with disenchantment. Whitman's person apart is "simple" only in the sense of being "average" or typical of those whose individuality perennially comes to term in a democratic society and is perpetually just within reach of that self-discovery or creation of one's self that always must be one more step ahead. Though Whitman's ideas of identity and individuality and of separateness, we might conclude, lean heavily on the side of "[e]ach singing what belongs to him or her and to none else," as he puts it in "I Hear America Singing" (9), we should not mistake his "simple separate person" for an abstraction.[18] Whitman's person is neither so precious nor so precocious as one whose being need not depend upon the world for becoming the individual whose accomplishment is to evolve out of himself in ways that are meaningful philosophically. Whitman's "simple separate person" is merely the *ostensible* beginning of his work.

By the time Whitman composes the first line of "Inscriptions" for *Leaves of Grass*, the "I" already is a "We," though to express in this way the logic of identity and individuality as he understands it is to crush his simple separate person under the weight of vulgar sociology. Rather, it should be said that Whitman's separate person is already a "world," as he says often in various ways, though never more clearly than in "Song of Myself" with the assertion, "I exist as I am, that is enough, If no other in the world be aware I sit content, And if each and all be aware I sit content" (413–15). Whitman sees himself and each of us as a world surrounded by worlds, each world taking notice of worlds circling about them, or not paying notice, as they please. To be a world is to possess the *means* to be aware, Whitman is suggesting, the *means* to identify other worlds, to represent one's own world to others, and to represent to oneself one's own world independent of recognition by others. For there to be the world that is each one, in other words, another and antecedent and common world that all worlds together share as the means for representation is required.

It is this common world, Whitman explains very importantly in "Song of the Open Road," that contains "objects that call from diffusion my meanings and give them shape!" (26).[19] Whitman's idea of a common world plays on Wittgenstein's impression of the relationship between language and world. Whereas Wittgenstein proved that to speak a language is to inherit a world, Whitman is saying that to share a world is to inherit a language, a language whose words, or meanings, are the worlds or "objects" that form our common world. The possibilities for meaning offered by this language are never less than the meanings belonging to our common world's own diversity of worlds, and potentially are far greater. Looking to the world we share for the means for individuality to call from diffusion and shape our meanings, Whitman transforms all "objects"—all worlds—appearing in our common world into metaphors that constitute a language through which the individuality belonging to each of us can discover and create ourselves as worlds. With the use of metaphors, the meaning of the common world we share and the meaning of every world within it, hence the meaning of the world we each become, are bounded only by the figurative limits of poetic construction, as we soon shall learn.

Individuality and identity begin, then, where our inquiry into poetic form first began, by "representing a world," an "object," aesthetically. The creativity of aesthetic representation is confined receptively to surfaces, inimical to approaches that presume that the in-itself of a world can be known. Oriented descriptively to the surfaces of worlds or of objects as they appear, aesthetic representation is receptive to the indeterminacy of their meaning, receptive to the fathomless difference in each world constituting the radical diversity of all. Aesthetic representation's creativity is inclusive of the meanings of different and diverse "objects that call from diffusion [our] meanings and give them shape!" Approached aesthetically, each of the world's objects is no less than a reservoir of metaphorical meaning for every individual, a world in-itself that represents interpretive possibilities for individuality's acts of self-discovery and self-creation through which individuals can "present" themselves as worlds. Each of us is a being who through its individuality can present a world because we are rooted in the world, and insofar as we orient ourselves *inclusively* to every world of meaning in our common world according to the receptivity of an ethic that preserves through its veneration for appearances the world's objects as a language for becoming. No one, consequently, is simply "simple" or "separate," though Whitman does not mislead us. On the contrary, singing of a simple separate person Whitman prepares us for his view that for an individual to be a part of the world and apart from the world is already and always potentially to become a world. "I am large," we remember Whitman exclaims in "Song of Myself." "I contain multitudes" (1326).

By tying individuality's being and becoming, its acts of self-creation or "presentation," to the aesthetic representation of the world and its worlds as a language of indeterminate meanings for individualization, Whitman intends for each of us to discover our forms of life through poetic forms. Relating to the world as the poet relates to the world, through poetic forms of representation, individuality would relate to the world aesthetically from the point of view of the artist. Descriptive and metaphorical forms of representation bear considerable weight. As poetic forms they model for individuality forms of life that are aesthetic, and as embodiments of a definite ethical orientation to the world, the aesthetic forms of life modeled entail the same ethic of appearances. It may be difficult to imagine a more indissoluble connection between ethics and aesthetics, forms of life and forms of art.[20]

Forcing Surfaces and Depths

Against this background of identity and individuality formed through an aesthetics of self-creativity, whereby each of us is able to create or present ourselves as a world by becoming receptive to the surfaces of worlds that provide our language of self-creation, we can understand what Whitman means when he declares in "Song of Myself,"

> Flaunt of the sunshine I need not your bask—lie over!
> You light surfaces only, I force surfaces and depths also. (987–88)

Dramatizing both the boundaries of the intelligible world with the metaphorical object of "sunshine" lighting surfaces only and an enlightened commitment to an ethic of appearances as well, Whitman first brackets individuality's receptivity to the surfaces of the world beneath which its unlit depths remain in darkness. Enlightenment limits representation to surfaces. Whitman remains aligned with Adorno. Yet Whitman playfully imagines other surfaces whose depths he "forces" are within range of his vision. As are all surfaces, Whitman's "forced surfaces" would be illumined, too, while his verse distinguishes "forced depths" that are removed from the light that illuminates "surfaces only." "*Forced* depths" thus are within sight though at the same time out of light's reach, a formulation that would be paradoxical, and a violation of an ethic of appearances, if the depths to which Whitman is referring belong to the surfaces of the worlds surrounding us. But the formulation is not paradoxical, for with "forced depths" Whitman is not orienting himself to depths that all along he has maintained are unseen and unknown. With the extraordinary declaration, "You light surfaces only, I force surfaces and depths also," Whitman makes it perfectly clear to whom forced surfaces and forced depths belong, and as he does so he highlights the dimensions of the philosophical framework within which he forms his verse. The idea of a depth remaining in darkness, unlit by a light lighting surfaces only, the idea of depth at the core of Adorno's aesthetics, we now see is united with the aesthetics of surfaces and depths at the center of Nietzsche's formulation of the aesthetic problem from the point of view of the artist (the creator).

Forced depths are uniquely intelligible, as are the forced surfaces they lie beneath in darkness, for they are the dark depths and bright surfaces that belong to each of us, which through the individuality belonging to each one of us we are able to force, or "create," forcing ourselves into existence. Forced surfaces are the selves we can create for others to see, appearances to which others are confined receptively as our surfaces protect from illumination the depths of a self that is unseen and unknown by all save the "*Is*" who would "force [their own] depths also." Forced depths are the concealed selves whose meaning individuality creates metaphorically out of the surfaces of the world to which it relates us receptively, out of "objects that call from diffusion my meanings and give them shape," as Whitman puts it. The meaning of the forced depths our individuality creates disappears into the darkness of an indeterminate figurative language and becomes inscrutable and unknown to all but the author of the meaning itself. Forced surfaces are the surfaces we create to be included with the rest, selves we create to which others may orient themselves receptively, "objects that call from diffusion [others'] meanings and give them shape," to paraphrase Whitman. Each such surface we create through our individuality offers to others yet another world of the appearances of which our common world consists, and which others may use creatively to create regions of the self that will remain deep or rise to the surface as their authors please.

Recalling our earlier discussion of the rhetorical strategy of Whitman's "Calamus" poems, for example, we learned that the self about whom he pledges to tell us is revealed and concealed at one and the same time, so that all we know of him for certain is that his appearance does not correspond to who he really is.[21] With the introduction of the language of "forced surfaces and forced depths," we see now that often when Whitman speaks of himself he presents himself brightly, as a surface, as he does in "Behold This Swarthy Face," and at the same time intimates as a difference from his appearance a depth too dimly lit to be made out with certainty.²²

> Behold this swarthy face, these gray eyes,
> This beard, the white wool unclipt upon my neck,
> My brown hands and the silent manner of me without charm;
> Yet comes one a Manhattanese and ever at parting kisses me
>   lightly on the lips with robust love,
> And I on the crossing of the street or on the ship's deck give a
>   kiss in return,
> We observe that salute of American comrades land and sea,
> We are those two natural and non-chalant persons. (1–7)

Or through imagery borrowed from the surfaces of the world, as in "Scented Herbage of My Breast," Whitman presents himself by concealing metaphorically, revealing obliquely, in his "own way," a depth "under," as he says.²³ Whitman creates an obscure, perhaps fragile existence beneath a surface that is not to be mistaken for the whole and that is to be received, aesthetically, in place of the life beneath.

> Perennial roots, tall leaves, O the winter shall not freeze you
>   delicate leaves . . .
> O slender leaves! O blossoms of my blood! I permit you to tell
>   in your own way of the heart that is under you . . . (4, 7)

Through Whitman's use of the language and images of surface and depth, our discussion now settles on concepts that serve as a point of convergence for arguments that together can further explicate his "Miracle of miracles," the miracle of "identity," and the idea of individuality as "presenting a world." To respond to that mysterious "quality of BEING" in oneself, to discover and develop one's "own central idea and purpose" is to "force" oneself as a surface and a depth. Through the individuality belonging to each of us, to "force" oneself as a surface and a depth is to create oneself aesthetically as a world by first becoming aesthetically receptive to the world as to a surface, as though *we* were Whitman's suns lighting surfaces only. By respecting the world's opacity, recognizing the world's indeterminacy, in short, being *receptive* to the world as a surface beneath which lies a fathomless difference, we can cultivate the world as a metaphor through which we find the possibilities to *create* ourselves as worlds, to which others may orient themselves receptively and creatively in turn. Creating ourselves aesthetically as worlds through an individuality aesthetically receptive to the world, we resemble Whitman's poetic forms, which include the dual aesthetic orientations of *receptivity*, belonging to Adorno, and *creativity*, belonging to Nietzsche. Whitman's poetic forms incorporate aesthetic strategies, descriptive and metaphorical forms, to create surfaces and depths, images of life belonging to his "simple, separate person," to himself and to each of us. Created as surfaces and depths, as the creations of an aesthetic individuality we can think of ourselves in ways that facilitate insight into areas of our identities that are mysterious to us and that enable us to identify both who we are and who we might become.

Whitman often demonstrates this poetically. In "That Shadow My Likeness," for example, an entry in the "Calamus" collection, Whitman initially expresses puzzlement about what appears to him to be an absence of coherence in his identity.[24] At first appearing, reflexively, as a self divided against himself, he graduates insightfully to the thought that he is necessarily divided. By intuiting from a visible surface seen as a depth that is either unseen or ascends to the surface as accident and his will permit, Whitman is guided to self-discovery about the divided nature of his being, that there is a part of him living unknown in partial darkness, a metaphorical "shadow." And he is led further by his intuitions to the rediscovery and affirmation of those with whom both he and his work, his "livelihood," prosper and develop as a community, where the obscurity of the partial darkness of his being is lifted.

> That shadow my likeness that goes to and fro seeking a livelihood, chattering, chaffering,
> How often I find myself standing and looking at it where it flits,
> How often I question and doubt whether that is really me;
> But among my lovers and caroling these songs,
> O I never doubt whether that is really me. (1–5)

Whitman's insight recalls the sentiments of "Earth, My Likeness," where the metaphorical image of the world's surface insinuates a depth, "something fierce in [him] eligible to burst forth" (4).[25] That depth, a deep depth about which Whitman "dare not tell . . . in words" (7), remains submerged in darkness, as though to resonate there, a reality frozen for all time as that moment of self-understanding in "That Shadow My Likeness" before he moved beyond it to develop and affirm new possibilities. Again, in "That Shadow My Likeness" and "Earth, My Likeness," we notice his practice of revealing and concealing by apprehending the world metaphorically to convey unseen depths that reveal Whitman to himself as *distinctly* as his figurative language presents himself to others *mysteriously*. Similarly, opening "Calamus" with "In Paths Untrodden," Whitman boldly commits himself to speak throughout this collection of a secret life that has made "Clear to me now standards not yet publish'd" (6), but to speak of this secret life from a "secluded spot" (10).[26] Proposing to reveal "the life that does not exhibit itself," and which "contains all the rest" (11) of his lives yet to be lived, by steadfastly concealing his life through the "seclusions" of metaphor, Whitman divulges his habit of consistently creating himself poetically as a depth—though surely not in verse only!

Taken together, "That Shadow My Likeness," "Earth, My Likeness," and "In Paths Untrodden" confirm Whitman's technique of forcing surfaces and depths for the purposes of self-clarification about the actualities and possibilities of his identity and individuality, and to obliquely confide his self-discoveries. Whitman's metaphorical configurations of depth, of course, are especially important, as depths hold the secret of our identities and individualities, who we really are and who we possibly can become. Intimating the presence of an indeterminate bottomlessness, surfaces set off depths, standing as sentries to what it is about each of us that is mysterious and wonderful. Whitman, in fact, frequently privileges depth, as he does conspicuously on two occasions in "Song of Myself." Presenting himself as a world by saying, "It is time to explain myself—let us stand up" (1134), the individual identity whose disclosure he promises is no sooner swallowed up by the multiplicity of the figurative "us," then it virtually disappears into the metaphor Whitman relies upon most often to convey indeterminacy.

> It is time to explain myself—let us stand up,
> What is known I strip away,
> I launch all men and women forward with me into the Unknown. (1134–36)

What Whitman is, and is yet to be, he consigns to the "Unknown," his metaphor for what is unseen, little seen, or never seen, for the darkness that traces the fathomless depths and unbounded space for self-creativity.

As though his figure of the "Unknown" may fail to express the pathos of creating in darkness, however, Whitman draws together creation, depth, and darkness in one of the most beautiful though painful images in all of his poetry. With a jarringly poignant metaphor Whitman captures the bittersweet joy of creating in space forms of creation normally denied space, creating in space whose depths and darkness remove creativity from harm's way on the surface but not so completely that creator and creativity entirely escape injury or the fear and threat of injury. As Whitman sings in "Song of Myself,"

> [B]ecoming already a creator,
> Putting myself here and now to the ambush'd womb of the shadows. (1052–53)

Securing a haven for creativity, though not one entirely immune to danger, the "ambush'd womb of the shadows" locates creativity metaphorically within the vulnerable space of the womb. Within the creative space of the womb, however, lies yet another space, the metaphorically dark, shadowy space of the unknown and fathomless, as though it were indeterminacy itself being creatively nurtured there. If individuality's creativity relies, as Whitman proposed its creativity must, upon our common world's "objects" to "call from diffusion [our] meanings and give them shape," what meaning has been given shape by the objects "womb" and "shadows"? As a metaphor for what is contained within metaphor, "womb" of the "shadows," "creativity" of the "Unknown," as it were, installs into creativity itself, as its very inception, the indeterminacy that belongs intrinsically to metaphor. A metaphor for what is contained within metaphor, as a space for an indeterminate space, "womb of the shadows" infinitely "deepens" creativity by infinitely deepening as the unknown the space within which creativity takes place.

"Forced depths" now become more a metaphor for the individuality of creativity than a concept only suggesting that there is something about individuals more than and different from what appears on the surface. With "womb of the shadows," Whitman pours into creativity what is required to create ourselves individually as the worlds he makes each of us out to be. It is the fathomless, indeterminate depth in the womb of our own individual creativity that constitutes the enigmatic, unknown quality defining the "in-itself" of our identities and the mystery that compels the individuality that creates our own central idea and purpose. As such a deep depth, individuality possesses the capacity for creating every possible meaning that must be created to be the world of metaphorical meaning that continues to be shaped by the equally unfathomable worlds belonging to others who inhabit our common world. So creative is depth, in "Song of Myself" Whitman reflects,

> Nor do I understand who there can be more wonderful than
>   myself. (1282)

So deep is individuality's creativity, so much does each self have within itself all the creativity required to create a world, in "Song of the Open Road" Whitman asserts,

> To see no being, not God's or any, but you also go thither. (173)

Attachment and Self-Creativity

With creativity approaching infinite measure, despite the weight Whitman assigns to "womb of the shadows," to "depth," the "Unknown," the "unseen," and to similar figures of speech, his ideas of identity and individuality would be underdetermined if creativity were tied exclusively to these or other metaphors. For each of us through our individuality to become the boundless world Whitman traces metaphorically, a *world* of metaphors is necessary to embody our likenesses, a world of worlds, of "objects that call from diffusion [our] meanings and give them shape." Individuality, we discover, relates us to the world in a unique way. To become a world we must be attached to the surfaces of the world, the surfaces of its "objects," to each world our common world possesses so that it might become a means through which our individuality forces our own surfaces and depths and their meanings into existence. It is as though the world we share with all others and other things, with all "objects," were midwife to our being and becoming. Nowhere is Whitman more explicit about individuality's creative attachment to the world's surfaces than in "Salut au Monde!" where the world Whitman himself becomes evolves magnificently in proportion to the breadth of his attachment to the surfaces of the world about him.[27]

> What widens within you Walt Whitman?
> What waves and soils exuding?
> What climes? what persons and cities are here?

Who are the infants, some playing, some slumbering?
Who are the girls? who are the married women?
Who are the groups of old men going slowly with their arms about
  each other's necks?
What rivers are these? what forests and fruits are these?
What are the mountains call'd that rise so high in the mists?
What myriads of dwellings are they fill'd with dwellers?
Within me latitude widens, longitude lengthens ... (5–14)

Within me zones, seas, cataracts, forests, volcanoes, groups,
Malaysia, Polynesia, and the great West Indian islands. (20–21)

All you continentals of Asia, Africa, Europe, Australia, indifferent
  of place! (190)

And you each and everywhere whom I specify not, but include just
  the same! (193)

Each of us limitless ... (197)

As the world expands gigantically, inwardly and outwardly, Whitman's own world, his "latitude" and "longitude," "zones, seas, cataracts, forests, volcanoes, groups ... ," his creative possibilities, expand in step, his being becoming as fertile as the being of the world.

Perhaps it is evident here that while individuality creates its own world by attaching itself to the surfaces of the world, our common world and all the worlds within it *inspire* individuality's creativity and its attachment. Surfaces appear to act as a "quality of BEING," to borrow from Whitman, that is external though equal to that mysterious internal quality of being-in-itself to which individuality necessarily responds when developing its own central idea and purpose. No intuitions we might have of the magnitude of the world's surfaces could prepare us for Whitman's conception of the breadth of possibilities for individuality's self-creation that surfaces metaphorically represent and the attachment to the world they inspire. As Whitman imagines in "Night on the Prairies," individuality's creative possibilities and attachment to the world swell as the worlds about it proliferate.[28]

I was thinking the day most splendid till I saw what the not-day
  exhibited,
I was thinking this globe enough till there sprang out so noiseless
  around me myriads of other globes. (9–10)

"Not-day" is the source of Whitman's inspiration. Not-day traces his creative possibilities through the image of worlds—globes—appearing in time beyond that globe attracting his fascination and affections during the day. Not-day is night and not only the night. Not-day is all time that is not day, today or any day. Not-day is all the possibilities all time will exhibit beyond those exhibited by every day. Not-day is measureless time and hence time's measureless possibilities not-identical to thinking's measures of time. Not-day is nonidentity, it is infinity. Is it any wonder that Whitman sometimes feels overwhelmed by the world and by his love for the world, and that he holds individuality, whose creativity looms as large as the worlds circling about him loom large, to be productive of worlds not less overwhelming, nor less inspiring. "Dazzling and tremendous how quick the sun-rise would kill me," Whitman muses in "Song of Myself," "If I could not now and always send sun-rise out of me" (560–61).

Of infinite breadth, the world to which individuality is creatively attached permits each of us to become as "worldly" as the surrounding world, our breadth the parallel of the breadth of the world. Whitman's limitlessness and the limitlessness of each one of us follow as the conclusion from a limitless world, however, only when we remember that the "objects that call from diffusion [our] meanings and give them shape" are, to Whitman's mind, each unfathomable, worlds in themselves. Unknown and fathomless worlds, waves and persons and cities and infants and girls and old men and forests and rivers and zones, to recall but a few of the worlds Whitman invokes in "Salut au Monde!" become the indeterminate, metaphorical surfaces through which he creates himself as a world.

Where worlds become metaphors, the *infinite breadth* of their surfaces becomes an *infinite depth*. Not only does the world and all its worlds within provide Whitman's individuality with the surfaces through which he can create himself as a world, as metaphors the worlds' surfaces enable Whitman to create himself *differently* from the worlds that give shape to his meanings. As metaphors, surfaces permit Whitman to create himself differently by concealing his identity and individuality, the identity of his difference, behind metaphorical "likenesses," the likenesses of earth and shadow, as we saw, among others. Then the breadth of the world and the breadth of Whitman's attachment to the surfaces of the world become the *depth* of his own world, and the world that Whitman becomes unfolds infinitely beneath the world whose likeness he appears as on the surface. Speaking figuratively in "Song of Myself," for example, Whitman says,

> Of every hue and caste am I, of every rank and religion,
> A farmer, mechanic, artist, gentleman, sailor, quaker,
> Prisoner, fancy-man, rowdy, lawyer, physician, priest,
> I resist any thing better than my own diversity. (346–49)

Whitman calls upon the world's surfaces to serve as his likenesses, to give metaphorical shape to the diversity of his meanings so that he may be and become always more than he appears to be to others and to himself. Whitman invokes the multiplicity of surfaces to insinuate a space, a nonidentical, metaphorical space, within which he locates a *difference* between his representations of any and all of these diverse worlds and his *own* identity, the identity he assumes individually and apart from them. Surely Whitman is saying here, to be unable to resist my own diversity is to be unable to resist the ways in which the world provides his individuality with the breadth of opportunities to become a diverse being. Just as surely he is saying, to be unable to resist my own diversity is to be unable to resist the ways in which the world provides the opportunities to become a *different* being, a being who seeks depth as well as breadth to develop his *own* diversity, or as Whitman says in *Democratic Vistas*, his "own central idea and purpose." To become a diverse world, Whitman argues in "Song of Myself," is to become a world of difference.

> All I mark as my own you shall offset it with your own,
> Else it were time lost listening to me. (392–93)

As metaphors to present ourselves as diverse worlds and worlds of difference, the surfaces of worlds to which individuality becomes attached furnish possibilities for meaning abstractly. Surfaces are forms that through our individuality we resemble or choose to resemble, resemble closely initially, perhaps, then vaguely as we become not just increasingly individualized within our chosen forms but different from these forms as the nature of form allows. In our depths where the diversity of our differences develops, we resemble our surfaces less and less. Whitman often stresses how open and indefinite remain the possibilities for individuality to create new meaning within existing forms of meaning, as he does in "Assurances," speaking in a manner characteristic of Nietzsche.[29]

> I do not doubt interiors have their interiors, and exteriors have
>   their exteriors, and that the eyesight has another eyesight,
>   and the hearing another hearing, and the voice another
>   voice . . . (7)

It merely falls to each of us to use our other eyes, other ears, and other voices to see, hear, and speak the new interiors and exteriors endlessly latent in the visible interiors and exteriors circulating about us. Whitman makes this point precisely where he presents himself through the metaphorical world of "A Noiseless Patient Spider," in his poem by that name.[30] Like the spider, Whitman is "Surrounded" but "detached, in measureless oceans of space," poised to "explore the vacant vast surrounding," "Ceaselessly musing, venturing, throwing, seeking the spheres to connect them" (7, 3, 8). Whitman's presentational metaphor wonderfully shapes his idea of a universe of inexhaustible meaning distributed among the surfaces of countless worlds, wherein lay our individuality's own infinite possibilities for meaning, and to which we seek to attach ourselves as noiseless patient spiders attach their webs.

Discontinuity

Whitman returns often to this theme, so that he may put an even finer point to it. The indeterminacy of metaphorical meaning through which we author our own identity guarantees the creativity of this achievement, but more importantly it defines its individuality. Where Whitman sees himself and all others as diverse worlds and worlds of difference, in other words, his images are of potentially more interesting, certainly more mysterious and wonder-filled worlds, each a diversity of differences. On many occasions Whitman deliberately accentuates the importance of difference, explicating diversity as the diversity of differences. Verse 15 of "Song of Myself" shares the rhetorical strategy of "Salut au Monde!" in all but its three concluding lines. Fully sixty-one lines draw from our common world an extraordinary panorama of forms of life, as illustrated here, diversely different worlds ("objects") whose surfaces provide Whitman with forms of being through which he might develop his own identity.

> The pure contralto sings in the organ loft . . . (264)
>
> The lunatic is carried at last to the asylum a confirm'd case . . . (273)
>
> The western turkey-shooting draws old and young, some lean on their rifles, some sit on logs . . . (283)
>
> The young sister holds out the skein while the elder sister winds it off in a ball, and stops now and then for the knots . . . (293)
>
> The bride unrumples her white dress, the minute-hand of the clock moves slowly . . . (303)
>
> The floor-men are laying the floor, the tinners are tinning the roof, the masons are calling for mortar . . . (313)

Clearly, Whitman seems intent simply on displaying the mere diversity of life's different possibilities, life as variation, perhaps, until he finishes his scenario with this.

> And these tend inward to me, and I tend outward to them,
> And such as it is to be of these more or less I am,
> And of these one and all I weave the song of myself. (327–29)

"[O]f these more or less I am," as he puts it, Whitman individualizes himself through a multiplicity of forms of life by first attaching himself to each and then distinguishing and differentiating himself from every one. "[O]f these one and all I weave . . . myself" as a diverse self, Whitman is singing, but a diverse self "more or less" different from each of the many selves from which he is woven.

Depth is difference, Whitman leads us to understand, as it must be if depth is to be meaningfully differentiated from what appears on the surface. By contrast, a *merely* diverse self, possessing a diversity that is not also a "more or less," or a diversity of *differences*, as is Whitman's self, is something of a "shallow depth," to borrow Hegel's phrase, one whose depth is spread out upon the diverse surfaces it has adopted. Depth as difference further clarifies the purpose of Whitman's distinction between forcing surfaces and forcing depths. Though it provides individuality with the space for the creation of a diverse self, depth especially provides for the creation of an identity that avoids the normalizing pressures of surfaces. Whitman is not reluctant to press this argument one step further. Depth as difference sets standards for individuality. Our identities are more perfectly individualized when created as differences outside the conventional order of meaning. Whitman proves this by invariably using metaphor to create depth as difference where he maps out the deep space within which the presentational opportunities for difference can be invented metaphorically. "Collecting I traverse the garden the world," Whitman reports in "These I Singing in Spring," "but soon I pass the gates" (4).[31] Passed the gates, Whitman continues, we enter the "pond-side" (5), where, as Whitman explained in "In Paths Untrodden," grows the unseen life that has "Escaped from the life that exhibits itself" (3). In part, then, individuality is realized as a struggle beneath the surface for discontinuity with images of the self prevailing in society at large. Yet, individuality is also a struggle for discontinuity with one's *own* identity, an identity Whitman believes must be created over and over, indifferent to individuality's creative struggles in the past and despite the suffering brought on by creating oneself differently time and again. Reflecting on his own struggles for a discontinuous life, in "O Living Always, Always Dying," Whitman confides uncertainly,[32]

> O living always, always dying!
> O the burials of me past and present,
> O me while I stride ahead, material, visible, imperious as ever;
> O me, what I was for years, now dead, (I lament not, I am
>   content;)
> O to disengage myself from those corpses of me, which I turn
>   and look at where I cast them,
> To pass on, (O living! always living!) and leave the corpses
>   behind. (1–6)

Is it likely that more than a few would have known many of Whitman's deceased, or that anyone would have known them all? Surely the departed generations composing his self-identity that Whitman recalls were largely private matters, "forced depths," as he teaches. I believe Whitman is saying there can be no depth without difference, just as he has said there can be no individuality without depth. If for Whitman the identity individuality creates is a diversity it cannot resist, a diversity that must be what lies in the heart of identity as its mysterious quality of being, it is more importantly a diversity of differences, a diversity of identities as different as life and death.

By saying "as different as life and death," I deliberately play on Whitman's intimations of his own discontinuity as "living always" and "always dying" to dramatize what is entailed by his understanding of identity and individuality. Unless presenting a world is thought of as creating not only a diverse self but a self composed of a diversity of *differences*, we can appreciate neither Whitman's idea of "world" nor his idea of "individuality." To be a world requires forcing depth, a difference discontinuous with what appears on the surface and without which there is no depth, that marks fathoms and is also fathomless, and ultimately distinguishes individuals as differences from one another. Difference is the essential characteristic of individuality. With an aim toward the development of difference individuality develops the proportions of a world.

From the aesthetic point of view of Whitman, the artist (the creator), it is by virtue of its creation of difference that we truly can speak of an aesthetic *individuality*, of individuals creating themselves as different worlds through the creativity entailed by their representations of the worlds of difference who are others. Individuality creates its own depths through an attachment to the surfaces of worlds it represents, where it finds the interpretive possibilities within metaphorical space to form its identity discontinuously as a diversity of differences. Attached to the surfaces of worlds, individuality's representation of the world's appearances forgoes interest in identifying or representing worlds as they are different in themselves. Both of these dimensions of individuality's creation of difference define it aesthetically. Individuality creates itself differently through the images it creates of the appearances of different worlds encircling it, whose identities individuality's representations allow to remain hidden in their depths. Individuality is able to present itself differently through representation that is *indifferent* to its *reconciliation* with the identity of difference.

According to this formulation of aesthetic individuality, aesthetic *representation* is the condition and perhaps the telos of aesthetic *presentation*, the telos of the emancipation of the individual from an identitarian relation to the world. Through a concept of individuality whose relationship to the world is formed as Whitman forms his poetry, an aesthetic receptivity to the world that Adorno confined to the artwork is incorporated into Nietzsche's idea of an aesthetic relation to the world from the point of view of the artist (the creator), which is qualitatively altered in the process. By offering a model of how individuality's originality and self-creativity can be implicated in a genesis whose possibilities for becoming different are unlimited, as does Nietzsche, and that does not permit the individual's own world to be created at the expense of other worlds, following Adorno, Whitman's poetic forms thus provide the key to what makes individuality aesthetic. Like Whitman's poetic forms, individuality is aesthetic when its creativity is regulated by an ethic of appearances orienting it receptively to the surfaces of the world through which it discovers forms that both enable a process of becoming different and defend the world's depths against representation that imposes form on the world. Expressing this in yet another way further highlights the tight philosophical relationship between Whitman, Adorno, and Nietzsche. We can say that the idea of individuality based on Whitman's poetic forms confirms the insights into an aesthetic receptivity to the world that is based on Adorno's theory of the aesthetics of the artwork and Nietzsche's concept of the aesthetic from the point of view of the artist (the creator). Aesthetic individuality is possible where individuality creates from the aesthetic point of view of the artist, that is, through aesthetic form, though through an aesthetic form that relates individuality to the world as art relates to the world. From the point of view of the artist individuality creates itself through an aesthetic form oriented receptively to appearances, attached to surfaces, indifferent to reconciliation, protective of depths, so that the forms of all the worlds' surfaces can become the forms for the depths and differences of one individual world.

Almost without exception, Whitman adopts just this aesthetic relation to the world within which he "forces" his own individuality to unfold. Remembering that Whitman becomes always "more or less" like those in whose worlds he discovers his own possibilities, more or less different and discontinuous from the forms of life through which he imagines he can form his own life, in "Song of Myself" we see him looking to surfaces to create his own depths. Reflecting on the fate of an escaped slave, for instance, Whitman thinks, "I am the hounded slave" (838). After seeing himself mirrored in the image of the slave, he then anticipates how he would feel as the victim by saying, "I wince at the bite of dogs" (838), a forethought that precipitates a frightful reverie.

> Hell and despair are upon me, crack and again crack the marksmen,
> I clutch the rails of the fence, my gore dribs, thinn'd with the
>   ooze of my skin,
> I fall on the weeds and stones,
> The riders spur their unwilling horses, haul close,
> Taunt my dizzy ears and beat me violently over the head with
>   whip-stocks. (839–42)

As though to allay doubt that he is not simply describing what he once witnessed but developing the scenario as though it were his own, Whitman concludes, "I do not ask the wounded person how he feels, I myself become the wounded person" (845). Not "asking," or, rhetorically speaking, "not asking *himself*" how the injured slave feels, is no failure to empathize on Whitman's part. On the contrary, Whitman refuses to ask because, recognizing the slave as a fathomless difference, he expresses regard for the "appearance" of the slave by dismissing the presumption that he could know another, fathom the depths of another so maligned. Instead of attempting to represent what lies deeply in the existence of the slave, Whitman relates to the slave receptively, as a surface that offers a metaphorical likeness of his own being through which he can create himself as a diverse but also a different world, "more or less" resembling, in its depths, the world of another. Perhaps this is the form empathy takes within the framework of an ethic of appearances.

Recalling "an old time sea fight" in "Song of Myself," Whitman adopts the same presentational strategy to invent his own courage as that of a crew member inspired by the heroic act of a captain of a frigate caught fire in battle.

> Now I laugh content, for I hear the voice of my little captain,
> *We have not struck*, he composedly cries, *we have just begun our
>   part of the fighting.* (915–16)

Similarly, Whitman reports in "Song of Myself," I "See myself in prison shaped like another man" (948), thus working once again with his idea that objects call forth his meaning and give them shape. In both of these cases we find that Whitman orients himself receptively to the appearances of worlds before him so that he might see his own reflection, imagine his own depths, in their surfaces. Surfaces are the forms in the metaphorical depths of which Whitman creates and conceals a discontinuous life, a life more or less the life shaped "like" his, whose surfaces conceal their own depths, in turn. After adopting the surfaces of many worlds for forms of what he can become—bridegrooms and brides, mothers and martyrs, slaves and prisoners, firemen and artillerymen, captains and crewmen and workmen, among others—Whitman provides a final affirmation of their unknown depths, and of his own unseen depths to be, as well. "And might tell what it is in me and what it is in you," Whitman concludes, "but cannot" (992).

A Constitutive Interest in Difference

Although individuality is indifferent to the identity of difference in-itself, inasmuch as individuality develops its own identity through an aesthetically creative and receptive relation to the world, it expresses a constitutive interest in difference, an interest in the bearing of difference on how its identity can become different, as is apparent in the passages above from "Song of Myself" and as we saw earlier in "Salut au Monde!" and other poetry. Where Whitman's verse relates his individuality to the world aesthetically, a constitutive interest in difference is displayed through the descriptive representation of the diversity of the world's surfaces and is intimated as the metaphorical depth of the surfaces described. A descriptive orientation to surfaces represents surfaces thematically, in other words, and by so doing implicitly refers to difference as depth, the unknown, the presence of an absence, the nonidentical. Speaking aesthetically of a constitutive interest in difference penetrates to the very essence of Whitman's ideas of identity and individuality. If the worlds about him were not different, or if he could not invent ways to represent and relate to all the difference in the world, Whitman could not himself become different, nor enrich the world by adding, personally, to its difference so that others may become different as well. For there to be identity and individuality, we learn from Whitman, there must be difference, and the greater the diversity of difference the greater the possibilities for individuality to develop its own identity as a breadth and depth of differences. We can become wonderful if the world is wonder-filled, mysterious and colorful if there are mysterious and colorful worlds, splendid if the world is splendid. Difference must be sustained. We must see, hear, and speak to—relate to—worlds so that they remain divided as surfaces and depths. Identities (representations) and differences are necessarily divided, infinitely, as interiors having interiors, exteriors having exteriors. Individuality should discern no uniformity among a world's surfaces and between a world's surfaces and depths, but rather should suppose their diversity and discontinuity. Any such uniformity would be an illusion individuality imposes on difference from without, the illusion of reconciliation that does violence to difference and to the individuality whose creativity relies on the diversity and discontinuity of differences so that it, too, can become different.

At the same time, it is important to recall again, though aesthetically identity and individuality require for their constitution that there be worlds of difference about us, this does not also mean for Whitman that our identities require difference in order to be. Where identity requires difference in order to be, as Connolly argues in *Identity\Difference*, or where "identity is organized through the differences it demarcates," as he puts it elsewhere, to construct our identities we must find in difference a contradiction, something we are not from which we can distinguish ourselves.[33] If difference serves as an antithesis through which identity is constituted dualistically, even where it is not subsequently transcendentalized and converted into otherness, difference is converted into what is "opposite," a sort of nontranscendentalized other. What is opposite, in other words, is not representative of difference but rather of what the construction of identity requires difference to be. Requiring difference in order to be, we should say, not only requires difference to exist, but requires it to be some "thing" in particular. If identity and difference are related as antinomies, the difference required for an identity in order to be is a difference whose meaning is defined in advance by the logic of the relationship. Requiring difference to be contradictory, antithetical, identity's negation, or just opposite, polar, identity's contrast, in whole or in part obscures, swallows up, or suppresses what actually is different about difference. Like the illusion of reconciliation, wherever identity requires difference to be demarcated, it replicates the logic of identitarian thought by imposing form on difference from the outside.

Relating to the world aesthetically, on the other hand, individuality does not require that difference be anything in particular so that identity can be distinguished by being demarcated from difference. Aesthetic individuality relates to the surface of a difference only, to the appearance of difference. Its interest is in *mere* difference, difference that is nothing more nor nothing less than difference, difference that never varies from itself and remains absolutely different. For aesthetic individuality, what would distinguish differences from one another other than their mere difference, what difference possibly could mean, remains concealed beneath the surface of difference, a depth out of sight and out of mind to which individuality is indifferent and that it leaves alone. On the basis of reconceptualizing the relation between identity and difference as a relation between surface and depth, aesthetic individuality encourages a special constitutive sense of the relation between identity and difference. Aesthetic individuality attaches itself to the surface of difference, finding there the metaphorical space to create an identity whose possibilities are not related to mere difference in any definite way. Rather than demarcating its identity from a particular difference, which constructs identity by reconstructing difference as a nontranscendentalized other, aesthetic individuality creates identity *through mere* difference, allowing its identity to become any and every difference. Attached to surfaces, aesthetic individuality is indifferent to the depths of differences of other worlds, indifferent to difference as a particular, definite difference, and creates its identity in relation to itself.

In *Democratic Vistas*, Whitman articulates this sense of identity created in relation to itself by referring to the principle of individuality as "the pride and centripetal isolation of a human being in himself—identity—personalism."[34] Whitman appears to be using the term *centripetal* in a deliberate way, indicating we are to conceive of individuality as developing identity *inwardly*, as though depth were developed through individuality's creation of identity as a diversity of discontinuous differences that circle in revolutions ever more closely to what forms its center. Developing an identity's differences centripetally, ever more inwardly, individuality moves increasingly in relation to its own central idea and purpose undetermined in relation to purposes, to *differences*, outside of it.

Does this special sense of identity and individuality not also entail the idea of world that Whitman's poetry conveys? Is Whitman's sense not that of an individuality attached to men and women and the earth and everything upon it as they are, so that through this world as it appears before it, leaving the world alone and unchanged, individuality creates the identity of its own world, a different world, as mysterious and unknown as the world that inspires it? And does this special sense of identity and individuality not also entail his conception of each of us as a world *sui generis*, a world that is self-originating in relation to our *own* being-in-itself? Consistently meeting his desideratum of world, Whitman's special sense of identity and individuality meet the desideratum of Adorno's "togetherness of differences," while installing Adorno's ideal in Nietzsche's ideal of individual creativity. Through the limitless possibilities for being offered by surfaces, aesthetic individuality creates identity as a difference that leaves the differences of other identities be.

The Aesthetic Value of Surfaces and Nietzsche's Marriage of Light and Dark

Does it now seem, perhaps, both to ensure individuality's creative potential and to see that it is not realized at any expense to difference, that Whitman so carefully forms the aesthetics of individuality within the metaphorical space provided by depths only to trivialize the aesthetic value of surfaces? Focusing the discussion on individuality's self-creativity, on presenting a "world," may unwittingly create the impression that surfaces are, in an as-yet-unforeseen way, only of instrumental value, forever means and never ends, the accidental victim of an aesthetic rationality not entirely free of identitarian thought. We should not forget, however, that in its orientation to the world as a surface and to the surfaces of all worlds the world contains, presenting a world presupposes representing a world receptively according to an ethic of appearances. Aesthetic individuality abides by a regulatory ideal that confines its attachment to the worlds' surfaces in response to their mystery and wonder.

This point cannot be made too strongly if the aesthetic value of surfaces is to be estimated along with the distinctiveness of aesthetic individuality, namely, its creativity and release from identitarian thinking. Aesthetic individuality *cannot* separate its own creativity from a receptive orientation that takes the world and everything upon it *as it appears on the surface*, which releases the world from interpretations, representations, and identifications that take it, contrarily, to be some "thing" and definite rather than any thing and indefinite. Surfaces create and preserve and protect an indefiniteness of metaphorical possibilities possessed by worlds of unfathomable depths lying beneath them. Without surfaces there are no depths. Without receptivity to the surfaces of worlds there are not the indefinite possibilities belonging to their depths. So although Whitman privileges depths as the place within which individuality without intrusion can create itself, individuality cannot lay claim to this sanctum without first turning receptively toward the worlds' surfaces. Distinguishing his approach from those of others who also by vocation are led to examine how worlds appear, in "Song of Myself" Whitman affirms the aesthetic value of the worlds' surfaces by drawing attention to his own peculiar relation to appearances. We recall Whitman's poetic commentary on science and scientists.

> Your facts are useful, and yet they are not my dwelling,
> I but enter by them an area of my dwelling.
>
> Less the reminders of properties told by words,
> And more the reminders they of life untold . . . (491–94)

Appearances are the indispensable surfaces without which there are no "entrances" to the unseen, the unknown, the untold, to the lives living within a world as possibilities for individuality's creativity.

To appreciate their aesthetic value, we may understand "surfaces" to be Whitman's generic metaphor for the creative opportunities provided when worlds are approached receptively, in his words, opportunities provided by "objects that call from diffusion [our] meanings and give them shape." Occasionally we find in Whitman's exploration of those surfaces to which he feels some special attachment an effort to explicate the enormous metaphorical weight "surfaces" bear. When poeticizing "occupations," for example, more than fifty in his "Song for Occupations," Whitman insists that every occupation, from presidents to scholars, flour grinders to sail makers, thieves, or prostitutes, to the "hourly routine of . . .

any man's life" (127), offers as many possibilities for self-creativity as any other. Affirming the creative potential of surfaces *per se*, Whitman knits together several ideas that clearly point to individuality's relation to the world of occupations (objects) as an aesthetic relation, to its self-creativity through occupations as aesthetic creativity, and to the identities it creates through occupations as aesthetic creations. Individuality's aesthetic character is secured through Whitman's treatment of occupations as surfaces ("shows"), as creative opportunities offered us that can be realized through an aesthetic attachment to every occupation (surface) of which we might conceive. These ideas are wonderfully captured by the image of occupations as "realities" and "poems for you and me."

> A song for occupations! (1)
>
> These shows all near you by day and night—workman! whoever you are, your daily life! (128)
>
> In them realities for you and me, in them poems for you and me . . . (130)
>
> In them the development good—in them all themes, hints, possibilities. (132)

An equally powerful affirmation of the creative value of surfaces, Whitman's "In Cabin'd Ships at Sea" invokes the image of the surface of the sea, the "boundless blue on every side expanding," to convey an expanse of creative possibilities for *"voyagers' thoughts"* (2, 9).[35] With *"tones of unseen mystery,"* the sea intimates "vague and vast suggestions of the briny world" beneath (13), of the depths always entailed by Whitman's surfaces, the faithful "reminders they of life untold," to recall the lesson of "Song of Myself" (494). Within these depths *"liquid-flowing* syllables" enable thought to create the "ebb and flow of *endless* motion" felt "*beneath* our feet" (13, 12, 11). Again, surface integrates several images that spring from the idea of individuality's aesthetic relation to the world. Surface becomes a metaphor for open-ended possibility, for a world of creative possibilities for being that, in constant motion, is constantly becoming. At the same time, the surface becomes a passageway that thought enters to ponder what reality such possibilities eventually may lay claim to. Or the surface becomes a passageway through which thought enters the depths to create there "new realities and new poems," to paraphrase "Song for Occupations" (130), just as Whitman here has created the *"ocean's poem,"* as he lovingly puts it ("In Cabin'd Ships at Sea," 16).

In the context of surfaces' enormous metaphorical value for aesthetic individuality, we can understand the deep care Whitman expresses for the being of the world. Where Whitman sings, in "Song of Myself,"

> To cotton-field drudge or cleaner of privies I lean,
> On his right cheek I put the family kiss,
> And in my soul I swear I never will deny him. (1003–5)

with democratic intent he would attach himself equally to every surface of every difference, foregrounding the aesthetic necessity for individuality's receptivity to difference. Taking *everything*, cotton-field drudge and privy cleaner included, *upon* the earth *as it is*, taking every thing on the surface of the world as it appears to be itself a surface, Whitman finds no surface to be aesthetically less meaningful than any other. Every surface provides us with objects for the metaphorical creation of our own difference, a world offering each of us another world of possibilities. Perhaps Whitman believes that to "deny" any world would be to deny the one world through which one of us could create our own and different world as surfaces and depths. If so, perhaps he believes that to exclude any world is to exclude any possible world and is an act of aggression against the idea that each of us is a world, ruining being's chances for becoming and risking the ruin of being.

Taking the metaphorical value Whitman attributes to surfaces together with his intense care for being, what earlier appeared more simply as aesthetic individuality's constitutive interest in difference now more precisely becomes its interest in the richness of the diversity of the surfaces of differences. Surfaces are individuality's aesthetic opportunities for "realities" and "poems." Pursuing identity aesthetically, is individuality not then obliged, according to the ethics of an aesthetic attachment to surfaces and for the sake of identity's aesthetic possibilities, not only to recognize and care for difference but to enrich the surfaces through which its own differences can appear metaphorically? Should the identity that aesthetic individuality creates as a difference at a depth not find its way to the surface, becoming as a new surface part of the surface of the world? Would Whitman have surfaces mask difference and conceal depths only, or are they ultimately to become the public forum for our self-creations? Surely Whitman includes among the meanings of "I force surfaces and depths also" that the depths we force are to be forced to the surface as well, forced out of the darkness and into the bask of the sun that lights surfaces only. Indeed, in "Song of the Open Road" Whitman warns of the "secret silent loathing and despair" we each suffer when our other, "duplicate" self goes "skulking and hiding ... everywhere" (196, 198, 201).

> Keeping fair with the customs, speaking not a syllable of itself,
> Speaking of any thing else but never of itself. (204–5)

Arguing in a way reminiscent of Nietzsche in *Beyond Good and Evil* and *Thus Spake Zarathustra*, Whitman admonishes us not to "allow the hold of those who spread their reach'd hands toward you" regardless of the "ironical smiles and mockings" with which our independence might be received" (148, 146). Equally remonstrative in "One Hour to Madness and Joy," Whitman urges us "To be absolved from previous ties and conventions," "To escape utterly from others' anchors and holds!" (12, 17).[36] "Whoever you are," Whitman exclaims in "Song of the Open Road," "come forth! or man or woman come forth!" (189).

> You must not stay sleeping and dallying there in the house,
>   though you built it, or though it has been built for you.
>
> My call is the call of battle, I nourish active rebellion ... (190, 211)

What difference there is in each of us that constitutes our depths we must force to the surface, Whitman is arguing, whether that difference is created in the depths as the "house" that each of us builds or inherited as "houses" built for us, as our ethnic, racial, gender, or other identity determines our fate. Yet Whitman seems to impose the burden of "active rebellion" so that we might abandon "the whole past theory of [our lives] and all conformity to the lives around [us]," to paraphrase a line from "Whoever You Are Holding Me Now in Hand" (10).[37] Forcing our depths to the surface, in Whitman's estimation, may square more with the imperative of living our lives on our own terms than with contributing to the diversity of surfaces for the sake of an individuality aesthetically interested in the creation of difference. Of course, the thought that we must be reconciled to ourselves often enough comes to Whitman's mind, though it seems not to be his only or primary reason for rebellion, at least not a reason for rebellion that is its own end. Rather, for an even more fundamental reason not only must depths rise to the surface, but surfaces and depths must exchange positions.

Although aesthetic individuality's creation of difference finds in the depths a space for becoming often unavailable to it on the surface, Whitman presses the view that if creativity is to have a continuous life what is created as the unseen must become the seen, what differences each of us create at a depth must become our surface. In Whitman's charming "Unseen Buds," for instance, he draws upon the metaphorical space of the unflowered bud to distill what he says throughout his verse about creativity.[38]

> Unseen buds, infinite, hidden well,
> Under the snow and ice, under the darkness, in every square or
>   cubic inch,
> Germinal, exquisite, in delicate lace, microscopic, unborn,
> Like babes in wombs, latent, folded, compact, sleeping;
> Billions and billions, and trillions and trillions of them waiting,
> (On earth and in the sea—the universe—the stars there in the
>   heavens,)
> Urging slowly, surely forward, forming endless,
> And waiting ever more, forever more behind. (1–8)

Creativity's most important elements here appear together—darkness and the unseen intimating depths and the unknown; darkness, the unseen, depth or the unknown as infinite in expanse and infinitely creative in possibilities. Is Whitman not saying that the unseen, "Urging slowly, surely forward," becomes the seen, the unknown becomes known, darkness becomes light and depth becomes the surface? It must be no coincidence that Whitman positions his poem "Grand Is the Seen"[39] immediately prior to "Unseen Buds." "Grand is the seen, the light, to me," Whitman sings, "But grander far the unseen soul of me"—"*Lighting the light*" (1, 4, 5; my italics). So the worlds seen before us are the illuminations of what once were our unseen depths, the worlds created as depths of difference come to the surface, surfaces now seen as lights that as differences in their depths formed the soul lighting the light.

And, finally, what becomes of surfaces, of the depths we present as our surfaces? Surfaces are Whitman's "joys," the joys of "thousands of globes," he sings in "Song of Joys" (9), the joys presented by engineers and horsemen and strong-brawn'd fighters and mothers and miners and soldiers and whalemen and orators and old manhood and ripen'd womanhood and music and dear companions and perfect comrades and solitary walks and solemn musings and time and space and death.[40] From these thousands of globes, he explains, recalling an earlier idea in another form, he will be "receiving identity through materials and loving them, observing characters and absorbing them" (98). Depths that come to the surface, becoming now "objects that draw from diffusion [our] meanings and give them shape," are the globes through which we create our new depths, or in Whitman's own words in "Song of Joys," are the objects from which we "receive identity," our "life henceforth [becoming] a poem of new joys!" (157). Thus Whitman forces surfaces and depths, depths that come to the surface as unseen buds urging slowly forward out of the darkness to become the globes where individuality's possibilities lie for its creation of yet new depths, new globes, and new joys, as the "grand seen" becoming "the grander far" that will again light the light on the surface. Thus through the creativity of an aesthetic relation to the world is individuality the marriage of light and dark.

EIGHT

DEMOCRACY AS AN AESTHETIC FORM OF LIFE

That we receive our identities through thousands of globes, that the world and its objects draw from diffusion our meanings and give them shape, requires discussion about aesthetic individuality to be inclusive of the politics of surfaces as well as the aesthetics of surfaces. Does Whitman not mean by his entreaty to take men and women and the earth and everything upon it as they are that individuality should have *access* to the *entirety* of the earth and to the *entirety* of its surfaces, so that the world we share with all of its globes can provide creatively for the world that each of us can become? Had not Whitman, himself, through his poetry appeared to have, real or imagined, precisely that access? The surfaces and depths that Whitman forces in verse are forced from all the surfaces of the earth present from its beginning, from the time before we as a species were born, and from all surfaces that we newly create from depths. Whitman's surfaces and depths are forced from the whole of the earth's facts and artifacts.

Yet, Whitman's representation of the earth in its entirety and of the entirety of everything upon its surface is dependent upon the structure of his poetic forms. Whitman forces surfaces and depths by first acquiring access to the entirety of the world through descriptive and metaphorical forms that are exquisitely *democratic* forms of poetic representation. As the aesthetic point of view of the artist (the creator), aesthetic form represents differences (individuals, genders, races, religions, ethnicities, cultures, occupations, geographies, and so forth) that Whitman appears to visualize as originally either separated or scattered throughout the world by drawing diverse differences near together. Aesthetic forms of representation democratically enable differences to appear together.[1] Whitman even invents ways for descriptive and metaphorical forms to mark the presence of what cannot be represented, so that what aesthetic form leaves out of representation it does not also exclude. Aesthetic form thus defines the nonidentical, the unknown, as aesthetically significant for creativity. If Whitman then means to tie the measure of the worlds that aesthetic individuality can enable each of us to become to the measure of the globes about us, how can individuality gain access to the earth in its entirety in the manner of Whitman's verse? Is the surface of the earth and every surface upon it within reach of aesthetic individuality's creativity and receptivity, or are the surfaces of the world we share beyond the grasp of the world that is each one of us? Perhaps democracy may prove as indispensable to an aesthetics of individuality as democratic forms of representation have to the aesthetics of Whitman's verse.

TECHNOLOGY, MODERNITY, AND DIFFERENCE

As were many nineteenth-century thinkers, Whitman was alert to the great historical divides introduced by the development of modern technology. Technology was singularly responsible, in Whitman's estimation, for nothing less than a massive break with all previous world history. In "Passage to India," Whitman enthusiastically applauds technology for its creation of a "New World."[2] Though the world once was composed of lands that, owing to geographical separations, to various extents were unacquainted with cultures foreign to their own, through technology the world was now to be "spann'd" and "connected" and finally "welded together" (32, 35). Technology constructed a "network" (32) that drew the diversity of all the world's cultures within range of one another. Technology issued in the practical realization of "a ceaseless thought,"

> Along all history, down the slopes,
> As a rivulet running, sinking now, and now again to the surface
>   rising ...
> Thou rondure of the world at last accomplish'd. (72–73, 80)

Whitman does not celebrate this technological achievement because it offers promise for some sort of new world order in which all member cultures exchange their particularistic norms for a common set of thick substantive principles. Rather, as is clear from his descriptive representations of the heterogeneous and radically heterodox cultures that technology has brought within reach of one another, Whitman is excited by the ever-expanding diversity of cultural differences that the New World is proved increasingly to possess. "Our modern wonders," as Whitman describes technology in "Passage to India" (4), acquaint us with the entirety of the earth and everything upon it. And if "the word En-Masse," the word that means taking everything together as a whole, is "a word of the modern," as he argues in "Song of Myself" (478), then technology ushers in what Whitman believes to be the defining characteristic of modernity.[3] As the consequence of a science able to tie together the diversity of worlds of difference within the boundaries of a single known world, there is now a single *modern* world, a modernity defined by the diversity of the earth's cultural identities collected together under the identity of the New World. Technology, modernity, the New World all refer to different dimensions of this same form of historical progress—drawing the entirety of the earth's diversity of cultural differences within range of one another. What to Whitman's mind appears to be of overriding importance, in other words, is what is aesthetically significant about technology, modernity, and the New World. As it has been within the creative reach of Whitman's poetry, all the differences in the world, each globe the globe contains, the earth and everything upon it are now drawn together in its entirety by technology to become accessible to the aesthetic creativity of all.

DEMOCRACY, MODERNITY, AND DIFFERENCE

At the same time, Whitman is hardly sanguine about the New World's capacity to advance the project of modernity through a commitment to technology alone. Technology appears to be a necessary condition for the creation of modernity, albeit insufficient to secure the identity of the diversity of differences of which the New World is composed. In "Thou Mother with Thy Equal Brood," Whitman turns to America, to which he refers as the "Brain of the New World," to "formulate the Modern—out of the peerless grandeur of the modern, Out of thyself" (34–36).[4] If Whitman valorizes America, it is because in his view it is distinguished by its commitment to democracy and its democracy is distinguished by its commitment to diversity. Indeed, both commitments appear to Whitman to be straightforward and unequivocal. Whitman explains in *Democratic Vistas* that he will "use the words America and democracy as convertible terms," by which he does not mean that his idea of democracy is simply modeled on America but that in his view America is the embodiment of the idea of democratic life.[5] And when challenging America to "formulate the Modern ... Out of thyself" in "Thou Mother with Thy Equal Brood," he advises how it should do so. "Sail, sail thy best, ship of Democracy," Whitman recommends, for America is a "Land tolerating all, accepting all" (47, 98). In *Democratic Vistas* Whitman credits America's "universalism" for its openness to "recruiting myriads of offspring."[6] In "Thou Mother with Thy Equal Brood" America's universalism appears in Whitman's references to its "moral wealth," out of which America vests authority in "no single bible, savior, merely," but approves an "all-supplying, all-enclosing worship," with "saviors countless" and "bibles incessant within thyself" (87–89).

So when Whitman explores the theme of technological progress in "Song of the Exposition," which along with "Passage to India" was first completed in 1871, he considers the relationship between technology, modernity, and the New World in the context of democracy in America.[7] "Passage to India's" celebration of technology's creation of a diverse New World is developed in "Song of the Exposition" to accord with Whitman's thinking about America, democracy, and diversity in such works as *Democratic Vistas*, published in 1871, and "Thou Mother with Thy Equal Brood," first completed shortly afterward. Whitman's "Song of the Exposition" playfully extends to the "Muse," who throughout the history of the world has inspired the greatest creations in the arts and sciences, an invitation to visit America to consider the "lessons of *our* New World" (5, 10; my italics). Welcoming the immortal Muse to America "In liberty's name," Whitman teaches that as a "Union holding all, fusing, absorbing, tolerating all," America has itself become "a World," an ensemble of diverse worlds that through its universalism has been "Rounded by thee," America, "in one" (62, 169, 171, 173). Though Whitman remains attentive to "the spirit of invention everywhere" (195) in America, "Song of the Exposition" clearly emphasizes his concern that America formulate the modern out of itself. Technology's rounding of diverse worlds into one New World is again thematized (especially lines 160–65[8]), though technology's New World is now subordinate, even harnessed to America's own rondure, whose democratic universalism provides "One common indivisible destiny for All" (174), in which science and invention will find creative freedom. ("Our farms, inventions, crops we owe in thee!" 237)

Whitman is careful to argue, however, that America's universalism, in his words an "idiocrasy" that sets its democracy apart from all others, does not also promote a common identity that discriminates against difference.[9] Not only does America's universalism foster inclusiveness of diversity and difference, but it fosters an equality that sustains difference rather than encouraging the identity of every difference to conform to a hegemonic norm. In "Thou Mother with Thy Equal Brood," for example, Whitman says that although the American states share "one identity only," they do so while remaining "varied" and "different" (2). America's great achievement, in Whitman's estimation, lies in cultivating a universalism that is sufficiently abstract to accommodate all differences while providing the outline of a common identity. "Accommodate" may state Whitman's case too weakly, though, for often he appears to favor the uniqueness of American universalism precisely because its radical inclusiveness of diversity guarantees differences the opportunity to oppose authority and aggressively press their own ideas and interests, as he indicates in "Still Though the One I Sing."[10]

> Still though the one I sing,
> (One, yet of contradictions made,) I dedicate to Nationality,
> I leave in him revolt, (O latent right of insurrection! O quenchless
>   indispensable fire!) (1–3)

We also learn in "Song of the Broad-Axe" that Whitman so admires America because its peoples "think lightly of the laws" and because, for Americans, "outside authority enters always after the precedence of inside authority" (119, 123).[11] Whitman conceives of universalism as supporting no legitimate power to which any form of difference need yield its own position. In the final analysis, it simply may be reasonable to suspect that if universalism means anything substantive at all for Whitman, it means no more than that diversity shares the identity of difference, an identity constituted by the tolerant and accepting togetherness of differences.

Without a doubt, then, the preeminence that democracy, or democracy in America, enjoys in Whitman's thought seems due largely, if not entirely, to the entitlement he believes its universalism provides for bringing together unconditionally and under a common emblem the broadest possible diversity of differences. If Whitman's allegiance to his image of America as radically universalistic is unequivocal, it is because he believes its democracy incapable of circumspection with regard to the extent of diversity and difference it embraces, a point that cannot be stressed too greatly. Whitman even goes so far, for example, as to *equate* democracy with universality and the idea of taking everything together as a whole, as he does in "One's-Self I Sing" by saying, "Yet [I] utter the word Democratic, the word En-Masse" (2).[12] And as though to complete the task that he recommended in "Thou Mother with Thy Equal Brood" of "formulating" the modern, the diverse world writ large, he proceeds to root the very idea of modernity in democratic universalism by concluding "One's-Self I Sing" with the line "The Modern Man I Sing" (8). Similarly, America possesses "the genius of the modern," Whitman elaborates in "Song of the Redwood-Tree," because it is "Clearing the ground for broad humanity" (103–4).[13] And he favors the democratic politics of the New World, we learn in *Democratic Vistas*, because it allows "full play for human nature to expand itself in numberless and even conflicting directions," and by so doing incorporates the "greatest lessons of Nature . . . the lessons of variety and freedom."[14] Finally, if Whitman's loyalty to democracy and America and his conceptions of universality and modernity are not yet satisfactorily rooted in his receptivity to diversity and difference, it may be useful to add this. Often Whitman speaks, too, as though his mission "to define America" and "prove this puzzle the New World," as he puts it in "To Foreign Lands" (2, 1),[15] is best accomplished by relentlessly foregrounding the democratic scope of America's diversity, as he does in "Our Old Feuillage." A poem remarkable for Whitman's refusal to spare just one of its eighty-two lines for any task other than descriptively capturing America's natural and social diversity, "Our Old Feuillage" concludes by justifying "foliage," a representation of diverse and different leaves, flowers, and plants, as the appropriate metaphor to express what lies at the heart of democracy.[16]

> These affording, in all their particulars, the old feuillage to me
>   and to America, how can I do less than pass the clew of
>   the union of them, to afford the like to you? (80)

Few poems devoted to democracy or America in Whitman's entire collection publicize the centrality of diversity and difference as expressively as "Our Old Feuillage."

By way of summary, we return full circle to the possibility posed hypothetically at the outset of this discussion, namely, that democracy proves to be as indispensable to an aesthetics of individuality as democratic forms of representation do to the aesthetics of Whitman's verse. At the heart of Whitman's deep affections for America lie passions of a very particular sort, which are expressed in two intimately related or overlapping images of democracy. Democracy in America displays an intense fidelity to a universalism that represents diversity and difference without qualification. Doing so, democracy also secures the identity and promise of a modernity whose world-historical significance resides in its distinction as a world of diverse differences brought together to form a New World. We should say that revolving around differences and their diversity and togetherness, Whitman's images of democracy reproduce what Adorno means by a "togetherness of differences."[17]

Drawing him near to Adorno in this way already suggests that Whitman conceives of democracy as an aesthetic form of life and, as well, that Adorno's aesthetics opens to the consideration that there is an important sense in which an aesthetic form of life spreads throughout democracies committed to difference. By bringing together a diversity of differences, democracy imitates poetry's representational capacity for creativity and becomes poetic, aesthetic, in precisely the way that Whitman's poetry, its aesthetic forms, are democratic. Representing the entirety of the earth's surfaces, as does Whitman's poetry, democracy is aesthetically receptive to "men and women and the earth and all upon it." Such universalistic, democratic receptivity to differences through which individuals may create themselves differently permits the aesthetic individuality belonging to each the same access to an infinite range of possibilities for self-creativity that belongs to poetry. I believe Whitman had this in mind when he argued in his preface to the 1855 edition of *Leaves of Grass* that the "Americans of all nations at any time upon the earth have probably the fullest poetical nature."[18] Democracy, Whitman is saying by drawing our attention to the "poetic form" of American character, affords its progeny access to the same diversity of different worlds represented democratically by poetic forms as he constructs them, through which poetry is able to create diversely different images. America's poetical nature, rooted in its democratic fealty to diversity and difference, perhaps constituted that "artistic identity" Whitman believed in *Democratic Vistas* to be the only "reliable identity" and one that could help furnish a "common skeleton, knitting all close."[19] "Poetical nature," "artistic identity," the "United States themselves [as] essentially the greatest poem," as he says also, Whitman's claim is that democracy knits a togetherness of differences that ensures the aesthetic foundation for aesthetic individuality's creative life.[20]

DEMOCRACY, DIFFERENCE, AND POETRY

Against this background, there appear to be occasions when Whitman further fleshes out the idea of democracy as an aesthetic form of life by focusing on the relationship between democracy, diversity, and poetry. Encouraging us to think about this relationship, another of Whitman's poetic "Inscriptions" explaining his purposes in *Leaves of Grass*, "On Journeys through the States," speaks reflexively to its readers about the verse collected.[21] Whether it is his poetry that travels or we who travel poetically or we who travel by reading his poetry, Whitman's idea, expressed with some deliberate ambiguity to intermingle these three interpretive possibilities, is that poetry gives each of us access to the world when it journeys through a democratic society. In other words, we form an *aesthetic* relation to the world from the point of view of the artist (the creator) when, as *democracy* permits, we are able, as poets, poetry, and readers of poetry are able, to have access to the world's diversity of differences. Whitman's song deserves to be cited in full for the adroitness with which it expresses this idea.

> On journeys through the States we start,
> (Ay through the world, urged by these songs,
> Sailing henceforth to every land, to every sea,)
> We willing learners of all, teachers of all, and lovers of all.
>
> We have watch'd the seasons dispensing themselves and passing on,
> And have said, Why should not a man or woman do as much as the seasons, and effuse as much?
>
> We dwell a while in every city and town,
> We pass through Kanada, the North-east, the vast valley of the Mississippi, and the Southern States,
> We confer on equal terms with each of the States,
> We make trial of ourselves and invite men and women to hear,
> We say to ourselves, Remember, fear not, be candid, promulge the body and the soul,
> Dwell a while and pass on, be copious, temperate, chaste, magnetic,
> And what you effuse may then return as the seasons return,
> And may be just as much as the seasons. (1–14)

How interesting the special care Whitman takes to highlight the aesthetic relationship between the access to the diversity of differences that becomes available to us in a democracy and the diverse beings that we, as individuals, can become. Journeying through different states, diverse cities, towns, and geographies, conferring with different men and women, and through these differences exposed receptively to a diversity representing the world, each man and woman comes to contain as much as is contained by the passing of the seasons. Each one of us contains and expresses all others.

Certainly Whitman attributes his own explosive creativity to the diversity and difference that he discovers in America, the unbounded field for the democratic play of the diversity of differences. Striking up for a "New World" (14), adopting "an American point of view" (85), pursuing an argument and adopting an approach resembling "On Journeys through the States," in "Starting from Paumanok" Whitman again describes the diversity of differences characteristic of what he calls "Democracy's Lands" (193), and declares,

> New Politics, new literatures and religions, new inventions and arts.
> These, my voice announcing—I will sleep no more but arise,
> You oceans that have been calm within me! how I feel you, fathomless, stirring, preparing unprecedented waves and storms.[22] (250–52)

Whitman thus matches the surfaces and depths his individuality creatively forms within him to the surfaces and depths without to which democracy provides him access. The diversity of the surfaces and depths of the world he will become is his individuality's creative response to the diversity of the democratic world of differences from which he receives his creative inspiration and creates his identity.

DEMOCRACY AND AESTHETIC EDUCATION

As Whitman thinks of the relationship between democracy, the diversity of differences, individuality, and creativity, he offers us no reason to believe that anyone endowed with the rights and protected by the laws of a democratic society should be too modest to assess their own creativity as some measure of his. Though Whitman is to be included among the greatest poetic voices, as a poet he is, and considers himself to be, first and foremost the product of a democratic society. Democracy, its representation of a diversity of differences, is the condition for a "poetical nature," as he calls it, for an aesthetic receptivity to the world through which one's self is created as a world. Democracy is the best friend of aesthetic individuality. To be assured the creative possibilities of an aesthetic individuality, it appears to be enough, Whitman seems to maintain, simply to live in a democratic society and have access to the diversity of differences it provides. To be sure, Whitman does believe democracy in America to have become a diverse, democratic society, holding it to have surmounted, with the resolution of the American Civil War, the "only foes it need ever fear (namely, those within itself, the interior ones)."[23] Here Whitman cuts to the root of the image of America pervading his work. Its democracy is aesthetically unique because it creates an identity—a "Union"—for a diversity of differences, in his view proving its uniqueness dramatically in 1865 by narrowly avoiding splitting apart the differences it draws near together.

Perhaps we should say that preoccupied with its democratic condition, Whitman naively overlooks obstacles to aesthetic individuality rampant in democratic societies, in America surely, where among other obstacles opportunities for exploiting possibilities for self-creativity are distributed unevenly. If Whitman appears inattentive to such obstacles, he is so only relatively. *Democratic Vistas* does warn sternly against believing that "the establishment of free political institutions . . . [will] yield to our experiment of democracy the fruitage of success."[24] And in a variety of ways and places in his work Whitman cites the dangers to individuality posed by capitalism (materialism and mass culture), on the one hand, and by what we today call the politics of normalization, on the other. Though Whitman believed democracy in America to have achieved an aesthetically significant diversity, he believed, too, that democracy's commitment to diversity and difference was tendentious, as then would be the creative possibilities for aesthetic individuality it provided.

In *Democratic Vistas*, for example, Whitman divides up the development of the New World into three stages, believing that by his time the first two had been completed and the third to be showing definite signs of emergence. Whitman describes the first stage as the "American programme," the "planning and putting on record the political foundation rights of immense masses of people—indeed all people,"[25] clearly anticipating his reference in "Thou Mother with Thy Equal Brood" to America as the "Brain of the New World" (34). The second stage "relates to material prosperity," generally to a wide range of technological advancements, which to his satisfaction, as we have seen in "Passage to India," not only had spread throughout but had constituted the New World, at least physically.[26] Whitman's final stage was characterized by the "democratizing" of America according to the "interior and vital principles" belonging to a democratic society. "Original authors and poets ... American personalities, plenty of them, male and female," would inaugurate the task of "dissolving the old."[27] A literary vanguard would found a "Religious Democracy," a civil religion organized around individuality's creativity—the "pride of man in himself," a "new and greater personalism"—which the "needs and possibilities of American imaginative literature" would develop "in reference with."[28] Inspired aesthetically, individuality could create potentially new surfaces within the depths of its "interior life," eventually replacing or "sloughing off surfaces" belonging to "a nation of practical operatives, law-abiding, orderly and well off."[29]

Democratization, we see, according to Whitman clearly consists of an aesthetic education for the immense mass of individuals who have yet to learn of the possibilities for creativity available in a democratic society. It does not refer to extending opportunities for the realization of these possibilities by first eliminating political inequalities. Could it be that Whitman did not believe there would be opposition to democratization as it evolved during democracy's later modernity as a political and juridical process through which the demands for recognition by diverse groups are met? After all, Whitman did recommend politics as a purposeful avocation, which suggests he believed democracy in America to be responsive to pluralizing pressures.[30] And he did observe that, politically, America "may be ... doing very well upon the whole." Even if Whitman did fear opposition to democratization, however, since his conception of aesthetic individuality privileges depth, the "interior life," life beneath the surface where individual creativity originates and flourishes, it would not necessarily occur to him or he would not feel compelled to politicize democratization around the issue of equalizing opportunities for self-creativity if they did not appear to be essentially connected to interiority. As the "mother of the true revolutions, which are of the [individual's] interior life," in Whitman's estimation democracy in America would adequately enable individuality, first by drawing together a diversity of differences and then through an aesthetic education that taught of democracy's creative possibilities.[31] Whereas the "American programme" had consummated democracy's allegiance to an aesthetically diverse dimension of existence, at this first stage of democratization individuality's aesthetic education had barely begun. Until individuality learns through literature and poetry of the aesthetic value of the worlds of difference surrounding it in the democratic world, its interior, aesthetically self-creative life would remain undeveloped. And "so long as the spirit is not changed," Whitman asserts in *Democratic Vistas*, "any change of appearance is of no avail."[32]

Given the enormous weight that Whitman has an aesthetic education bear, what lessons ought it to consist of? How are the "new Literature, perhaps a new Metaphysics, certainly a new Poetry," in his estimation to become the "only sure and worthy supports and expressions of the American Democracy?"[33] Literature, especially poetry, Whitman argues, needs to express "Nature." Because nature involves "questions of the aesthetic," "Nature, true Nature, and the true idea of Nature" must become "fully restored" so that it can "furnish the pervading atmosphere to poems, and the test of . . . aesthetic compositions."[34] If the aesthetic is represented by nature, indeed, if the aesthetic finds its meaning in nature so that nature becomes the test of what is and what is not aesthetic, what, then, according to Whitman, is Nature? Nature is the "All" and the "idea of the All," Whitman explains, speaking in *Democratic Vistas* about nature precisely as he speaks of democracy.[35] Nature, "containing all," containing being in all of its diversity and difference, ideally, paradigmatically democratic, becomes democracy's standard-bearer and the example poetry is to offer when teaching lessons about the nature of democracy.[36] Individuality will learn from poetry what poetry learns, and as Whitman himself has learned, from nature. Individuality learns that that which *contains all* enables its poetical, aesthetic nature, as Whitman describes the nature of Americans, to become the "caresser of life wherever moving," as he has become "the caresser of life," and to weave the song of itself from the worlds made available by nature and a democratic form of life. Whitman teaches us this lesson when he follows these lines from verse 13 of "Song of Myself,"

> In me the caresser of life wherever moving, backward as well as forward sluing,
> To niches aside and junior bending, not a person or object missing,
> Absorbing all to myself and for this song [,] (232–34)

with nearly a hundred lines describing nature's worlds (235–62) and the worlds composing a democratic world (263–326), and then says, concluding verse 15, "And of these one and all I weave the song of myself" (329).

As transparently as Whitman intends for poetry to tie nature's universality to democracy and its universality, he also deepens this connection by tying nature to aesthetic form, as we might expect since he thinks of aesthetic form as expressing his and modeling our own democratic relation to the world. Describing nature in *Democratic Vistas* as "the only complete, actual poem," Whitman is saying that to contain all, as nature contains all, is to relate poetically, aesthetically to what all is contained, as though nature, by leaving nothing out, relates aesthetically, to All, to being in its universality.[37] Surely, Whitman orients himself to the world aesthetically through descriptive and metaphorical forms of poetic representation designed to include all that the world contains. And by marking the presence of what eludes representation and remains unknowable (nonidentical), poetic representation even includes the nonidentity of that which falls outside the limits of representation. So poetry is like nature, *completely* poetic, *completely* aesthetic, when it is oriented to All, when, like democracy, it contains all differences, the identifiable and the nonidentifiable, differences whose identities are known and differences whose identities are unknown, all surfaces and depths. By meeting Whitman's criterion for the aesthetic—nature's "All"—poetic form provides an aesthetic education by exemplifying an interpretation of a democratic form of life! As Whitman's "On Journeys through the States" teaches (a poem he intends to be quite obviously didactic), to journey "through the States" is to journey "through the world, *urged by these songs*" (1, 2; my italics). In other words, to journey democratically, to *live* a democratic life, is to journey as poetry journeys, as *Leaves of Grass* journeys, by means of an aesthetic, democratic form of representation that relates to the world All-inclusively.

If nature teaches the poet what it means to be completely poetic, completely aesthetic, then through poetic form the poet teaches, as Whitman's songs teach, what it means to be completely democratic. To live democratically means to pass through the world as poetry passes through the world, oriented to all as poetry is oriented to All, becoming like nature, and like poetry has become like nature, "the only complete, actual poem." To live democratically means to draw differences together as nature and poetry draw differences together, aesthetically. Then in the way that nature's All becomes accessible to a poetry that forces surfaces and depths, do all the differences in the world become aesthetically accessible to individuality, as objects that draw from diffusion its meanings and give them shape. Nature teaches what it means to be aesthetic, poetic; poetry teaches what it means to be democratic; and democracy, containing within it all possible worlds through which individuality can create itself aesthetically, is the world to which an aesthetically educated individuality becomes creatively receptive.

DEMOCRATIC TIME, DEMOCRATIC SPACE

From the pedagogical alliance of nature and poetry, each of us is to learn that individuality's creative possibilities for becoming different through its receptivity to the diversity of differences surrounding it are stretched across a democratic frame that is, in every direction, limitless. Since democracy, like nature and poetry, contains all and comes to be known as containing all, it would appear to exhaust the creative possibilities for individuality's aesthetic relation to the world and to itself as a world. Could we imagine another world that would open individuality to creative possibilities beyond the limitless horizon of those offered by democracy's universality of diversity and difference? Even with this extraordinary image of an endless democratic horizon tracing the possibilities for being and becoming, however, Whitman would be unprepared to accept a formulation of democracy as an aesthetic form of life nonpareil that risked omitting what else he believes makes democracy truly exceptional. For democracy's togetherness of differences would be of diminished creative value to our individuality if there were not some sense in which individuality's aesthetic experience of democratic universalism could enable it, in *actuality*, to become universal as well. Whitman recognizes that individuality's incitement to orient itself to the world creatively and receptively is also the promise that democratic universalism holds out for aesthetic individuality to become different without limit or exception.

Although the worlds democracy draws near together provide access to limitless possibility, individuality's creativity is restricted to possible meanings construed from worlds of difference existing in its own time and its own space, worlds continuing from an individual's past, belonging to its present and to what of its future remains. Mortality, in other words, limits individuality's creativity in time and space. Encountering limits to individuality's universality in time and space, individuals would be disposed to think of themselves not as universal but as finite. They would conceive of themselves less as aesthetic achievements, less as beings able to become different without limit and without exception of any difference, than as beings whose contingency is circumscribed and whose opportunities for becoming different are enclosed and ultimately foreclosed by time and space. Finiteness would threaten the undoing of aesthetic individuality's self-creativity by encouraging us to become receptive not to difference without exception but only to those far fewer differences to which a mortal life must confine itself. In order to then justify a life that must be lived in certain ways because it cannot be lived in different ways, each individual might seek to privilege the identity of its own particular differences, perhaps inventing transcendental warrants to secure the certainty of its own way of life. Life's finiteness would spoil a receptivity to the world according to an ethic of appearances that orients individuality aesthetically to all differences as they appear, and appear equally, as possibilities for creating its identity differently.

Appearing to anticipate the danger to aesthetic individuality that mortality threatens, Whitman incorporates into his idea of a democratic form of life an aesthetic experience of diversity and difference that relativizes time and space. The aesthetic access to difference democracy provides allows individuality to distill the transcendental from its finite, transitory experience of diversity and difference, but not for the purposes of privileging or justifying or establishing the truth of the identity individuality creates. Rather, owing to some further and extraordinary consequence of an access to the diversity of differences belonging to the universalism of democratic life, an access excluding no difference, individuality overcomes its finiteness. Whitman already hinted at this consequence in *Democratic Vistas*, where he argued that Nature, the "All, and the idea of All," is accompanied by the "idea of eternity," thus suggesting a connection between nature's universality of differences and the thought of our lives as going on forever. As we learned, though, nature's All is only the lesson of universality poetry enables individuality to discover through democratic life. What, then, is the further connection between *democratic* universalism and individuality's immortality?

In "Song of the Answerer," Whitman says,

> What always indicates the poet is the crowd of the pleasant company of singers, and their words,
> The words of the singers are the hours or minutes of the light or dark, but the words of the maker of poems are the general light and dark ... [38] (56–57)

Songwriters sing of eras, epochs, of time as it "indicates itself in parts" (55), whereas Whitman is interested in *all* time. Time is infinite, and space, too, is infinite. "See ever so far," Whitman directs us in "Song of Myself,"

> there is limitless space outside of that,
> Count ever so much, there is limitless time around that. (1196–97)

What is of interest to Whitman is not time and space *per se*, however, but the relationship of time and space to being as it unfolds in time and space. Because time and space are infinite, the being that unfolds in time and space is infinite. As Whitman explains in "Song of Myself,"

> There is no stoppage and never can be stoppage,
> If I, you, and the worlds, and all beneath or upon their surfaces,
> were this moment reduced back to a pallid float, it would
> not avail in the long run,
> We should surely bring up again where we now stand,
> And surely go as much farther, and then farther and farther. (1190–93)

Being contains all because time and space contain all. For this reason Whitman wants all time, for to have all time is to have all being, all worlds, the world that is the time of his world, and the worlds of past and all future times. Hence in "Song of Joys" Whitman sings,

> O to make the most jubilant song!
> Full of music—full of manhood, womanhood, infancy!
> Full of common employments—full of grain and trees.
>
> O for the voices of animals—O for the swiftness and balance of fishes!
> O for the dropping of raindrops in a song!
> O for the sunshine and motion of waves in a song!

> O the joy of my spirit—it is uncaged—it darts like lightning!
> It is not enough to have *this* globe or a *certain* time,
> I will have *thousands* of globes and *all* time.[39] (1–9; my italics)

And to have all space, "to realize space," as he explains further on, is "To emerge and be of the sky, of the sun and moon and flying clouds, as one with them" (112, 114). Having all time and all space, Whitman has all being, all the worlds and globes that being contains, all "objects" that could call from diffusion his meanings and give them shape. Individuality's universe of creative possibilities expands toward the infinite.

Yet, how is Whitman to have all time and all space? As Whitman in *Democratic Vistas* has led us to expect, poetry takes on the project of acquiring time and space. Since the idea of eternity accompanies the idea of the All embodied by Nature, it is in keeping with the pedagogical alliance between poetry and nature that poetry should represent eternity as it represents all else belonging to nature. "Starting from Paumanok" expresses this more precisely. Alluding at one point to his ambition for *Leaves of Grass*, Whitman promises that "I will make the true poem of riches," by which he intends, among other things, to "thread through my poems that time and events are compact" (162, 170). Whitman offers a clue as to how poetry "compacts" time and space.

> But I will make poems, songs, thoughts, with reference to ensemble,
> And I will not sing with reference to a day, but with reference to
>   all days . . . (173–74)

Whitman's thought is that by composing verse about the future and what might be, or about the past and what has been, or about the present and what is, in his words by poeticizing "with reference to all days," poetry refers to "ensemble." Taking "ensemble" to mean all together at the same time (as an ensemble of instruments play together at the same time), Whitman is explaining that he writes with reference to everything happening at the same time. While at first this may sound odd, it is considerably less so when we realize Whitman is saying that poetry includes, at the particular time and in the particular space (place) that it is written or read, the time and space *belonging* to the times and places *about* which the poem is written, that is, the time and space during which an individual, a culture, a nation, and so forth, became what it was, is what it is, or becomes what it will be.[40] Poetry acquires, or contracts to its own time and to its own place, the time and space belonging to whatever it represents!

Consider "Crossing Brooklyn Ferry," for instance, where Whitman, as he crosses from shore to shore, thinks of others who reading his poem long after will experience through him his time and his place as he at the moment of his poetic reflection also imaginatively experiences theirs.[41] It is as though through poetry he and his readers share the same time and the same place, becoming together an ensemble.

> What is it then between us?
> What is the count of the scores or hundreds of years between us?
>
> Whatever it is, it avails not—distance avails not, and place avails
>   not . . . (54–56)
>
> Closer yet I approach you,
> What thought you have of me now . . . (86–87)
>
> Who knows, for all the distance, but I am as good as looking at
>   you now, for all you cannot see me? (91)

When we now recall from *Democratic Vistas* that poetry, after nature, is to include All, as Whitman's poetic forms of representation include all, we can see that by including All poetry likewise includes the time and space belonging to All. Taking the next step, we appreciate how extraordinary is Whitman's idea. By *representing* All, and thus through representation including the time and space belonging to All, poetry includes all time and all space. Can we not then understand what Whitman means when he insists, in "Song of Myself," that "I know I have the best of time and space, and was never measured and never will be measured" (1201). Through poetry that includes all time and all space Whitman believes himself to overcome his own time and his own space, the mortality of his time and place, and his own mortality! Again Whitman provokes us, perhaps never more than here. If being unfolds throughout infinite time and infinite space, then through poetry's aesthetic forms of representation, which represents All and in so doing includes being's universality of diversity and difference, we inherit the time and space belonging to universality, belonging to the being that universality contains. Poetry teaches that through a poetic, aesthetic relationship to the world, through an access to diversity that excludes no difference, we shall become timeless. Because Whitman intends poetic representation to model the way we can relate to the world in a democratic society, to say that through poetry we inherit the time and space belonging to the being of universality, that we become timeless, is already to address the relationship between democracy and time and space. It is to raise the possibility that in a democracy the absoluteness of time and space undergoes a transformation not unlike the transformation of time and space that occurs in poetry owing to its aesthetic forms of representation. It is to raise the possibility of a "democratic time" and a "democratic space."

Let us express the possibility of a democratic time and space (my terms) in the form of a question. Does democracy, like poetry, contract time and space? In "Song of Myself" Whitman explains, "I speak the pass-word *primeval*, I give the sign of democracy" (506). Democracy persists from the beginning of time, I believe Whitman is arguing, because a democratic society can include what the world includes from time's beginning, all the diversity of differences appearing throughout time. By including the diversity that time itself includes, democracy inherits the time belonging to all the differences it includes, the time during which these differences became what they are. It were as though democracy were the key opening the door to time. So here we discover that democracy is related to time as poetry is related to time, namely, that both *democratic and poetic forms of representation* are inclusive of the world's differences in a way that also includes the time belonging to those differences, the time from the world's beginning. Following poetry's example, in other words, it is precisely democracy's aesthetic receptivity to the diversity of differences that earns it, at every moment, time in addition to any moment.

So often does Whitman invent ways to express this idea of "democratic time" that it becomes, as he promised, a thought woven like a thread throughout his poetry ("Starting from Paumanok," 162, 170). In *Democratic Vistas* we again find the aesthetic receptivity to diversity and difference related quite explicitly to the contraction of time. As a result of its "idiocrasy of universalism," which Whitman describes as the "true child" of America, he proposes that *"now and here,"* at *that particular moment* in which he lives and writes, democracy is "journeying through Time."[42] Nowhere in Whitman's work, though, is there a more polished image of how a diversity of worlds entails a diversity of times than in his preface to the 1855 edition of *Leaves of Grass*. Referring to democracy in America Whitman argues,

> [H]ere at last is something in the doings of man that corresponds with the broadcast doings of the day and night. Here is not merely a nation but a teeming nation of nations. Here is action untied from strings necessarily blind to particulars and details magnificently moving in vast masses.[43]

Is not all time, are not all nights and all days contained in the "broadcast doings of the day and night"? Does not the "general light and dark," as Whitman refers to all time in "Song of the Answerer" (57), belong to the swarm of differences within a nation of nations that each possess its own time?

In this light, perhaps Whitman ceases to be enigmatic when, referring to America's "idiocrasy of universalism" as its "unseen moral essence" in "Song of the Redwood-Tree" (58), he says,

> *You that, sometimes known, oftener unknown, really shape and*
> *mould the New World, adjusting it to Time and Space.* (58–59)

Democracy is "adjusted to time and space" by way of an aesthetic receptivity to the world that, inclusive of universality's diversity of differences, includes *at any one time* all the time and space belonging to universality's diverse forms of life as they unfold. So when Whitman speaks of space in "Our Old Feuillage,"

> *Encircling all*, vast-darting up and wide, the American soul . . . (47; my italics)

> The certainty of space, increase, freedom, futurity . . . (66)

and in "Thou Mother with Thy Equal Brood,"

> As a strong bird on pinions free,
> Joyous, the amplest spaces heavenward cleaving [,] (14–15)

he does not have in mind physical space, such as the geographical space between seas and coasts. Rather, he is thinking of the compaction of all space within "democratic space," the space belonging to and inherited with the representation of the togetherness of differences, spaces within which diverse differences became what they are and that were at one time or another spread out or scattered and separated throughout space. And when speaking of time in "Thou Mother with Thy Equal Brood,"

> While thou, Time's spirals rounding, out of thyself, thyself still
>   extricating, fusing,
> Equable, natural, mystical Union thou . . . (119–20)

Whitman is thinking of the time compacted and absorbed by a democratic world that has become the "globe of globes" (126), of the time belonging to each world that becomes "Time's *spirals*" when worlds are drawn near together and globes are included one *within* another as they are in a democratic world.

Now, receptive to and creating itself through globes, or worlds—through the diversity of differences—that democracy has absorbed into its own world, an aesthetic individuality, too, could absorb a world of worlds, and thus a time of times and a space of spaces belonging to these worlds. Out of these globes individuality's own Time would spiral as the times and spaces of all differences are drawn together within its one identity. By offering individuality access to a world of worlds, by offering it the opportunity to create itself differently through All the differences in the world according to an ethic of appearances and from the aesthetic point of view of the artist (the creator), democracy offers individuality the opportunity "to conceive no time, however distant, but what you may reach it and pass it" (171), as Whitman in "Song of the Open Road" recommends each of us consider our own time.[44] Democracy offers aesthetic individuality immortality, the opportunity to overcome its own finiteness. As Whitman sings in "Thou Mother with Thy Equal Brood," through democracy, "the immortal reality!" the "Thought of man justified" as "the immortal idea!" (32, 31, 33).

Surely, though we hardly could imagine it possible, Whitman means to say even more than democracy offers immortality, for his poetry makes it clear that if immortality is to have any meaning at all it must lead toward life, and its meaning will be found in the life immortality increases. Instead of immortality, then, let us think of the time that democracy makes available to an individuality aesthetically receptive to the world as an infinity, however not, as though it were immortality, an infinity of time. Rather than an infinity of time, democracy bestows upon individuality the infinite possibilities for creating itself differently that are contained in democratic universalism's globe of globes, its world of diversely different worlds. Infinity is the democratic promise for an individuality that will acquire a "peerless capacity for creativity," to recall Whitman's thought of democracy in America as realizing the "peerless grandeur of the modern, Out of thyself," in "Thou Mother with Thy Equal Brood" (35–36). Aesthetic individuality's creativity realizes democracy's promise of universalism through a receptivity to the worlds of difference to which democratic forms of representation provide singular access, the limitless objects that draw from diffusion individuality's limitless meanings and give them shape.

NINE

Aesthetic Individuality as a Democratic Achievement

For democracy truly to be an aesthetic form of life, it is not enough that its universalism provide individuality with access to worlds of difference to which it can form an aesthetic relation as the poet through poetry forms an aesthetic relationship to the world. As an aesthetic form of life democracy must do more than draw near together the differences that can call from diffusion individuality's limitless meanings and give them shape. Before democracy's togetherness of differences can become aesthetically meaningful, individuality must become receptive to the world according to an ethic of appearances and creative from the aesthetic point of view of the artist (the creator) whose aesthetic forms incorporate a sensibility to the violence in creativity. Democracy must be productive of an aesthetic individuality so that individuality can begin to form its relations to the world aesthetically. Our question then becomes, can aesthetic individuality be the achievement of democratic society? Surely Whitman believes it can be, though he offers two different answers to our question.

In *Democratic Vistas*, we recall, Whitman argues stridently that each individual should be the beneficiary of an aesthetic education.[1] A "new Poetry" would teach that the development of each individual and of American civilization as a whole relies upon the creation of a "varied personalism," "identity," or "individuality" that "democracy *alone*" produces "on anything like Nature's scale," by "break[ing] up the limitless fallows of human-kind."[2] Put simply, poetry's lesson is that individuality in all of its great diversity of differences, in all of its "unimpeded branchings," in Whitman's words, flourishes best under a democratic form of life, which allows American civilization to flourish in turn. Whitman explains that poetry teaches individuals its lesson about democracy by mimicking the "aesthetic" quality of nature. Poetry, the representational or "image-making faculty," as he thinks of it, ascends to an aesthetic level when like nature it democratically represents "the All, and the Idea of All."[3]

Of obvious note here is that Whitman privileges poetry's *form* of representation rather than any lesson poetry might explicitly offer. Poetry does not teach its lesson simply by saying poetically that by affirming the norm of democratic equality American civilization will be inclusive of the individuality upon which its prosperity depends. Rather, poetry teaches that it is *individuality* that flourishes in all of its diversity and difference when, in the manner of poetry, individuals form their concepts and images of the world on the basis of a democratic ideal. The individuality of each must be as all-inclusive as nature. If civilization prospers, it is on the basis of an individuality that flourishes by representing all of individuality's possibilities, an individuality that is inclusive, as poetry and democracy are inclusive, of nature's diversity of differences. Specifically, the individuality of each one is created, "presented," as it were, by including or "representing" the *individualities of all the rest*. Being so inclusive, then individuality, like the concept of nature on which poetry and democracy are based, is aesthetic.

Whitman's proposal in *Democratic Vistas* that the development of individuality and America ultimately rests upon an aesthetic education is preceded by an even more provocative claim, one going to the more immediate relationship between individuality and democracy. In his preface to the 1855 edition of *Leaves of Grass*, Whitman observes,

> The Americans of all nations at any one time upon the earth have probably the fullest poetical nature. The United States themselves are essentially the greatest poem.[4]

In view of Whitman's later insistence in *Democratic Vistas* on the contribution to be made by an aesthetic education, the idea that Americans *already* are poetical, already are aesthetic, without the instruction of the artist and art, is quite remarkable. Whitman's observation suggests, moreover, that the poetical nature of Americans is related to something poetic in nature belonging to democracy in America. Indeed, Whitman closes his preface by arguing passionately that "an individual is as superb as a nation when he has the qualities that make a superb nation"—which is to possess the "soul" of the nation that becomes the "wealthiest and proudest" by going "half-way to meet [the soul] of its poets." The soul of the individual becomes as poetic as the soul of the nation, Whitman concludes metaphorically, if the nation absorbs the poet! "If the one is true," Whitman declares, "the other is true." If the nation is poetic, in other words, the individual is poetic. If the nation is aesthetic, the individual is aesthetic.

Though Whitman's extraordinary preface suggests that by producing a "poetical" people democracy in America had absorbed the poet to become "the greatest poem," he does not explain how a democratic society can produce such a people, how, metaphorically speaking, America can absorb the poet. Rather, his preface is devoted to an explanation of how the poet can "absorb" a democratic America so that poetry can express its soul. Following up on Whitman's suggestion, I want to pursue the possibility that democracy in America produces a "poetical" people, an "aesthetic individuality" as I have described it, and attempt to explain how it does so, thus fleshing out one of the figurative senses in which it can be said that America has absorbed the poet. I am going to pursue this possibility in the way I believe poses difficult challenges to this thesis, through a reconstruction of the work of a thinker who is one of America's most seminal critics. Alexis de Tocqueville's *Democracy in America* possesses an authority that is uncontested. Even by today's theoretical standards, very few important aspects of American democracy are omitted from his analysis, few institutions and their institutional principles, few practices and the beliefs that underlie them. Given the way in which Tocqueville constructs his analytical framework, any evidence that can be found for aesthetic individuality in his critique of democracy in America will help to prove that it is a democratic achievement. My approach to Tocqueville's great work will be to redescribe his argument in the aesthetic terms I have laid out in the preceding three chapters, to determine if there is a correspondence between the aesthetic form of Whitman's poetry and the form of individuality as it is actually produced by democracy in America as Tocqueville understood it.

TOCQUEVILLE'S AESTHETIC SENSIBILITY

Neither *aesthetic* nor *individuality* are terms that occupy any place of prominence in *Democracy in America*, and *aesthetic individuality* is a term unique to my own approach to conceptualizing individuality. *Aesthetic* is absent entirely, omitted even from Tocqueville's appraisal of the arts in America, though by assessing American literature, poetry, drama, and architecture in light of their contribution to an ideal of beauty he implicitly introduces a conventional sense of aesthetics into his discussion, one quite different from that developed here. *Individuality*, not to be confused with the democratic *individualism* of which Tocqueville is so famously critical, appears rarely enough, discouraging a reading of his work interested in discovering, at least at the manifest level of his text, evidence of individuality in democratic America.

Toward the end of the first volume of *Democracy in America* Tocqueville describes a "distinct individuality" that emerged during the Middle Ages. Medieval peoples, provinces, cities, and families were "broken up," he argues, when bound together exclusively by a religious tie. By itself, religious commonality is insufficient to suppress the development of differences among them.[5] In this context Tocqueville is clear that individuality means to be different from the rest, for he goes on to complain of a "tendency to assimilation" since the medieval period, whereby there is increasingly "less difference" among nations. Following the train of thought adopted by Whitman in "Passage to India" roughly thirty-five years later, Tocqueville attributes this advance toward "unity" to "[o]ur means of intellectual intercourse [that] unite the remotest parts of the earth" (*DAI*, 433). Tocqueville also speaks of the destruction of the Roman Empire as issuing in the resumption of the "individuality" belonging to each nation antecedent to its incorporation into the Roman world. Individuality is reasserted through the emergence of a rank order among the former empire's states, whose "different races were more sharply defined," that is, their differences were accentuated, once having lost the colonial bonds that established reciprocal ties and a deeper commonality.[6] Beyond these occasions Tocqueville speaks explicitly of individuality only once more, where it again alludes to difference. "Individuality" is destroyed by philosophical systems of thought teaching that all things are simply parts of a greater whole possessing eternally constant qualities in relation to which what is individual and different, he implies, becomes insignificant and its presence obscured" (*DAII*, 31–32). Here Tocqueville is critical of a democratic people's inclination to favor the general over the particular, to overlook "individuals to think only of their kind," which is characteristic of their fascination with "pantheism."

Because he fails to discover any direct evidence for the "aesthetic" qualities of an individuality to which he devotes little attention in other terms as well, it nevertheless would be premature to conclude that Tocqueville contributes nothing to the concept of aesthetic individuality I have elaborated in this work. To locate a point of entry into *Democracy in America* that permits us to engage Tocqueville in a discussion about aesthetic individuality, we are alerted to certain conceptual possibilities by his references to individuality as "difference." Conceptually, difference appears at the very center of what I have argued is aesthetic individuality's creative and receptive orientation to the world. Individuals receptive to the world's diversity of differences are oriented aesthetically, an orientation through which they create themselves differently while not subjecting the diverse forms of difference through which they become different to the violence of formal rationality. If Tocqueville were found to be interested in difference in ways conceptually relevant to this argument, the omission of any discussion of either aesthetics or individuality may erect only a superficial barrier to efforts to draw him into an inquiry into the aesthetics of individuality in a democratic society.

To begin with, Tocqueville's association of individuality with difference already invites speculation that the presence or absence of difference in a democratic society is a measure of the presence or absence of individuality. Within a democratic society, moreover, the orientation of individuals to differences with which they are surrounded might mark the presence of what we understand to be aesthetic individuality, though Tocqueville did not describe relations among individuals in democracy in these terms specifically. If we search Tocqueville's text for proof of an interest in difference relevant conceptually to individuality as an aesthetic problem, we may bring *Democracy in America* to bear on the question of whether aesthetic individuality could be a democratic achievement.

To fix the importance of difference in Tocqueville's thinking, we first note the point he makes, rather emphatically, of explaining that he believes a cognitive interest in difference to be a superior quality of mind. "God," Tocqueville proposes,

> surveys at one glance and severally all the beings of whom mankind is composed; and he discerns in each man the resemblances that assimilate him to all his fellows, and the differences that distinguish him from them. God, therefore, stands in no need of general ideas; that is to say, he never feels the necessity of collecting a considerable number of analogous objects under the same form for greater convenience in thinking. (*DAII*, 13)

Proceeding to think in the manner he ascribes to the deity, Tocqueville then recognizes a difference between the human intellect and God's, stressing that if man is to think at all he must have "recourse to an imperfect but necessary expedient." "General ideas" provide the ordering mechanism that saves the human mind from becoming lost in the "immensity of detail" were it "to attempt to examine and pass a judgment on all the individual cases before it." As he is unable to attend to "difference(s)" among these cases, man's dependence upon general ideas guarantees the insufficiency of an intellect that must "pass a rapid judgment on a great many objects at once" and settle for notions that "are never other than incomplete," causing the "mind to lose as much in accuracy as it gains in comprehensiveness." But what of the paradox in which Tocqueville with obviousness implicates himself by distinguishing a divine from a human intellect, a difference that, by his own account, his human nature ought make it impossible for him to conceive?

Surely Tocqueville would have been aware of this contradiction, so that if his intention were to argue coherently about mankind's intellectual disabilities rather than highlight his interest in difference, he would have refrained from continuously identifying and focusing our attention on differences that neither he nor anyone, he ostensibly claims, has the ability to appreciate. When describing the exterior form of North America, for example, Tocqueville speaks of "[n]ature in her infinite variety," by which he means, as he later seems to explain, again anticipating Whitman, that "there are in nature no beings exactly alike" (*DA*I, 21; *DA*II, 13).[7] Tocqueville thinks in similar ways of the emigrants arriving at various periods to settle America, who "differed from each other in many respects," and of American dramatists and their native audience, "a multitude," he observes, "composed of elements so different" (*DA*I, 28; *DA*II, 81). Considering the advantages of American federalism, by contrast he raises the political and administrative issues that arise when the uniformity of laws legislated by centralized nations are imposed upon the "diversity of customs" belonging to their people (*DA*I, 163). Indeed, Tocqueville's interest in difference is acute to the extent that he distinguishes, with reproach to the Americans, between a classic architectural creation and its North American copy, a *difference among similarities*, we should say, becoming apparent when he goes out of his way to inspect the design "more closely" (*DA*II, 52). And he worries that his European readers will construe *Democracy in America* as portraying a model of democratic institutions that should be imitated by all democratic communities (*DA*I, 329–30). Doing so would be to ignore perhaps his deepest and most fundamental concern, the correspondence between a people's customs and its political constitution, that cultural differences among nations are irreconcilable with the universal adoption of an invariable set of institutional arrangements.

Taking these several instances of Tocqueville's own intellectual practices together, can we not say that he displays, and quite deliberately it seems, the very interest in difference he so highly and explicitly valorizes as a superior quality of mind? Yet, simply thematizing Tocqueville's "interest" in difference may do him an injustice by obscuring the sensibility that underlies and informs it, a sensibility to the way difference is suppressed representationally in ideas, by thinking in general, as we have seen, and that corresponds to the sensibility cultivated by Whitman and Adorno. Tocqueville's interest in difference, in other words, reflects a sensibility with aesthetic overtones, and no doubt is an understated description of an orientation to difference deeply inspired by his impression of the way nature and its world and everyone and everything in it are constituted diversely.

TOCQUEVILLE'S BLINDNESS TO DEMOCRATIC DIFFERENCE

Once Tocqueville's interest in difference is foregrounded, his analysis of the fate of difference in a democratic society, always remarkable, becomes all the more so, leading us to suspect that there may be other factors at work in the background of his analysis blunting his sensibility to the presence of difference in democracy. While Tocqueville concedes that democracies cannot be rid of the division between the "wealthy," "those who have little or no property," and those "in easy circumstances," so that "the people may always be mentally divided into three classes," for all intents and purposes, in his view, class differences disappear (*DA*I, 213). Democratic institutions foster a "two-fold revolution" abolishing aristocratic society's distinctions of rank, whereby the nobility hereditarily positioned at the top descend toward a midpoint collecting those ascending from the bottom social layers (*DA*I, 6). "Every half-century brings [the distinctions of class] nearer to each other," Tocqueville estimates, "and they will soon meet," though he offers other prognoses that are less cautious, as when he concludes that the first half-century of democratic revolution destroyed "the last trace of hereditary ranks and distinctions" (*DA*I, 6, 50–51). In America, where the collapse of these class and cultural differences has advanced furthest, the "distinctions of rank . . . in political society . . . are nil" and "in civil society are slight" to a vanishing point, as Tocqueville suggests by saying, "for, so to speak," in civil society "there are no longer any classes" (*DA*II, 172, 4). It is with these developments in mind that Tocqueville must feel pressed to convert the sociology of an order of rank, or class analysis, into a purely "mental" construct with its tripartite division between the wealthy, those in easy circumstances, and the poor. To Tocqueville's way of thinking, a framework of differences explaining the relationship between class structure and cultural formation must give way to one simply highlighting the aberrant inequalities produced by democratic society that no longer correspond historically to the obsolete structural differences between classes.

To democracy, then, there corresponds the erosion of differences in rank, the breakdown of differences between classes. Spatially less territorial and internally less insular, classes gradually "approach" and "mingle" with one another, Tocqueville explains, so that their "members become undifferentiated and lose their class identity for each other" (*D*AII, 99). As class ceases to serve as the difference around which identity is constituted, individuals disappear "in the throng" and are "easily lost in the midst of a common obscurity," Tocqueville concludes, bringing into sharper focus the trajectory of a dynamic within democratic society leading to the formation of "one single mass" (*D*AI, 328; *D*AII, 239). While on occasion he stops just short of characterizing this deindividualized democratic mass as completely homogeneous, adding, for instance, that the elements of which it is composed are "analogous though not entirely similar," his overall judgment is considerably harsher. "Variety"—difference—"is disappearing from the human race" as a consequence of the progress of democracy, Tocqueville announces stunningly, so that "the same ways of acting, thinking, and feeling are to be met with all over the world," increasingly resembling "something nearer to the constitution of man, which is everywhere the same" (*D*AII, 229). Surveying democracy's "countless multitude of beings," Tocqueville reports that "the sight of such universal uniformity saddens and chills me and I am tempted to regret that [aristocratic] state of society which has ceased to be" (*D*AII, 332). Given Tocqueville's views on the disappearance of variety and the universality of uniformity in democracy, we might recall his claim that the Deity stands in no need of general ideas because a divine mind expresses regard for mankind not as a whole, but for the differences distinguishing each of the beings of which it is composed (*D*AII, 13). From his analysis of the fate of difference in democratic society, it were as though Tocqueville were arguing that democracy produces a uniform people for whom God could have no regard.

Without a doubt, among all the features of democracy in which Tocqueville shows fascination, we learn that there is not one more important to him than the eclipse of difference. He reveals this dramatically by saying that it is precisely because aristocratic society exhibits none of democracy's uniformity that he is "tempted to regret" aristocracy's passing. Such a confessional remark is shocking, especially as it arrives at the very conclusion of his two-volume study, perhaps inviting, though certainly forcing, us to reassess his analysis of democracy in view of the aristocratic prejudice it unabashedly discloses to be the standpoint from which he determines that difference has disappeared in democratic America. If we are shocked, we are not surprised by his prejudicial remark. Throughout his work and often with little subtlety Tocqueville valorized aristocratic institutions as a prelude to judging the merits and defects of democratic society. So that when in favor of America he at last says, "A state of equality is perhaps less elevated, but it is more just: and its justice constitutes its greatness and its beauty . . ." we would not read him unfairly as damning democracy with faint praise (*D*AII, 333). After all, the image of democracy Tocqueville presents is of a society not less elevated but, on the contrary, *far* less elevated than the aristocratic order with which it is invidiously compared throughout his work. Aristocracy's elevations, as typical of the moral codes of its everyday life as of its arts and sciences, to Tocqueville's mind are no less rooted in the presence of difference than what interests him about democracy is rooted in its absence. Rich and poor in aristocratic nations are no less than different "species," as Tocqueville puts it more than once, and "astonishingly unlike each other," he argues, "their passions, their notions, their habits, and their tastes are essentially different" (*DA*II, 231, 228). By eventually rejecting the possibility that differences within aristocratic regimes, no matter how profound, could be rooted in human nature rather than in societal conditions, however, Tocqueville retreats from the essentialist position in which he is frequently implicated by his language. Considering the class system he grants that aristocratic institutions "*made* the beings of one and the same race so different" (*DA*II, 163; italics added). And referring to castes within the aristocratic class he explains that codes of honor originate contextually in the "special habits and special interests of the community" in which men are collected together (*DA*II, 235). Differences among men and women likewise are not natural, but the consequences of "birth and fortune" (*DA*II, 205).

Curiously, the methodological sophistication Tocqueville displays by his grasp of the social construction of difference does not carry over beyond his concluding reflection on the prejudicial role played by aristocratic difference in his determination of the absence of difference in a democracy. As we discover from the closing paragraphs of the second volume of *Democracy in America*, although Tocqueville is not only aware of his prejudice but aware that as its consequence he stumbles into methodological errors despite his insight into the great extent to which it necessarily blinds him to dimensions of democratic life, he allows his analysis of democratic society to conclude without revision. Methodologically self-conscious about his approach to studying democracy in America, Tocqueville admits to a sympathy for "men of great importance," "great wealth," and "great learning," as he describes the European aristocracy who comprised the normative and empirical standpoint for his analysis of the democratic form of life. He accounts for his methodological one-sidedness, in his own words a "weakness," by comparing his analytical abilities with those of God, who once again serves as Tocqueville's standard-bearer for how the mind can and cannot think. Whereas the "gaze" of the "Almighty and Eternal Being . . . surveys distinctly, though all at once, mankind and man," Tocqueville is "unable to see at once all that is around" him, so that he is "allowed thus to select and separate objects of [his] predilection from so many others" (*DA*II, 332). Then addressing the implications of his all-too-human prepossession, Tocqueville concedes that his examination of democracy was shaped by a prejudgment that could compromise his ability to appreciate the originality of democracy in America.

> What appears to me to be man's decline is, to His eye, advancement; What afflicts me is acceptable to Him. . . . Care must therefore be taken not to judge the state of society that is now coming into existence by notions derived from a state of society that no longer exists; for as these states of society are exceedingly different in their structure, they cannot be submitted to a just or fair comparison. (*DA*II, 333)

Recommending a studied impartiality far too late to have any bearing on the construction of his investigation, in light of his admission and account of his aristocratic prejudice Tocqueville without further revision only inserts, "I *would strive*, then, to raise myself to this point of the divine contemplation and thence to view and to judge the concerns of man" (Ibid.; italics added).

No doubt the odd placement of Tocqueville's efforts at self-criticism could be explained by a consideration of the rhetorical structure of his text, guided by his methodological reflections, and its relationship to the observations, arguments, and conclusions of his analysis. As such a study is beyond my immediate interests, at this moment I can contribute only a few leading remarks. If Tocqueville did not mean for his concluding methodological reflection to call the validity of his work into question and to imply the obligation to undertake textual revisions, we must infer that by retrospectively dividing his analysis into what he *has* done (judge democracy to be man's decline) versus what he *would strive* to do (judge democracy to be man's advancement), he intends *Democracy in America* for two distinct audiences. Europeans would be advised by Tocqueville's inquiry, as it stands, to avoid or manage those democratic institutions and practices that catalyzed the decline of man by, among other things, eliminating variety or difference from the human race, into which a chilling, universal uniformity as a consequence is introduced. Americans, whose democratic principles Tocqueville believes set them on an irreversible historical course toward uniformity, might be persuaded by his attempt to mask his aristocratic bias by deferring to a divine intellect who judges to be an "advancement" what he prejudicially condemns as a "decline" and an "affliction." Perhaps Tocqueville had counted on their Christian faith, which he credited as the primary cause of the maintenance of democracy in America, to dispose Americans to accept his explanation for his prejudice and to discount it accordingly.[8]

Whether one is American or not, overlooking a bias only the Almighty could avoid, however, does not make it less definitive of the architecture of Tocqueville's work. Although in view of Tocqueville's admission of prejudice the disappearance of difference in democracy may newly appear as an advancement and not a decline, against a background of aristocratic difference, difference in democracy has still vanished. Notwithstanding Tocqueville's error, and in spite of his obviously disingenuous account of his inability to suspend his ungodlike "predilection," as he refers euphemistically to his prejudice, his confessional remarks are instructive. From Tocqueville we learn that if we are to allow *Democracy in America* to shape our sensibility to the presence of difference in a democratic society, since he did not treat of democratic difference independently of aristocracy, we first must understand how in his arguments the disappearance of difference in democracy is relative to the aristocratic context in which his measure of difference is formed. Discovering how the disappearance of difference in democratic society is relative to Tocqueville's concept of aristocratic difference will allow us to appreciate just how "exceedingly different in their structure," to borrow his words, these two forms of difference may be, so that what difference seems to disappear relative to one context may have a presence and a life of its own in another. To be sure, if democracy were as free of difference as Tocqueville contends, aesthetic individuality, whose fundamental receptive orientation to the world is to a world filled with differences in all of their diversity, would be without a world to form and in which to form itself creatively. Our point of departure, then, is to arrive at a clearer idea of Tocqueville's concept of difference, of the aristocratic properties it assumed, so that we may begin to see democratic difference in a different light.

The Large Differences of Aristocratic Societies

Aristocracies produce individuals who "gradually become so dissimilar that each class assumes the aspect of a distinct race" (*DA*II, 14). Recalling that Tocqueville does not subscribe to the view that differences, at least most human differences, are natural, we may be puzzled by his selection of terms that entail the view he rejects. "Race," "species" (*DA*II, 231), and "essentially different" (*DA*II, 228) may have been chosen by Tocqueville to convey the idea that the socially constructed differences of aristocracies are naturelike, in the sense of a historically manufactured second nature as seemingly durable as nature itself. Tocqueville's language serves another purpose as well, that of underscoring the permanence of the social inequalities from which naturelike differences arise. Differences that at bottom are artificial class differences are to impress us as shaping the destiny of a people when, as historically acquired "essential" and "racial" characteristics, over the long course of time they determine its fate. As qualities distinguishing one class from another, "differences," "dissimilarities," "astonishingly unlike," or the "essentially different," as Tocqueville speaks of difference synonymously, only develop in the wake of inequalities that are permanent (*DA*II, 242, 228). For Tocqueville, in other words, there is a reciprocally necessary connection between the development of difference and the existence of permanent inequality or "inequality of conditions," as he often refers to inequality to emphasize its social origins and consequences. Permanent inequality produces difference, while difference, more to the point of Tocqueville's explanation for the disappearance of difference in democracy, presupposes permanent inequality.

Anchored in feudal property relations, in the hereditary privileges and powers attached to families possessing property, and in the doctrine that rights are inherent in individuals, the permanent inequalities of aristocratic class differences remained unchanged for centuries. As Tocqueville expresses it in one of his many attempts to capture the inertia of aristocracy, "[m]en then believed that families were immortal; men's conditions seemed settled forever, and the whole of society appeared to be so fixed that it was not supposed anything would ever be stirred or shaken in its structure" (*DA*II, 188). Tocqueville's admiration for aristocracy was based in large part on the endurance of its material and political inequalities, as it enabled the inequality of condition to be reproduced in extreme forms at the cultural level. Permanently released from material cares, the privileged ranks could apply themselves to "more arduous" and "habitually lofty" undertakings, leading individuals to "superior intelligence, learning and enlightenment" (*DA*II, 128, 245, 10). Valuing cultural achievements above all, which in his view justified aristocracy's permanently unequal conditions, Tocqueville excused permanent inequality by proposing that when "all conditions are unequal, no inequality is so great as to offend the eye" (*DA*II, 295). He grudgingly endorsed democratic equality because he believed it to be both historically inevitable and consistent with the teachings of Jesus Christ (*DA*II, 334, 15).

Over time, Tocqueville stresses, through the great concentrations of wealth, education, and power fostered by permanent inequality, aristocracy becomes insular, developing into a community whose exceptional position he frequently prefers to describe as a "caste" rather than a class. Through permanent deprivation of wealth, education, and power the lower classes become as insular and their position as exceptional, so that the different classes are "like vast enclosures, out of which it is impossible to get, into which it is impossible to enter," and between which there is "no communication" (*DA*II, 216). From his adoption of powerful descriptive language, we form a clear idea of the significance Tocqueville attaches to the insularity and closure of classes that develop around the permanent inequality of condition. Strongly marked and permanent, for example, each of the "classes of an aristocratic people . . . is regarded by its own members as a sort of lesser country, more tangible and more cherished than the country at large" (*DA*II, 98). Relations between these "countries" proceed as though along "two parallel lines, which neither meet nor separate," a metaphor with which Tocqueville underscores the absence of communication and interchange between social enclaves (*DA*II, 179).

As disintegrated as are these classes taken as a whole, each in itself is tightly knit within, "closely binding every man to several of his fellow citizens," as is suggested by Tocqueville's use of "community" to describe the aristocratic caste (*DA*II, 98, 239). Tocqueville pays special attention to the intellectual and moral existence nurtured within the well-integrated, enclosed world of the aristocracy. All ideas circulating within the aristocratic class originate inside its borders and erect "lofty stationary barriers" impenetrable from without and protective of its form of life and ideological integrity (*DA*II, 216). No question or issue is so general that it cannot be considered from the foreshortened perspective of the particular rights and idiosyncratic practices of the aristocracy as they are at any particular time (*DA*II, 93). What is true of the aristocracy is true of the powerless as well, as Tocqueville illustrates by pointing to the "notions and manners" belonging to the "distinct class" of servants in fealty to the aristocracy (*DA*II, 177). So internal to each class and self-absorbed is its form of life, neither class has sight of the other or thinks of itself as sharing any of the characteristics that would include the other (*DA*II, 14–15). Each class is virtually out of sight, out of mind of the other, an extraordinary consequence of a social order that resembles a *de*

AESTHETIC INDIVIDUALITY AS A DEMOCRATIC ACHIEVEMENT

facto apartheid when we recall Tocqueville's view that permanent inequality renders classes so dissimilar that each assumes the traits of a distinct race.

Indeed, Tocqueville goes to the extreme of arguing that aristocratic forms of life are sufficiently enclosed and self-referential to introduce large breaches in the shared meanings constituted intersubjectively between classes.

> Each of these classes contracts and invariably retains habits of mind peculiar to itself and adopts by choice certain terms which afterwards pass from generation to generation, like their estates. The same idiom then comprises a language of the poor and a language of the rich, a language of the commoner and a language of the nobility, a learned language and a colloquial one. The deeper the divisions and the more impassable the barriers of society become, the more must this be the case. (*DA*II, 67)

Moral sentiments also vary with the forms of life peculiar to each caste. Aristocratic closure nurtures the capacity for sympathetic feelings among members of the same class, and among members of the same class *exclusively*, "for real sympathies," Tocqueville reasons, "can exist only between those who are alike," between those "considering themselves as children of the same family" (*DA*II, 163, 162). "Generosity" rather than sympathy is the moral sentiment the privileged express for those of different classes. Tocqueville's distinction between generosity and sympathy again highlights the differences between classes, while it also indicates that the similarities of individuals within their respective classes breed a like-mindedness on which certain moral sentiments turn. As an additional measure of the degree of ideological similitude among members of the privileged class, Tocqueville comments on the "weakness" of the aristocracy's "social authority," a weakness rooted in its inability as a class to rise above its private interests to attend to the "interests of the public," by which he means the protection of the privileged class's unencumbered right and power to reproduce social relations through which entirely different and unrelated forms of life can be perpetuated (*DA*II, 328). For nothing supraterritorially "public" could be imagined by a closed community of like minds as he describes the aristocracy.

By a "social authority of extreme weakness" Tocqueville should not be taken to imply, as I may appear to suggest, that the hegemony of the privileged class is not expressed through the universalization of its beliefs and values. Though the ruling class does not take its own qualities to resemble any held by other classes, the permanent position "above the multitude" it enjoys allows it to entertain "vast ideas" of "the dignity, the power, and the greatness of man" and "to conceive a sublime, almost a divine love of truth" (*DA*II, 44). Again insinuating a connection between the ideas of the ruling class and truth, Tocqueville refers wistfully to how the images of man reflected in aristocratic art provide a "glimpse of the Divinity" (*DA*II, 52). In an interesting variation on Marx, Tocqueville's argument seems to be that although through its concept of truth the ruling class universalizes the beliefs and values internal to its own form of life, the universalized ideas of the ruling class do not become the ruling ideas. Rather, Tocqueville insists, as we have seen, that

> [a]mong an aristocratic people each caste has its own opinions, feelings, rights, customs, and modes of living. Thus the men who compose it do not resemble the mass of their fellow citizens; they do not think or feel in the same manner, and they scarcely believe that they belong to the same race. (*DA*II, 163)

Even more precisely he reports that the "notion of a uniform rule equally binding on all the members of the community was almost unknown to the human mind in aristocratic ages" (*DA*II, 289). Owing to the perfectly self-contained and totalistic character of the privileged class's form of life, then, paradoxically the dominant aristocratic class universalizes ideas that neither are intended to be applicable universally to all classes nor are universally embraced, as the powerless have their own form of life unseeded by aspirations from the one above. Social authority is consequently weak in the extreme *despite* the universalization of beliefs and values of the ruling class, and is only secured, Tocqueville explains, by powerful nobility able to restrain the private interests of their caste in favor of a public interest equated with the status quo (*DA*II, 328).

Other than affirming the value of the aristocratic model of cultural achievement, of what significance is the universalization of aristocratic ideals if it does not strengthen social authority by promoting the public interest? An answer to this question is provided where Tocqueville indirectly uncovers a relationship between the universalized beliefs and values of the privileged class, or its identity, let us say, and the construction of class differences within permanently enclosed communities whose self-containment suppresses the awareness by each class of the other's presence and discourages each from thinking of itself as belonging to the same "species" or "race" as the other. Tocqueville fastens on the way a "notion of honor," for example, corresponded to "dissimilarities and inequalities" between aristocratic classes and "identified" in the minds of those constituting the upper class "all that distinguishes their own position," so that honor seemed to them to be "the chief characteristic of their own rank" (*DA*II, 242, 240). Notions of honor and their detailed rules of application proliferated in keeping with the development of the needs, wants, and general requirements of the privileged class, and functioned to reinforce its self-understandings and to rationalize the inequality of condition on which its unchanging position was based. So political obligation, like social authority generally, is thinly and precariously constructed out of the sense of honor with which the privileged classes meet their responsibilities to the powerless wherever they reserve their deeper moral sentiments, like sympathy, for those who are alike.

Tocqueville's discussion of aristocratic honor thus clarifies several features of the process in which the identity of the privileged class is constructed through universalized norms that in very precise terms specify its difference from the under classes. To begin with, through universalized codes of honor, the idea constructed by the privileged of their difference from the powerless is so absolute, we understand why the ideas of what it means to be human produced by the ruling class do not establish even an abstract commonality between the classes, as Tocqueville argued. Likewise, the precision of aristocratic codes of honor explains why each member of each rank is fixed in a position that cannot be surrendered. To put these two points somewhat differently, from such universal values as honor an ideological division arises between the classes shutting up each within its own world, resulting in a spatial separation whose boundaries neither class can cross. A static relationship ensues between classes whose members are immobile beyond the limited movement afforded within their well-defined territories (*DA*II, 228). Immobile, members of the privileged class neither would fear becoming nor members of the under class would hope to become like their counterparts. Neither would those occupying different ranks *within* the privileged class hope to become like those positioned above nor fear becoming like those positioned below. Regardless of how narrowly circumscribed are the possibilities for each individual born into its class system, however, as Tocqueville presents it, aristocracy near to its end remained a civilization virtually without discontents of the sort that such a rigidified social apparatus might provoke. For the principle that there is a hereditarily predetermined place for everyone (perhaps the one belief shared by all classes) convinced all individuals that each is the measure of man or, in Tocqueville's words, that "the utmost limits of human power are to be discerned in proximity to himself" (*DA*II, 33). Finally, ideologically and spatially separated, the shallow mutual acquaintance of the classes forced each to "imagine" what those composing the other class are like and to "represent them with some addition to, or some subtraction from, what they really are" (*DA*II, 73). By virtue of the inequality of their condition, Tocqueville appears to be saying, classes are fated to misrepresent one another, as each is constrained to identify those who are different in images of otherness reducible to the idiopathy of its own one-sided situation.

To fully appreciate how exaggerated is the inward turn of mind belonging to each class within aristocratic society, we should consider Tocqueville's remarks on the relationship between identity and memory. With the position and condition of each class remaining unchanged for centuries, "often on the same spot," as Tocqueville puts it, "[a]ristocracy naturally leads the mind to a contemplation of the past and fixes it there" (*DA*II, 98, 72). Fixated on the past, he argues, "all generations become, as it were, contemporaneous. A man almost always knows his forefathers and respects them; he thinks he already sees his remote descendants and he loves them" (*DA*II, 98). Tocqueville's point is that the perpetual coexistence of past and present in memory prevents anything from being forgotten and creates a cumulative memory that weds each individual to a self-identity that is projected into the future as the center around which all social relations are constructed and interpreted. Anchoring an individual identity that remains continuous with itself at all times and in all places, memory infuses and seals off the space occupied by each class, a space within which each class constructs its own world of meanings that distinguish it from the other in near absolute terms.

Perhaps the formative power of class-based memory is demonstrated most effectively by the one significant instance Tocqueville mentions where classes hold memories in common. Families of aristocratic classes brought together as master and servant often remain together for several generations, during which time "they are connected by a long series of common reminiscences" (*DA*II, 179). Under these conditions, where the classes are "always distinct and always in propinquity," a shared history develops that "modifies the mutual relations" between the two classes so that they "grow alike," meaning that servants imaginatively assume the master's personality and learn to regard themselves from the master's point of view (*DA*II, 179, 177). As the one variation of aristocratic relations of domination through which classes associate with one another to form common recollections, master-servant relations underline the degree to which their normally unshared memories isolate the classes from one another. Master-servant relations serve, as well, as one of two exceptions that prove Tocqueville's more general claims regarding the construction and coexistence of class differences in ideologically and spatially separate, unequal, and unrelated worlds. Beyond the master-servant relationship, Tocqueville finds only one other cultural practice that draws together classes in ways that foster the same development of intersubjectively constituted meanings. At the theater, Tocqueville reports, the privileged classes mix with the underclasses, whose loudly expressed opinions of dramatic performances often influence those of the cultivated (*DA*II, 79–80). Neither drama nor master-servant relations, however, create meanings that bridge the distance and overcome the isolation between class differences outside the narrow confines of the estate or the theater.

To summarize, when the cardinal features of Tocqueville's image of aristocratic society are assembled, it is apparent that his analysis of its infrastructure yields a concept of difference that rests on his understanding of the construction of *large, class differences*. Large differences are class differences founded on permanent inequality, seemingly natural, enclosed communities, each of which develops its own self-contained beliefs and values, institutions and practices, "languages" or worlds of meaning. Sharing nothing as worlds apart, large differences are qualitatively different forms of life between which there is such little communication they remain largely invisible to one another, so alien to one another that the impressions each forms of the other must rely on the work of the imagination. Individuals' identities conform to the way their forms of life are largely different from each other, and are imprisoned by memories that bring the history of who they have been to bear determinatively on who they are in the present and who in the future they will continue to be, further insulating each class and guaranteeing the uniqueness of its existence. Though its culture legitimated its form of life to the minds of the privileged, and to Tocqueville's satisfaction, its universalized valuation was a mere reflection of ruling-class self-absorptions and a decisive obstacle to its recognition of the need for social authority, whose vacancy was filled by powerful and gifted nobility who tended to the status quo. What commonality in beliefs and values prevails among those within the privileged class as the source of their sympathy exclusively for others of their kind only underscores their large difference from those for whom generosity, their moral sentiment for the "other," must be cultivated. So large are the differences between classes, Tocqueville was moved to conclude that "in olden society *everything was different*; unity and uniformity was nowhere to be met with" (*DA*II, 328; italics added). Large, class differences are thus totalities, each occupying its own space and ideologically incommensurable with the other, into which there is no entry and from which there is no exit, and within which for the privileged class there is as little movement between ranks. For Tocqueville, difference was equated with these large, class differences. Despite its cultural achievements, the aristocratic society Tocqueville admired, where no one could move or hope to move between large differences to become different from what they were, was an unaesthetic form of life, a conclusion to be revisited when the aesthetic dimensions of individuality in a democratic society are fleshed out. And aristocracy serves as the bright background against which Tocqueville's reading of democracy and the disappearance of difference in democracy is framed as a silhouette.

The Small Differences of Democratic Society

"Among the novel objects that attracted my attention during my stay in the United States," Tocqueville reports, "*nothing struck me more forcibly than the general equality of condition among the people*" (*DA*I, 3; italics added). In a phrase Tocqueville discloses his point of departure for understanding democracy in America. Equality of condition, "principle of equality," "equality," the "social condition" of Americans, the "democratic principle," "the republican condition," the "democratic condition," used synonymously throughout his work, strike him with incomparable force because of the permanent *inequality* of condition that founded his own civilization and shaped its every dimension as it shaped his thinking (*DA*I, 6, 46, 53, 290, 311). Tocqueville finds the equality of condition to have a similarly formative impact on democracy, a belief conveyed in words expressing awe at a form of life that seems to him so entirely foreign and mysterious. A "primary fact" exercising a "prodigious influence ... on the whole course of society," equality gives a "peculiar direction to public opinion" and a "peculiar tenor to the laws," "imparts new maxims to the governing authorities and peculiar habits to the governed." Its effect "extends far beyond the political character and the laws of the country," and creating "opinions," giving birth to "new sentiments," and founding "novel customs," equality of condition has "no less effect on civil society than on the government," modifying whatever it does not produce. Equality of condition is the "fundamental fact from which all others seem to be derived and the central point at which all my observations constantly terminated," Tocqueville explains, and it has become "not only predominant, but all-powerful" (*DA*I, 3, 53).

So novel is the equality of condition of democratic society, Tocqueville recognizes the need for and promises to apply none but "novel ideas" to democracy. Now that the novelty of Tocqueville's ideas has been questioned by tracing their aristocratic origins, however, it seems clear that as the historical backdrop of his analysis of democracy his ideas did not permit him to conceptualize a democratic form of life independently of aristocracy, a task short of which its real novelty would be lost, as we saw him concede.[9] Because Tocqueville's ideas belong to an older world in relation to which the new world is its precise and absolute negation, though, his ideas at least offer him a logic and a language with which he is able to fully deduce and describe the novelty of democracy in light of the ways it is the *antithesis* of aristocracy.

Equality of condition proceeded directly from the abolition or "negation" of feudal privilege, meaning that property ceased to be the tenure of those whose claim to it rested on their birthright. Once property was no longer an inherent right, the rights and privileges attached to property were annulled along with the indelible class distinctions they underpinned, summarily distinguishing noble and lowborn. Property was redistributed on the basis of a democratic principle of right, so that none need suffer the abject poverty stemming from irremediable propertylessness. In "America," Tocqueville says flatly, "there are no paupers" (*DA*I, 245). Property rights, which created a taste for "well-being" or "physical well-being," as Tocqueville speaks of material comforts, are accompanied by other universal civil and political rights with which no one can be barred from that to which property gives economic access (*DA*I, 245–46, 251; *DA*II, 137, 253). Rights provide access to property, in other words, and to other values property brings within reach and that, acquired through rights, are used by each to fashion a way of life through political activity as well as within the private space of civil society. For Tocqueville, rights mean that in principle no one is retained in place, where "place" refers both to a class position fixed *de jure*, and to any *de facto* social position that can be changed through the exercise of civil or political rights. Universal rights establish the equality of condition, in the sense of constituting its presuppositions though not the equality of condition itself, a distinction that must be observed to appreciate the nature of the equality Tocqueville is describing.[10] If Tocqueville attaches a greater significance to rights than this, as he may appear to do on occasion, it is that by virtue of being endowed with rights a people is driven spontaneously to establish an equality of condition among themselves.

Equality of condition thus turns on the achievement brought within reach of those possessing rights or that rights induce each without exception to realize. A movement launched through rights then advances through the least education, to which rights provide access, which Tocqueville believes completes the prerequisites for achieving the equality of condition. Freedom and education enable the intellect to become the "source of strength and of wealth" through which "every addition to science, every fresh truth, and every new idea," including "[p]oetry, eloquence, and memory, the graces of the mind, the fire of imagination, depth of thought" all serve "the advantage of democracy" (*DA*I, 5). Reflecting on the contribution to the intellectual development of all forged by the alliance of democracy and enlightenment, Tocqueville argues that "we shall scarcely find a single great event of the last seven hundred years that has not promoted the equality of condition" (Ibid.). And though the development of the intellect "leans on one side to the limited, the material, and the useful," the "multitude" become wealthy in the broader sense, able in different degrees as individual material circumstances allow to "indulge in the pursuits and pleasures of the intellect" (*DA*II, 38–39). Despite inequality in natural endowments and variations in material circumstances, Tocqueville stresses that through the subdivision of wealth the multitude find equal means or opportunity for putting their intellectual abilities to work (*DA*I, 52). "America," Tocqueville concludes at one point,

> exhibits in her social state an extraordinary phenomenon. Men are there seen on a greater equality in point of fortune and intellect, or, in other words, more equal in their strength, than in any other country of the world, or in any age of which history has preserved the remembrance. (*DA*I, 53)

As equality of condition, or equality in "fortune and intellect" through freedom and education, leads to physical well-being, ambition is unleashed and with it the desire for greater well-being and its satisfaction through the creation of vast markets that emerge in response to the formation of new patterns of consumption (*DA*II, 159–60, 244–45). With "ambition . . . the universal feeling," economic activity further distributes real property and the desire to increase physical well-being among an expanding multitude whose immense numbers form an "intellectual world [that] starts into prodigious activity" (*DA*II, 244, 39, 253–54). Rights and the redistribution of property and of intellectual resources have enabled individuals to think of themselves as self-reliant and in control of their own destiny (*DA*II, 99). Under this social condition none are ever satisfied with the position they attain and as they are "always free to leave it," Tocqueville explains, "they think of nothing but the means of changing their fortune or increasing it" through the resources the equality of condition places at their disposal (*DA*II, 45). Wealth consequently "circulates with incredible rapidity," so that there is constant movement along a social scale whose vicissitudes of success and failure all remain within the range mapped by the equality of condition. Tocqueville's recurring image of equality is of an incessant and irrepressible movement in which all are irresistibly involved, such that classes become "more and more undifferentiated" and "intermingled" and finally are "obliterated"

(*DA*I, 328; *DA*II, 187, 129). As classes become closer and the "more the conditions of men are equalized and assimilated," each individual "conceives a more lofty opinion of his rights," so that the cycle of rights, the redistribution of property, well-being, ambition, new wants and satisfactions, and the erosion of gradations in the social scale continue unabated (*DA*II, 26, 189).

Tocqueville does not claim, of course, that the equality of condition is the actual elimination of classes. To the contrary, as we have seen, he insists that people may always be divided "mentally," that is, analytically, into "three classes," the "wealthy . . . those who are in easy circumstances . . . [and] those who have little or no property and who subsist by the work they perform for the two superior orders" (*DA*I, 213). Rather, equality of condition means that the "proportion of the individuals in these several divisions may vary according to the condition of society," with the middle class continuing to swell in size. Although on this one occasion Tocqueville refers to the tripartite division of classes, more often he simply notes the ineradicable presence of the polarities of wealth and poverty, intelligence and ignorance, at either end of the social scale. Conditions can never be so equal that there could never be "some members of the community in great poverty and others in great opulence," rich and poor, though, importantly, here he alerts us to his use of "poor" in the relative sense (*DA*II, 252). By the standards of nineteenth-century Europe, where the equality of condition had not made the same progress, the poor in America "would often appear rich," highlighting the extent to which Tocqueville considers the larger of the two American extremes, in particular, to be thinning out and collapsing toward the middle (*DA*I, 214, footnote 7). Whether he speaks of democracy divided analytically into three or two classes, however, it is the "innumerable multitude" in between the two withering extremes of the wealthy propertied and propertyless poor, and the whole population between the learned and the ignorant, who attract virtually his entire attention (*DA*II, 253). Regardless of what differences might prevail, in Tocqueville's estimation the "fortunes of men" and their intellectual acquirements are "equal" or "nearly equal" and "nearly alike," or "becoming more equal." Virtues and vices likewise become more alike as do manners, which generally draw those once related to one another as superior and inferior "daily towards the same level" (*DA*II, 39, 6, 25, 194). Individuals have "learned the same things together" and "lead the same life," so that no one is able to "rise above himself" to stand out from the rest. In brief, it is in face of the steady advancement of the equality of condition pulling all ranks toward a common center that we find Tocqueville concluding that the greater the equality the more do individuals "simultaneously arrive at something nearer to the constitution of man, which is everywhere the same" (*DA*II, 229).

As Tocqueville's description of the equality of condition is brought into focus, it is clear that it is not only the disappearance of the poor that he takes to be relative to another historical measure. When silhouetted against the historical fate of the large, class differences of aristocratic society, *all* differences among individuals in a democracy seem to disappear, which Tocqueville acknowledges by saying, the "[e]quality of conditions turns servants and masters into new beings, and places them in new *relative* positions" (*DA*II, 180; italics added). And he acknowledges relativizing the disappearance of difference against class also by arguing that "as each class gradually approaches others and mingles with them, its members become undifferentiated and lose their class identity for each other," thus inferring that the identity of difference is conceptually and historically meaningful only as the difference of a fixed class identity (*DA*II, 99).

Once Tocqueville's concept of the disappearance of difference is clarified as a development that is relative to the disappearance of large, aristocratic class differences, we then are left with differences in democracy other than large differences that have not disappeared but to which a conceptual framework equating difference with large differences would have been blinded. *Small differences,* as I will refer to them, are those differences in democratic society that lie beyond the conceptual boundaries of Tocqueville's large, aristocratic class differences, and which *neither appear nor disappear relative to the disappearance of classes*. Small differences include the entire range of nonclass social differences—multicultural differences, and pluralized differences constructed through the constitution of hegemonic cultural identities, such as racial and gender differences.[11] Small differences also include all nonclass ideological and idiosyncratic intellectual differences according to which individuals identify themselves. And they include, as well, the differences in material circumstances from which individuals can escape to the ones above or fall to the ones below as the equality of condition varies, possibly significant differences appearing insignificant only when they are measured in relation to large, class differences. As a whole, nonclass small differences are not small in any relative sense but are so called only to distinguish them from the large, aristocratic class differences that conceal them from Tocqueville's view. As differences that are nonclass differences, small differences are surely "large" in another sense, as through their social evolution cultures or genders or races become largely, qualitatively different.

On the occasions when Tocqueville does recognize the nonclass small differences of race and gender, he does so only because socially and politically the "Negro" and the "Indian," and women politically, are denied the equality of condition responsible for eliminating difference in a democracy.[12] Indeed, Tocqueville admits to concerning himself with racial differences only as "collateral topics," for as the condition of the races is "American without being democratic," they are unrelated to his conceptual framework, or in his words they are "connected with [his] subject without forming a part of it" (*DA*I, 331). Because he frames difference and its disappearance in class terms, such racial and gender differences would disappear *conceptually* from Tocqueville's view at the very point that Afro-Americans, Native Americans, and women would be granted and begin to benefit from the same equality of condition that affects citizens in their various class positions. For at that point Tocqueville's framework only would measure their differences from others strictly in class terms, as is proved by a scandalous comparison he draws between the ways in which intellectuals in Europe and America view women in the wake of democratic progress.

> There are people in Europe who, confounding together the different characteristics of the sexes, would make man and woman into beings not only equal but alike. They would give to both the same functions, impose on both the same duties, and grant to both the same rights; they would mix them in all things—their occupations, their pleasures, their business. It may readily be conceived that by thus attempting to make one sex equal to the other, both are degraded.... It is not thus that the Americans understand that species of democratic equality which may be established between the sexes. They admit that as nature has appointed such wide differences between the physical and moral constitution of man and woman, her manifest design was to give a distinct employment to their various faculties; and they hold that improvement does not consist in making beings so dissimilar do pretty nearly the same things, but in causing each of them to fulfill their respective tasks in the best possible manner.... In no country has such constant care been taken as in America to trace two clearly distinct lines of action for the two sexes and to make them keep pace one with the other, but in two pathways that are always different. (*DAII*, 211)

Here Tocqueville betrays the weakness of his conceptual scheme. In Europe gender differences become invisible to his conceptual framework whose operating assumption is that because difference is to be defined only in class terms, differences necessarily disappear with the equality of condition. In America gender differences become visible to Tocqueville once again when class inequality persists, as though only with the persistence of inequality of condition does difference persist. As Tocqueville argues, by making man and woman *equal*, as they are made by many Europeans, they necessarily are made *alike*, which is to say their differences disappear; only where they are unequal, as they are in America, do they appear to Tocqueville to be different and their differences appear. While equality may make genders alike in some ways, though, there will remain small differences between them. These are differences that do not become the same, that do not disappear, in other words, by becoming equal, contrary to Tocqueville who reasoned that equality meant sameness, because in an aristocracy, where there was no equality, everyone was different.

It is fascinating to observe the way Tocqueville circles around the small differences he believes disappear with equality of condition. It were as though moving about in democracy while wearing conceptual blinders, he could not help but nearly stumble upon differences his framework concealed in the dark, which then left their telltale signs in his text. During his American journey, for example, Tocqueville became acquainted with "races of men who are nearly strangers to each other in their language, their religion, and their modes of life," the successive waves of émigrés who "in their language, their religion, their manners differ" (*DA*I, 199, 292). Alluding to this plurality of American cultures, instances of what I have called nonclass small differences, he laments the universalism of democratic laws failing to do justice to the peculiarities of "populations which have as yet but few points of resemblance" (*DA*II, 290). And Tocqueville's earlier noted reflections on the love of drama in democratic nations reveal his further struggle with difference in American cultural pluralism, as we find him commenting on the "multitude" of authors and spectators "composed of elements so different and scattered in so many places" they cannot acknowledge the same literary rules and conventions. Tocqueville also admits that manners are characterized by diversities that proliferate precisely because they do not resemble fixed class patterns, though he qualifies his assessment by saying that these differences among manners must be "lesser diversities" as they emerge from the "same social condition" (*DA*II, 218). With the limits of his conceptual framework in mind, however, we can put this judgment into perspective by adding that the common social condition he believes forms "less" diverse manners could be any of the nonclass social and cultural positions in which manners can be rooted when their fixed class roots are destroyed. Tocqueville at first discerns small differences in manners by noting their departure from class "patterns." He then takes differences in manners to be less articulated than they actually may be as he ties them to social conditions that appear to be the "same" simply because they are equal, rather than fixed, as they are in aristocracies. Just at the moment he appears about to escape from aristocratic categories to recognize a unique property of democracy, he falls back into the aristocratic standpoint from which he consistently conceptualizes each aspect of a democratic form of life.

A final example of democratic differences that spill over the borders of Tocqueville's conceptual framework are those who become wealthy through industry established to meet the demands of markets fueled by the equality of condition. Tocqueville observes how members of the American "manufacturing aristocracy" grow "more different" from one another owing to their material and intellectual resources, while those depending upon them "grow more alike" (*DA*II, 160). Importantly, he explains that this aristocracy of manufacturers does not resemble the European aristocracy that preceded it. By this Tocqueville means that as the American wealthy possess none of the features we found associated with fixed class enclosures, the differences among them are more individuated than the differences among their European "counterparts." Moreover, Tocqueville's wealthy who become different from one another by virtue of their resources are not narrowly confined to democracy's exceptional example of the manufacturing aristocracy. The wealthy include a "multitude of people enjoying opulence" and who are "not so closely linked to one another as the members of the former aristocratic class of society," who are not like-minded, that is (*DA*II, 38). And Tocqueville's association of wealth and the development of difference makes explicit the subtle connection running throughout *Democracy in*

America between the newly found intellectual independence of individuals and the restricted access to the arts and sciences equality of condition affords. Intellectual independence is constrained by the material resources accompanying equality that gives "some resources to all the members of the community," though "prevents any of them from having resources of great extent" (*DA*II, 244–45). Read in light of his association of wealth and difference, the implication here (also insinuated where Tocqueville argues that the "greater or lesser ease with which people can live without working is a sure index of intellectual progress") is that if democracy were able to achieve greater affluence for greater numbers, the intellectual differences among those better off would proliferate (*DA*I, 200).

Several other such examples from *Democracy in America* could be furnished of differences that should not be recognizable within a text whose conceptual framework, by equating difference with class difference, enables Toqueville to establish their disappearance relative to the equality of *class* condition. Tocqueville, however, makes it unnecessary to produce them. Having well established his indictment of democracy's dissolution of difference, in what appears to be a self-critical or at least a cautionary reflection on the conclusion that his readers will draw from his description of the equality of condition, Tocqueville says,

> It might be supposed that the final and necessary effect of democratic institutions would be to identify all the members of the community in private as well as in public life and to compel them all to live alike, but this would be to ascribe a very coarse and oppressive form to the equality which originates in democracy. No state of society or laws can render men so much alike but that education, fortune, and tastes will interpose some differences between them. (*DA*II, 215)

Then proceeding to describe the associational life of democracy within the sphere of civil society, Tocqueville conveys the understated nature of his cautionary note by concluding that "private society is infinitely varied" (*DA*II, 216).

THE AESTHETICS OF SMALL DIFFERENCES

Including all differences falling within the conceptual space mapped by the duality between aristocracy's inequality of condition, on the one side, and democracy's equality of condition, on the other, Tocqueville's analytical framework is now revised to be inclusive of all differences—"large, class differences" *and* all nonclass "small differences." Large, aristocratic differences rooted in class inequality are embodied within linguistically, normatively, and culturally incommensurable forms of life, closed communities whose perpetuity desensitizes large, class differences to one another's existence, so that the foreignness of each is accessible only through the other's imagination. Individuals' identities correspond to large, class differences, are narrowly constituted by their insular forms of life, and are sealed off further by a history of experience whose recollections overwhelm who each becomes in the present and future. Time is reduced to a constellation of undifferentiated images in which identity sees its reflection. Neither is there physical nor intellectual movement between or within large, class differences, the ultimate consequence of a stasis upset by democracy's introduction of the equality of condition. Substituting universal for inherited rights, equality of condition galvanizes movement between classes by providing individuals with access to material and intellectual well-being, which releases ambition and propels needs and wants and satisfactions whose constantly changing form transcends class position. Transcending class position, this new form of life created by the equality of condition means that forms of life that once were different are different no longer. Differences—large, class differences—disappear, as does the linguistic, normative, and cultural form each class assumes, the mutually alien and impermeable identities the form of life belonging to each class sustains, and the opportunities to collect a history of experience contributing to the reproduction of class identity in its established form. But what of the small differences of democratic society originally situated beyond the parameters of an analytical framework attuned only to the presence or absence of class differences, which now come into view when their conceptual extraterritoriality is illuminated against the class background on which Tocqueville's concept of difference is based? While large differences may disappear with the equality of condition, at least the permanent aristocratic class differences Tocqueville described, what impact does the equality of condition have on small differences? If we are to answer this question, we must look more closely at the logic of equality, specifically at how the equality of condition shapes the relationship between those who are different in small ways.

Democracy's Mimetic Dimension—Self-Creativity and Aesthetic Presentation as Imitation, or Individuality From the Point of View of the Artist (the Creator)

Democracy possesses its own peculiar pedagogy, Tocqueville contends. Simply by virtue of living in a democracy individuals are taught certain lessons, as it were, much as through an individual's acquisition of language cultural habits are shaped. Living in a particular society, for Tocqueville, appears to go hand in hand with learning its way of life and as a pedagogical consequence for that way of life to cultivate in its inhabitants ways of thinking and acting or inclinations to thinking and acting, and particular feelings and emotions. Though any idea or practice belonging to a democratic way of life can have pedagogical consequences, equality of condition is pedagogically singular, as it is definitive of the nature of democracy. The uniqueness of equality of condition in this regard can be appreciated best by recalling the terms Tocqueville uses synonymously to designate its centrality to democratic society—"principle of equality," "equality," the "social condition" of Americans, the "democratic principle," "the republican condition," the "democratic condition," and so forth. And also to be recalled is his announcement at the outset of his second volume, that "among the novel objects that attracted my attention during my stay in the United States nothing struck me more forcibly than the general equality of condition among the people."

Focusing on equality of condition's pedagogical features, Tocqueville refers to his analytical strategy in *Democracy in America* by explaining that he has "not undertaken to point out the origin and nature of all our inclinations and all our ideas; I have only endeavored to show how far both of them are *affected* by the equality of men's conditions" (*DA*II, vi; italics added). Then considering the ways that equality of condition pedagogically "affects" ideas, inclinations, and actions, Tocqueville argues, for example, that it "*suggests* to the human mind several ideas that would not have originated from any other source, and *modifies* almost all those previously entertained" (*DA*II, 33; italics added). Equality of condition "makes men *feel* their independence, *shows* them their own weakness ... *teaches* them that although they do not habitually require the assistance of others, a time almost always comes when they cannot do without it" (*DA*II, 175; italics added). It "*inspires* a spirit of independence," "*lodges* in the very depths of each man's mind and heart ... the instinctive inclination for political independence," "*reminds*" every citizen that he lives in society, "*impresses*" duties upon his mind, "*naturally disposes*" individuals to adopt certain maxims, and "has *created* in their minds many feelings and opinions which were unknown in the old aristocratic societies of Europe" (*DA*II, 288, 105, 4, v; italics added). And to "affects," "suggests," "modifies," "feel," "shows," "teaches," "inspires," "lodges," "reminds," "impresses," "naturally disposes," and "has created," Tocqueville adds "renders," "exposes," "leads," "fosters," "produces," "imparts," "awakens," "impels," and "encourages," among many other pedagogical features belonging to the equality of condition. With each pedagogical feature Tocqueville's purpose is the same, to demonstrate that in a democracy individuals are taught to think and act or inclinations to think and act as a "consequence" or "effect" or "result" of an equality of condition that suggests, modifies, teaches, inspires, imparts.... Indeed, Tocqueville draws *Democracy in America* to a close by indicating that the purpose of his work depended on his "having shown what ideas and feelings are *suggested* by the principle of equality" (*DA*II, 287; italics added).

Democratic institutions, Tocqueville now contends, "awaken and foster a *passion for equality*" (*DA*I, 201; italics added). The pedagogical consequence of the equality of condition, in other words, democracy creates in each individual an "ardent, insatiable, incessant, invincible" feeling and conviction that the equality each possesses in principle is an equality that can be possessed in fact (*DA*II, 97). Driven by a passion for equality individuals are not satisfied with the formal equality afforded by rights or education. Formal equality only enables them to "discover that they are not confined and fixed by any limits which force them to accept their present fortune," to "conceive the idea of increasing it," and to "attempt" to do so (*DA*II, 38). As the object of a passion for equality, moreover, not only does equality mean more than being able to imagine improving or attempting to improve one's economic circumstances. Its meaning *exceeds* even the achievement of the same *material* condition or position of another individual. Pursued passionately, equality translates into an unflagging determination to overcome any and every *difference*—material and otherwise—between oneself and others, as Tocqueville proposes more and less explicitly.

On one occasion Tocqueville argues quite powerfully, for example, "the slightest dissimilarity is odious in the midst of general uniformity; the more complete this uniformity is, the more unsupportable the sight of such a difference becomes" (*DA*II, 295). Similarly, though he believes conditions could never be reduced to a "perfect level" regardless of what efforts individuals make, Tocqueville speculates that even if equality of position were to be "absolute and complete," other inequalities would persist (*DA*II, 138). Pointing broadly to differences among individuals rather than disparities in material conditions as the object of the passion for equality, in this context Tocqueville specifically mentions the persistent inequality of minds that would continue beyond the utopian achievement of economic equality. Elsewhere Tocqueville gestures again toward a more expansive sense of difference. The same equality of condition that creates the desire to abolish difference, he goes on to suggest, continually proliferates new differences that offer ever-changing forms of inequality for the passion for equality to overcome. As a consequence of the independence that rights and education bestow upon each, Tocqueville explains, an individual "may choose his own path and proceed *apart* from all his fellow men" (*DA*II, 252; italics added). Democracy is so productive of difference, in fact, Tocqueville describes democratic ages as "times of rapid and incessant transformation," which only follows from his expectation that the multitude would begin "to take an interest in the labors of the mind" as a consequence of the "restless ambition that equality begets" (*DA*II, 252, 29). Surely, when Tocqueville proposes that "men will never establish any equality with which they can be contented," he is thinking not simply of democracy's residual material inequalities in condition and position. He is thinking also of the infinite variety of differences he observed within civil society that not even the most ardently, insatiably, incessantly, and invincibly passionate individuals could entirely overcome, who thus are each left ever passionately determined to do so (*DA*II, 138).

Despite his practice of equating difference with class, then, Tocqueville's interpretation of the passion for equality born from the equality of condition identifies the inequalities to be overcome as not exclusively economic or material inequalities or "large differences." Inequalities to which the passion for equality is directed are inclusive of "differences" in a wider sense, so that if Tocqueville does not recognize all "small differences" that I have revised his framework to include, his discussions of the passion for equality move us in that direction and permit us to consider small as well as large differences as the objects of the strongest desire fostered by democratic institutions. As Tocqueville says, even though the passion for equality is expressed with particular intensity as the "love of well-being" that favors an exact equality of material conditions and position, the taste for comfort must be regarded only "as the *original* source of that secret disquietude which the actions of the Americans betray" (*DA*II, 137; italics added). From this point on in our argument, then, as we consider the differences the passion for equality drives individuals to overcome, we will include the small as well as the large, class differences of which Tocqueville spoke.

While no individual's passion for equality is equal to the task of overcoming all large and small differences between the individual and others, as inequalities are surmounted no one's passion goes unrequited, which Tocqueville conveys through language that stresses movement in a democratic society. Movement is one of Tocqueville's most regular themes, especially in his second volume, and "constant motion," "constant activity," "everyone in motion," "universal tumult," "agitation," "such mobile elements," the "tumultuous intercourse of men," and many other similar expressions depict the movement of individuals overcoming differences and crossing thresholds into new levels of equality. Though differences are overcome with great energy and at such great speed, the passion for equality is not in the least subdued. To the contrary, Tocqueville insists that "it is natural that the love of equality should constantly increase together with equality itself," thus indicating that the equality of condition possesses a logic stubbornly independent of any achieved equality (*DA*II, 295). As equality rapidly progresses, soon members of the community "all live in close intercourse," coming to "stand so near" to each other that "all [are] closely seen," so that individuals become proportionately more sensitive to differences among them and turn their attention toward these other forms of inequality (*DA*II, 258, 216, 4). Tocqueville eloquently formulates the logic of increasing equality, individuals being drawn increasingly within sight of one another, and an increasing appetite for equality in all possible forms, by saying,

> it is certain that every member of the community will always find out several points about him which overlook his own position; and we may foresee that his looks will be doggedly fixed in that direction. When inequality of conditions is the common law of society, the most marked inequalities do not strike the eye; when everything is nearly on the same level, the slightest are marked enough to hurt it. Hence the desire of equality always becomes more insatiable in proportion as equality is more complete.[13] (*DA*II, 138)

Unable entirely to satisfy the passion for equality it awakens and fosters, equality of condition projects an ideal of complete equality that serves as a continual incitement to each individual to become equal to every other by overcoming every large and small difference that achieved levels of equality bring into sight. And the ideal of complete equality is an illusion from which no one is exempt, as everyone is implicated in the logic of equality owing to the "scantiness and insecurity of fortunes" in a democracy and the necessity for each having to work (*DA*II, 237).

How does the passion for equality propelled by the logic of equality of condition express itself? Or to ask this question in another way, what actually occurs when individuals overcome a large or small difference they discover between themselves and others? Living "so closely together" and able to "communicate and intermingle every day" so that they develop an intimate awareness of the differences from themselves in which others appear, members of the classes "imitate and emulate one another," Tocqueville observes (*DA*II, 39). Being near to one another "suggests to the people many ideas, notions, and desires that they would never have entertained if the distinctions in rank had been fixed and society at rest." Importantly, the many ideas, notions, and desires imitated and emulated by someone, or *adopted*, as imitation and emulation imply, do not necessarily belong to someone else of another class *per se*, or someone's sensitivity to a difference leading to the imitation of another is not necessarily rooted in either's class position. By the time individuals are thrown together so closely that they become acutely aware of the forms of differences taken by others, class distinctions already have been eroded by the equality of condition, to the point, as we have seen, that Tocqueville concludes that classes have disappeared. Equality of condition increasingly relates individuals to one another as the independent members of a people or a mass, albeit a people highly differentiated by the "many ideas, notions, and desires"—the many small differences—that distinguish them. Accordingly, Tocqueville's illustrations of the forms of small differences that are imitated and emulated mix examples of those having had a class basis with small differences that exceed a class definition.

He explains, for example, that in democratic countries the poor imitate the rich and the servant the master, but those who are farmers emulate those who are townsmen and those in the provinces imitate those in the metropolis. And even more generally, those who "read," Tocqueville notes, include "all the people," by which he means that many of the "many ideas, notions, and desires" individuals imitate they find in the literature read by others. As they "do not read with the same notions or in the same manner as they do in aristocratic societies," those in a democracy read whatever anyone else is reading regardless of the economic condition or position that once might have been associated with their newly acquired literary interest. So much do different literary genres circulate throughout the people that Tocqueville complains that Americans have "properly speaking, no literature," that is, no class-based literature or literatures that correspond to the particular interests of different classes (*DA*II, 56). Various literatures, like the adoption of "many ideas, notions, and desires," are thus among the non-class small differences—differences in cultural beliefs and values, ideological differences, and idiosyncratic intellectual differences—that are being imitated and emulated in a democratic society. No one, it seems, imitates primarily out of a need to better a class condition or position, but rather does so as the means of overcoming any and all small differences between himself and others that are perceived at close hand. Tocqueville makes a point of saying, in fact, that imitation occurs within a social context where no one "allows himself to be reduced to the mere material cares of life" (*DA*II, 39).

Democracy, we now begin to understand clearly, possesses a "mimetic dimension," as I will call it, through which individuals "imitate and emulate" each other, or as Tocqueville also says, "borrow" and "copy" from one another, and in doing so come to resemble those differences they imitate (*DA*II, 39, 74, 282, footnote 2). In the perpetual throe of a passion for equality awakened and fostered by the equality of condition, individuals *overcome differences* between themselves and others by *becoming different*, specifically by *adopting the form of difference taken by another*. To formulate Tocqueville's argument in the terms I have introduced earlier to conceptualize the aesthetics of Whitman's poetry, in a democracy individuals are aesthetically receptive to one another from the point of view of the artist (the creator).[14] The form of small difference in which every individual appears is imitated by others who do so to form themselves, their meanings and values, differently. In Whitman's language, the form of small difference in which every individual appears to others is an "object" that "draws from diffusion their meanings" and "gives them shape."

It would be inaccurate, then, to read Tocqueville, as he is so often read, as simply arguing that democratic society molds all its members in the same identical image so that eventually there will be no differences among them. This is an incomplete and misleading picture of the way in which individuals form themselves in a democracy as Tocqueville describes it. Individuals create themselves through a mimetic relation to others, indeed, through a mimetic relation to "all others," as we learn from Tocqueville when he says that in democratic ages "the whole assemblage [of individuals and communities] presents to the eye of the spectator one vast democracy, each citizen of which is a nation" (*DA*II, 74–75). "Each citizen of which is a nation" is a truly remarkable phrase with which Tocqueville conveys the image of each individual in a democracy becoming different in *all* the ways *all* others in society are different. It is an image of an individual who, becoming different, is at the same time himself and someone else, himself and many others, who "hopes," as Tocqueville puts it in other words, "to appear what he is not" (*DA*II, 51). Becoming different in the ways others are different and different in those ways from himself, each individual in a democracy develops identities that are many "identities"—many ideas, notions, and desires—in one. The consequence of the aesthetically receptive activity of copying and borrowing, imitating and emulating small differences, is that individual identity becomes multiple or plural. From Whitman's point of view, the aesthetic point of view of the artist (the creator), individuals become diverse through the diversity of different forms (appearances, surfaces) they adopt, just as Whitman becomes diverse through the diversity of different forms he adopts.¹⁵ Tocqueville offers additional support for my redescription of his work in aesthetic terms when he claims that in democratic communities "each man instantly sees all his fellows when he surveys himself" (*DA*II, 73). Each individual sees himself, in other words, in the form of the differences that originally belonged to others and that, overcome as the passion for equality compelled, enabled him to create himself differently from what he is.

Once uncovered, and then formulated from Whitman's aesthetic point of view, the mimetic dimension of democracy's passion for equality provides a dramatically revised perspective on Tocqueville's critique of democratic society. Differences do not disappear in democracy as Tocqueville had alleged. By becoming equal to, the same as, or resembling others, individuals actually become different in the way others are different, which means that when we take all individual differences together, collectively differences are sustained. For each individual, differences are pluralized or multiplied; hence for the mass, differences are undiminished. In light of the aesthetically receptive, mimetic relationship between identity and difference, Tocqueville's images of democratic homogeneity and uniformity also can be revised. Democracy's "mass" is not one, consistent, unvaried form. Both mass and the individuals collected together as the mass are composed of small differences, differences distinguished from one another not in terms of their magnitude, which only would reduce their variations to a third term (class), but in terms of their kind, type, or quality, as was Whitman's "old feuillage."¹⁶

Many of those claims made by Tocqueville seemingly at odds or irreconcilable with his strong image of a homogeneous and uniform mass are now more intelligible. When he remarks, for instance, that it "seems natural that in a democratic community men, things, and opinions should be forever changing their form," Tocqueville's comment may be taken as a description of the way a diversity of small differences varies in relation to the way in which those who make up the mass exchange appearances with one another through perpetual imitation and emulation. Would individuals who are constantly changing their forms by adopting the forms of others not appear together as a collectivity changing its form? What is true for Tocqueville's image of the mass is especially true for his image of the individual. In a phrase that from our revised perspective seems stunningly postmodern, Tocqueville declares that individuals in a democratic society "perpetually differ from themselves" (*DA*II, 58). Tocqueville, obviously our "contemporary," from our revised perspective is referring to what we think of as the "discontinuity" characterizing late modern individuals whose identities integrate different forms of meaning and value originally belonging to different forms of life that had been *exclusive* of one another and often *opposed*. Neither society nor the individual could be more diversely different from the uniform mass they appear to be to Tocqueville, who also conceives of the diverse forms of meaning and value formed within democracy—and thus offered as possible forms of life each individual can imitate—as displaying the measure of "mankind for the first time in the broadest light." "All that belongs to the existence of the human race taken as a whole . . . its vicissitudes and its future," and Tocqueville includes fortunes, feelings, wants, professions, opinions, beliefs, and thoughts among the social forms whose diversity democracy encourages, become forms of difference through which individuals mimetically form themselves, becoming different from who they are, so that they perpetually differ from themselves (*DA*II, 75).

To appreciate the immense breadth of small differences connoted by "mankind" and "human race" that an individual's passion for equality would dispose him to imitate requires a clearer impression of what Tocqueville means by the "movement" democratic society generates and the consequences it entails. Confronted with an ever-changing diversity of differences, each individual's aesthetically receptive activity of imitation, the movement of overcoming differences by creating oneself through the forms of others, would be uninterrupted and endless. If we now multiply the uninterrupted and endless movement of the one by that of the many, we arrive at a composite of what Tocqueville must have believed he was witnessing when he described relations among individuals in a democratic society with language such as "tumultuous." What appeared to Tocqueville as tumultuous likely appeared even more so to each of those intimately involved in mimesis and surrounded by others similarly involved. Such mimetic movement would be overwhelming, at least to the extent that no one could avoid concluding that change is constant and the only constant or, in Tocqueville's words, each would come to believe that the "prevailing notion is that nothing abides" and would be "haunted by the thought of mutability"(*DA*II, 188).

One consequence of living in constant anticipation of change, "the image of an ideal but always fugitive perfection presents itself to the human mind," Tocqueville argues, a belief in "an indefinite faculty for improvement" or "indefinite perfectibility of the human race," as he also refers to it (*DA*II, 34, 73). "Indefinite perfectibility," Tocqueville appears to be saying, is the belief that there are no limits to the equality of overcoming difference by becoming different, for which democracy creates such a passion. At some, more than implicit level of understanding, Tocqueville's argument suggests, imitation would be understood to be without limits, identity would be seen as able to be limitlessly different, as Whitman envisioned, and "becoming" someone different rather than "being" always the same one would become the norm.[17]

Working in harmony with the idea of indefinite perfectibility to promote mimesis, there are also consequences to memory and to the perception of time that follow from the expectation of unremitting movement and change. Incessantly changing themselves, surrounded by others changing and only anticipating change, each individual, Tocqueville proposes, becomes "unattached to that of his fellows by tradition," and ties that unite one generation to another are "relaxed or broken" (*DA*II, 58, 4). Being forgotten, the values and ideals of past generations cease to influence the present, which then alone "engages and absorbs" each one so that his passion for equality and for its aesthetic practices of imitation unfold free of the aristocratic burden of creating a present that perpetuates the past" (*DA*II, 247). Unfettered by memory, the individual is released from limitations on continually becoming different from himself in the present. The present is repeated as an unending series of changing forms that extends into a future, whose constantly changing form becomes indistinct from the present and hidden. Unencumbered by the past with the future collapsed to the present, the repetition of becoming different through imitation allows the individual to know but one measure of time, the time in which the mimesis of becoming different without limitation recurs, the "democratic time" as which Whitman encourages us to think of time in a democratic society.[18]

With the idea of democracy's "mimetic dimension," as I call it, I begin the task of *redescribing*, in the aesthetic terms I developed through Whitman's poetic forms, Tocqueville's conceptualization of the relations among individuals encouraged by the equality of condition, the passion for equality that the equality of condition awakens and fosters, and the imitation of difference that expresses the desire for equality. Tocqueville's concepts largely focus our attention on each individual's becoming different in sight of others, where each one seeing others at close hand allows him to become aware of their small differences, which provide the forms of difference through which each forms himself differently through imitation. In aesthetic terms, the practice of imitation orients individuals receptively to the forms of difference in which others appear on their surfaces (which will be considered more extensively later), and enables each on his own surface to adopt a different form in which to appear in plain view. Since Tocqueville's argument focuses for the most part on the surface forms of aesthetic presentation individuality creates through its adoption of the surfaces of others, he offers few insights into aesthetic individuality's self-creativity beneath the surface, in its depths, where individuality forms its own meanings and values for the diverse forms of difference it imitates. And what insights he does provide into the deeper levels of self-creativity do not correspond to aesthetic counterparts quite as readily as imitation, emulation, copying, and borrowing do with the aesthetics of an individuality creating and presenting itself differently on its surface.

Despite these qualifications, however, we are not left without a trail of evidence for presentational self-creativity at the deeper layers of individual existence. In particular, while invoking his familiar image of members of a democratic community who "never differ much from each other and naturally stand so near that they may all at any time be fused in one general mass," Tocqueville speaks of the "numerous and artificial distinctions [that] spring up by means of which every man hopes to keep himself aloof lest he should be carried away against his will in the crowd" (*DA*II, 216). Tocqueville's context for this remark is his discussion of the "multitude of small private circles," or private forms of association, that arise in opposition to the dominant tendency for the "state of society or laws," that is, for the equality of condition and its passion for imitation, to "render men so much alike" (*D*AII, 215). Reformulating Tocqueville's observations in aesthetic terms, he appears to want us to imagine individuals' reactions to the increasingly widespread adoption and appearance of forms of feeling, opinion, belief, and thought that occur through their own as well as others' practices of imitation and emulation. At a level beneath their surfaces, whose forms through imitation come to resemble the plurality of surfaces of others who are different, individuals would create "numerous and artificial distinctions," independently authored meanings and values, they would later bring to the surface to present as variations of the originally borrowed and copied forms. Although Tocqueville does not introduce precisely analogous terms for the aesthetic idea of individuals' creating in the depths of their existence, his examples of variations in the surface forms of difference move in that direction where he reveals elements of autonomy and originality in individuals' self-creativity and presentation.

Describing variations in the "manners" of a democratic society, for instance, he explains that rather than being "molded . . . upon an ideal model proposed for general imitation," manners lack coherence because they are based upon the "feelings and notions of each individual," who "behaves after his own fashion" (*D*AII, 217–18). To "behave after one's own fashion," of course, means to form something in one's own way, in a way, in other words, that is rooted in who one is, in one's identity, which is visible on the surface in manners and in other forms of feeling, opinion, belief and thought, but is more and deeper than what is revealed on the surface. If "manners are characterized by a number of lesser diversities, but not by any great differences," as Tocqueville argues, if manners are distinguished by small, democratic rather than large, aristocratic differences, accounted for aesthetically the differences in the forms of manners on the surface must originate in the differences in the forms of manners at a depth. What diverse forms of difference individuals are receptive to on the surface and imitate they draw beneath the surface, to be fashioned after their "own fashion" in their depths before being presented on the surface for the imitation and deeper forms of self-creativity by others.

Perhaps the language of individuation and individualization would further clarify the levels on which the aesthetics of individuality's self-creativity unfolds. *Individuation*, individuals differentiating themselves from one another on the surface, occurs through the self-creativity of *individualization* in their depths, where individuals create highly personal meanings and values through the forms of difference they imitate and adopt (in Whitman's words, through "objects that draw from diffusion [their] meanings and give them shape"). Hence we can understand why Tocqueville says that in a democracy, where master and servant are "naturally almost alike" owing to the equality of condition, they also almost "always remain strangers to one another" (*D*AII, 179). Becoming alike on the surface as a consequence of mimesis, master and servant are without the "common reminiscences" that had established resemblances at a deeper level of identity between their aristocratic counterparts. Rather than formed as common memories through a common history, the depths of individuals—as in the case of master and servant—whose social positions and ties are no longer fixed by large, class differences, are now formed by each independently, or individualized. When individuals then bring these depths to the surface, they would seem as "strangers" to one another, to whom their "foreignness" would be the mark of individuation differentiating them from one another on the surface and proof of the individualization occurring below in their depths. Along with imitation through which the forms of individual differences unfold, individuation and the individualization in which it is rooted reflect the self-creativity of an aesthetic individuality.

Redescribed as democracy's mimetic dimension, Tocqueville's description of the equality of condition brings to light individuals regularly engaged in the aesthetic activity of forming and creating and presenting themselves differently on the surface and in their depths as a consequence of their membership in a democratic society. Aesthetic individuality appears to be a democratic achievement. Permitting individuals movement between social positions and assembling all together within sight of one another, the equality of condition creates a passion for equality that encourages each individual to become different by adopting the forms in which others appear to be different in small ways. Out of such an aesthetically receptive desire to become different and within view of and viewing all others, individuals develop an acute sensitivity to differences as they appear on the surface, which accelerates the movement with which each looks receptively to the surfaces of the small differences of others for forms to become different themselves. On their surfaces and in their depths, in their forms of appearance and where they hide themselves from view, individuals become plural through the plurality of different surfaces they imitate, and the frenetic movement of the aesthetic activity of all persuades each that change is itself immutable. From the impression that change is immutable arises the notion of indefinite human perfectibility, and from the reality of immutable change a forgetting of the past occurs. That individuals know that no one is or can be perfect, and through forgetting rescue their identity from submersion in images from the past, further releases their individuality from limitations on creating it aesthetically in different forms. Individuals then present themselves aesthetically in forms of difference whose multiplicity may parallel the breadth of small differences embodied by the nation or by mankind. By constantly becoming different through the aesthetics of individuality's self-creativity, individuals cannot but discover themselves in part, and thus their identity remains a mystery for which they discover as its final answer only that their self-creativity and self-discovery are indistinguishable, which corresponds to the relationship between individuality and identity as Whitman understood it.[19]

Democracy's aesthetic features highlight the unaesthetic qualities of an aristocratic form of life. Democracy is inclusive of small differences within a framework of an equality of condition that breaks down social distinctions by creating a dynamic through which the individual forms its self and its identity differently. Aristocracy establishes large differences within a framework of inequality of condition that maintains permanently enclosed communities whose exclusivity freezes identity in its socially determined form. Whereas democracy makes individuals in their different forms visible to all others in theirs, aristocracy makes individuals in their different positions unaware of all others in theirs. Whereas democracy encourages each to become different, and makes each intently aware of the possibilities for becoming different in the forms of difference that surround the individual, aristocracy makes the form of difference in which each one appears seem to be unchangeable. Whereas democracy encourages individuals to view whatever form they become to be an imperfect presentation that always is improved upon by becoming different yet again, depending on the class of which an individual is a member aristocracy encourages each one to view his or her form as perfectly natural or capable of a higher perfection, either of which sets an absolute limit to what one may become. Whereas democracy further encourages becoming different by encouraging forgetting and starting over each time anew, aristocracy is wedded to memories that provide models for who one must continue to be in the present and the future. Whereas from the outside democracy appears as an infinitely variegated and constantly changing montage of small differences, aristocracy appears as a mosaic of inert primary colors from whose essential differences no other colors can be formed. Whereas democracy facilitates ever-quickening movement, aristocracy is perpetually immobile. Democracy substitutes "becoming" for the "being" of aristocracy, and replaces aristocracy's static relationship between classes with an ecstatic relationship between individuals. Democracy makes individual identity plural, discontinuous, in contradiction and nonidentical with itself. Aristocracy makes individuality unitary, continuous, consistent and identical with itself. Democracy is productive of an aesthetic individuality. Individuality in an aristocracy is artless.

Representing Difference: A Sensibility to Violence in the Aesthetics of Individuality

Aesthetic individuality, which now appears to be the creation of a democratic society as Tocqueville describes it, discovers in others the different forms through which it becomes different from itself. Individuality cannot create itself differently, however, without first creating images of those differences whose forms it desires to adopt. Individuality's self-creativity on its surface and in its depths, its aesthetic *presentation*, in other words, requires the *representation* of forms of difference belonging to others. What are the consequences meted out to those who are different by an individuality whose aesthetic presentations require the representations of the forms in which the differences of others appear? Is there not only creativity in the aesthetic individuality Tocqueville enables us to find in a democratic society, but a sensibility to violence in the ways this individuality represents difference as it forms itself aesthetically? Does the individual, whose membership in a democratic society enables its self-creativity to be receptive to others from Whitman's aesthetic point of view, also display the artist's sensibility to violence in creativity that is embodied in his poetry's forms of representation? Although an answer to this question will be best found in Tocqueville's argument by examining the logic of the relationship between identity and difference as it is formed in a democracy by an individuality receptive to others aesthetically, he also takes up the issue indirectly and offers some clue as to what that examination likely will show.

As was evident in our discussion of democracy's mimetic dimension, however closely the equality of condition throws individuals together, each individual who becomes different from himself originally stands apart from others, independent of those whose differences provide the forms for his individuality's self-creativity. Tocqueville is fascinated by this independence, which is the basis for his famous critique of democratic "individualism." Contrary to the interdependency of individuals he associated with the interconnected ranks and castes of the privileged class in an aristocracy, Tocqueville believed the principal characteristic distinguishing the individual in America was the appeal "only to the individual effort of his own understanding" (*DA*II, 3). Tocqueville described this independence of mind in several ways.

"Everyone shuts himself up tightly within himself and insists upon judging the world from there," Tocqueville reports; "they acquire the habit of always considering themselves as standing alone, and they are apt to imagine that their whole destiny is in their own hands" (*DA*II, 4, 99). Americans' "natural Cartesianism," though, as Tocqueville described their habit of making judgments independently and thus displaying an implicit belief in Descartes's solitary *cogito*, slides into certain "dangerous propensities" (*DA*II, 22). Intellectually independent to the point of having to rely more or less completely on themselves, individuals begin to form judgments without taking the views of others into consideration, which leads them to develop a somewhat arrogant self-confidence. And such complete independence of all to obey "no other guide than their own will" can slip further into the tendency of each to become isolated from every other, to become self-absorbed and to "concentrate . . . [his] attention upon himself" (*DA*II, 287, 22). Inflated self-confidence, isolation, and self-absorption are at the heart of "individualism," that disposition of each to "sever himself from the mass of his fellows and to draw apart with his family and friends, so that after he has thus formed a little circle of his own, he willingly leaves society at large to itself" (*DA*II, 98). Taken together, these several forms of independence, the initial independence of judgment and self-reliance and the extreme propensities to arrogance, isolation, self-absorption, and the withdrawal from public life marked by individualism, are consequences following from the right to "judge of all things for oneself" granted by the equality of condition (*DA*II, 194; see also, for example, 5–6, 287).

Yet, as we have seen, other consequences of equality, specifically the passion for equality and the inclinations to the imitation and emulation of differences it awakens and fosters, oppose the individual's extreme tendencies to independence. Imitation and emulation, individuality's aesthetic receptivity to difference, draw individuals near to one another by making each aware of and dependent upon others whose differences he would emulate, others who are outside the narrow circle of family and friends and who are distributed throughout civil society. At the same time, while aesthetic individuality's self-creativity enables it to avoid the extremes of independence expressed as arrogance, isolation, self-absorption, and individualism, it is not hostile to independence as such. Aesthetic individuality presupposes an individual who stands apart from others, and through its independence is able to survey and be mimetically receptive to the diversity of forms in which differences appear.

Most importantly, the independence that is presupposed by aesthetic individuality also seems to be one of its ends, as though the independence individuality requires for becoming different from oneself must necessarily be defended in the process of its self-creativity. It is here, in a struggle for independence that its aesthetic receptivity makes it impossible to escape, that individuality's sensibility to violence in the representation of difference seems to be born. Tocqueville argues, as we recall from what was said earlier, that "numerous and artificial distinctions spring up by means of which every man hopes to keep himself aloof lest he be carried away against his will by the crowd." In aesthetic terms, Tocqueville appears to be suggesting that the activity of individuals becoming different from themselves is also a form of *resistance* to the pressure each feels to lose one's identity to a collective or hegemonic cultural identity, an identity Tocqueville thought of as the "tyranny of the majority." An individual appears to safeguard his independence through resistance to the pressure to conform to a shared identity by creating himself differently in the diversity of forms, in the diversity of "numerous and artificial distinctions," in Tocqueville's words, that proliferate within the sphere of private life. In the struggle for independence against a collective identity through individuality's aesthetic self-creativity, an individual's conflict with hegemony would seem to entail a twofold recognition. Individuals may recognize, if only tacitly, that just as the identity of one's own difference for which it struggles exceeds the shared, collective identity of the society as a whole, each form of difference belonging to others also exceeds the identity attributed to it. And it may recognize as well, again if only implicitly, that identity is imposed on difference wherever it is equated with the difference it represents, much as a shared cultural identity is an imposition on differences distinguishing individuals. Hence, aesthetic individuality appears to be a creation of democratic society through which individuals maintain the independence of their identities in a way that at some level entails an awareness of the violence associated with the representation of difference.

If a sensibility to the violence in representation is truly characteristic of individuality, though, it will be evident from an examination of all aspects of the *form* of individuality's aesthetic relationship to difference as it creates its identity through a mimetic receptivity to others. What will come into view, in other words, are the representational logic of individuality's aesthetic relation to difference as it creates its identity mimetically and the consequences of its logic of representation for others who are different in small ways. If the logic of individuality's aesthetic relation to difference mirrors Whitman's poetic forms of representation, the sensibility to violence embodied in Whitman's poetry should also appear in individuality's aesthetic relationship to the world.

Individuality's Orientation to the Surfaces of Small Differences

From Tocqueville's description of the relations among individuals imitating one another's differences, individuality appears to be aesthetic not only in the ways it creatively forms itself but in its receptivity to others whose small differences it represents as the forms through which it then will become different. Assembling individuals near to one another, we have learned, democracy calls the senses into play. Tocqueville speaks of individuals in a democracy "listening" to each other, and his descriptions of the close intercourse of members of democratic societies encourage us to imagine an awareness of each by others as involving all the senses (*DAII*, 74). Among the senses, though, democracies appear to privilege vision, as Tocqueville conveyed by saying that living "so closely together" and coming to "stand so near," "all [are] closely seen," and with other language stressing the significance of seeing and being seen in democratic ensembles. Tocqueville mentions the "rapid glance" with which the daily incidents of democratic life are appreciated. He notes the excitement with which democratic nations each "survey" one another. And he describes the speech, dress, and daily actions of the denizens of democracies as "too familiar" to become subjects of poetry, which should concern itself not with what is ordinarily seen but only with that which can be idealized (*DAII*, 43, 73, 75). The importance of vision demonstrates that individuals in a democratic society are receptive primarily to the ways each other *appears*, and receptivity to the appearance of difference is receptivity to its *surface*. Tying vision and receptivity to surfaces together explicitly, Tocqueville supports this conclusion by saying that "there is nothing upon which men set more store" in a democracy than "the outward form of human actions" (*DAII*, 217). Drawing out the aesthetic implications of aesthetic individuality's receptivity to surfaces, we can say that as each individual forms its self differently through the forms of small difference others take, it does so by representing these differences in images as they appear on the surface, just as Whitman's poetic forms of representation represent differences as they appear on the surface.[20]

Individuality's All-Inclusive Orientation to Small Differences

If the form of aesthetic individuality's receptivity to the small differences presented by others is to the surfaces of differences, does an aesthetically receptive individual represent surfaces selectively, including some differences and excluding others, or is there another principle at work in individuality's relationship to difference? As individuals imitate and emulate one another, creating themselves differently through receptivity to the diverse surfaces of others, each comes to resemble every other so as to constantly differ from himself, as Tocqueville explained. Relating to one another aesthetically, all become "similarly different," we should say, each individual separately presenting a plurality of different forms culled from the diversity of small differences with which all are visibly and commonly surrounded. In the midst of this equality of condition, where "each individual man becomes more like *all* the rest," Tocqueville argues, "a habit grows up of ceasing to notice the citizens and considering only the people, of overlooking individuals to think only of their kind," of forming "general ideas" (*DA*II, 31, 13–17; italics added). Surrounded by others like oneself, by individuals whose aesthetic receptivity enables each to become similarly different or "more like *all* the rest," each individual's receptivity to the similarity of small differences presented by every other individual encourages receptivity to all differences together at the same time. Aesthetic individuality appears to shift attention from "any one portion of mankind" to the "whole," from the "multitude of different objects," as Tocqueville puts it, to the idea of "unity," from the diversity of particulars to the universal (*DA*II, 15, 31). Through its aesthetic receptivity, then, individuality's representation of some differences leads it necessarily to the representation of all other differences as they appear on the surface. The form of individuality's receptivity to surfaces is to be all-inclusive of their diversity, as though to be different in any way means to be different in any and all of the ways every other is different, or to reiterate Tocqueville's words once again, "to be more like *all* the rest." Receptive to differences all-inclusively, aesthetic individuality excludes no surface as a difference through which it may become different itself, and thus reproduces the representational practice of all-inclusiveness characteristic of Whitman's poetic forms of representation.[21]

Individuality's Orientation to the Equality, Sufficiency, and Uniqueness of Small Differences

To judge from Tocqueville's description of the inclination of each individual to shift his attention from the part to the whole, which I have *redescribed in* aesthetic terms as individuality's all-inclusive representation of small differences, aesthetic individuality's receptivity appears to represent all differences as being equal. Since individuality's image of universality can be formed from its aesthetic interest in "*any* one portion of mankind," on its face there is nothing to suggest that the representation of the whole individuality forms is inclusive of parts, of differences, that it in any way believes to be unequal. This is only to beg the question, however, whether individuality's aesthetic receptivity relates it to the small differences of which it is representationally all-inclusive as though each were the equal of every other. In Tocqueville's estimation, as the equality of condition progresses and the passion for equality enables each to become more like all the rest, "the less prone does each man become to place implicit faith in a certain man or a certain class of men" (*DA*II, 10). In aesthetic terms, we might say that because differences on their surfaces all appear to be the same, since all appear to be similarly different, in other words, no surface offers an individual reason to privilege its representation as being in any way more valuable than any other. Individuals receptive to others aesthetically would not be receptive to others *differently* by virtue of their surfaces being different. Or as Tocqueville expresses it in a direct reference to democracy in America, capturing perfectly individuality's representation of the equality of differences in its aesthetic receptivity to all, "an American ... does not think himself bound to pay particular attentions to any of his fellow citizens" (*DA*II, 172). Quite like Whitman's poetic forms, individuality represents every small difference as equal to every other, and thus no difference is less eligible than any other for aesthetic representation.[22]

Moreover, as a consequence of its aesthetic receptivity to the equality of differences, although individuality is aesthetically inclined to discover and recognize the differences in others as ways in which it may itself become different, it does not take its own form of difference to be less than adequate, as might be suspected of those who are constantly changing their form. Because the equality of condition and its passion for equality aesthetically orient each to every other receptively as to someone who is different though equal, individuality's aesthetic representation of the equality of small differences seems to encourage each to think of himself as equal to every other appearing differently. Individuality does not exclude its own difference from the equality it attributes aesthetically to the differences of others. So when Tocqueville argued that in the context of an equality of condition an American "does not think himself bound to pay particular attentions to any of his fellow citizens," he added that neither "does he require such attentions from them towards himself." Can we not conclude that individuals who believe themselves to be equal to all others and consequently are in no need of any special recognition surely must feel their own forms of difference to be sufficient? To be sure, individuality's feeling of sufficiency or sense of adequacy must be what Tocqueville acknowledges when in America he observes that individuals who "meet by accident ... do not care to display any more than to conceal their position in the world" (*DA*II, 169). It were as though the air of nonchalance an individual expressed in the presence of others was rooted in his belief that since the indefiniteness of perfectibility converted perfection to an ideal against which he and all others could never be measured, no one could be more perfect than he or anyone else. Perpetually differing from himself, each always was as perfect as he could be, and thus in all respects as sufficient as Whitman's poetry found to be all the differences the world contained.[23]

Finally, though we already have considered Tocqueville's claims about the acute sensitivity to difference created by the passion for equality, the aesthetic aspect of this sensitivity should be highlighted. Moved by a passion for equality, individuals are inclined to seek out differences aggressively, to recognize in what ways others are different from themselves, regardless of how apparently insignificant these differences may be. The determination to discover and recognize difference is animated by an aesthetic impulse. Receptive to others through an aesthetic interest in becoming different, individuality *sees differences*. Redescribed in aesthetic terms, then, by reason of its aesthetic nature an individuality driven by a passion for equality is necessarily receptive to the way in which others on their surfaces appear different—distinctive, peculiar, unusual, in a word, unique—just as the representational practices of Whitman's poetry found all surfaces to be different.[24]

Individuality's Receptivity to Small Differences

Every aspect of aesthetic individuality's relationship to difference that has been considered thus far as a consequence of the equality of condition appears to be governed by a logic of representation encouraging individuals to be open to one another without exception or qualification, just as Whitman's poetic forms of representation open his art to the world and to all the worlds of meanings the world contains. "Receptivity" is summarily redescriptive of the aesthetic features of such openness to the world. Certainly, without proceeding any further, by itself "imitation" immediately conveys receptivity, which Tocqueville affirms by introducing the phrase "assimilate him *to* all his fellows" to describe individuals imitating and emulating one another (*DAI*, 13; italics added). Yet, receptivity does not only mean an interest in becoming different through the differences with which one is surrounded. Beyond this fundamental receptivity to forms of difference, individuality's receptivity is expressed in each of the formal elements of its aesthetic relationship to the world of differences.

Aesthetic individuality's orientation to the surfaces of difference expresses a receptivity toward every small difference that can be heard or felt, especially seen, that our every sense makes us aware of. Individuality's resemblance to any particular difference or portion of the whole surrounding it leads it to form an all-inclusive orientation toward every difference forming the whole, as we saw, a receptivity to small differences that would allow individuality to become as unrestrictedly different as the whole. Individuality's disposition to view all small differences with which it is surrounded as being equal, indicates that its aesthetically receptive sensibility does not find any difference more or less valuable or meaningful than any other difference through which it can become different. And since an individuality aesthetically receptive to difference recognizes each to be equal to every other, its principle of including all small differences opens it to an interest in every particular difference. What is aesthetically striking and attractive in the details of every difference would not be wasted upon an individuality that is intensely sensitive to differences in all their uniquely demonstrative forms. Nor is an individuality so aesthetically receptive to the differences of others in the least reticent or shy about displaying its own newly acquired forms of difference. Apparently the strongest inclination encouraged by the equality of condition, the passion for equality expressed as an aesthetic interest in imitating others likewise encourages all to "feel extreme pleasure in exhibiting" the ways in which they distinguish themselves from the small differences of others (*DA*II, 226). An individual taking pleasure in such exhibitions must be confident of the sufficiency of the different forms in which he appears, and no doubt has been taught by the equality of condition that encourages each to be receptive to all other forms of difference that all will be similarly receptive to him.

Aesthetic receptivity has a variety of consequences. Where the equality of condition prevails, Tocqueville argues, "men unacquainted with one another are very ready to frequent the same places and find neither peril nor advantage in the free interchange of their thoughts" (*DA*II, 169). Aesthetic receptivity seems to be at work here, for Tocqueville seems to be describing far more than the simple democratic tolerance of different ideas. Conceptualized in aesthetic terms, he appears to suggest that equality removes both the fear (the "peril") of the unknown that leads thinking to abolish what is different by equating it with one's own beliefs and the instrumental interest (the "advantage") that distorts the meaning and value of the different views received. As a second and similar effect, Tocqueville describes the "sympathies" that individuals form for one another under the equality of condition, specifically the capacity of each to "think and feel in nearly the same manner," to "judge in a moment of the sensations of all the others," to enter into every possible form of "wretchedness" (*DA*II, 165). This "softening" or "mildness" in "customs," as he also refers to the development in each individual of sympathies for all, is a response to others that "can exist only between those who are alike," or in aesthetic terms between those who come to resemble the ways in which each other differently appears. Clearly, the sympathetic identification of each with the feelings of others Tocqueville is describing, and that he includes prominently among the motivations that enable one individual to come to the assistance of another, seems to be empathy, which can be redescribed aesthetically as an extreme form of receptivity.

Last, Tocqueville underscores though regrets the disappearance of "notions of honor" that follows from democracy's equality of condition. In aristocracies, different ideas of honor were associated with different castes, each idea articulating what those occupying a particular rank held to be valuable and estimable, thereby establishing codes of behavior ensuring the exclusivity of their group. Against this aristocratic background the disappearance of honor as an *aesthetic* phenomenon is readily apparent. In aesthetic terms, receptivity, we might say, wants for the "honor" that affirms being one way to the complete exclusion of becoming any other way. For want of codes of honor and similar disciplines stipulating who can and who cannot share in the identity of a group, receptivity destroys the normative boundaries of groups that create a territory whose diversity of small differences are off-limits to others who would find them aesthetically interesting.

Attachment and Intimacy

Individuality's aesthetic receptivity to the diversity of differences with which it is surrounded dissolves any boundaries that stood as a barrier to identity's formative adoption of the forms of small difference lying outside of it. In its inclusiveness of small differences as the means for overcoming inequality by becoming different, receptivity also expresses the *dependency* upon difference characteristic of an individuality that creates itself differently through the imitation of the forms of small difference in which others appear on the surface. Receptivity expresses the "attachment" to the surfaces of difference without which individuality could not become different from itself, the same attachment to the world expressed in Whitman's poetic representation of all that lay outside of him.[25] Having seen how the equality of condition creates the passion for equality from which individuality's aesthetic receptivity to diversity and its attachment to difference arise, we should follow Tocqueville one step further to discover if individuality's aesthetic attachment to difference is secure. After all, it seems clear from Tocqueville's argument that as the defining property of democracy, equality of condition appears to press individuality predominantly in the direction of an imitative, aesthetic receptivity to difference as its means of overcoming inequality, so that we would expect its attachment to small differences to be undisturbed. Does this mean that individuality's aesthetic receptivity would prevail over all other inclinations, interests, or allegiances that might disrupt its attachment to surfaces, regardless of how powerful they may be?

With regard to this question, Tocqueville's description of the consequences of equality for the individual's relation to God is especially important. Strong religious convictions could surely impose moral restrictions on the different forms of life to which individuals could be aesthetically receptive. And it is in this respect that the importance of God is foregrounded in Tocqueville's work, when we consider that he was preoccupied with the exceptional contribution that "customs," specifically religion, made to the maintenance of democracy. Religion, above all for Tocqueville, provided a source of moral authority that guided the individual's understanding and use of rights. Within a democratic society, at least in light of Tocqueville's argument, the place that God occupies in an individual's life thus becomes the test case for determining whether his aesthetic attachment to difference created by the equality of condition can be dislodged.

Tocqueville found that however singular the authority of God in the lives of individuals, at least in America, as a source of morality the supernatural, as he so

AESTHETIC INDIVIDUALITY AS A DEMOCRATIC ACHIEVEMENT

often refers to God, over time is eroded by the equality of condition and eventually acquires a precarious standing. Describing the exaggerated intellectual self-reliance he traced to the equality of condition, Tocqueville added that as a result of the habit of "fixing the standard of their judgment in themselves alone," individuals

> conclude that everything in the world may be explained, and that nothing in it transcends the limits of the understanding. Thus they fall to denying what they cannot comprehend; which leaves them ... an almost insurmountable distaste for whatever is supernatural. (*DA*II, 4)

Encouraging an antipathy to the supernatural, toward the invisible, we might say, the equality of condition orients the individual toward the visible. Tocqueville makes this point differently by arguing that the equality that "begets in man the desire of judging of everything for himself ... gives him in all things a taste for the tangible and the real," a claim he later reiterates by saying that "equality does not destroy the imagination, but lowers its flight to the level of the earth" (*DA*II, 41, 208). So the receptivity that equality encourages, as we now learn again but from another perspective, is to that which is directly available to the senses. To redescribe Tocqueville's argument in aesthetic terms, it is a receptivity, an "attachment," to what is sensuous, a dependency upon the surfaces of that whose tangible, real, and earthly immediacy provides the indispensable forms through which individuality creates itself. By also nurturing a "distaste for whatever is supernatural," equality prevents it from interfering with individuality's attachment to what is sensuous, or the distaste for the supernatural is evidence of such an attachment. In either case an interest in the supernatural and an attachment to differences are opposed to each other, with equality securing the latter and displacing the former. Tocqueville does not deny the importance to America of Christianity and its concept of God, of course. He does stress, however, that Christianity's influence increasingly extends only to certain well-established dogmas beyond which it does not venture for fear of fatally colliding with democracy's naturally Cartesian independence of mind and the distaste for the supernatural it fosters. Yet even within the limits of its influence Christianity indirectly encourages the attachment to the sensuous through its emphasis on material prosperity, Tocqueville notes, anticipating Weber's analysis of the Protestant ethic. "But the American preachers are constantly referring to earth," he observes, "and it is only with great difficulty that they can divert their attention from it" (*DA*II, 127).

To flesh out the aesthetic nature of attachment, it is not quite enough to think of it as individuality's steadfast and sensuous dependency on the surfaces of diverse small differences it imitates. Although individuality cannot become different from itself without its attachment to the surface, the way in which the equality of condition fosters attachment also suggests an intimacy that enhances the attachment to differences that individuality forms. Tocqueville's many images of individuals being thrown closely together in a democracy, seeing and hearing and touching and talking and sympathizing with one another, and his images of the acute sensitivity to difference each feels, all suggest an association of each with others that breeds a familiarity with what can be sensed on the surface. Such a familiarity closely resembles the intimacy with which the world's diversity of differences are represented in Whitman's poetic forms.[26] Indeed, Tocqueville's frequent comparisons of the distance between individuals and classes in an aristocracy and the eclipse of distance between individuals and classes in democratic society seem deliberately intended to thematize the experience of intimacy. As the equality of condition progresses, what was once distant to each—feelings, experiences, beliefs, judgments, the small differences of others in all their forms—is brought near, Tocqueville explains. And this togetherness of differences is further accentuated by the development of science and technology. Science and technology, whose pursuit Tocqueville once describes as an "addiction" of democracies, is the precondition for the prosperity and redistribution of property that facilitates the unremitting and frenetic movement with which individuals overcome inequality through imitation and emulation (*DA*II, 41–47). Technology puts individuals in sight of and in touch with one another. Redescribed in aesthetic terms, technology facilitates the intimacy that issues from the aesthetic attachment of each one to every other.

Individuality's Indifference to Difference in Its Depths, the Unknown, and the Indeterminacy of Surfaces

Each element of individuality's aesthetic form of representation orients it creatively and receptively to the surfaces of small differences. Drawn near together to surfaces to which it is attached as the media for creating itself differently, individuality finds all small differences on the surface to be equal and none less perfect than others as forms through which it can become different. Aesthetic individuality is sensitive to the small differences among surfaces distinguishing individual differences from one another, and it is receptive to the surfaces belonging to all. There can be no question that individuality's possibilities for creating itself differently are due to an aesthetic form of representation that, like Whitman's poetic forms, is both consistently receptive to surfaces and receptive with a democratic intent to include all the forms of small differences assumed by others.

As we now shall learn, individuality's possibilities for self-creativity are expanded still further, because its aesthetic form of representation is not merely receptive to surfaces democratically. In the exact same manner as Whitman's poetic forms of representation, individuality's form of representation *confines* it to the surface as well, and with the same aesthetic consequences that attend Whitman's poetry. The equality of condition in which both individuality's desire to become different and its logic of aesthetic representation are rooted also encourages individuality to relate to truth in a way that fosters its indifference to difference in its depths, a disinterest in the identity of difference as it is, in-itself.[27] Through its indifference to the identity of difference, individuality's creativity is confined to the surface. As the aesthetic consequence of its confinement, individuality is permitted to remain innocent of the violence to difference that accompanies every effort to say what difference is in its depths, and what lies below is permitted to remain unknown. And with the identity of difference unknown, the surface is uncoupled from a foundation whose depth, if it had been thought to be intelligible instead of opaque, would have legislated the meaning and value of difference once and for all. Divided from its depths, the surface to which individuality's creativity and receptivity are confined becomes open to interpretation, indeterminate in meaning and value, limitless in the possibilities it offers individuality's self-creativity, an aesthetic consequence of an equality of condition that begins by shaping individuality's relation to truth and concludes by shaping its use of language.

As we have seen, from the individual's natural Cartesianism—from "the desire of judging everything for himself" created by the equality of condition—grows his "contempt for tradition and forms." Intellectually independent, Tocqueville elaborates, individuals develop a hostility to cultural forms in all their symbolic representations, secular as well as religious, that act to "conceal or to set off truths that should more naturally be bared to the light of day" (*DA*II, 25). While individuality's intellectual self-reliance does not involve the rejection of truth, in other words, it does entail the rejection of all attempts to shield truth from constant examination, as though the individual's desire to judge everything for himself were expressed more in the manner of John Stuart Mill than Descartes. According to Tocqueville's description of the individual's disposition to truth encouraged by equality, it first seems that truth quite nearly serves as a mere rationalization for a critical activity that places authority permanently into question and in abeyance. At the same time, since truth must appear to individuals without the benefit of cultural symbolism that establishes it as an ideal or standard worthy of loyalty and exempt from criticism, Tocqueville concluded that

> they like to discern the object which engages their attention with extreme clearness; they therefore strip off as much as possible all that covers it; they rid themselves of whatever separates them from it, they remove whatever conceals it from sight, in order to view it more closely and in the broad light of day. (*DA*II, 4)

Tocqueville's language is consistent with his earlier description of the sensuous receptivity of each individual to all others. For an individual to represent the truth of "objects," of the world and everyone and everything within it in all of its diversity, means to move beyond the prejudices of cultural forms that block the view of objects as they actually *appear*, that is, as they can be seen and seen clearly and closely on the surface. On the one hand, then, the critical disposition of each to truths held by any other makes it unlikely that any "truth" would be accepted as such, while on the other hand the idea of what constitutes truth orients the understanding only to what can be seen. In aesthetic terms, on both counts individuality's relation to truth can be redescribed as an indifference to difference in its depths, an indifference to difference not as it appears on its surface but to its identity as it is, in-itself. What the identity—the "truth" or "reality"—of anything is, how it is different from its appearance on the surface and from individuality's representations of its surface, seems not to be the concern of the intellectually self-reliant and critically disposed individual. And this indifference to difference in its depths confines individuality to the different surfaces to which it is aesthetically receptive "in the broad light of day," which leaves the depths of differences out of sight and outside of individuality's sphere of representation. Coincidentally, Tocqueville describes relations among individuals in terms that capture the aesthetic qualities of their relation to truth, when he speaks of the members of a democratic community who are "*indifferent* to each other" (*DA*II, 228; italics added).

It is not only as a consequence of their intellectual independence, though, that individuals become indifferent to the identity of small differences, but by virtue of their independence and self-reliance at a more practical level as well. As all are constantly in motion, spurred by a passion for equality to become different from what they are, "the habits of the mind that are suited to an active life are not always suited to a contemplative one" (*DA*II, 43). Under such regularly changing circumstances as are created by equality, the mind is "annoyed" and "disturbed," Tocqueville proposes, but not "excited" or "elevated," and the pursuit of abstract truth, which requires an aristocratic form of life unmoved by the passion for equality, becomes unfeasible. Equality disrupts the "meditation" and "calm" necessary to "unceasingly pursue one sole object" and to produce the "deeper combinations of the intellect" (*DA*II, 42). It forces each to "embrace several objects at once," all of which are different, and demands that all "know a great deal quickly" rather than "anything well." Everyone inspired by democracy's equality of condition is "readily satisfied with imperfect notions," and no one has the "time" or the "taste to search things to the *bottom*" (*DA*II, 223, 224; italics added). No one, in other words, has the opportunity or interest to know someone or something in its depths.

Both at an intellectual and practical level, then, the equality of condition encourages a relationship to truth that can be redescribed in aesthetic terms as individuality's indifference to difference in its depths, the same indifference to difference expressed in Whitman's poetic forms of representation, and with the same aesthetic consequences. Although under the pressure of the equality of condition individuality does not abandon the idea of truth, the idea that difference possesses identity, by fostering its indifference to the depths where the identity of difference is beyond its reach, equality relieves individuality of a concern with the identity of small differences. Confining its representation of difference to the surface through indifference, individuality abstains aesthetically from representing the identity of difference. Like Whitman's poetic forms, as a consequence of its aesthetic receptivity to surfaces, which does not equate the appearance of difference with its identity, individuality expresses an aesthetic sensibility sparing difference the violence of representing its identity as other than it is. For all of its "representational" intents and purposes, as does Whitman, individuality relates to difference aesthetically as though its identity were unknown. With the identity of difference tacitly acknowledged to be unknown, the surface of difference has no foundation on the basis of which individuality could with certainty determine its meaning and value. As difference appears to individuality on the surface, its meaning and value consequently seem indeterminate, as it seems to Whitman to be indeterminate. Essentially, the surface of every small difference would become a metaphor to which individuality could assign a plurality of meanings. Not only would individuality be surrounded with a plurality of forms of difference through which it could create itself differently, but each different surface would possess a plurality of meanings, indefinitely multiplying the ways in which individuality can create itself aesthetically on its own surface and in its depths. If individuality's representation of small differences is confined aesthetically to the surface, thus expressing a sensibility to the violence in representing the identity of difference and tacitly acknowledging that the identity of difference is unknown, there should be evidence of individuality's aesthetic intuition of indeterminacy. It is therefore significant that Tocqueville allows us to find indeterminacy in the way individuals are encouraged to use language in a democracy.

As Tocqueville argues, the competition among individuals encouraged by the equality of condition to acquire the intellectual and material means to imitate and emulate others produces new ideas, inventions, and developments that are made sense of through the introduction of new meanings into language. Only an aristocracy would remain sufficiently unchanged that language would remain in repose to the same extent (*DA*II, 65). With new meanings given to words and expressions that are already in use in a democratic society, a "doubling" of meaning occurs, so that the original as well as the new meaning is rendered "ambiguous." Ambiguity "is a deplorable consequence of democracy," Tocqueville concludes, and then declares that he "had rather that the language should be made hideous with words imported from the Chinese, Tartars, or the Hurons than that the meaning of a word in our own language should become *indeterminate*" (*DA*II, 67; italics added). Hence Tocqueville finds in language as it is shaped by democracy that very aesthetic quality that belongs to an individuality confined to the representation of the surfaces of small differences. Language would dispose if not compel individuality to interpret the meaning of each new and different "surface" or "object" (as Whitman speaks of persons and things), it encounters to be indeterminate. Language would encourage individuality to be aesthetically receptive to each surface as though it offered all the possibilities for self-creativity that could be offered by a form of difference whose meaning is forever uncertain. Because he once said that "I readily admit that the Americans have no poets," in the context of his critique of the democratic configuration of language, it is ironic that where he reflects on the origin of poetry Tocqueville recognizes indeterminacy as an aesthetic quality (*DA*II, 74).

> If man were wholly ignorant of himself, he would have no poetry in him; for it is impossible to describe what the mind does not conceive. If man clearly discerned his own nature, his imagination would remain idle and would have nothing to add to the picture. But the nature of man is sufficiently disclosed for him to know something of himself, and sufficiently obscure for all the rest to be plunged in thick darkness, in which he gropes forever, and forever in vain, to lay hold on some completer notion of his being. (*DA*II, 76)

Is Tocqueville not saying that we invent poetic forms when the meaning and value we discover in one another are found to be indeterminate? If so, then although they may not become poets to Tocqueville's satisfaction, perhaps the aesthetic offspring of democracies instead form a poetic relationship to the world whose meaning it finds to be indeterminate.

The Logic of Identity "as" Difference

From the aesthetic point of view of the individual, the artist (the creator) produced by democracy's equality of condition, individuality's logic of aesthetic representation does not implicate individuality in a relationship through which its identity is constituted by excluding difference. Through its aesthetic representation of difference, individuality creates its identity as a visible surface and an unseen depth through the plurality of forms of difference in which those around it appear. As identity assumes the plurality of forms of difference belonging to the surfaces of others, what once was uniform becomes diverse, what was continuous becomes discontinuous and contradictory. Identity is constituted *as* difference through an aesthetic form of receptivity that integrates what is outside with what is inside, and is an aesthetic achievement because the creative, mimetic form of its relationship to difference enables it to do so. Receptive to small differences all-inclusively, making no exceptions, individuality's aesthetic form creates its identity so that it mirrors the diversity of meanings and values belonging to the surfaces of small differences encircling it. Sensitive to how each is different from itself, from others, and from the whole, aesthetic individuality recognizes that the identity of every small difference possesses its own unique meaning and value in its depths, that it is a world in-itself, and that by orienting itself inclusively to difference in these respects individuality is able to create itself differently and uniquely. Acknowledging all differences included to be of equal value, aesthetic individuality is free of the desire to establish the greater or lesser value of any form of difference and to fix value as grounds for exclusion. Believing itself to be sufficient, to be no less perfect than others, aesthetic individuality does not resent others who are different and does not exclude others out of resentment. Intimately acquainted with all small differences to which it is attached, aesthetic individuality is not *more* attached to and *better* acquainted with some rather than others because they are different *per se*, but is attached to and acquainted with all inclusively because each is different *per se*. Indifferent to difference in its depths and confined to the surface to which it is receptive aesthetically, individuality is free of the violence of identifying difference by equating the surface of difference with difference as it is, in-itself. Leaving every small difference alone and unknown, individuality understands difference to be indeterminate in meaning and in the possibilities it offers each individual for becoming different from what he is.

Because every element of individuality's aesthetic form of representation orients it to difference *inclusively*, its identity is not constituted by distinguishing it from difference as that which it is *not*, which would require that difference be excluded. Without requiring the exclusion of difference, in other words, the relationship between identity and difference in which aesthetic individuality is implicated moves beyond the logic of contradiction. Beyond contradiction, the logic of constituting identity *as* difference allows aesthetic individuality to constitute its identity without converting difference to otherness either transcendentally, to establish the certainty of identity, or contingently, both of which require that identity exclude difference from the outset, that identity relate to difference as its contradiction. Nor does aesthetic individuality convert difference into something other than it is in the mere act of representation. Unknown, the identity of difference is never the same as aesthetic individuality's representation of its surface. Unknown, the identity of difference is never the same as aesthetic individuality's thought of it.

The elements of individuality's aesthetic form of representation all appear to be immune to a logic that implicates identity in the exclusion of small differences, whereby otherness is created out of a difference from which identity distinguishes itself through contradiction. There is one element in particular, however, that may not be immune. Despite the sense of sufficiency aesthetic individuality acquires as a consequence of the idea, encouraged by the equality of condition, that because perfectibility is indefinite no individual could be more perfect than the next, would there not be evidence of the superiority of some that an aesthetic receptivity affirming the equality of difference could not ignore? Would individuality not then be prone to resent those perceived to be superior, and to a slave morality that victimizes difference by imposing the stigma of otherness upon those who do not, cannot, or will not conform to the values of the dominant culture?

Tocqueville anticipates the possibility of a slave morality in a democracy. The passion for equality that "tends to elevate the humble to the rank of the great" by teaching each to imitate and emulate others, he argues, is matched by a "depraved taste for equality, which impels the weak to attempt to lower the powerful to their own level and reduces men to prefer equality in slavery"

(*DA*I, 53). At the same time, though, Tocqueville dispels the fear of slave morality by suggesting that where there is an equality of condition the "general notion of a superior becomes weaker and less distinct" (*DA*II, 194). So long as there is an equality of condition that enables each to imitate every other, he appears to say, no one would form the idea that what distinguishes another is a *permanent* distinction and a mark of superiority. Democracy undermines the image of a superiority whose perception creates the resentment that urges some to universalize their own way of life at the expense of those whose form of life is beyond their reach. An anecdote Tocqueville relates offers poignant confirmation of the success with which democracy's equality of condition can enfeeble the idea of superiority and stem the resentment that precipitates a slave morality.

> He has been informed that the conditions of society are not equal in our part of the globe, and he observes that among the nations of Europe the traces of rank are not wholly obliterated, that wealth and birth still retain some indeterminate privileges, which force themselves upon his notice while they elude definition. He is therefore profoundly ignorant of the place he ought to occupy in this half-ruined scale of classes, which are sufficiently distinct to hate and despise each other, yet sufficiently alike for him to be always confounding them. He is afraid of ranking himself too high; still more he is afraid of being ranked too low. This twofold peril keeps his mind constantly on the stretch and embarrasses all he says and does. (*DA*II, 173)

Tocqueville is describing Americans traveling abroad at a time when the equality of condition had not advanced to the same degree in European democracies as it had in the United States. Not having known the limitations of a system of permanent inequality, ill at ease in democracies whose anachronistic practices of making class distinctions they do not share, and unaccustomed to think of themselves as superior or to view others as superior, Americans would be disinclined to "rank themselves too high or too low." Put in aesthetic terms, their embarrassment would be the price of an individuality whose aesthetic sensibility neither defines its self-identity by saying no to others nor allows the identity of others to be defined by saying no to them, and is thus averse to the logic of a slave morality, as Nietzsche conceptualized it.[28] Once again we find irony here, for early in *Democracy in America* Tocqueville confessed to imagining a society "removed alike from pride and servility," which according to his own words seems to be the consequence of an aesthetic individuality that is a democratic achievement (*DA*I, 9).

AESTHETIC INDIVIDUALITY AS A DEMOCRATIC ACHIEVEMENT

Hence we have individuality conceived from Whitman's aesthetic point of view, the point of view of the artist (the creator), who composes poetry through the forms in which we find individuals in a democratic society creating themselves and their world, their meanings and their values, with a sensibility to the violence in their creativity. Democracy orients individuality receptively to the surface of the world so that it leaves the world's depths, its identity, alone. Democracy thus produces an individuality that meets Adorno's criterion for an aesthetic sensibility that avoids doing harm to difference. Democracy also orients individuality to the surface creatively, because in its recognition of the unknown, individuality's creativity is not weighed down by a depth whose identity imposes limits on the meanings and values individuality may create. Democracy thus produces an individuality that meets Nietzsche's criterion for creativity. Though his contribution to a concept of aesthetic individuality has proved to be far richer than the sum of these parts allows, through Whitman we have found a form of individuality that marries Nietzsche's idea of aesthetic creativity on the surfaces of the world to Adorno's idea of an aesthetic receptivity that protects its depths. Creative on the surface, in the broad light of day, respectful of the darkness of the depths below, the aesthetic individuality democracy creates, to borrow from Nietzsche, is a marriage of light and dark.[29]

Redescribing Tocqueville's work in aesthetic terms, we discover that democracy provides the aesthetic education for which Whitman had hoped. With the elements of Whitman's poetic forms reproduced in individuality's aesthetic receptivity to its world and in its creativity, we now understand why "Americans," in particular, perhaps, as Whitman believed, though more generally the progeny of a modern democratic society, can be said to "have probably the fullest poetical nature." Of course, not every element of Whitman's poetic forms belongs to individuality's aesthetic receptivity to the world as it is produced by democratic society, which is to say that the concept of aesthetic individuality I have developed from the aesthetic point of view of Whitman, the artist (the creator), is deeper and broader than the form of it for which we find evidence in democracy. Wonder, in particular, appears to be absent from an individuality whose receptivity to democracy's diversity of different surfaces is driven by a passion to overcome differences by overcoming inequality. Though there is no evidence for it in Tocqueville's argument, however, it would not be idle to speculate that individuals so consistently receptive to the surfaces of a world of differences tacitly recognized to be unknown and mysterious would respond with wonder to their fathomless depths. How could an individuality receptive to the world as Whitman's poetic forms are receptive to the world not find the wonder in the world that Whitman's poetry finds? Yet, even if wonder were not part of individuality's aesthetic experience of difference, to have the qualities that make a superb nation, to recall Whitman's 1855 preface to *Leaves of Grass*, an individual need go only halfway to meet the soul of its poets.

TEN

Conclusion:
INDIVIDUALITY AFTER THE HOLOCAUST

Once *Democracy in America* has been reconstructed according to the aesthetic criteria we inherit from Adorno, Nietzsche, and Whitman, several theoretical conclusions can be drawn regarding the historical possibility for an aesthetic form of individuality in late modern democratic society. First, aesthetic individuality is what an individualism rooted in equality of condition and the passion for equality eventually would become, and perhaps to a significant extent. For if the equality of condition and the passion for equality have been at the center of democratic life since Tocqueville's great work appeared in the first half of the nineteenth century, as he prophesized it would, then aesthetic individuality should have become increasingly prominent. Second, as aesthetic individuality prevailed in democratic societies, difference would be less victimized by the burden of "otherness." What Adorno believed to be a utopian ideal, the possibility that identity could be constituted without becoming implicated in a logic of contradiction and exclusion, would be the consequence of an individuality able to create its identity differently through an aesthetic receptivity to difference. Individuality would create the identity of the self on its surfaces and in its depths through the surfaces of every difference to which it became aesthetically receptive. Finally, the democratic society whose passion for equality had fostered the development of aesthetic individuality would have erected a barrier to the evil of demonizing difference and to its apocalyptic expression, holocaust and genocidal extermination.

No matter how robust the passion for equality unleashed by the equality of condition in modern democratic society, however, and how kinetic the aesthetic form of individuality that would be fostered as a result, aesthetic individuality would not go unchallenged. To be sure, as were its earlier stages, modern democratic life continues to be fed by multiple sources of morality. Some of these sources would encourage the conversion of difference to otherness in the contribution they make to the constitution of individual and group identity.[1] By so doing they would threaten the undoing of aesthetic individuality and the evil that aesthetic individuality opposes. Yet, it would be hasty to assume that morality in democracy cannot work differently from the way Nietzsche had claimed. While Nietzsche had a complex theoretical and philosophical appreciation of morality and its dynamics, arguably his understanding of democracy is relatively thin in comparison, though I do not have the opportunity in this work to give this matter the attention it deserves. I adopt a circuitous approach to this issue; for my purposes it is sufficient to examine the question of whether democracy does not only produce slave morality. Contra Nietzsche, I want to ask whether democratic society also facilitates the creation of moral beliefs and practices that are not hostile to aesthetic individuality and may even be allied with it. By way of considering this possibility I want to turn to a seminal work that bears directly on this question, George Kateb's *The Inner Ocean: Individualism and Democratic Culture*.[2]

A MORALLY DISTINCTIVE DEMOCRATIC INDIVIDUALITY

At the heart of "democratic individuality," as Kateb refers to it, lies a certain "moral identity," which individuals acquire by learning particular "moral lessons" they are taught as a consequence of their participation in a representative and constitutional form of democratic government. To begin with, the electoral system, which Kateb takes to be the fundamental institution of representative democracy, encourages the development of specific attitudes and dispositions toward authority. In their role as citizens in establishing political authority through their electoral activity, individuals receive instruction about the meaning of authority within democratic contexts. Whenever political authority is "regularly recreated," as it is during elections, Kateb argues, its "artificial nature" is highlighted, so that it is "demystified or desacralized."[3] Electoral politics thus teaches that authority is conventional and constructed, so that authority undergoes a metamorphosis. By participating in elections, individuals learn that authority is not merely given, beyond their influence, and simply to be obeyed. Authority loses the hold it otherwise would have if it were not understood to be made through a type of political action that also allows it to be unmade.

What Kateb calls the "moral distinctiveness" of representative democracy is rooted in the way individuals' orientations to authority are shaped by an electoral system of politics. To learn, as does an active electorate, that political authority is conventional because it is created through democratic procedures is to grasp the fundamental insight that the authority granted to leaders by the electoral process is "regularly revocable" and hence "temporary and conditional." Although this connection between the construction of political authority and its meaning that electoral arrangements enable individuals to make may seem rudimentary, as a consequence of such insight a "major moral distinctiveness enters the life of society." As individuals learn that a democratically constituted authority is temporary and conditional because revocable, they are encouraged to be skeptical of authority, to be reluctant to defer to authority, and to believe that those who possess authority ought to be skeptical of their own exercise of authority.[4] It seems that the morally distinctive quality of representative government lies in its encouragement of moral attitudes that combine to "chasten" authority, a result that yields further moral consequences by sponsoring "distinctive moral phenomena in the life of society." In Kateb's words,

First of all, there is independence of spirit . . . the independence that ordinary people show in their extraordinary moments—moments that help to give a larger sense to their whole lives. The chastening of political authority encourages individuals to be less fearful of all authority, whether concentrated in particular figures of authority or impersonally present in given rules and conventions. The positive expression of independence in the face of personal and impersonal authority can be called *autonomy*. . . . Autonomy is acting on one's own, making one's life one's own, freely making commitments, accepting conventions known to be conventions, and straining to construct the architecture of one's soul. . . . The negative expression of independence is the disposition to say no, to dissent, to engage in acts of principled or conscientious disobedience or resistance or rebelliousness, whether in acts of citizenship or in the rest of life.

Second, the mere status of citizen which enables one to run for office and to vote in the contested elections for office is a continuous incitement to claim the status of citizen—or something analogous—in all nonpolitical relations of life. Indeed, the incitement is to politicize the nonpolitical relations of life and thus to democratize them.

The third moral phenomenon follows from the electoral system's partisan or factional basis. In a representative democracy, political authority is in essence partial (to leave aside the judiciary). A part—a party or faction or coalition—is temporarily allowed to stand for the whole. Parts take turns standing for the whole and giving it a temporary moral emphasis or coloration. The very association of authority and partisanship promotes a sense of moral indeterminacy . . . the belief that within a frame of settled commitments, a number of contrasting and competing responses or answers to morally tinged questions are to be expected and welcomed. . . . A struggle against those in authority understood as defenders of one possible right answer rather than the only possible right answer is thus encouraged. Disseminated into society, this notion not only intensifies the demand to democratize all relations but cultivates a general tolerance of, and even affection for, diversity: diversity in itself, and diversity as the source of regulated contest and competition.[5]

Each of these "moral phenomena" is a pedagogical consequence of representative government, and when they are taken together, they in part constitute the moral identity at the core of Kateb's concept of democratic individuality. If there is a defining moral quality among this rich constellation of moral phenomena, it appears to be the quality of "autonomy" or "independence" taught to individuals when they participate in electoral practices that rely upon and encourage independent expression. Because autonomy is taught by the electoral practice of either creating or revoking authority, individuals are able to shed their fear of authority and to consider its limits, or to resist or contest authority once it is chosen. Learning, if only implicitly through their participation in electoral politics, that citizenship fosters their independence, individuals may resolve to expand their role as citizens and to insinuate that independence into private—personal, family, and professional—as well as public relations. And having learned that authority is limited by those who independently constitute it through the electoral process, individuals may come to view the moral positions attached to authority and to those who contest it as both limited and open to the moral reasoning that all participants in the electoral process may contribute.

It is evident why Kateb speaks of the "enormous alteration" in political authority for which democracy is responsible. An alteration in the authority that political institutions, leaders, and policies command—political authority in the broadest sense, in other words—is traceable to the creation of a moral autonomy and independence that originate in a prior and equally comprehensive alteration in the individual's beliefs and understandings about authority, and in the attitudes and behavior that they support. In a phrase, it is traceable to the creation of what according to Kateb's argument is a "morally distinctive democratic individuality" (my term).

With autonomy, or independence, foregrounded as the defining characteristic of a morally distinctive democratic individuality, to further articulate the protean forms, levels, and aspects that individuality assumes in a democracy Kateb distinguishes between positive, negative, and impersonal forms of individuality, each of which goes to the meaning of autonomy and its turns of mind.

Positive individuality refers to the beliefs and attitudes engendered by the chastening of authority that may dispose individuals to independently examine social conventions that partially constitute their personal identities. Implicit in this disposition is the aspiration to take responsibility for oneself by determining if such conventions would enable one to conduct oneself morally and to have morally valuable experience, such as discovering the ethical limitations of one's own conventional moral codes. Negative individuality refers to the disposition to disobey unjustifiable conventions and unjust laws by means of dissent and heresy, among other forms of disobedience.

While the positive and negative forms of individuality pertain to the democratically learned inclinations to differentiate one's own identity from the ready-made identities available through social conventions, impersonal individuality moves beyond the tendency to make oneself over and increasingly to become the author of one's experiences and relations with others. Rather than having to do with reconstituting the boundaries of personal identity, impersonal individuality has everything to do with exceeding or negating those boundaries. Impersonal individuality is the love of the world for what it is, and it is expressed through what Kateb provocatively describes as an "almost promiscuous acceptance of one thing after another, almost no matter what." Its art lies in nourishing that which is superior to an individuality that ever changes its identity: the soul. Receptive without discrimination to all that it embraces, impersonal individuality forges a qualitatively different relationship to the world, "which may be described as either a philosophical or poetical relation to reality."[6]

Whereas positive and negative individuality are not strange in the everyday, ordinary doings of democratic societies, impersonal individuality is somewhat rare, as we should expect from the way Kateb develops it conceptually. Impersonal individuality incorporates individuality's finest though most exceptional aspects, and there are three in particular that characterize its philosophical and poetical relationship to reality. An *overtly moral* aspect of the relationship, Kateb explains, is represented by an individual's ability to "see all persons as human, as able to suffer, and to sympathize with them in their ardors and their travails." There is an *existential* dimension that "pertains not only to how one should perceive and understand but also to how one should act. A belief in one's inviolability allows one to take chances, to transform dead seriousness into play," into experimentation. Last, there is the *aesthetic* aspect of the poetical relation, which is to see "all persons as beautiful, even when by conventional definition they are not."[7] Kateb understands these elements of individual expression to be uncommon, though democracy is not less productive of morally distinctive democratic individuality for that reason. To the contrary, in his estimation democracies lay the foundations for individuality's most advanced forms of expression, so that as a poetical relation to reality individuality becomes a possibility within the womb of democratic society for the many and not merely for the few.

In order to convey the idea that impersonal individuality lies within the reach of the numbers whose morally distinctive democratic individuality in his view justifies the existence of a democratic way of life, Kateb distinguishes forms of individuality according to various levels, each of which is intended loosely to represent its actual or expected presence in a democracy. Kateb positions impersonal individuality as falling largely within a *transcendent* level of democratic achievement. Transcendence is not being used here to refer to that which surpasses the horizon of the many, but rather means that through impersonal individuality the egoistic sense that one is better or more valuable than anyone or anything that lies outside one's self is discarded or overcome. Indeed, this highest level of individualist expression is actually the next step up from other, preparatory levels upon which it rests, notably the *extraordinary* and *normal* levels of morally distinctive democratic individuality. As examples of the former, Kateb includes self-reliance, independent thinking, and unexpected creativity as its positive forms, civil disobedience as its negative form, and the bestowal of sympathy and the effort to see beauty in everything as its impersonal form of individuality. As with the transcendent level of individuality, extraordinary refers less to the fact that it is confined to the few, which it is not or is only for a time, than to the episodic or occasional experience of this level of individuality for the many, which in a democracy would become more common in time. Of the three, Kateb's so-called normal level of morally distinctive democratic individuality appears to be the most striking, though not merely because it is the most common or democratic in the ordinary sense.

CONCLUSION: INDIVIDUALITY AFTER THE HOLOCAUST

The normal level is the most interesting because its common eloquence erases all doubt that our everyday experiences of individuality are not impossibly removed or disconnected from the transcendent and extraordinary levels of individuality. As positive expressions of normal individuality, those living in democratic societies quite commonly think of themselves as individuals and suspend or perhaps abandon their identities and adopt new personas. It has become more common for those who are members of marginalized, victimized, or stigmatized groups to express their individuality negatively, in Kateb's sense of the term, by saying no to their condition and insisting that every member of any group is an individual and not a mere member of a category. And individuals who discover within themselves an all-forgiving tolerance practice an impersonal individuality that must only be different in degree and not in kind from its extraordinary and transcendent levels.

Kateb deepens our appreciation of the pedagogical virtues of representative government by introducing another conceptual scheme that further captures its moral dimensions. If the electoral process teaches moral lessons, he believes, then it also must contain values or possess intrinsic value, and does so by *accommodating*, *embodying*, and *expressing* values. Where he had argued that the electoral system instructs citizens about the moral limitations of political positions formed through an electoral process that is essentially partial (as are campaigns, party platforms and caucuses, public opinion, pressure and protest groups), intrinsic to this instruction is the accommodation of a plurality of contested values that provides individuals with the opportunity to learn about a range of moral claims, their strengths and weaknesses.[8] Or where he had proposed that individuals learn that authority is constituted through the electoral opportunities offered by citizenship, intrinsic to that lesson is the embodiment of the value that the individual counts, counts only as one, and is always owed an account. Finally, where Kateb had tried to show that individuals take the lessons of citizenship out of public life and into their professional and private lives, intrinsic to those teachings is the insight that representative government expresses values that work on the imaginations of its participants by acting as a "continuously potent force of suggestiveness." Democratic individuality's complexity is obvious from Kateb's more expansive interpretation of the moral lessons taught by representative government and the moral qualities they instill in individuals. A morally distinctive democratic individuality would most likely possess a complex moral identity composed of multiple layers of moral beliefs and understandings and moral dispositions. While no one individual would possess them all, each one would possess some and perhaps many, though not necessarily the same ones. The exception, of course, would be that the democratically schooled moral individuality of each would possess as its animating force the autonomy or independence that appear to be the constant moral qualities that accompany every moral lesson taught by electoral processes.

Electoral processes do not work alone to create and nurture morally distinctive democratic individuality, but rather in alliance with other democratic institutions that augment its breadth and depth. Constitutionally protected legal procedures, especially due process, in Kateb's view make up the second of the two most salient pedagogical components of representative government.[9] As does the electoral process, due process certifies representative government's intrinsic value by accommodating, embodying, and expressing values. Due process accommodates the values of impartiality, deliberation, and the serious play of agonistic debate, which are taught to judges, lawyers, and jurors by rule-governed procedures that impose constraints on their behavior. Due process also accommodates the value of human dignity through the respect for suspects, defendants, and prisoners it requires of all participants in the legal system. Among other ways, due process embodies the values of justice and fairness by forbidding authority to treat any individual as having relinquished certain rights or as having a diminished status before the law, regardless of crimes committed; by preventing it from employing any expedient to achieve what it considers to be a worthy outcome; and by requiring it to strengthen its adversary to ensure a good contest. And taken as a whole, Kateb maintains, the procedures of due process express values by teaching the sum of its valuable lessons. The practice of restraint is taught by the values accommodated and embodied collectively by due process, which encourage individuals in their public and private roles to imitate government procedures by exercising the self-doubt and self-correction that restraint entails. Together with the lessons taught by electoral processes, those taught by constitutional procedures complete the moral identity of democratic individuality.

Perhaps the most attractive feature of Kateb's argument is what I would describe as its quasi-empirical foundation. To put it differently, much of the force of his argument flows from his claim that morally distinctive democratic individuality is actually created by representative government and constitutionalism. This does not mean, however, that every citizen in a democracy necessarily would develop the forms, elements, and aspects of individuality to the extent indicated by Kateb's concept of democratic individuality. Rather, to say that the institutions and practices of representative government and constitutionalism create democratic individuality is also to say that they create a *culture* of democratic individuality, a collection of opportunities and possibilities that await individuals who become more or less involved in a democratic form of life. It follows that no individual's experience of a democratic form of life could be like any other's. It would vary according to the widest variety of sociological and idiosyncratic factors that influence and characterize an individual's existence. The lessons representative government and constitutionalism teach would be understood on different levels, expressed in different forms, inclusive of different aspects. And the notion of a political culture internalized differently by different individuals is consistent with the spirit of democratic individuality.

Would it not be contrary to the idea of individuality for it to appear uniformly throughout the society that engenders it? Because it is foremost a collection of opportunities and possibilities belonging to a "culture" of democratic individuality created by representative government and constitutionalism, and only afterward an individuality that is the consequence of both this culture *and* the contingencies that shape each individual's life, can we comprehend the expansiveness and indefiniteness of democratic society's moral distinctiveness and of the morally distinctive democratic individuality it creates.

THE MORAL AND THE AESTHETIC

One way to discover if aesthetic individuality could flourish in an environment where democratic institutions foster the development of a morally distinctive democratic individuality is to consider the similarities in meaning Kateb and John Stuart Mill attach to the "morality" of individuality. In *On Liberty*, Mill speaks of the "moral courage" belonging to individuality.[10] Above all, a "morally courageous individuality," now to paraphrase Mill, is experimental, not only able but willing to explore new ways of thinking and acting, new ways of being. Such moral courage depends on the presence of other intellectual qualities. Individuals not only must have a sense that the beliefs they hold may be in error, but also must be willing "to take precautions" against their fallibility.[11] Each one who assumes personal fallibility, Mill is proposing, must beware of discarding personal beliefs in favor of trusting, alternatively, in the infallibility of the world in general. Here Mill no doubt is responding to Tocqueville's concern that the intellectually self-reliant individual created by democracy's equality of condition is also burdened by a certain insecurity when his or her solitary judgment is threatened by the pressures of mass opinion. Since the assumption of fallibility should carry with it the understanding that all beliefs, at best, are partial truths, no one should feel that the beliefs held collectively by others are any more secure than his or her own, or any less eligible for correction. And just as the assumption of fallibility is the source of the individual's resistance to the imposition of the beliefs held by the many on the beliefs held by the one, so too does it compel the individual to abstain from imposing personal views on others. By acknowledging their own fallibility, individuals likewise acknowledge that they have no authority to decide questions "for all mankind."[12] No one or no collectivity, in other words, may *universalize* its own beliefs at the expense of others, because the particular that is sacrificed to the generalizable not only may be sacrificed to error but also may itself contain a portion of the truth whose loss would allow error to be perpetuated.

Assuming their beliefs may be in error, individuals then must be willing to contest their views in order to arrive at less imperfect understandings. Minimally, contestation requires individuals to be open to all views contrary to their own, and their openness, moreover, is to be demonstrated by their interest in seeking out a diversity of beliefs, so that they ultimately would "neglect nothing" that might be said against them. Making the connection between forming true opinions and contesting a diversity of views, individuals learn that diversity is a good in itself and contestation, rather than social intolerance, the preferred way to eliminate untruths. Successfully defending one's own beliefs is only part of what is entailed by eliminating error through contestation, however, which likewise supposes the attempt to refute the views held by others and a willingness at least to suspend one's own judgment if others' views cannot be refuted. Yet, no revised understanding arrived at even after consulting, contesting, and refuting all contrary opinions would justify dispensing with the assumption of fallibility. Contrary beliefs and opinions may appear at some future time, and, though they failed to appear, it is in every event necessary to continue to contest a view held to be true lest it cease to be connected to the inner life of a human being. Unless a truth is permitted through contestation to become rooted in the "imagination, the feelings, and the understanding," as Mill explains, it becomes a dead belief unable to inform and animate the individual's existence.[13] For Mill, a truth for the living is a living truth, a truth kept alive by being contested, even though its history of contestation in every case has reaffirmed its truth.

Individuals who assume the fallibility even of their strongest convictions, and who display their receptivity to diversity by entertaining other views, allowing their own views to be contested and contesting the views of others, are morally courageous. Yet, where, more precisely, does the *moral courage* lie in these intellectual qualities? Such qualities constitute moral courage because they either enable the individual to oppose or are themselves expressions of opposition to the "despotism of Custom," the "modern *regime* of public opinion," as Mill refers to the imposition on individuals of systems of moral belief through which "life is reduced nearly to one uniform type."[14] Evidence that the moral qualities enabling the individual to oppose the universalization of moral beliefs would also complement, if not foster, "aesthetic individuality" is offered by Mill's assertion that to contest their own views morally courageous individuals throw "themselves into the mental position of those who think differently from them [to consider] what such persons have to say."[15] Have we not seen that the ability to adopt the form of life in which another individual appears is the essence of an individuality aesthetically receptive to the world's diversity of differences? Further evidence of the complementarity between Mill's concept of individuality and aesthetic individuality is his proposal that moral courage very often requires that in the pursuit of truth individuals come to hold conflicting and contradictory beliefs. Doing so cannot be avoided by an individual sincerely interested in arriving at the truth, because rather than one doctrine being entirely false and another entirely true, Mill argues, it is "the commoner case [that] conflicting doctrines . . . share the truth between them."[16] Thus Mill indicates that morally courageous individuals, in a manner that resembles the self-creativity characteristic of aesthetic individuality, become diverse by reflecting the diversity of forms of life surrounding them.

It is apparent that in important respects Mill's "morally courageous individuality" and Kateb's "morally distinctive democratic individuality" are conceptually symmetrical. What is demonstrably *moral* in both Mill's idea of individuality and in Kateb's are those qualities that enable the individual to resist authority. Largely as a pedagogical consequence of representative government and constitutionalism, as we saw, a morally distinctive democratic individuality possesses the ability to penetrate the mystifications of authority. Rather than appearing as a brute fact, simply given as something to which one must be resigned, authority is recognized by individuals to be artificial, conventional, constructed, and thus conditional, temporary and revocable, originally made and thus something that can be remade or unmade, as seems warranted. Individuals develop a skepticism toward authority, a reluctance to defer, and believe that those who hold power ought to be similarly skeptical of their own authority. Subjected to a metamorphosis by democratic institutions through which it is stripped of its sacred aura, authority's radical chastening weakens its grip over individuals, whose learned fearlessness of authority they express in ways that mutually reinforce one another. Fearlessness takes the form of independent thinking, specifically a willingness to consider the limits of authority and a corresponding openness to views that compete and contrast with the single-minded views defended by authorities. Receptivity to other than authoritatively approved views evolves into a tolerance of and affection for a diversity of beliefs. Fearlessness graduates to a sense of autonomy and self-reliance oriented toward creating one's own values, and toward a regular disposition to nay-saying and an occasional disobedience toward authorities that would thwart such independence. Finally, this multifaceted oppositional stance toward political and public authority, which expands imaginatively as individuals learn the obligations associated with the role of democratic citizenship, is extended to civil society. Within the sphere of civil society individuals' antiauthoritarianism challenges the structure of authority in all areas of private life and, supported by the restraint, self-doubt, and self-correction taught by constitutionalism, challenges their own personal authority as individuals as well.

Whether we speak of democratic individuality's *moral courage* or its *moral distinctiveness*, then, the essence of each is individuality's oppositional stance toward authority. In both cases, there is an intimate connection between an individual's questioning of external forms of authority and her questioning of her own authority. For Mill, morally courageous individuality begins with the individual's assumption of personal fallibility. It ends with the individual's assuming the fallibility of all authority, including all privately held and public opinions, custom and convention, the authority of the state. For Kateb, morally disctinctive democratic individuality begins with the ordinary operations of the democratic political system teaching individuals the conventional nature of all authority, political, public, and private. It ends with democratically schooled individuals inferring the conventional nature of their own authority and intuiting a sense of the contingency of their own identities when they are based on such artificial authority. As the morally distinctive democratic individual intuits the limits of the authority underpinning his or her own identity, the sense of autonomy acquired through opposition to authority is balanced by the sense that one is an individual only and obliged to relinquish any other sense one may have had of superiority to others. Once having discovered the limits of one's own identity, and inspired by the recognition that since other authorities are not, each individual is responsible for his or her own fate, morally distinctive democratic individuality no less than morally courageous individuality creates the self anew by adopting new personas, creating new identities. So the complex synthesis of becoming autonomous by learning the limits of external authority, recognizing the equal authority of others while discovering the limits of one's own authority, and becoming the architect of one's own life out of an intuition of the constructed nature of one's identity, issues in individuality's turning outward toward the diversity of differences in the surrounding world. Perhaps what is thus most distinctive about Kateb's morally distinctive democratic individuality is its inclination, in the absence of an authority whose certainty is undisputed, to recreate relations with others whose terms want for the authority to exclude anyone or any value. Morally distinctive democratic individuality displays not only an "all-forgiving tolerance," as Kateb puts it, of all forms of life, but an "almost promiscuous acceptance of one thing after another, almost no matter what." It displays an unqualified receptivity to the world's diversity of differences.

Democracy, we find, may not only produce an aesthetic form of individuality that serves as a barrier to the evil of holocaust and genocidal extermination. Democratic society may also foster a morally distinctive democratic individuality that, like Mill's morally courageous individuality, does not oppose aesthetic individuality, while it may also promote it.

NOTES

ONE

1. Max Horkheimer and T. W. Adorno, *Dialectic of Enlightenment* (New York: Herder and Herder, 1972).

2. Stephen White draws our attention to an early modern thinker whose work integrates an aesthetic dimension and a critique of modernity that anticipates Horkheimer and Adorno's *Dialectic of Enlightenment*. See Stephen K. White, *Edmund Burke: Modernity, Politics, and Aesthetics* (Thousand Oaks, Calif.: Sage, 1994), especially 84.

3. Friedrich Nietzsche, *Twilight of the Idols* (Middlesex, England: Penguin, 1975), 33.

4. I recommend Terry Eagleton's *Ideology of the Aesthetic* (Oxford: Blackwell, 1997), for one of the most thoughtful and provocative accounts of the relationship between Adorno's reaction to Fascism and its impact on his work, particularly his aesthetic theory. Eagleton considers the possibility that Adorno's work reflects an "overreaction to Fascism" (358).

5. In a recent work on what he refers to as "receptive generosity," which is a highly original attempt to reconsider the ethics and politics of generosity, Romand Coles tacitly recognizes the peculiar aesthetic nature of reason that Adorno is trying to explicate through his critique of enlightenment. Although Coles does not refer to "aesthetic" reason explicitly, he argues that for Adorno "thinking is not *about* the nonidentical but is a *relation with* the nonidentical," thus capturing aesthetic rationality's relational character to difference. It is in the context of a discussion of *Negative Dialectics* that Coles recognizes that the nature of thought has to do with its relation to difference, and he subsequently traces this formulation into Adorno's *Aesthetic Theory*. See Romand Coles, *Rethinking Generosity: Critical Theory and the Politics of Caritas* (Ithaca, N.Y.: Cornell University Press, 1997), 93. Chap. 2 is recommended for its grasp of Adorno's concept of thinking in *Dialectic of Enlightenment* through *Negative Dialectics* to *Aesthetic Theory*.

6. I view Zygmunt Bauman's *Modernity and the Holocaust* as an excellent companion volume to Horkheimer and Adorno's explanation for the centrality of formal rationality in modernity and the relation of modernity to the Holocaust. Unlike Horkheimer and Adorno, though, he seems to slip between two arguments, at times arguing that by virtue of the position formal (instrumental) reason occupies in modernity the Holocaust becomes possible, while at other times he appears to make the stronger argument that the Holocaust becomes inevitable. See Zygmunt Bauman, *Modernity and the Holocaust* (Ithaca, N.Y.: Cornell University Press, 1989), especially chap. 4.

7. Friedrich Nietzsche, *On the Genealogy of Morals*, trans. Walter Kaufmann and R. J. Hollingdale (New York: Vintage, 1967), 103.

8. With its emphasis on the centrality of aesthetic, particularly poetic form, the formulation of individuality as an aesthetic problem from the point of view of the artist (the creator) is a version of what Alexander Nehamas refers to as Nietzsche's urging "that we fashion our lives in the way artists fashion their works." See Alexander Nehamas, *Nietzsche: Life as Literature* (Cambridge: Harvard University Press, 1985), 194, especially chap. 6.

9. For example, see Friedrich Nietzsche, *Thus Spake Zarathustra*, trans. Thomas Common (Mineola, N.Y.: Dover, 1999), 132; *On the Genealogy of Morals*, 78; *Beyond Good and Evil*, trans. R. J. Hollingdale (Middlesex, England: Penguin, 1984), 82.

10. Nietzsche plays on both senses of "light" in *Thus Spake Zarathustra*, 84.

11. Walt Whitman, "Song of the Open Road," in *Leaves of Grass* (New York: Norton, 1973), 150 (line 26), hereafter referred to as *NCE* (the Norton Critical Edition).

12. As my approach to individuality as an aesthetic problem draws out and upon the relationship between aesthetic form, aesthetic individuality, democracy, and America as they appear in Whitman and Tocqueville, it may be construed to be an American exceptionalist argument. At an *explicit* level of analysis, at least, this argument is not intended, as I do not mean to privilege democracy in America as the aesthetic form of life that makes aesthetic individuality possible.

13. George Kateb, *The Inner Ocean: Individualism and Democratic Culture* (Ithaca, N.Y.: Cornell University Press, 1992).

TWO

1. Johann Wolfgang von Goethe, *The Sorrows of Young Werther* (New York: Vintage Classics, 1990), 64, 66 (translation slightly altered).

2. Max Horkheimer and T. W. Adorno, *Dialectic of Enlightenment* (New York: Herder and Herder, 1972), 105.

3. Horkheimer and Adorno, *Dialektik der Aufklärung* (Frankfurt am Main: Fischer Verlag, 1966), 22.

4. Ibid., 44.

5. Horkheimer and Adorno, *Dialectic of Enlightenment*, 15.

6. Ibid.

7. Adorno, *Negative Dialektik* (Frankfurt: Suhrkamp, 1973), 151, 152.

8. Horkheimer and Adorno, *Dialectic of Enlightenment*, 15 (my italics).

9. See the discussion in chap. 3, "Reconciliation and the Alliance between Kant and Hegel, or Hegel without the Absolute, Kant without the Supersensible."

10. Horkheimer and Adorno, *Dialectic of Enlightenment*, 9.

11. Ibid., 16.

12. Ibid., 17.

13. Ibid., 12.

14. Ibid.

15. Ibid., 15.

16. Ibid., 65.

17. Ibid., 11.

18. Concerned about the absence of any discussion of women in much of the literature on Horkheimer and Adorno's *Dialectic of Enlightenment*, Nancy Love shows that women figure prominently in the major theoretical arguments of their text. I recommend Love's article for its excellent discussion of Horkheimer and Adorno's treatment of the Sirens episode, through which she develops her argument. See Nancy Love, "Why Do the Sirens Sing?: Figuring the Feminine in *Dialectic of Enlightenment*," *Theory and Event* 3, 1 (1999).

19. Horkheimer and Adorno, *Dialectic of Enlightenment*, 43.

20. Ibid., 46.

21. Ibid., 55.

22. Ibid., 46 (translation changed).

23. Ibid., 29.

24. Ibid., 60.

25. Ibid., 46.

26. Ibid., 60–61.

27. Ibid., 49.

28. Ibid., 5.

29. Ibid., 7.
30. Ibid., 93 (my italics).
31. Ibid., 5.
32. Ibid., 86.
33. Ibid., 16.
34. Ibid., 37.
35. See the discussion in chap. 3 entitled "Reconciliation and the Alliance between Kant and Hegel, or Hegel without the Absolute, Kant without the Supersensible."
36. Horkheimer and Adorno, *Dialectic of Enlightenment*, 85.
37. Ibid., 25.
38. Ibid., 13.
39. Ibid., 26.
40. Ibid., 83.
41. Ibid., 96, 94.
42. Ibid., 103.
43. Ibid., 97.
44. Ibid., 117.
45. Ibid., 106.
46. See Adorno, "Cultural Criticism and Society," in *Prisms*, trans. Samuel and Shierry Weber (London: Neville Spearman, 1967), 11–34.
47. Horkheimer and Adorno, *Dialektik der Aufklärung*, 128.
48. Horkheimer and Adorno, *Dialectic of Enlightenment*, 120.
49. Ibid., 124.
50. Ibid., 140.
51. Ibid., 143.
52. Ibid., 136.
53. Ibid., 124.
54. Ibid., 145.
55. Ibid., 156.
56. Ibid., 167.
57. Ibid., 123.
58. Ibid., 86.
59. Ibid., 187.
60. Ibid., 188, 193.
61. Ibid., 194.
62. Ibid., 170 (my italics).
63. Ibid., 23.
64. Ibid.

THREE

1. Max Horkheimer and T. W. Adorno, *Dialectic of Enlightenment* (New York: Herder and Herder, 1972), 208.
2. Ibid., 11.
3. See chap. 2, the section entitled "Difference and Mythical Thinking."
4. Horkheimer and Adorno, *Dialektik der Aufklärung* (Frankfurt am Main: Fischer Verlag, 1966), 55.
5. Prior to the discussion in this section, I also take up the metaphorical significance of Odysseus in chap. 2, the section entitled "Difference and Mythical Thinking."
6. Although preanimistic and magical thought do not set off the unending process of

enlightenment and hence do not have the same developmental relationship to enlightenment as myth, there is yet some small evidence at these stages that what appears to be a historical struggle of abstract principles of reason also can be understood as a conflict of the faculties within the self. See my discussion in chap. 2 in the sections entitled "Difference and the Birth of Thinking" and "Difference and Magical Thinking."

7. Horkheimer and Adorno, *Dialectic of Enlightenment*, 59.
8. Ibid.
9. Ibid., 58 (my italics).
10. Ibid., 32.
11. Ibid., 46.
12. Ibid.
13. Ibid., 36.
14. Ibid., 47.
15. Ibid., 33, 35.
16. Ibid., 33.
17. Ibid., 48.
18. Ibid., 54.
19. Ibid.
20. Ibid., 72.
21. Ibid., 63.
22. Ibid., 56 (my italics).
23. And as such the groundwork for Adorno's later critique of thinking as "identitarian" in *Negative Dialektik* (Frankfurt: Suhrkamp, 1973).
24. Horkheimer and Adorno, *Dialectic of Enlightenment*, 25, 30.
25. Homer, *Odyssey*, trans. Robert Fagles (New York: Penguin, 1997), 277 (line 208).
26. Ibid., line 215.
27. Horkheimer and Adorno, *Dialectic of Enlightenment*, 34.
28. Ibid., 156.
29. Friedrich Nietzsche, *Beyond Good and Evil*, trans. R. J. Hollingdale (New York: Penguin, 1984), 143.
30. Friedrich Nietzsche, *On the Genealogy of Morals* (New York: Vintage, 1967), 70 (my italics in first line).
31. Ibid., 21.
32. See ibid., especially 72–73. I have followed Jacques Derrida's translation of Nietzsche's use of "Aufhebung" (*Writing and Difference*, trans. Alan Bass [London: Routledge & Kegan Paul, 1978], 251–77). On the importance of Derrida's translation, see Sarah Kofman, *Nietzsche and Metaphor*, trans. Duncan Large (Stanford, Calif.: Stanford University Press, 1993), 164.
33. Horkheimer and Adorno, *Dialectic of Enlightenment*, 23.
34. Ibid., 31–32.
35. Nietzsche, see *On the Genealogy of Morals*, especially 25–26.
36. Horkheimer and Adorno, *Dialectic of Enlightenment*, 38–39.
37. Ibid., 39, 32.
38. Ibid., 20–21.
39. Ibid.
40. Ibid., 22.
41. Ibid., 104.
42. Ibid., 121–22.
43. Ibid., 47 (my italics).
44. Ibid., 78.
45. Ibid., 41.
46. Ibid., 131.

47. Ibid., 87.
48. Ibid., 136 (my italics).
49. Ibid., 132, 148.
50. Ibid., 149.
51. Ibid., 90, 89.
52. Ibid., 153.
53. Ibid., 198.
54. Ibid., 107.
55. Ibid., 106.
56. Ibid., 113.
57. Ibid.
58. Ibid., 116.

FOUR

1. See my discussion in chap. 6, the sections entitled "Nietzsche's Pure Surfaces" and especially "The Creative Will and Its Destruction of Depth."
2. I recommend Peter Dews's examination of the parallels between the poststructuralist and Adorno's critique of identity for its recognition of the ways in which philosophical positions that Nietzsche maps out in *The Birth of Tragedy* eventually appear in Adorno's work, notably *Negative Dialectics* and *Against Epistemology*. Dews does not, however, develop any parallels between *The Birth of Tragedy* and *Dialectic of Enlightenment*. See Peter Dews, "Adorno, Post-Structuralism and the Critique of Identity," in *Mapping Ideology*, ed. S. Zizek (New York: Verso Press, 1994), 46–65. And though he does not recognize parallels between *Dialectic of Enlightenment* and *The Birth of Tragedy*, Gunter Rohrmoser notes similarities between the latter work and Adorno's *Aesthetic Theory* with regard to the relationship between art and reconciliation. See Gunter Rohrmoser, *Herrschaft und Versöhnung: Aesthetik und die Kulturrevolution des Westens* (Frieburg: Romach, 1972), chap. 1, especially 14.
3. Friedrich Nietzsche, *The Birth of Tragedy*, in *Basic Writings of Nietzsche*, trans. and ed. with commentaries by Walter Kaufmann (New York: Modern Library, 1968), 33.
4. Ibid.
5. Ibid.
6. Ibid., 35.
7. Ibid., 34.
8. Ibid., 35.
9. Ibid., 36.
10. Ibid.
11. Ibid., 37.
12. Ibid., 104, 99.
13. Ibid., 37.
14. Max Horkheimer and T. W. Adorno, *Dialectic of Enlightenment* (New York: Herder and Herder, 1972), 35.
15. Horkheimer and Adorno, *Dialektik der Aufklärung* (Frankfurt am Main: Fischer Verlag, 1966), 41; Nietzsche, *The Birth of Tragedy*, 36, 38.
16. Nietzsche, *The Birth of Tragedy*, 33 (my italics).
17. Ibid., 38.
18. Ibid., 40.
19. Ibid., 39.
20. Ibid., 40.
21. Ibid., 41, 40.

22. Ibid., 42.
23. Ibid., 42, 41, 43.
24. Ibid., 46.
25. Ibid.
26. Ibid., 47.
27. Ibid., 44, 45.
28. Ibid., 39.
29. Ibid.
30. Ibid., 47.

31. Ibid., 46. In his commentary on Nietzsche's *The Birth of Tragedy*, David Lenson wonderfully reinterprets Nietzsche's "tossing bark" metaphor (which originates in Schopenhauer's *World as Will and Representation*) in the context of the rigidity of the Doric reaction to the Dionysian threat, which I now cite because it works to support the connection I am establishing between *The Birth of Tragedy* and *Dialectic of Enlightenment*. In view of Nietzsche's introduction of Sparta as evidence of the "dictatorial" power of the Apollinian, his "calm man in the boat, weathering the stormy sea," Lenson suggests, is now *"chained to the oarlocks just in case"* (Lenson, *The Birth of Tragedy* [Boston: Twayne, 1987], 49; my italics). While I cannot say if he had the Sirens episode in mind, Lenson's trope reminds us of Horkheimer and Adorno's characterization of Odysseus tied to his ship's mast while his oarsmen, their ears plugged with wax, row without fearing the danger of the Sirens' song.

32. Nietzsche, *The Birth of Tragedy*, 55.
33. Ibid., 55, 49.
34. Ibid., 56.
35. Ibid., 56, 57.
36. Ibid., 59.
37. Ibid., 59, 64.
38. Ibid., 59.
39. Ibid., 64.
40. Ibid., 61.
41. Ibid., 64.
42. Ibid., 65 (my italics).
43. Ibid., 66.
44. Ibid.
45. Ibid.
46. Ibid., 67, 66.
47. Ibid., 66 (my italics).
48. Ibid., 67.

49. Adorno, *Aesthetic Theory*, eds. Gretel Adorno and Rolf Tiedemann, trans. and ed. with an introduction by Robert Hullot-Kentor (Minneapolis: University of Minnesota, 1997), 109.

50. Nietzsche, *The Birth of Tragedy*, 103, 104.
51. Ibid., 45, 44.
52. Ibid., 104.
53. Ibid., 83.
54. Ibid.
55. Ibid., 87, 95 (my italics).
56. Ibid., 88.
57. Ibid., 97.
58. Ibid., 88–89.
59. Ibid., 93.
60. Ibid., 97.

61. Ibid., 91, 65, 99–100, 86.
62. Ibid., 100.
63. Ibid., 102.
64. Ibid., 74 (my italics).
65. Ibid., 52.
66. Ibid., 62, 65 (translation altered).
67. Ibid., 37 (my italics).
68. From this point to the conclusion of this chapter I will continue to place the word *concept* in quotation marks, to indicate that Horkheimer and Adorno are speaking about the *idea* of the "concept" rather than any particular concept *per se*.
69. Horkheimer and Adorno, *Dialectic of Enlightenment*, 39.
70. Ibid., 39.
71. Ibid., 187 (italics added).
72. Ibid., 188.
73. Ibid., 189.
74. Ibid (my italics).
75. Horkheimer and Adorno use both the first (1781) and second (1787) editions of Kant's *Critique of Pure Reason*, using one or the other depending on the argument being made, although often their interpretations of Kant omit references to either of the two editions, which are different in important ways. Regarding the Kantian features of their notion of "conscious projection," I suspect they have in mind Kant's statement in the first edition that "[f]or that unity of consciousness would be impossible, if the mind, in the knowledge of the manifold, could not become *conscious* of the identity of function, by which it unites the manifold synthetically in one knowledge." *Critique of Pure Reason*, trans. F. Max Muller (New York: Anchor, 1966), 105 (my italics).
76. An excellent discussion of Adorno's critique of Kant is offered by Diana Coole in *Negativity and Politics* (New York and London: Routledge, 2000). See chap. 5, "Subject-Object Relations Again: Identity, Non-Identity and Negative Dialectics."
77. Horkheimer and Adorno, *Dialectic of Enlightenment*, 27.
78. Ibid., 193.
79. Ibid., 190.
80. Ibid., 195.
81. Ibid., 24.
82. Ibid., 15.
83. Ibid.
84. Ibid., 24.
85. G. W. F. Hegel, *Phenomenology of Spirit*, trans. A.V. Miller (Oxford: Oxford University Press, 1979), 479–93.
86. Horkheimer and Adorno, *Dialectic of Enlightenment*, 194.
87. Hegel, *Phenomenology of Spirit*, 46.
88. In Kant's opening words to "What Is Enlightenment," "Enlightenment is man's leaving his self-caused immaturity. Immaturity is the incapacity to use one's intelligence without the guidance of another. Such immaturity is self-caused if it is not caused by lack of intelligence, but by lack of determination and courage to use one's intelligence without being guided by another." *The Philosophy of Kant: Immanuel Kant's Political and Moral Writings*, ed. with an introduction by Carl J. Friedrich (New York: Modern Library, 1949), 132.
89. Horkheimer and Adorno, *Dialectic of Enlightenment*, 195 (translation altered; my italics).
90. Ibid., 23 (translation altered).
91. Ibid.
92. On the Christian concept of reconciliation see the Bible, "New Testament Letters," 2 Cor. 5 ("The Ministry of Reconciliation"), where Paul makes it clear that God and world are

reconciled through Christ, and John 14 ("Last Supper Discourses"), where Jesus says that to know him is to know God.
93. Horkheimer and Adorno, *Dialectic of Enlightenment*, 179.
94. Horkheimer and Adorno, *Dialektik der Aufklärung*, 177.
95. Horkheimer and Adorno, *Dialectic of Enlightenment*, 187.
96. Ibid., 200.
97. Ibid., 41.
98. Ibid., 158.

FIVE

1. T. W. Adorno, *Negative Dialektik* (Frankfurt: Suhrkamp, 1973), 151, 152.
2. J. Habermas, *The Theory of Communicative Action I* (Boston: Beacon Press, 1984), 373–74.
3. On Habermas's understanding of the concept of "reconciliation," see Seyla Benhabib, *Critique, Norm, and Utopia* (New York: Columbia University Press, 1986), 311–12, and 405 (footnote 76).
4. Karl Marx, *Early Writings*, trans. and ed. T. B. Bottomore (New York: McGraw-Hill, 1963), 31.
5. See my discussion in the previous chapter, in the section entitled "Aesthetic Individuality and the Destruction of the Jews."
6. Fred Dallmayr reverses, I believe, the respective approaches to the possibility of reconciliation held by Adorno and Habermas, seeing the former as an advocate for what he calls "an emphatic type of reconciliation" and the latter critical of such a view. In large part, I believe, Dallmayr's argument is informed by the view that we can speak of varying degrees of reconciliation. But though there may be a sense in which this is true in Adorno's work, for Adorno the meaning of reconciliation changes decisively if it is relativized in this way, and in my estimation would not alter the fact that, in the first as well as final analysis, and despite the work that "hope" for reconciliation plays in his model of thinking, Adorno is an unwavering opponent of reconciliation for the violence it inflicts on the objects of thought. My disagreements with Dallmayr, however, cannot be developed here. See Dallmayr's excellent discussion of reconciliation in *Between Freiburg and Frankfurt: Toward A Critical Ontology* (Amherst: University of Massachusetts Press, 1991), chap. 3, which takes up the concept of reconciliation in critical theory as a whole, and especially 78–85.
7. Habermas, *The Theory of Communicative Action* I, 387.
8. Adorno, *Negative Dialektik*, 9 (my italics).
9. One of the finest early accounts in English of Adorno's writings on aesthetics, including his *Aesthetic Theory* and the relationship of this work to his social theory is Frederic Jameson's *Marxism and Form* (Princeton, N.J.: Princeton University Press, 1971), chap. 1.
10. As any further consideration of the relationship between art and theory is beyond the focus of my argument, I would recommend Susan Buck-Morss, *The Origin of Negative Dialectics* (New York: Free Press, 1977) for a further exploration of this important subject in Adorno's aesthetics. See especially 132–35.
11. Adorno, *Aesthetische Theorie* (Frankfurt: Suhrkamp, 1974), 531.
12. On Horkheimer and Adorno's views on "expectation," see my discussion in the previous chapter in the section entitled "Reconciliation and the Alliance between Kant and Hegel, or Hegel without the Absolute, Kant Without the Supersensible."
13. Adorno, *Aesthetic Theory*, eds. Gretel Adorno and Rolf Tiedemann, trans. and ed. with an introduction by Robert Hullot-Kentor (Minneapolis: University of Minnesota, 1997), 73.
14. Thomas Mann, *Doctor Faustus*, trans. H. T. Lowe-Porter (New York: Vintage, 1971), 180. In the words of Mann's narrator, Serenus Zeitblom, "[it] is work: art-work for appearances

sake—and now the question is whether at the present stage of our consciousness, our knowledge, our sense of truth, this little game is still permissible, still intellectually possible . . . whether the work as such . . . whether all seeming, even the most beautiful, even precisely the most beautiful, has not today become a lie."

15. Adorno, *Aesthetic Theory*, 35.
16. Adorno, *Negative Dialektik*, 398.
17. Adorno, *Aesthetic Theory*, 111.
18. Ibid., 109.
19. At a performance of Beethoven's Sixth Symphony in Lenox, Massachusetts (Tanglewood) several years ago, I had an experience that (in retrospect) dramatically clarified the meaning of Adorno's concept of "spirit." Through the first two movements and well into the third the weather rapidly changed for the worse until, just before Beethoven's famous storm began, the orchestra was nearly overwhelmed by nature's genuine version. Rather than urging his musicians to compete with real rain, wind, thunder, and lightning, the conductor (Klaus Tennstedt) made a shocking move. He put down his baton, turned to the audience, and orchestra and audience listened silently to the surrounding drama. As the last of nature's own counterpoint slipped into the distance, the orchestra returned to Beethoven's *Pastoral*. It was only at that moment, when the "storm passage" was "repeated," that the "spirit" of Beethoven's music nearly caused the dividing line between art and nature, which suddenly had been made visible to us, to vanish.
20. Adorno, *Aesthetic Theory*, 112.
21. Ibid., 115.
22. Ibid., 135 (translation changed).
23. Ibid., 55 (translation changed).
24. Ibid., 69.
25. Ibid., 131.
26. Ibid., 46.
27. Ibid., 76–77.
28. F. Nietzsche, *Beyond Good and Evil* (Middlesex, England: Penguin, 1984), 169. An aesthetic of reconciliation is present in different forms in other of Nietzsche's works. An especially provocative examination that illustrates what is entailed philosophically by such an aesthetic and what its implications are for the possibilities of human life in modernity is Tracy B. Strong's "Nietzsche's Political Aesthetics," in *Nietzsche's New Seas*, eds. M. Gillespie and T. B. Strong (Chicago: University of Chicago Press, 1988). Though, appropriately, Strong does not describe Nietzsche's project in *The Birth of Tragedy* as an aesthetic of reconciliation, it seems clear to me that in his study of Nietzsche the aesthetic dimension in tragedy prefigures Nietzsche's later conception of what I have described here as a dream of reconciliation. In his *Fin-De-Siècle Vienna* (New York: Vintage, 1981), Carl Schorske's reading of the influence of *The Birth of Tragedy* supports the direction of Strong's argument. Schorske reports that Gustav Klimt, searching for a new life orientation in visual form, drew inspiration and instruction from Nietzsche's great work. Klimt believed Nietzsche was arguing on behalf of an aesthetic language having the power to achieve harmony and reconciliation. See chap. 5, particularly 221. In chap. 4 of this work I defend Nietzsche against the charge that there may be an aesthetic of reconciliation in *The Birth of Tragedy*. See the section entitled "Reconciliation and the Alliance between Kant and Hegel, or Hegel without the Absolute, Kant without the Supersensible."
29. Adorno, *Aesthetic Theory*, 343.
30. Nietzsche, *Beyond Good and Evil*, 256, especially 171.
31. *The Nietzsche-Wagner Correspondence*, ed. Elizabeth Forster-Nietzsche (New York: Liveright, 1949), chap. 1.

32. For an overview of Adorno's critical understanding of Schoenberg's music, see Martin Jay, *Adorno* (Cambridge: Harvard University Press, 1984), especially 27–29, 40–42, 150–53, although the book as a whole is to be recommended highly for its overall presentation of Adorno's critical theory.

33. Adorno, *Philosophy of Modern Music*, trans. A. G. Mitchell and W. V. Blomster (New York: Seabury, 1973), 39.

34. Ibid., 49–50.

35. A historical examination of the Frankfurt School that highlights the more general philosophical themes present in Adorno's philosophy of music and describes the relationship of Adorno's music theory over the course of his life to Schoenberg's compositions is Rolf Wiggershaus, *The Frankfurt School: Its History, Theories, and Political Significance*, trans. Michael Robertson (Cambridge: MIT Press, 1994), especially 508–19.

36. Adorno, *Philosophy of Modern Music*, 102 (my italics).

37. Ibid., 53 (my italics).

38. Ibid., 64, 113, 66 (my italics).

39. Ibid., 103.

40. Ibid., 104 (my italics).

41. Ibid., 133.

42. David Roberts expresses this nicely by saying, "Schoenberg's radicalism denounces the reconciling subsumption of the individual reader under the general, which constitutes for Adorno the innermost principle of musical illusion (*Schein*)." David Roberts, *Art and Enlightenment: Aesthetic Theory after Adorno* (Lincoln: University of Nebraska, 1991), 52, and pt. 1 for an excellent discussion of Adorno's *Philosophy of Modern Music* and the status of aesthetic theory in its wake.

SIX

1. On Nietzsche's relationship to Horkheimer and Adorno, see chaps. 3 and 4 in their entirety.

2. Friedrich Nietzsche, *Thus Spake Zarathustra*, trans. Thomas Common (New York: Modern Library, 1999), 132.

3. Ibid., 201.

4. Nietzsche, *On the Genealogy of Morals*, trans. Walter Kaufmann and R. J. Hollingdale (New York: Vintage, 1967), 78.

5. Nietzsche, *Beyond Good and Evil*, trans. R. J. Hollingdale (Middlesex, England: Penguin, 1984), 175.

6. Nietzsche, *Twilight of the Idols*, trans. R. J. Hollingdale (Middlesex, England: Penguin, 1975), 72.

7. Ibid.

8. Nietzsche, *On the Genealogy of Morals*, 103.

9. Ibid.

10. Nietzsche, *The Will to Power*, trans. Walter Kaufmann and R. J. Hollingdale (New York: Vintage, 1968), 419.

11. Ibid.

12. Nietzsche, *Beyond Good and Evil*, 64.

13. Nietzsche, *Thus Spake Zarathustra*, 49.

14. Ibid., 153, 39.

15. Ibid., 20.

16. Nietzsche, *Beyond Good and Evil*, 197.

17. In *The Will to Power* Nietzsche speaks of art as an "interpretive, additive, interpolating, poetizing" will to power (424).
18. Nietzsche, *Thus Spake Zarathustra*, 84.
19. Ibid., 95.
20. Ibid., 112.
21. Ibid., 233.
22. Nietzsche, *Beyond Good and Evil*, 204.
23. Ibid., 176.
24. Ibid., 196.
25. T. W. Adorno, *Negative Dialektik* (Frankfurt am Main: Suhrkamp Verlag, 1973), 153.
26. Nietzsche, *On the Genealogy of Morals*, 36–37.
27. Ibid., 39–40.
28. Nietzsche, *Twilight of the Idols*, 135 (my italics).
29. Nietzsche, *Thus Spake Zarathustra*, 36.
30. This is William Connolly's formulation of the constitution of identity in relation to difference. See *Identity\Difference: Democratic Negotiations of Political Paradox* (Ithaca, N.Y.: Cornell University Press, 1991), 64.
31. Nietzsche, *Beyond Good and Evil*, 141.
32. Adorno, *Negative Dialektik*, 153.
33. Nietzsche, *Thus Spake Zarathustra*, 76.
34. Nietzsche, *Twilight of the Idols*, 36.
35. See my discussion of morbid or false projection in chap. 4, the section entitled "Reconciliation and the Alliance between Kant and Hegel, or Hegel without the Absolute, Kant without the Supersensible."
36. Nietzsche, "Nachgelassene Fragmente," in *Nietzsche: Werke Kritische Gesamtausgabe*, eds. Giorgio Colli and Mazzino Montinari (Berlin and New York: De Gruyter, 1967), 4, 554; cited in Sarah Kofman, *Nietzsche and Metaphor*, trans. Duncan Large (Stanford, Calif.: Stanford University Press, 1993), 28.
37. I consider Kant and Hegel's relationship to Adorno and Horkheimer's concept of thinking in chap. 4, the section entitled "Reconciliation and the Alliance between Kant and Hegel, or Hegel without the Absolute, Kant without the Supersensible." I treat the matter of the relationship of Nietzsche's early writing to Adorno and Horkheimer in chap. 4.
38. Nietzsche, *The Will to Power*, 434.
39. Nietzsche, *The Gay Science*, trans. Walter Kaufman (New York: Vintage Books, 1974), 329; also see Nietzsche, *The Will to Power*, 445–46.
40. Nietzsche, *The Will to Power*, 446.
41. See Nietzsche, *On the Genealogy of Morals*, second essay, section 17, 87.
42. Nietzsche, *The Will to Power*, 42.
43. Nietzsche, *Thus Spake Zarathustra*, 76.
44. Nietzsche, *Twilight of the Idols*, 36.
45. Nietzsche, *Thus Spake Zarathustra*, 76.
46. Nietzsche, *Beyond Good and Evil*, 141.
47. Nietzsche, *Thus Spake Zarathustra*, 83.
48. Ibid., 96–97.
49. Nietzsche, *Twilight of the Idols*, 39.
50. In *Nietzsche and Political Thought* (Cambridge: MIT Press, 1988), Mark Warren captures this point by saying that for Nietzsche "the artist takes appearances seriously, not looking 'behind' the world for its content, as do metaphysical views of the world" (179).
51. Nietzsche, *Twilight of the Idols*, 41.
52. Nietzsche, *The Will to Power*, 435.

53. Nietzsche, *Thus Spake Zarathustra*, 134–35, in the section entitled "The Spirit of Gravity."
54. Walt Whitman, "Song of Myself," in *Leaves of Grass* (New York: Norton, 1973), 73; hereafter referred to as *NCE* (the Norton Critical Edition).
55. Whitman, "A Song of the Rolling Earth," *NCE*, 219.
56. Whitman, *Democratic Vistas*, in *Leaves of Grass and Selected Prose* (London: Everyman, 1994), 552; "Song of the Redwood-Tree," *NCE*, 207.
57. Whitman, "Are You the New Person Drawn toward Me," *NCE*, 123.
58. Whitman, "Among the Multitude," *NCE*, 135.
59. Whitman, "The Sleepers," *NCE*, 427.
60. Whitman, "Of the Terrible Doubt of Appearances," *NCE*, 120.
61. Whitman, "Song of the Open Road," *NCE*, 148.
62. Whitman, "A Song for Occupations," *NCE*, 211.
63. Whitman, "Passage to India," *NCE*, 411.
64. Whitman, "Darest Thou Now O Soul," *NCE*, 441.
65. Whitman, "To Think of Time," *NCE*, 434.
66. Whitman, "Salut au Monde!" *NCE*, 137.
67. Whitman, "Song of the Exposition," *NCE*, 195.
68. Whitman, "Preface 1855 to *Leaves of Grass*, First Edition," *NCE*, 721.
69. Ibid.
70. See my discussion in chap. 4, in the section entitled "Reconciliation and the Alliance between Kant and Hegel, or Hegel without the Absolute, Kant without the Supersensible."
71. Whitman, "Earth, My Likeness," *NCE*, 132.
72. Whitman, "I Dream'd in a Dream," *NCE*, 133.
73. Whitman, "In Paths Untrodden," *NCE*, 112.
74. Whitman, "Scented Herbage of My Breast," *NCE*, 113.
75. Whitman, "Whoever You Are Holding Me Now in Hand," *NCE*, 115.
76. Whitman, "Journeys through the States," *NCE*, 10.
77. Whitman, "Beginning My Studies," *NCE*, 9.
78. Whitman, "One Hour to Madness and Joy," *NCE*, 105.
79. Whitman, "Preface 1855 to *Leaves of Grass*, First Edition," *NCE*, 718.
80. Whitman, "Starting from Paumanok," *NCE*, 15.
81. Whitman, "Crossing Brooklyn Ferry," *NCE*, 159.
82. Whitman, "Our Old Feuillage," *NCE*, 171.

SEVEN

1. Walt Whitman, "Eidolons," in *Leaves of Grass* (New York: Norton, 1973), 5, hereafter referred to as *NCE* (the Norton Critical Edition).
2. Whitman, "Song of Myself," *NCE*, 28.
3. For a discussion of the differences between Adorno's and Nietzsche's concepts of depth, see my discussion in chap. 6 in the first three sections entitled "Up from the Depths, Onto the Surfaces of the World," "Nietzsche's Pure Surfaces," and "The Creative Will and Its Destruction of Depth."
4. Whitman, "Song of the Answerer," *NCE*, 166.
5. See chap. 6, the section entitled "The Sufficiency, Equality, and Uniqueness of Appearances."
6. Whitman, "Preface 1855 to *Leaves of Grass*, First Edition," *NCE*, 719.
7. Whitman, "Passage to India," *NCE*, 411.
8. T. W. Adorno, *Negative Dialectics*, trans. E. B. Ashton (New York: Seabury, 1973), 5.
9. Whitman, "A Paumanok Picture," *NCE*, 461.

10. I discuss Whitman's idea of the "sufficiency" of appearances in chap. 6, in the section entitled "The Sufficiency, Equality, and Uniqueness of Appearances."
11. Whitman, "A Song for Occupations," *NCE*, 211.
12. Whitman, *Democratic Vistas*, in *Leaves of Grass and Selected Prose* (London: Everyman, 1994), 530.
13. Ibid.
14. See my discussion in chap. 6 in the section entitled "Into the Unknown."
15. Whitman, *Democratic Vistas*, 530.
16. Ibid.
17. Whitman, "One's-Self I Sing," *NCE*, 1.
18. Whitman, "I Hear America Singing," *NCE*, 12.
19. Whitman, "Song of the Open Road," *NCE*, 149.
20. On the indispensability of aesthetics to ethics, see Jane Bennett's "'How Is It, Then, That We Still Remain Barbarians?': Foucault, Schiller, and the Aestheticization of Ethics," *Political Theory* 24, 4 (1996), 653–72.
21. See my discussion in the section entitled "Appearance and Difference" in chap. 6.
22. Whitman, "Behold This Swarthy Face," *NCE*, 126.
23. Whitman, "Scented Herbage of My Breast," *NCE*, 113.
24. Whitman, "That Shadow My Likeness," *NCE*, 136.
25. Whitman, "Earth, My Likeness," *NCE*, 132.
26. Whitman, "In Paths Untrodden," *NCE*, 112.
27. Whitman, "Salut au Monde!" *NCE*, 137.
28. Whitman, "Night on the Prairies," *NCE*, 452.
29. Whitman, "Assurances," *NCE*, 447.
30. Whitman, "A Noiseless Patient Spider," *NCE*, 450.
31. Whitman, "These I Singing in Spring," *NCE*, 118.
32. Whitman, "O Living Always, Always Dying," *NCE*, 450.
33. William E. Connolly, "Suffering, Justice, and the Politics of Becoming," in *Culture, Medicine and Psychiatry* (Dordrecht, Netherlands: Kluwer Academic, 1996), 20, 262.
34. Whitman, *Democratic Vistas*, 529.
35. Whitman, "In Cabin'd Ships at Sea," *NCE*, 2.
36. Whitman, "One Hour to Madness and Joy," *NCE*, 105.
37. Whitman, "Whoever You Are Holding Me Now in Hand," *NCE*, 115.
38. Whitman, "Unseen Buds," *NCE*, 557.
39. Whitman, "Grand Is the Seen," *NCE*, 556.
40. Whitman, "Song of Joys," *NCE*, 176 (lines 10, 16, 22, 24, 62, 65, 73, 86, 88, 94, 122, 124, 129, 131, 132, 139).

EIGHT

1. I find a voice sympathetic to my own approach to Whitman in Martha Nussbaum's compelling *Poetic Justice: The Literary Imagination of Public Life* (Boston: Beacon Press, 1995). In those discussions focusing on Whitman, Nussbaum explores the poet's relationship to the world as a basis for exercising judgment in a democratic society. In my view, Nussbaum's reading of Whitman is especially poignant for its sensitivity to his poetry as providing the *form* for how judgment ought to be exercised democratically. See 79–83 and 118–21 particularly.
2. Walt Whitman, "Passage to India," in *Leaves of Grass* (New York: Norton, 1973), hereafter referred to as *NCE* (the Norton Critical Edition), 411.
3. Whitman, "Song of Myself," *NCE*, 28.
4. Whitman, "Thou Mother With Thy Equal Brood," *NCE*, 455.

5. Walt Whitman, *Democratic Vistas*, in *Leaves of Grass and Selected Prose* (London: Everyman, 1994), 506.
6. Ibid., 532.
7. Whitman, "Song of the Exposition," *NCE*, 195.
8. With latest connections, works, the inter-transportation of the world,
   Steam-power, the great express lines, gas, petroleum,
   These triumphs of our time, the Atlantic's delicate cable,
   The Pacific railroad, the Suez canal, the Mont Cenis and Gothard
       and Hoosac tunnels, the Brooklyn bridge,
   This earth all spann'd with iron rails, with lines of steamships
       threading every sea,
   Our own rondure, the current globe I bring ("Song of the Exposition," *NCE*, 160–65)
9. Whitman, *Democratic Vistas*, 532.
10. Whitman, "Still Though the One I Sing," *NCE*, 13.
11. Whitman, "Song of the Broad-Axe," *NCE*, 184.
12. Whitman, "One's-Self I Sing," *NCE*, 1.
13. Whitman, "Song of the Redwood-Tree," *NCE*, 206.
14. Whitman, *Democratic Vistas*, 505.
15. Whitman, "To Foreign Lands," *NCE*, 3.
16. Whitman, "Our Old Feuillage," *NCE*, 171.
17. For an elaboration of the meaning of Adorno's concept of a "togetherness of differences," see the section entitled "No Trespassing" in chap. 5, the section entitled "Nietzsche's Pure Surfaces" in chap. 6, and the sections entitled "Every Existence Has Its Idiom," "The Distant Brought Near," and "A Constitutive Interest in Difference" in chap. 7.
18. Whitman, "Preface 1855 to *Leaves of Grass*, First Edition," *NCE*, 711.
19. Whitman, *Democratic Vistas*, 510.
20. Whitman, "Preface 1855 to *Leaves of Grass*, First Edition," *NCE*, 711.
21. Whitman, "On Journeys through the States," *NCE*, 10.
22. Whitman, "Starting from Paumanok," *NCE*, 15.
23. Whitman, *Democratic Vistas*, 511.
24. Ibid.
25. Ibid., 544.
26. Ibid.
27. Ibid.
28. Ibid., 544, 546, 539.
29. Ibid., 544, and especially 534–35.
30. For an opposing interpretation of Whitman on politics, see George Kateb, "Democratic Individuality and the Claims of Politics," in *The Inner Ocean: Individualism and Democratic Culture* (Ithaca, N.Y.: Cornell University Press, 1992), 77–105.
31. Whitman, *Democratic Vistas*, 545.
32. Ibid.
33. Ibid., 550.
34. Ibid (spelling changed from "esthetic" to "aesthetic").
35. Ibid., 553.
36. Ibid.
37. Ibid.
38. Whitman, "Song of the Answerer," *NCE*, 166.
39. Whitman, "Song of Joys," *NCE*, 176.
40. Here is an example of the contraction of time and space Whitman has in mind. When we read a book we not only absorb its contents but, in Whitman's sense of contraction, inherit the time it took to write the book, as well as all the time required to have the experience and

acquire the knowledge making it possible for its author to write it, and the space that was occupied and impressed itself on the writer's thinking during the time such experience and knowledge were acquired. The contraction of time and space is no different in our acquaintance with any "object" (person, occupation, gender, race, and so on). Through the relations with the diversity of different objects provided us by poetic forms of representation, we inherit the time and space belonging to them, the time and space during which they became what they are.

41. Whitman, "Crossing Brooklyn Ferry," *NCE*, 159.
42. Whitman, *Democratic Vistas*, 532.
43. Whitman, "Preface 1855 to *Leaves of Grass*, First Edition," *NCE*, 711.
44. Whitman, "Song of the Open Road," *NCE*, 149.

NINE

1. See chap. 8, the section entitled "Democracy and Aesthetic Education."
2. Walt Whitman, *Democratic Vistas*, in *Leaves of Grass and Selected Prose* (London: Everyman, 1994), 550, 529.
3. Ibid., 553.
4. Whitman, "Preface 1855 to *Leaves of Grass*, First Edition," in *Leaves of Grass* (New York: Norton, 1973), 711, hereafter referred to as *NCE* (the Norton Critical Edition).
5. Alexis de Tocqueville, *Democracy in America*, vol. I, trans. Henry Reeve and corrected by Francis Bowen and Phillips Bradley (New York: Knopf, 1997), 433. Hereafter all references to citations from the Reeve text of *Democracy in America*, vol. I, are incorporated into the text of this chapter and designated as *DAI*, with the corresponding page number.
6. Tocqueville, *Democracy in America*, vol. II, trans. Henry Reeve and corrected by Francis Bowen and Phillips Bradley (New York: Knopf, 1997), 24. Hereafter all references to citations from the Reeve text of *Democracy in America*, vol. II, are incorporated into the text of this chapter and designated as *DAII*, with the corresponding page number.
7. See Whitman, "Song of Myself," *NCE*, 35 (line 134).
8. For a different view of the audience for whom Tocqueville wrote *Democracy in America*, see Alan Ryan's excellent introduction to Tocqueville's work. Though I disagree, Ryan argues powerfully that *Democracy in America* was written only for French readers, and not for the Americans or British. See Alan Ryan, Introduction to Alexis de Tocqueville, *Democracy in America*, vols. I and II, (New York: Everyman, 1994), ix–xlvii.
9. See the discussion earlier in this chapter in the section entitled "Tocqueville's Blindness to Democratic Difference," where I argue that Tocqueville is aware of the presence of a prejudice in this thinking that compromises his ability to separate his assessment of democracy in America from the Aristocratic perspective rooted in his background, and hence the extent to which he can determine the originality of the American experience.
10. If universal rights are presupposed by the equality of condition, they are not presupposed necessarily. Tocqueville imagines two cases in which the equality of condition can occur, one democratic and the other undemocratic. In the first case, of which America is Tocqueville's premier example, universal rights enable the equality of condition to be established, whereas in the second case, where no one is granted any rights, the absence of rights *is* the equality of condition (i.e., "equality in slavery"), since no other condition could arise when the right to change one's condition is denied. See *DAI*, especially 53–54.
11. On the pluralization of difference in relation to the constitution of hegemonic cultural identity, see William E. Connolly, *The Ethos of Pluralization* (Minneapolis: University of Minnesota Press, 1995), especially the introduction and chaps. 4, 5, and 6.
12. See *DAI*, "The Present and Probable Future Condition of the Three Races That Inhabit

the Territory of the United States," 331–434; and *DA*II, "How the Americans Understand the Equality of the Sexes," 211–14.

13. Or as Tocqueville puts it again later in his second volume, "Hence it is natural that the love of equality should constantly increase together with equality itself, and that it should grow by what it feeds on" (*DA*II, 295).

14. See chaps. 6 through 8 for the meaning and implications of this conceptualization.

15. See chap. 7, especially the section entitled "Presenting a World" and forward, and chap. 8.

16. For the work that Whitman's metaphorical "old feuillage" performs in conceptualizing difference, see chap. 8, the section entitled "Democracy, Modernity, and Difference."

17. For Whitman's idea of the limitlessly different forms identity can assume within a democratic society, see chap. 8, the section entitled "Democratic Time, Democratic Space."

18. I argue that Whitman offers us a notion of "democratic time" in chap. 8, the section entitled "Democratic Time, Democratic Space."

19. I believe that my configuration of the aesthetics of individuality in democratic America through the work of Whitman and Tocqueville finds a home within what Thomas Dumm refers to as the "politics of the ordinary," at least insofar as the ordinary is understood by Dumm to include all expressions of the desire for an existence that affirms life in all its diversity of differences. For a compelling idea of the ordinary that explodes the narrowly dimensioned ways in which it is customarily used by political and social theorists, see Thomas L. Dumm, *The Politics of the Ordinary* (New York: New York University Press, 1999).

20. Whitman's poetic representation of surfaces is discussed in chap. 6, in the section entitled "Into the Unknown" and forward.

21. The all-inclusive orientation of Whitman's poetic forms of representation is discussed in chap. 7, in the sections entitled "Representing Surfaces Descriptively" and "Representing Surfaces Metaphorically," and in chap. 8, the section entitled "Democracy and Aesthetic Education."

22. Whitman's poetic representation of the equality of differences is discussed in chap. 6, the section entitled "The Sufficiency, Equality, and Uniqueness of Appearances."

23. I discuss Whitman's poetic representation of the sufficiency of differences in chap. 6, in the section entitled "The Sufficiency, Equality, and Uniqueness of Appearances."

24. Whitman's representational interest in difference is discussed in chap. 7, the section entitled "A Constitutive Interest in Difference."

25. I discuss the attachment to the world formed through the representational practices of Whitman's poetry in chap. 7, the section entitled "Attachment and Self-Creativity."

26. I discuss the intimacy with the world created through Whitman's poetic forms of representation in chap. 6, in the section entitled "An Intimacy with Appearances."

27. The indifference to difference in its depths expressed in Whitman's poetic forms and its aesthetic consequences are discussed in chap. 7, the section entitled "Representing Surfaces Descriptively."

28. On identity and the logic of slave morality, see my discussion in chap. 6, the section entitled "Nietzsche's Pure Surfaces."

29. Friedrich Nietzsche, *Beyond Good and Evil*, trans. R. J. Hollingdale (Middlesex, England: Penguin, 1984), 204.

TEN

1. See William E. Connolly, *The Ethos of Pluralization* (Minneapolis: University of Minnesota Press, 1995), especially the introduction and chap. 1.

2. George Kateb, *The Inner Ocean: Individualism and Democratic Culture* (Ithaca, N.Y.: Cornell University Press, 1992).

3. Ibid., 36–37.
4. Ibid., 37–38.
5. Ibid., 39–40.
6. Ibid., 93.
7. Ibid., 93–95.
8. Ibid., 61.
9. By due process Kateb understands not only the minimal requirements of the nonarbitrary rule of law, but "enlarged" due process, which includes the adversarial system. Strictly speaking, his model of due process also would entail the rights and entitlements specified in Amendments Four to Eight, generously interpreted and read to include the exclusionary rule. This is less important, though, than the understanding that what he means by due process is distinct from the continental civil-law tradition and refers to an enlarged due process procedure patterned after the "due process model" conceptualized by Herbert L. Packer in *The Limits of Criminal Sanction* (Stanford, Calif.: Stanford University Press, 1968).
10. John Stuart Mill, *On Liberty*, ed. Currin V. Shields (Indianapolis, Ind.: Library of Liberal Arts, 1956), 82.
11. Ibid., 22.
12. Ibid., 21.
13. Ibid., 50.
14. Ibid., 86, 88, 90.
15. Ibid., 45.
16. Ibid., 56.

INDEX

absolute knowing, 112, 118
Adorno, Theodor W., 1. *See also Dialectic of Enlightenment*; negative dialectics
    aesthetic individuality as art and, 67–68
    aesthetic individuality as ideal form and, 60–62
    aesthetic reason, individuality and sensibility and, 5–7
    aesthetic theory, individuality and, 15–19, 194
    beauty, the unknown and, 122–124
    capitalism, violence to difference and, 79–84
    conflict of faculties, hierarchical resolution and, 55–58
    democracy and, 299
    difference, birth of thinking and, 29–33
    difference, enlightenment of modern times and, 40–51
    difference, magical thinking and, 33–35
    difference, mythical thinking and, 36–40
    equivalence and, 70–71
    expression, the unknown and, 128–130
    forgetting (repression) and, 72–75
    formal, aesthetic reason and, 2–4
    genealogy of reason and, 7–11
    the great divide (fathomless meaning of difference) and, 135–137
    homo natura and, 69–70
    identity as self-contradiction and, 55–58
    individuals with possession of ourselves and, 55
    marriage of light and darkness and, 145–146
    methodological reflection of aesthetic individuality and, 62–64
    modern subjectivity, artless thinking and, 65–67
    music, beauty, the soul and, 138–144
    nightmare of, 144–145
    rationality, mimesis, the unknown and, 125–127
    reason, darkness and, 130–133
    rhetorical overlay *vs.* linear historical narrative and, 52–55
    self-identity, formal reason and, 58–60
    spirit, the unknown and, 127–128
    sublation and, 71–72
    trace, the unknown and, 124–125, 166
    translation of process of enlightenment and, 68–69
    translation of subjectivity/individuality and, 69–70, 72
    trespassing barrier and, 133–135
    universalization of formal reason, capitalism and, 76–79
Aeschylus, 104
aesthetic education
    democracy and, 237–240, 248–250
aesthetic form
    as democracy, 230
    distinguish power from illusion in, 126–127
    emancipation and, 132–133
    forms of thought, aesthetic individuality and, 92–97
    objective aspiration of, 126
    reason, art and, 119
    reason happy in, 130–131
    reconciliation in, 130–131
aesthetic individuality, 1, 8, 12, 67–68, 152–144
    aesthetic form, forms of thought and, 92–97
    aesthetic form lacking in, 15–16
    aesthetic Socratism analogy for, 104–106
    Apollinian analogies and, 86–92

as art, 67–68
artist and, 221
attachment to surface of difference by, 223–225
Attic tragedy of, 86–87, 91, 94, 96–104
The Birth of Tragedy and, 86–87
comprised form of, 91–92
democracy and, 14–15, 22, 25, 312n12
differences and, 156–157
Dionysian analogies and, 86–92
ending of, 9, 12
enlightenment broken by, 146
evidence for, 14–15
finiteness limitation to, 241–242
formal reason integrated with, 103–104
Greek Dionysian festival analogies and, 92–97
historical possibilities of, 63–64
hope in, 54
ideal form of, 60–62, 63, 97–104
identity created in, 163
immortality, democracy and, 246–247
Jew's destruction and, 114–116
Kant and Hegel reconciliation with, 106–114
methodological reflections on, 62–64
murderous principle of enlightenment and, 104–106
noble, 154–155
nurturing, 26
obstacles to, 237
in possession of itself, 146
representations for, 220
Socratic reason with, 104–106
the unknown for, 162
aesthetic individuality, democratic, 298–299. *See also* equality; individuality, poetic form of
aesthetic education for, 248–250
aesthetics of small differences for, 270–271
artist (creator) point of view for, 276–277, 283
attachment, intimacy and, 290–292
difference and, 250–252
disappearance of difference in, 263, 267

equality of condition for, 280, 292, 294–295, 300
equality, sufficiency and, 286–288
indeterminacy of surfaces for, 295–296
indifference to difference in depths of, 290–296
large differences of aristocratic societies and, 257–263, 267
logic of identity as difference for, 296–298
mimetic dimension of, 271–282, 284–285, 292, 295
morality in, 26, 301–307
passion for equality for, 272–276, 278–279, 284, 288, 290, 300, 326n13
point of view of artist (creator) for, 276–277, 296, 298
receptivity to small differences of, 288–290
representing difference in, 282–285
self-creativity and imitation for, 275–277, 279–281, 283–284
sensibility to violence for, 282–285
small differences of democratic societies and, 263–270
surfaces of small differences in, 285–286
Tocqueville's aesthetic sensibility and, 250–253
Tocqueville's blindness to democratic difference and, 253–257
uniformity of difference and, 254
uniqueness of small differences of, 286–288
aesthetic reason. *See* reason, aesthetic
aesthetic receptivity, 6–7, 11, 16, 32, 115
aesthetic representation for, 20–21
appearances and, 172–173, 200–201
art, recollection and, 95–96
as art, 67–68
art and limitation of, 95
attachment with, 290
to being, 98
creativity, surfaces and, 156–157
democracy and, 22, 245
descriptive representation and, 198
destruction of, 12, 26

to difference, 300
Dionysian, 90–91, 95
enlightened self-possession with, 54–55
equality of differences of, 287–288
formal reason destruction of, 40
imitation for, 276
indifference in, 200–201
liberalism with, 81–82
magical thinking and, 35
openness of, 184
sacrifice of, 39–40
self-possession and, 64
sensitivity to differences in, 281
to small differences, 288–290, 296–297
steadying of, 177
to the surface, 18, 154, 285–286
surfaces with, 285–286
aesthetic reflection, 171
aesthetic Socratism, 104–106
aesthetic theory, 14–15, 117–120. *See also* music
   aesthetics of darkness in, 120–122
   art, not reason, basis of, 130
   beauty, the unknown and, 122–124
   creativity, nobility and, 154–156
   depth, surface and, 19
   distance between the world and its representation in, 194
   dream of, 138–140, 144–145
   expression, unknown and, 128–130, 141
   genealogy of reason to, 13–14
   the great divide (fathomless meaning of difference) of, 135–137
   limiting condition and, 133–135
   marriage of light and dark in, 145–146
   meaning of, 119–120
   music, beauty, the soul and, 138–144
   Nietzsche's dream, Adorno's nightmare for, 144–145
   rationality, mimesis, the unknown and, 125–127
   reason, darkness and, 130–133
   reconciliation denied in, 123
   reflection in, 119–120, 131, 136
   spirit, the unknown and, 127–128
   subjects, objects and, 134
   trace, the unknown and, 124–125, 166
   trespassing barrier and, 133–135
   the unknown and, 149
Aesthetic Theory (Adorno), 13, 15, 44, 119, 102, 124–125, 132, 149
agnostic reflection, 55
All. *See* infiniteness
America, 248
   aesthetic individuality, democracy and, 312n12
   as brain of the New World, 232, 234, 238
   democracy, aesthetic individuality and, 22–26
   diversity of differences in, 236–237
   equality in, 263
   exceptionalist argument of, 312n12
   federalism of, 252
   idiocrasy of universalism of, 245
   poetic nature of, 235
   staged development of, 237–238
   universalism of, 233–224
annihilation, 29–30
anthropology, philosophical, 56
anti-Semitism, 49
Apollinian analogies, 86–92
   dreams and, 88, 91
   formal reason and, 90–91
   individuation principle with, 88–89, 97
Apollinian culture, 11–12
   dictatorial power of, 316n31
   Dionysian culture union with, 96–104
   Dionysian culture *vs.*, 92–96
   illusion, self-discipline in, 93
   naive in, 93
appearances. *See also* surfaces
   aesthetic receptivity and, 172–173, 200–201
   difference and, 178–180, 189, 285
   equality, sufficiency, uniqueness of, 180–183
   ethic of, 164, 173–174, 187, 190, 194, 205, 206, 209, 220, 225, 246
   God, the unknown and, 171–173, 171–174
   intimacy of, 183–184
   like language, 168

meaning of, 161
mystery, wonder and delight in, 174–177
nonidentity, the unknown and, 166–169, 173
as other-worldly, 202–203
perspectivism, the unknown and, 169–171, 173
reality (depth) and, 45, 161
sufficiency of, 199, 200
violation of ethic, 210
aristocracy, 24
antithesis of, 263
as artless, 282
change in, 254–255
as glimpse of the Divinity, 259
honor of, 289–290
immobility of, 282, 295
lack of universality of, 259–260
large differences and, 257–263, 282
memory class-based, 261–262
prejudice for, 256, 325n9
social weakness of, 259–260, 263
art. See aesthetic theory
aesthetic individuality as, 9, 67–68
aesthetic receptivity limited to, 95
Apollinian lyric, 97–99
Apollinian, 88–89
artist and, 164
being and, 98, 149
breaking from enlightenment, 130
counter–intuitive attitude towards, 165
Dionysian, 88, 91
Doric, 94
as embodiment of reason, 119
enchantment through, 5
essence in, 127
ethical impulse in, 149
failing to illuminate darkness in, 127, 145
formal reason as guise of, 105
here and now of, 141
illusion of reconciliation in, 118, 130–131
liberalism with, 81
limits to enlightenment by, 14
as living manifold, 123
middle world of, 92–93
nature's relationship to, 102

nonconceptual yet communicative, 136
objects and, 191
prerepresentational life of, 124
recollection of aesthetic receptivity with, 95–96
reconciliation and, 95, 315n2
reconciliation's illusion shatter in, 123, 135
reflective view of itself in, 131
repression of life by, 123
self-preservation with, 94
subjectivity and, 125
truth and, 162
unity with, 92
vision/ image of, 120
will to power for, 150–151
art deities
aesthetic individuality, forms of thought and, 87–92
artist (creator)
aesthetic form for, 16–17, 311n8
aesthetic problem of, 151–152
art and, 164
cruelty of, 159
nobility and, 154–155
point of view of, 161, 163, 164–165, 186, 195, 200, 202, 204, 210, 220, 230, 236, 248, 276–277, 283, 296, 298, 321n50
surface representation by, 200
attachment, 326n25
aesthetic receptivity and, 290
to difference, 290–291
intimacy and, 290–292
self-creativity and, 214–217, 226
Attic tragedy, 11–12, 86–87, 91, 94, 97–104. See tragedy
birth of new aesthetic form in, 101
condensing of being in, 107
Dionysian and Apollinian culture united with, 96–104
image projections of, 106–107
transfiguration through, 100–103
visionary figure in, 101
autonomy, 302–303

Bacon, Francis, 41–42
barbarism, 1, 30, 33

Dionysian, 92, 94
beauty
  appearances as transcendent for, 203
  art-work as lie and, 318–319n14
  the soul, music and, 138–144
  the unknown and, 122–124, 127
becoming
  being and, 209
  ontology of, 150
Beethoven's Ninth Symphony, 123, 319n19
"Behold This Swarthy Face" (Whitman), 210–211
being
  aesthetic, 249
  art and, 98, 149
  Attic tragedy and condensing of, 107
  becoming and, 209
  disenchantment of, 158
  the divine and, 120
  fathomless nature of, 102
  in-itself, 206–207
  intuition merge with, 103
  oneness of, 108
  quality of, 211, 215
  representation of, 124
  thought difference from, 91
  time, space relationship to, 242, 244
Beyond Good and Evil (Nietzsche), 69, 86, 135, 138, 151, 154, 227, 319n28
The Birth of Tragedy (Nietzsche), 11–12, 30, 37, 43, 69, 96, 104, 106, 117, 315n2, 316n31, 319n28
  aesthetic individuality and, 86–87

"Calamus" (Whitman), 178–179, 210–212
capitalism, 10
  liberalism of, 79–83
  mass culture of, 47
  monopoly stage of, 80–82
  private property of, 77
  stages of competitive, 79–80, 82
  universalization of formal reason in, 76–80
  violence to difference and, 79–84
Cartesianism, 31, 32, 67, 283, 293
centripetal, 224
Christianity
  equality and, 258, 290–291
  known values, Jesus and, 114–115
Circe, 59, 64, 65
citizenship, 302, 305
class(es)
  collapse/erosion of, 253–255, 266, 269, 271, 275
  differences of, 253–255, 257, 260–261, 267, 270, 273
  imitation of, 275
  large, 24
  three, 266
  transcending of, 271
  undifferentiated, 267
concept(s), 116, 136
  dialectic correction of, 111
  divisive function of, 108–109
  individuality, subjectivity, enlightenment and, 113
  objects, cognition and, 110
conceptual thinking
  loss of, 114
  reconciliation vs., 109
cognition
  concept, objects and, 110
conscious projection, 110
constitutionalism, 306–307
consumers
  fitting in as, 80
  mass culture of, 48
creative will. *See also* will
  destruction of depth and, 157–165
creativity, 21. *See also* artist (creator); self-creativity
  depth and, 18–19
  haven (womb) for, 213–214
  individuality with, 151, 153
  infinite, 228
  noble, 154–156
  problem of, 17
  surfaces and, 18, 154, 156–157
creator. *See* artist
"Crossing Brooklyn Ferry" (Whitman), 184, 243–244
culture(s)
  collapse of identity of, 253–254
  linking of, 194
  as political foundation, 306–307
culture industry, 79, 80

repetition in, 48
ruthless unity of, 49
subjectivity and, 48–49
Cyclops, 38–39, 42, 65

darkness
  aesthetics of, 120–122
  failing to illuminate contents in, 127, 145
  as a limiting condition of nonidentity, 134
  marriage of light with, 145–146, 224–229
  reason and, 130–133
  trespassing barrier of, 134–135
dead truth, 113
deconstruction, 10
democracy, 227, 312n12. *See also* aesthetic individuality, democratic
  aesthetic education for, 237–240, 248–250
  as aesthetic form, 230
  aesthetic individuality in, 22–23
  as aesthetic (poetic) form, 237, 239–240
  alternation and, 303
  American, aesthetic individuality and, 22–23, 25–26
  creativity of, 22
  difference, modernity and, 232–235
  difference, poetry and, 235–237
  diversity of differences in, 236–237
  due process, constitutional protection and, 306–307, 309n9
  Jesus Christ teachings for, 258, 290–291
  judgment in, 323n1
  liberal, 116
  moral democratic individuality in, 301–307
  poetry of, 201, 249
  representative, 301–307
  science and technology in, 292
  slave morality in, 297–298
  small differences and, 263–270
  time, space and, 240–247, 324–325n40
  as universalism, 233–234, 239–242
Democracy in America (Tocqueville), 15, 23, 249–252, 255, 269–270, 272, 298, 300, 325n8
"Democracy's Lands" (Whitman), 236
democratic individuality, morally distinctive, 26, 301–307
  all-forgiving tolerance of, 310
  alternation and, 303
  autonomy for, 302–303
  continuous force of suggestiveness by, 305
  fallibility, diversity and, 307–308
  foundation for culture of, 306–307
  impersonal, 304–305
  living truth for, 307–308
  moral courage for, 307–310
  moral phenomenon for, 301–303
  negative, 303–304
  normal level of, 304–305
  positive, 303–305
  resistance utilized by, 304, 308–309
  restraint for, 306
  transcendent level of, 304
Democratic Vistas (Whitman), 167–168, 206, 217, 224, 232, 234–235, 237–238, 239, 242–245, 248–249
depth
  creative will and its destruction of, 157–165
  as difference, 218–219
  fathomless, 18, 180
  forced, 210–211, 214
  individualization at, 280–281
  infinite, 216
  meaning of, 161
  metaphorical, 222
  reflection vs., 17
  shallow, 218
  surface vs., 18–19
  surfaces and, 150–152, 157–165, 171, 173, 187, 209–217, 220, 222, 228–229
  the unknown, 19–20
Descartes, 66
dialectic. *See* negative dialectics
  correction of concept by, 111
Dialectic of Enlightenment (Horkheimer and Adorno), 2, 4, 9–14, 29, 31–32,

33, 36, 38, 43–44, 46–47, 52–56, 57, 60, 61–65, 67–70, 72–75, 77, 79, 85–87, 104–106, 132
difference(s)
  adoption of another's, 276
  aesthetic individuality and, 250–252
  among similarities, 252
  appearance and, 178–180, 189
  attachment of, 290–291
  birth of thinking and, 30–33
  class, 253–255, 257, 260–261, 267, 270, 273
  class vs. nonclass, 267, 270
  constitutive interest in, 222–224
  demarcation of identity from, 223–224
  democracy, modernity and, 232–235
  democracy, poetry and, 235–237
  democratic, 253–257
  depth as, 218–219
  destruction of, 52, 61, 78, 79–84, 115
  disappearance of, 23–24, 267
  diversity of, 219, 236–237, 246, 278
  enlightenment of modern times and, 40–51
  equality of, 326n22
  existence of, 188
  fathomless meaning of, 135–137
  fathomless diversity of, 145–146
  gender, 267–268
  identity integrated with, 98, 103, 220
  imitation and overcoming of, 24–25
  in-itself, 66, 197, 222
  indifference to, 197, 200–202, 292–293, 326n27
  Jewish, 118, 190
  logic of identity as, 296–298
  lost of receptivity to, 39
  magical thinking and, 33–35
  modernity and closing of, 191–193
  mythical thinking and, 36–40
  nonidentity and, 202
  opposite and, 223
  pluralization of, 277, 325n10
  poetry and insulation of, 189
  race, 267–269
  representing (democratic), 282–285
  row in music and, 144
  sufficiency of, 326n23
  sustaining of, 222
  technology, modernity and, 231–232
  terrifying nature of, 31
  togetherness of, 134, 157, 191, 193–194, 224, 235, 246, 248, 292, 324n17
  uniformity of, 254
  violence and representing, 282–285
  without hope of reconciliation, 195
  world of, 217
differences, large, 24
  aristocratic societies and, 257–263, 282
  meaning of, 267, 270
  overcoming of, 273–274
difference(s), small, 24
  adoption of another's, 276
  aesthetics of, 270–271
  all-inclusive orientation to, 285–286
  democratic societies and, 263–270
  indifferent to, 294
  meaning of, 267, 270
  overcoming of, 273–276
  orientation to surfaces of, 285–286
  receptivity to, 281, 288–290, 292, 296–297
  sufficiency, equality and, 286–288
  uniqueness of, 286–288
Dionysian analogies, 86–92
  aesthetic receptivity and, 90–91, 95
  barbarism of, 92, 94
  dissolution of identity with, 87–88, 95, 99
  enchantment (intoxication) of, 89, 91, 93–94
  festivals and, 92–97
Dionysian culture, 11–12
  Apollinian culture union with, 96–104
  Apollinian culture vs., 92–96
  oneness in, 97, 108
  tragedy and, 99–100, 101, 108
Dionysian transfiguration, 100–103, 104
discontinuity, 217–222, 223, 224, 277
division of labor, 76
domination, 29
Doric worldview. See Sparta
dramatic prologue, 105
dreams, 88, 91
due process, 306, 327n9

Dumm, Thomas, 326n17
"Earth, My Likeness" (Whitman), 178, 212
education, 265, 270, 275
"Eidolons" (Whitman), 185
electoral system
    conditional/temporal nature of, 301–302
    force of suggestiveness in, 305
    moral phenomena of, 302–303
    partisan or fractional basis of, 302
emancipation
    aesthetic subject and, 132
    political *vs.* human, 118
emotions
    sign language of, 71–72
enchantment, 5
    awe of, 32
    Dionysian, 89, 91, 93–94
    disenchantment of, 36, 40, 55–56
    experience of, 8
    experience *vs.* contemplation of, 8–9
    the unknown and, 116
Enlightenment
    capitalism and, 76–77
    enlightenment into, 70
    equalizing of differences in, 35
    Fascism as fulfillment of, 30
    formal reason for, 115–116
    as historical principle, 70
    Reason for, 65
    reconciliation as illusion of, 12–13
    social order and, 75–76
enlightenment, 10
    aesthetic individuality breaking of, 146
    aesthetic transformation for, 7
    art breaking from, 130
    destruction of difference by, 115
    dominance of, 72–75
    Enlightenment as accomplice of, 45
    Enlightenment barriers to, 44
    Fascism apotheosis of, 50
    formal reason in process of, 32
    genealogy of, 63
    Kant and, 317n75
    meaning of, 3
    modernity and, 9, 40–51
    mythical thinking and, 36–37
    process of, 4, 5, 6, 12
    purging of differences in, 13
    representation limited to surface by, 209
    science, irrationality and, 74
    suppression of, 97
    suppression of differences by, 35
    totalitarian value of, 33
    transformation of nature by, 41
    translation of process, 69–70, 72
equality
    Christianity and, 290–291
    of condition, 23–24, 263–267, 268–273, 274, 280, 292, 294–295, 300, 325n10
    democratic achievement, aesthetic individuality and, 14–15
    of differences, 287–288
    God and, 290–291
    movement towards, 274
    passion for, 23, 272–275, 276, 278–279, 284, 288, 290, 300, 326n13
    sufficiency, uniqueness of appearance and, 180–183
    sufficiency, uniqueness of small differences and, 286–288
equivalency, 35, 47–48, 55, 69–70, 71, 74
    nature, uniformity and, 105
    as universal rational/scientific principle, 74
Erwartung (Schoenberg), 140–142
essence, 127
    appearance of, 128
Euripides, 12, 104
experience, aesthetic
    lost of, 12
    Socratic logic and, 12
expression, aesthetic
    identity of, 141
expression, artistic
    unknown and, 128–130

faculties
    conflict of, 55–58, 314n6
faith, 154
fallibility, 307
false projection, 50
family, 82–83, 92

Fascism, 1
  defeat of, 117
  difference inimical to, 49–50
  Enlightenment fulfilled through, 30
  fitting in with, 80
  formal reason, madness and, 50–52
  Jew as negative principle for, 115
  liberalism and, 49
  love, pleasure and, 83–84
  murderous principle of, 51
  no truth to measure, 53
  paranoia, science and, 50
  rationalization of cultural systems by, 47
  reason basis of, 29
fear, 111–112
  Fascism and, 50
  nature, myth and, 72–74
  nature and healing of, 102
  unknown and, 2, 4, 12, 15, 31, 33, 52, 289
finiteness, 241
forgetting, 72–75
  reason, primordial fear and, 73–74
  self, 88, 90, 92, 97, 99
formal reason. *See* reason, formal
forms of thought
  aesthetic individuality, aesthetic form and, 92–97
Frankfurt school, 320n35
free choice, 57
freedom, love *vs.*, 83
Freud, Sigmund, 82

The Gay Science (Nietzsche), 159
gender, 267–268
genealogy, of reason, 6–7, 13–14
  aesthetic individuality as art with, 67–68
  aesthetic individuality as ideal form for, 60–62
  autonomy of formal reason, social order and, 75–76
  capitalism, violence to difference and, 79–84
  conflict of faculties, hierarchical resolution and, 55–58, 313–314n6
  enlightenment's system dominance and, 72–75

equivalence and, 70–71
forgetting (repression) and, 72–75
homo natura and, 68–70
identity as self-contradiction with, 55–58, 313–314n6
individuals with possession of ourselves an, 55
man back to nature for, 69–70, 85
methodological reflection of on aesthetic individuality with, 62–64
modern subjectivity, artless thinking and, 65–67
Nietzsche and, 69–74
reconstruction of history through, 9–10
rhetorical overlay *vs.* linear historical narrative with, 52–55
self-identity, formal reason and, 58–60
subjectivity back to individuality for, 85
sublation and, 71–72
translation of process of enlightenment for, 68–69
translation of subjectivity/individuality for, 69–70, 72
universalization of formal reason, capitalism, private property and, 76–79
God
  equality and, 290–291
  Jewish nameless value of, 51
  reconciliation of human and, 193–194
  superior mind of, 251–252, 255–256
  the unknown and, 171–173
Goethe, 33
"Grand Is the Seen" (Whitman), 228–229
Greeks, 1, 11. *See also* Apollinian culture; Dionysian culture
  philosophy of, 40
  religion of, 36

Habermas, J., 118–120, 130
heart, back to heart of, 99
Hegel, 75
Hegel, Georg, 75
  absolute of, 118
  dialectic of, 111
  Kant, aesthetic individuality and, 106–114

INDEX

without the absolute, 112
historicity, 62
History and Class Consciousness (Lukács), 77
Holocaust, 26–27. *See also* Jews
   culmination of enlightenment and, 2
   formal reason affect on, 4
Homer, 92
Homeric culture, 93–94, 100, 101, 103, 111–112
homo natura, 69–70
Horkheimer, Max, 1. *See Dialectic of Enlightenment*
   aesthetic individuality as art and, 67–68
   aesthetic individuality as ideal form and, 60–62
   aesthetic reason, individuality and sensibility and, 5–7
   capitalism, violence to difference and, 79–84
   conflict of faculties, hierarchical resolution and, 55–58
   difference, birth of thinking and, 29–33
   difference, enlightenment of modern times and, 40–51
   difference, magical thinking and, 33–35
   difference, mythical thinking and, 36–40
   equivalence and, 70–71
   forgetting (repression) and, 72–75
   formal, aesthetic reason and, 2–4
   genealogy of reason and, 7–11
   homo natura and, 69–70
   identity as self-contradiction and, 55–58
   individuals with possession of ourselves and, 55
   methodological reflection of aesthetic individuality and, 62–64
   modern subjectivity, artless thinking and, 65–67
   rhetorical overlay *vs.* linear historical narrative and, 52–55
   self-identity, formal reason and, 58–60
   sublation and, 71–72
   translation of process of enlightenment and, 68–69
   translation of subjectivity/individuality and, 69–70, 72
   universalization of formal reason, capitalism and, 76–79

identical individual,
   one identical world through, 59
identitarianism, 136, 156, 170, 220, 225
identity
   demarcation of difference from, 223–224
   development of inward, 224
   difference integrated with, 98
   discontinuity of, 219
   dissolution of, 87–88, 95, 99
   diversity of difference inclusive to, 103
   illusory form of, 15
   miracle of, 206–207, 211
   as representation, 202
   as self-contradiction, 55–58, 314n6
IdentityDifference (Connolly), 223
idiocrasies, 204
imitation, 24. *See* mimesis
   class, 275–277
immortality. *See* infiniteness
"In Cabin'd Ships at Sea" (Whitman), 226
"In Paths Untrodden" (Whitman), 179, 219
In the Unknown (MacNeil), 120, 121f
independence. *See* autonomy
indeterminacy, 208, 211, 213, 218–222
   metaphorical representative of, 204, 217
individual
   flight of, 38
individual identity
multiplicitious nature of, 25
individuality
   aesthetics of, 152–153
   after the Holocaust, 26–27
   creativity of, 20, 151, 153
   democratic, 1
   from depths to surface in identity for, 149–150
   destruction of, 1
   distinct, 250

diverseness, surfaces and, 21
  identity and, 207–208
  morally distinctive, 26
  negativity (dialectic) affirms existence of, 111–112
  nobility basis of, 17
  subjectivity, aesthetic dimension and, 106
  subjectivity transformation from enlightenment from, 113
individuality, aesthetic. *See* aesthetic individuality
individuality, democratic. *See* democratic individuality
individuality, poetic form of, 186–188
  attachment, self-creativity and, 214–217, 226
  constitutive interest in difference in, 222–224
  discontinuity/indeterminacy of, 217–222
  discontinuity of own identity in, 219–220
  distant brought near in, 188–194
  existence as own idiom for, 186–188
  forcing surfaces and depths in, 209–214
  limitlessness of, 215–216
  presenting a world of, 206–209
  representing a world by, 194–195
  representing surfaces descriptively by, 195–202, 209
  representing surfaces metaphorically by, 202–206, 208, 209, 217
  surfaces' aesthetic value in, 224–229
individualization
  depths and, 280–281
individuation
  Attic tragedy, and limits of, 102
  principle of, 88–89.95
  surfaces and, 280–281
inequality
  of condition, 257, 260–261, 263
  of mind, 273
  permanent, 257–258
infiniteness, 216, 242, 244, 246, 326n17
The Inner Ocean: Individualism and Democratic Culture (Kateb), 26, 301

"Inscriptions" (Whitman), 235
intellectual independence, 265, 270–272, 275, 283, 294, 307, 309
intimacy, 326n26
  attachment and, 290–292
intuition
  being and, 103

Jews
  aesthetic individuality, and destruction of, 114–116
  aesthetic reason by, 51
  democracy and, 1
  destruction of, 1, 13, 26, 49, 51–52, 68, 114–116
  difference of, 13, 118, 190
  religion, difference and, 51
Jews. *See also* anti–Semitism
Judaism
  connection to God in, 114
  expectation of, 114
  imageless God of, 114–116
  non-pronouncing of God's name in, 51, 114
  the unknown important to, 114

Juliette (Sade), 45–47, 83

Kant, Immanuel, 32–33, 48, 67
  concept and, 109–111
  conscious projection of, 110, 317n75
  enlightenment and, 317n75
  formalism of, 48
  Hegel, aesthetic individuality and, 106–114
  ontology of, 44–45
  perception, projection and, 50
  supersensible realm of, 113
Kateb, George, 26
  morally distinctive democratic individuality and, 301–307, 309–310, 327n9
knowledge
  reason pursuing, 3

language
  dialectical conception of, 166
  like appearances, 168
  limitations of, 165
  poetry outside, 165

large differences. *See* difference(s), large
Leaves of Grass (Whitman), 176, 181, 184, 189, 206–207, 235, 240, 243, 245, 248–249, 299
liberalism, 10, 116
  art with, 81
  capitalism and, 79–83
  family and, 82–83
  Fascism and, 49
liberty
  over authority, 82
light. *See* darkness
limitlessness, 215–216
linear historical narrative, 58, 62
  rhetorical overlay vs., 52–55
Lotus-eaters, 59, 65
love, 83
  sexuality and, 46–47

magical thinking
  aesthetic receptivity of, 35
  control over nature from, 35
  enlightenment and, 313n6
  equivalency and, 47–48
  nonidentity, identification and, 34
  preanimistic idea of mana for, 34
  social order and, 75–76
  spirit inhibiting nature in, 41
majority, tyranny of, 284
mana, 32, 51
  mythical thinking and, 36
  preanimistic idea of mana, 34
Mann, Thomas, 123, 318–319n14
Marxism, 10, 79
mass culture
  common identity in, 48
  modern capitalist in, 47
  sameness of, 77, 80
memory
  class-based, 261–262
  primordial fear as forgotten, 73–74
  unfettered by, 278–279
Mendelsohn's *Hebrides* Overture, 128
metaphors. *See* representation, metaphorical
Mill, John Stuart, 1, 307–310
mimesis, 34–35, 50, 110. *See also* imitation
  democracy and, 275–282, 284–285, 292, 295
  indefinite perfectibility with, 278–279
  music and, 142–143
  the unknown, rationality and, 125–127
miracle of miracles, 206–207, 211
"The Modern Man I Sing" (Whitman), 234
modern subject, 113
modern thinking
  social order and, 75–76
modernity
  American, democracy and, 22–23
  art in, 68
  closing of distances/differences in, 191–194
  critique of, 311n2
  as culture of self-preservation, 117
  democracy, aesthetic education and, 237–238
  difference, democracy and, 232–235
  difference, technology and, 231–232
  dilemma of, 33
  distortion from metaphysics to, 61
  enlightenment process of, 9
  reconciliation and, 117–118, 193–194
  reduced to formal reason in, 122
  subjectivity and, 65–67, 77–78, 113–114
  for Whitman, 191–192
Monet, Claude, 124, 137, 144
Morality. *See also* democratic individuality, morally distinctive
  courage of, 307–310
  noble, 156
  religion separated from, 44
  ressentiment, 156
  sentiments and, 259
  slave, 297–298
  transvaluation of, 46
muse, 232
music, 101, 135
  atonality and, 140–142
  beauty, the soul and, 138–144
  finished, though incomplete, 144
  Frankfurt school and, 320n35
  here and now of, 141
  illusion and, 320
  integration of difference and identity by, 97–98

mimetic potential of, 142–143
nature and, 145
reconciliation and, 139, 142
row in determination of, 143, 144
tonal centricity of, 139–140
tonic key and, 138
tragedy origin's in, 99
twelve-tone, 142–144, 145
variation as absolute in, 143–144
mystery, 225, 226
    delight in appearances and, 174–177, 222
myth, 5
    fear, nature and, 72–74
    fleeing from, 40, 55–56
    no unknown in, 43
    rationalization of, 41
    repressed, 72–73
    science and, 40–41
    subjectivity, formal reason and, 65
    terror rationalized by, 36
mythical thinking, 36–39, 38–39, 64
    aesthetic receptivity, formal reason and, 39–40
    ambiguity of, 95
    celebration of difference in, 36
    compromise with enlightenment for, 61
    ending process of enlightenment in, 54–55
    enlightenment process with, 36–37, 314n6
    escape from animistic forces in, 41
    mana and, 36
    Odysseus fleeing from, 40
    social order and, 75–76
    subjectivity vs., 67
    subversion receptivity of, 36

naive, 93
nature
    art relationship to, 87, 102, 126
    emancipation of repressed, 65
    end of denial of, 103
    formal reason and, 42
    healing of terrifying, 102
    man back to, 10, 69–70, 72, 85, 99
    miracle of identity with, 206
    musical domination of, 145
    myth, fear and, 72–74
    nonidentity of, 122–125
    poetry's expression of, 239
    repression of, 72–74, 76
    science and, 42
    subjugation to, 74
    as the unknown, 30
    as useful and terrifying, 32
negative dialectics, 127, 166–167
    reconciliation and, 118–119
    unity of art through, 124
Negative Dialectics (Adorno), 117, 119, 122, 132, 155
Nietzsche, Friedrich, 1–3, 10–12, 14, 16–17, 18–19, 25, 135. *See also specific works by*
    aesthetic form, Dionysian Festival and, 92
    aesthetic individuality and, 11–13, 85–87
    aesthetic Socratism and, 104–106
    aesthetic theory, 16–19, 138–140, 144–145
    Apollinian analogy for, 87–92
    Attic tragedy and, 96–104
    democracy and, 299
    Dionysian analogy for, 87–92
    dream of aesthetic theory of, 138–140, 144–145
    equivalence for, 70–71
    forgetting for, 72–74
    man back to nature for, 69–70
    marriage of light and dark by, 224–229
    morality and, 301–302
    music and, 138–140
    pure surfaces of, 150–157
    reconciliation and, 106–108
    social order and, 75
    sublation for, 71–72
    surfaces' aesthetic value and, 224–229
    surfaces, destruction of depth and, 157–165
"Night on the Prairies" (Whitman), 214
nobility, 154–156
    with creativity, 17
    as demonized otherness, 17
nodal point, 67
"A Noiseless Patient Spider" (Whitman), 217

nonidentity, 122–125, 135
   darkness as a limiting condition of, 134
   difference and, 202
   identity and, 202
   representation of, 127
   the unknown and, 166–169, 173, 204
not-day, 214–215

"O Living Always, Always Dying" (Whitman), 219
object, 15
   aesthetic approach to, 209, 213, 218, 225, 230
   aesthetic theory, subject and, 134
   art and, 191
   giving shape to, 210
   here and now of, 34
   reconciliation's violence to, 318n6
   truth of, 293–294
Odysseus, 5, 42, 62–63, 117, 162
   aesthetic receptivity as art for, 67–68
   ambiguity of mythical thinking for, 95
   art, aesthetic individuality and, 60–61
   compromise of, 9, 11
   conflict of faculties for, 56–57
   control of fame of, 8
   enchantment of unknown by, 116
   evolution of enlightenment through, 45–46
   fleeing from mythical being by, 40, 55–56
   formal *vs.* aesthetic thought for, 55–58
   homecoming of, 77
   lost of receptivity to differences by, 39
   as modern subject, 65
   self–identity of, 59–60
   self-sacrifice of aesthetic ability of, 38–40, 85
   Sirens overcome by, 37, 145
   temptation of self-abandonment of, 90
   as unified identity, 64–65
Odyssey, 5, 7, 36–38, 55, 64, 66–67, 90, 100
"Of the Terrible Doubt of Appearances" (Whitman), 167, 169
"On Journeys through the States" (Whitman), 179, 235–236, 240
On Liberty (Mill), 307

On the Genealogy of Morals (Nietzsche), 16, 71, 73, 86, 151, 152, 155
"On the Jewish Question" (Marx), 115, 118
"One Hour to Madness and Joy" (Whitman), 181, 227–228
"One's-Self I Sing" (Whitman), 234
ontology
   aesthetics and, 13
   phenomenal world vs. supersensible world of, 44–45
opposite
   difference and, 223
orientation
   formal *vs.* aesthetic, 8
otherness
   as demonized nobility, 17
"Our Old Feuillage" (Whitman), 183, 234, 245

paradox, 169
paranoia, 111–112
parental authority, 83
"Passage to India" (Whitman), 171–172, 191–194, 231, 238, 250
passion. *See* equality
"A Paumanok Picture" (Whitman), 195, 202
perception
   aesthetic, 199
   preconceptions and, 170
   as projection, 109–110
perfectibility, indefinite, 278
perspectivism
   the unknown and, 169–171, 173
Phenomenology of Spirit (Hegel), 112
Philosophy of History (Hegel), 75
Philosophy of Modern Music (Adorno), 119, 140, 320n42
Plato
   rationalization of myth by, 41
poetic creativity, 20
poetry *See also* individuality, poetic form of; Walt Whitman
   anticipation in, 201
   compacting of time and space by, 243, 324–325n40
   democracy, difference and, 235–237
   democracy and, 201, 237, 240

differences insulated by, 189
differences, unknown and, 19
expression of nature in, 239
inadequancy of language and, 165
love and, 180
lyric, 97–100, 108
outside language, 165
point of view of artist in, 164–165
reconciliation, modernity and, 193–194
relationship to world through, 25, 186–187
unknown unfoldment with, 19
politics of the ordinary, 326n19
Polyphemus, 36, 39–40, 55, 59
poor, 266
predestination, 57–58
presentation, aesthetic, 220, 282
presentational dimension, 25
projection
    conscious, 110, 317n75
    false, 115
    perception as, 109–110
property rights, 77, 264–265. See capitalism

race, 267–269
rationality. See reason
reader
    historical basis of, 10
    precarious, 6
reality. See depth
    appearance vs., 45
reason. See also genealogy, of reason
    absurd, 1–2
    aesthetic form, happiness and, 130–131
    art as embodiment of, 119
    barbarism and, 30
    darkness and, 130–133
    mimesis, the unknown and, 125–127
    reason beyond, 2
    self-referential critique of, 119
    unafraid, 4
    universalistic orientation of, 31
    the unknown and, 130–133
reason, aesthetic, 1–2, 4–5
    formal reason vs., 4, 37, 55–56
    formal reason displacing of, 67
    as heart of individuality, 13
    limit to enlightenment for, 15–16
    lost in art for, 145–146
    origin and decline of, 11
    receptive to differences by, 5–6, 9
    resistance of enlightenment by, 6
reason, formal, 3–4
    aesthetic reason displaced by, 4, 40, 67
    aesthetic reason vs., 4, 37, 55–56
    aesthetic receptivity destroyed by, 40
    Apollinian, 90–91, 95
    bridging divide by, 13
    capitalism and universalism of, 76–80
    contingency of history affect on, 7
    domination of, 8, 117
    enlightenment process in, 5, 32
    Fascism conclusion of, 50, 52
    genealogy, self-identity and, 58–60
    Holocaust from, 311n6
    integration of aesthetic individuality with, 103–104
    Marxism and, 10
    paradoxical, 6
    preservation of nature and, 42
    private property and universalization of, 76–79
    social order and autonomy of, 74–76
    Socratic reason as, 12
    subjectivity, myth and, 65
    technical rationality and, 132
    underlying value of, 13
    unreflective, 45
    without conscience, 46
receptive generosity, 311n5
reconciliation
    aesthetic, 134–135, 138, 319n28
    art, formal reason and, 95, 315n2
    Christian, 317–318n92
    conceptual thinking vs., 109
    critique of, 191
    differences without hope of, 195
    emphatic type of, 318n6
    expectation of, 114, 120
    as illusion/dream, 12–13, 118, 121, 123, 135, 168, 319n28
    indifferent to, 220
    between Kant and Hegel, 106–114
    as lie, 124
    modernity, poetry and, 193–194

modernity and, 117–118
music and, 139, 142
negative dialectics, 118–119
twelve-tone music and, 144–145
violence on objects by, 318n6
will to, 145
reductionist interpretation, 62
reflection
aesthetic theory and, 119–120, 131, 136
depth *vs.*, 17
first and second, 130
reification, 77
religion
civil, 238
moral principles separate from, 44
representation, 124
aesthetic, 199, 200, 204, 208, 209, 220
democratic, 245
descriptive, 195–203, 209, 230
as identity, 202
indifference to difference in, 201–202
metaphorical, 203–206, 208, 209, 214, 230
poetic, 245, 248, 285, 286, 290, 326n17–18, 326n22–23
surface limited by enlightenment with, 209
repression
capitalism and, 80
of myth, 72–74
of nature, 72–74, 76
resentment, 25
nobility and, 17
rhetorical overlay, 52–55, 62
linear historical narrative vs., 52–55
Roman empire, 250
romance, 83

sacrifice. *See* self-sacrifice
Sade, Marquis de, 45–46, 83
"Salut au Monde" (Whitman), 175, 214, 217, 222
satyr, 99–100
"Scented Herbage of My Breast" (Whitman), 179, 211
Schoenberg, Arnold, 140–142
Schubert's *Wintereise*, 128
science, 292

equivalency as principle and, 74
irrationality of enlightenment, 74
mastery over nature by, 42
no unknown in, 43
self-reflection lost in, 43–44
transition from myth to, 40–41
scientific abstraction
constructive principle of, 42
sculpture, 120–121
self
images of, 21
likeness of, 214, 216, 221
subjugation to, 74
self-abandonment
temptation of, 90
self-abnegation. *See* forgetting
self-confidence, 283
self-contradiction
identity as, 55–58, 314n6
self-creativity, 22, 25, 206–207, 209, 211–212, 213, 224, 226, 241
aesthetic presentation as imitation for, 275–277, 279–281, 283–284
attachment and, 214–217, 226
expansion of, 292
self-identity, 111
genealogy, formal reason and, 58–60
self-preservation and, 59
self-preservation
art form with, 94
myth, enlightenment and, 37–38
self-sacrifice and, 55, 57–59
threat to, 70
self-possession
compromised form of enlightened, 61–62, 64, 68
self-preservation, 2, 30
repression of, 74
self-identity and, 59
self-realization, 59
self-reflection
art and, 131, 136
science losing of, 43–44
self-sacrifice, 64
aesthetic ability and, 38–39, 55–56, 65
sexuality, 92
love, pleasure and, 46–47
shaman, 35

Sirens, 37–38, 55, 56, 58, 59, 60, 61, 64, 67, 68, 95, 96, 100, 117, 145, 316n31
"The Sleepers" (Whitman), 180
small differences. *See* difference(s), small
social authority
    of extreme weakness, 259–260, 263
social order
    formal reason and, 74–76
    modern, 117
socialism, 78
Socrates, 12
Socratic reason, 43, 104–106
"Song of Answerer" (Whitman), 245
"Song of Joys" (Whitman), 229, 242–243
"Song of Myself" (Whitman), 164, 166–169, 172, 173, 174, 176, 180–185, 195–196, 197, 199–200, 202, 204–205, 208, 209, 213, 214, 216–218, 221–222, 225, 226–227, 239, 242, 244
"A Song for Occupations" (Whitman), 170, 200, 225
"Song of Open Road" (Whitman), 169, 180, 214
"Song of Self" (Whitman), 186, 188
"Song of the Answerer" (Whitman), 186, 189, 196, 199, 242
"Song of the Broad-Axe" (Whitman), 233
"Song of the Exposition" (Whitman), 232
"Song of the Open Road" (Whitman), 21, 208, 227, 246
"Song of the Redwood-Tree" (Whitman), 167, 234, 245
"A Song of the Rolling Earth" (Whitman), 165–167
Sophocles, 104
The Sorrows of Young Werther (Goethe), 29–30
space
    being and, 242, 244
    poetry compacting of, 243, 324–325n40
    time and democratic, 244–247
Sparta, 94, 316n31
spirit, 319n19
    the unknown and, 127–128

"Starting from Paumanok" (Whitman), 182, 236, 243, 245
"Still Though the One I Sing" (Whitman), 233
subjectivity
    art and, 125
    artless thinking and modern, 65–67
    back to heart of nature with, 99
    culture industry and, 48–49
    enlightenment pressures individuality into, 113
    "I think" as, 66–67
    individuality, aesthetic dimension and, 106
    individuality back from, 85
    modern, 77–78, 113–114
    myth, formal reason and, 65
    mythical thinking vs., 67
    object and, 31–32
    object as part of, 66
    sacrifice individuality to, 61, 66
sublation, 71–72, 81
sufficiency
    appearances and, 199, 200
    equality, uniqueness of appearance and, 180–183
    uniqueness of small differences, equality and, 286–288
superior power, 32
supersensible realm, 113
surface(s). *See also* appearances
    aesthetic value of, 18–19, 187, 224–229
    artist representation of, 200
    attachment to, 214–215
    beneath *vs.* on, 157
    creative will, its destruction of depth and, 157–165
    depth and, 18–19, 150–152, 157–159, 171, 173, 187, 209–217, 220, 222, 228–229
    descriptive representation of, 195–202
    diverseness of, 21
    entirety of, 230
    ethic of appearances and, 173–174
    forced, 210–211
    imitation and, 279–280
    individuation at, 280–281

as likeness of self, 216, 221
metaphorical representation of, 202–206
mirror of, 150
Nietzsche's pure, 18, 150–157
pure, 150–151
receptivity to, 285–286
representation limited by enlightenment to, 209
the unknown and, 165
sympathies, 255, 289

technical rationality
formal reason and, 132
technology, 113, 292
modernity, difference and, 231–232
terror, 30
myth rationalizing of, 36
"That Shadow My Likeness" (Whitman), 212
"These I Singing in Spring" (Whitman), 219
"Thou Mother with Thy Equal Brood" (Whitman), 232–234, 238, 245–247
thought
critique of, 40
divisiveness of, 109
eluding, 2
emancipation of absolute from, 118
forms of, 92–97
in-itself, 32–33, 34, 37, 44, 51, 173
malformation of object of, 3
nature and, 87
neutrality of, 43
object and, 15
preanimistic stage of, 30, 31, 75
ruthlessness of, 33
as substitution, 35
terrifying nature of, 30
unbridgeable gap of known and unknown in, 15–16
violence and cognitive act of, 34
Thus Spake Zarathustra (Nietzsche), 150–157, 156, 159–160, 227
time
being and, 242, 244
poetry compacting of, 243, 324–325n40

space and democratic, 244–247
timeless of, 244, 246
Titans, 92–93
Tocqueville, Alexis de, 15, 23
aesthetic individuality, democracy and, 23–26, 312n12
aesthetic sensibility for, 250–253
aesthetics of small differences and, 270–271
attachment, intimacy and, 290–292
blindness to democratic difference by, 253–257
democracy, aesthetic individuality, and, 298–299
democracy's mimetic dimension of, 271–282
difference and, 250–252
equality, sufficiency, uniqueness of small differences and, 286–288
equality of condition and, 23–24, 263–273, 274–275, 325n10
God, superior mind and, 251–252, 255–256
indifference to difference in depths and, 290–296
indifference to indeterminacy of surfaces and, 290–296
large differences of aristocratic societies and, 257–263
logic of identity as difference and, 296–298
receptivity to small differences and, 288–290
representing difference and, 282–285
small differences of democratic societies and, 263–270
surfaces of small differences and, 285–286
tonic key, 108
trace
the unknown and, 124–125
tragedy
Apollinian, 101
death of, 106
Dionysian, 99–100, 101, 108
music and origin of, 99
transfiguration through, 99, 101
vision of, 100–101

transcendence, 32
transcendental apperception, 109
transfiguration, 100–103, 104
Tristan und Isolde (Wagner), 138–140
Trojan horse, 41
truth
   art and, 162
   living, 308
   of objects, 293–294
   universal moral, 17
Twilight of the Idols (Nietzsche), 1, 151, 156, 160
tyranny of majority, 284

Udeis (Nobody), 39–40, 55
unconsciousness
   understanding through, 99, 101
unity
   individual experience of, 92
   primordial, 89
   primordial contradiction with, 97–98
universal rights, 264, 325n10
universalism, 233–234, 239–242, 245, 286
   idiocrasy of, 245
the unknown. *See also* darkness
   affirmation divide of, 197, 198
   artistic expression and, 128–130
   beauty and, 122–124, 127
   deepening of, 213–214
   as difference of depth, 19–20, 222
   fear of, 2, 4, 12, 15, 31, 33, 52, 289
   God and, 171–173
   as identity of difference, 297
   indifference to difference in depths and, 290–296
   Judaism value of, 114
   known becoming, 228
   known from, 120, 176–177
   known *vs.*, 19
   as nature, 30
   nonidentity, 173
   nonidentity and, 166–169, 173, 204
   perspectivism and, 169–171, 173
   rationality, mimesis and, 125–127
   reason and, 130–133
   science and, 43
   spirit and, 127–128
   surfaces and, 21–22, 162, 165
   terrifying, 31
   trace and, 124–125
"Unseen Buds" (Whitman), 228

values
   transvaluation of, 46
violence
   aesthetic sensibility to, 25
   capitalism, difference and, 79–84
   cognitive act of thought for, 34
   to difference, 52, 53, 79–84, 163
   end of aesthetic individuality and creation of, 9
   free from, 10
   of representation, 164
   sensibility to, 21, 282–285
   subduing of, 21
vision
   aesthetic receptivity and, 285, 288

Wagner, Richard, 138–140
weakness, 1, 46
   social authority and extreme, 259–260
wealth, 265
Whitman, Walt, 15, 25. *See also specific works of*
   aesthetic education for, 237–240, 248–250
   aesthetic individuality, democracy and, 312n12
   aesthetic problem of artist for, 19–23
   attachment, self-creativity and, 214–217
   constitutive interest in difference in, 222–224
   counter-intuitive attitude towards, 165
   democracy, difference, modernity and, 232–235
   democracy, difference, poetry and, 235–237
   democracy, time, space and, 240–247
   democracy as aesthetic form for, 230, 237–240, 299
   difference, appearance and, 178–180
   discontinuity/indeterminacy and, 217–222
   distant brought near by, 188–194
   existence as own idiom for, 186–188
   forcing surfaces and depths with, 209–217

God, the unknown and, 171–174
intimacy of appearance for, 183–186
meeting of art and artist in, 164
for modernity, 191–192
mystery, wonder and delight in appearances for, 174
not-day of, 214–215
perspectivism of, 169–171
point of view of artist of, 19–23, 276–277
politics and, 238, 324n30
presenting a world of, 206–209
reconciliation, modernity, poetry and, 193–194
representing a world by, 194–195
representing surfaces descriptively by, 195–202
representing surfaces metaphorically by, 202–206
sufficiency equality, uniqueness of appearance and, 180–83
surfaces' aesthetic value in, 224–229
technology, modernity, difference and, 231-232
unknown, nonidentity and, 166–169
"Whoever You Are Holding Me Now In Hand" (Whitman), 179, 228

will
to power, 150–151, 158–159, 160, 161–162
to truth, 160

The Will to Power (Nietzsche), 151, 162
women, 312n18
world. *See also* object
creative living in unreconcilable, 195
orientation to appearance of, 205